GOSSAMER ODYSSEY

ERRATUM

The first sentence in the Foreword by HRH The Prince of Wales should read as follows:

As President of the Royal Aero Club and Honorary Fellow of the Royal Aeronautical Society I was delighted to have had the chance to meet Dr Morton Grosser when I presented Dr Paul MacCready and the rest of his team with the Kremer Trophy for their great achievement with the Gossamer Albatross.

GOSSAMER ODYSSEY

THE TRIUMPH OF HUMAN-POWERED FLIGHT

MORTON GROSSER

with a foreword by HRH Prince Charles

Michael Joseph LONDON

First published in Great Britain by Michael Joseph Ltd
44 Bedford Square, London WC1
1981

ISBN 0 7181 2033 7

Illustration credits on page 285.

Portions of this book have appeared in
Natural History and *Technology Review*.

Printed in the United States of America

To My Friends and Teammates
of the
Gossamer Squadron

Acknowledgments

LIKE THE HUMAN-POWERED AIRCRAFT PROJECTS it describes, *Gossamer Odyssey* has received generous help and cooperation from many people. First among them are the members of the MacCready family. They include Paul and Judy MacCready, with whom my wife and I have spent many hours as teammates and friends, their sons, Parker, Tyler, and Marshall, and Paul's sisters, Mrs. Isabelle Champagne and Mrs. Anne Plant. They have been unstinting with their memories, their patience, and their candor.

Our colleagues on the *Gossamer Condor* and *Gossamer Albatross* teams are each described in the book and listed in the appendix, but I would like to thank them collectively as well. Surely no expedition has ever assembled a more talented or better-natured group. I owe a special debt to Marvin and Beverly Allen, who opened their home and hearts to us, and to Ed and Bambi Schwartz, who first introduced me to Paul MacCready.

Although California is not usually considered part of the British Commonwealth, after the Gossamer teams received their second Kremer Prize from His Royal Highness Prince Charles, we began to feel as though he was our patron *pro tem*. It was especially gratifying to receive the awards from an experienced aviator who could appreciate both the technology and the human effort that went into the *Condor* and *Albatross* projects. We were honored to find that our mutual regard was high enough for the prince to overlook political boundaries and write a foreword to this account.

In the course of the project certain people have repeatedly gone out of their way to provide essential data and illustrations. They include Mrs. Margret Clarke of Du Pont U.K.; the officers and staff of The Royal Aeronautical Society, and especially Mrs. Eva Dane and the late Mr. Kenneth Clark; Mr. Don Monroe, whose photographs are the most complete visual record of the *Condor* and the *Albatross;* and Mr. Ron Moulton of Model & Allied Publications and the Man-Powered Aircraft Group Committee of the RAeS.

Anyone who has lost faith in the kindness and altruism of humanity should try building a human-powered airplane. The following list is so heterogeneous that to describe each person's contribution would fill another book. While working on the *Albatross* project I was offered, among other things, aircraft hardware; plastic adhesives; carbon-fiber sprockets; translations from Japanese and Greek; studio-quality tape transfers; photographs; slide bindings; first-day covers; publication rights; transportation by boat, plane, hovercraft, motorcycle, truck, and a wide variety of automobiles; excellent lodging, and many days' worth of hospitality, good companionship, food, and drink. The one thing that all of the donors had in common was their refusal to accept any payment for their kindness. This mention is an attempt to thank them without their being able to demur.

My grateful thanks to: The Honourable Edward Adeane; Mr. and Mrs. Joseph G. Arlington; Mr. Brooks Bauer and Dr. John Siddall of Zoecon Corporation; Mr. H. G. Bennison, O.B.; Mr. Joe Bilgri; Mr. Don Billett of Du Pont U.K.; Wing Commander and Mrs. Colin Campbell of R.A.F. Manston; Dr. Walter B. Cannon; Messrs. Jack Conmy, Roger Morris, Samuel L. Waltz Jr., and Richard J. Woodward of the Du Pont Company; Mr. Jack Cox of the Experimental Aircraft Association; Mr. Paul Dicken of British Hoverlloyd Ltd.; Mr. John Dubord; Mrs. Gwyn Dukes; Mrs. Jeanne Dumont, Mr. John Musante, and Mrs. Velma Washington of Eastman Kodak Company; Professor Albert Elsen of the Stanford University Art Department; Dr. Walter Englert of the Stanford University Classics Department; Mr. Richard J. Fouquet of Optima Publications; Miss Diane Giavia, Mrs. Susan Lukawski, and Mrs. Sally Palermo of Wang Laboratories, Inc.; Rear Admiral H. C. N. Goodhart, C.B.; Ms. Marguerite Grady of the Stanford Art Library; Dr. Wolfgang Gronen; Mr. Bill Hannan; Mr. James P. Harrington of the Franklin Institute; Mr. Anton Higgs; Mr. Frederick Hoerner of the Naval Air Test Center; Mr. Tom Horton; Mr. and Mrs. Raymond Humphreys of the St. Hilary Guest House, Ramsgate; Mr. Otis Imboden of *National Geographic Magazine;* Professor Hidemasa Kimura; Mr. John Krausz; Mr. Hiroyasu Kubota of the Stanford University Asian Languages Department; Professor E. Eugene Larrabee of the Massachusetts Institute of Technology Department of Aeronautics and Astronautics; Mr. A. N. Le Cheminant of the Canadian Aeronautics and Space Institute; Mr. Ralph Libby of the Palo Alto Library; M. et Mme. Jean Louf of the Chambre de Commerce de Calais; Dr. Joseph Mastropaolo of California State University at Long Beach; Dr. John McMasters of the Boeing Company; Chief Officer and Mrs. Peter Morris of Her Majesty's Coast Guard, Folkestone; Mr. Wolfgang Nothnagel; Miss Agnes F. Peterson of the Hoover Institution, Stanford University; Mr. John Pond; Mr. and Mrs. George Reiser and the staff of the Savoy Hotel, Ramsgate; Miss Mary Reynolds of the British Consulate General, San Francisco; Mr. Joel Rieman; Mrs. Vivienne Schuster of John Farquharson, Ltd.; Mr. and Mrs. Attilio Scubla of the Wear Bay Hotel, Folkestone; M. Daniel Seité of the Chambre de Commerce de Calais; Mr. and Mrs. Darrell C. Sonnichsen; Messrs. Harn Soper, David H. Porter, and Roger Wiersma of Music Annex Recording Studios; Mr. James A. Sugar; Mr. Hans-Dieter Teichmann; Mr. Willem Van Loon of Du Pont Netherlands; Mrs. Eleanor Velarde; Mr. John Worth of the Academy of Model Aeronautics; Dr. and Mrs. J. E. R. Young.

It is a profligate debt, but I owe an even greater one to my wife, Janet, and son, Adam. Their help and continuous encouragement were indispensable to the completion of the book. Thank you, everyone.

Morton Grosser

Menlo Park, California
June 1980

Contents

Illustrations   xiii

Foreword by H.R.H. Prince Charles, Prince of Wales   xvii

Introduction: Parallels   xix

PART I: THE GOSSAMER CONDOR

1. Stimulus: Forerunners of the Kremer Prize   3
2. The Kremer Prize: Human-Powered Flight 1938–1961   18
3. Competition: Kremer Prize Projects 1961–1976   32
4. Ground School: Paul MacCready Jr.   50
5. Genesis: The Origins of the *Gossamer Condor*   66
6. Eyrie: Mojave Airport   83
7. Fledgling: Mojave/Shafter   98
8. Adolescence: Shafter Airport   111
9. Practice: The Turning Point   125
10. Triumph: Winning the Kremer Prize   137

PART II: THE GOSSAMER ALBATROSS

11. Sequel: The Cross-Channel Prize   155
12. Evolution: The *Gossamer Albatross*   174
13. Endurance: The First Long Flights   192
14. Migrants: The Winds of Kent   209
15. Liftoff: The Edge of England   227

16. The Channel: Blériot, Nous Sommes Ici!   242
17. Epilogue: Some Reflections on the Gossamer Projects   256

Appendices:
    The Gossamer Squadron   269
    The Rules for the Kremer Competitions   270
    Members of the Man-Powered Aircraft Group
        Committee, Royal Aeronautical Society   279
Bibliography   280
Index   286

Illustrations

FOLLOWING PAGE 74

1. Gabriel Poulain and his *Aviette* when he won the *Prix Peugeot,* first prize for human-powered flight, Paris, July 9, 1921
2. *Mufli,* built by Helmut Haessler and Franz Villinger, flying near Frankfurt, August 1935
3. Enea Bossi's *Pedaliante,* Milano, March 1937
4. Henry Kremer and Robert Graham
5. *SUMPAC* made the first human-powered flight in Great Britain, November 1961
6. *Puffin II,* successor of *Puffin,* which flew 6 days after *SUMPAC*
7. *Linnet I,* first human-powered aircraft to fly in Japan, February 25, 1966
8. *Jupiter,* the most successful HPA ever built in Britain, set a world record on June 29, 1972
9. *Toucan* ("Two can fly if one cannot")
10. Dr. Paul Beattie MacCready and 15-year-old Paul MacCready Jr., New Haven, Connecticut, 1940
11. The future Dr. Paul MacCready Jr.
12. Bryan Allen, future bicycle racer and HPA pilot
13. Vern and Maude Oldershaw, en route to the National Model Airplane Championships, 1946
14. Vern Oldershaw, building a wing rib of the *Gossamer Condor,* 1977
15. Jim Burke, working on the final version of the *Gossamer Condor,* March 1977
16. Professor Kimura's *Stork B,* Shimofusa Naval Air Base, January 2, 1977

17. *Gossamer Condor* team after the successful Kremer Figure-of-Eight flight
18. HPA Factory I, Shafter Airport, July 1978
19. HPA Factory II, Terminal Island, Long Beach, March 1979
20. Part of the *Gossamer Albatross* team, American Embassy, London, May 16, 1979
21. Waiting for the weather, June 1979
22. *Gossamer Albatross* cockpit, just before the Channel flight, Kent, England, June 1979
23. The voyage begins
24. An hour into the flight
25. With both legs cramped, Bryan brings the *Albatross* past the rocks at Cap Gris-Nez, France
26. The reward

FOLLOWING PAGE 234

1. Forerunners, I. Nearly a perfect miniature analog of the Gossamer planes
2. Forerunners, II. Paul MacCready, hang gliding in 1975
3. Jim Burke, Kirke Leonard, and Paul MacCready, working on the first version of the *Gossamer Condor,* December 1976
4. Parker MacCready, flying the *Gossamer Condor,* December 26, 1976
5. *Condor* team's unsuccessful effort to improve the plane's lateral stability, January 1977
6. Greg Miller, pedaling the much-modified *Condor,* January 1977
7. Paul MacCready, Vern Oldershaw, Peter Lissaman, and Jack Lambie, working on the *Condor*'s fuselage
8. Crash of the modified *Condor,* March 1977
9. Bryan Allen and Greg Miller, after a bicycle race in 1979
10. Bryan Allen, working on an ergometer
11. Bryan, flying the *Condor,* with Sam Durán on chase bike
12. Bryan, flying the *Condor* over a height marker
13. Bryan, piloting the *Condor* on the Kremer Prize flight, August 23, 1977
14. The *Gossamer Condor* in the National Air and Space Museum, with the X-15, the Wright *Flyer,* and the *Spirit of St. Louis*

15. Beginning the *Gossamer Albatross,* March 1978
16. The first *Albatross,* ready for testing, July 1978
17. The *Albatross* flies beautifully right from the beginning
18. *Albatross* in its new home, Terminal Island, December 1978
19. An *Albatross* crash, February 1979
20. Hangar 522, Terminal Island
21. Bryan, flying the *Albatross* on the longest human-powered flight yet made, April 25, 1979
22. Building *Albatross 2,* R.A.F. Manston, Kent, England
23. The qualification flight for the Kremer Cross-Channel Competition
24. The *Albatross,* assembled in preparation for the Channel attempt
25. The broken front wheel being replaced
26. The *Albatross* lifts off, setting a course for France
27. Mid-Channel, far behind schedule
28. Bryan, signaling that he must give up and needs a tow
29. Bryan struggles on toward the coast of France
30. Over the beach at Cap Gris-Nez
31. The moment of landing

TEXT FIGURES

1. Dr.-Ing. Hans Seehase's proposed human-powered plane, designed in 1937   [12]
2. Human power output vs. time for bicycling and rowing   [34]
3. *Gossamer Condor 1,* as built and flown at Mojave Airport   [72]
4. Lissaman 7769 Airfoil   [85]
5. Kremer Prize-winning *Gossamer Condor 2*   [118]
6. Technique of forming carbon-fiber frame tubes for *Gossamer Albatross*   [166]
7. Skeleton of *Gossamer Albatross*   [170]
8. *Albatross,* in form in which it was flown across Channel [176]
9. Canard stabilizer of *Albatross* and its rigging   [190]
10. Drive train and flying controls of *Albatross*   [202]
11. Perspective of *Albatross* as erected at R.A.F. Manston   [212]
12. John Dubord's depiction of HPA cross-Channel race   [229]

FOREWORD
BY H.R.H. PRINCE CHARLES,
PRINCE OF WALES

BUCKINGHAM PALACE

As President of The Royal Aeronautical Society I was delighted to have had the chance to meet Dr. Morton Grosser when I presented him and the rest of his team with the Kremer Trophy for their great achievement with the Gossamer Albatross. For hundreds of years, if not thousands, the idea of man-powered flight has inspired countless brave men to design strange contraptions with which to rival the birds.

Finally, in 1979, the great moment came when human intelligence, based on the modern knowledge of aeronautics and other systems, triumphed over what had seemed impossible. In the context of the kind of earth-shattering inventions, sophisticated technologies and various space research projects to which we have become accustomed, this achievement may to some people seem funny, insignificant and of absolutely no value whatsoever.

The truth is that life presents us with a whole series of challenges which man cannot resist trying to overcome. The Gossamer project is a classic example of that wonderful spirit of adventure and determination which has led to the unveiling of so many of God's mysteries in this universe. Long may such dedicated enthusiasts and craftsmen continue to inspire us and fire our imagination! Without them we are doomed.

Charles.

Introduction

PARALLELS

IT IS A CLEAR MORNING in the spring of 1558. You are standing on a Flemish hillside above the Cretan Bay of Mérabellou, looking east to where the sun is rising out of a limpid Mediterranean Sea. Across the bay from your vantage point the buildings of what will become Nikólaos gleam pink and white against the cliffs. To your left, close enough to speak to, a plowman in a red blouse has just started his fourth furrow of the morning. He guides the wooden moldboard of his plow expertly through the dew-soaked earth, contouring the furrows to the curves of the sloping field. Except for the breeze, the only sound is the creak of the plow's wooden wheel and the clink of its draw chain.

The hill shelves out below the plowman's field, and a shepherd leans on his staff there, gazing raptly at the luminous sky. He doesn't look a great wit, but his gear is neat and compact, and his dog sits relaxed and attentive beside him. The sheep browse methodically, some venturing down the headland almost to the water's edge. To their right a fisherman leans forward to reset his line, a mug of breakfast mead on the grassy verge beside him. A large bird watches him from the overhanging branch of a tree.

Out in the bay the breeze is freshening. Two jachts on a broad reach are heeled to port, and a carrack runs seaward with her fore- and mainsails bellied out by the westerly wind. Just past the nearby headland another handsome carrack is starting her voyage. Her great foresail and lateen mizzen are pulling magnificently, and crewmen are out on the yards removing the gaskets from the main- and topsails. She slips through the water with the smooth wake of a well-kept hull. Except for one small detail, the whole scene is one of a world in harmonious order, a world of good craftsmanship.

A few yards from the grazing sheep, only a little farther from the fisherman, there is a roil of disturbed water. Two sturdy bare legs flail in the air; it is obvious that their owner is in dire distress, in fact is drowning. There is no cry. No one looks up. It is Icarus, in Pieter Bruegel's *Landscape with the Fall of Icarus,* and he drowns. In a world of good craftsmanship, the picture says, you must know what you're doing: Stick to your last.

*   *   *

It is a clear morning in June of 1979. You are standing on a French headland above the tidal beach of Cap Gris-Nez, looking northwest to where the cliffs of Dover are just visible as a hazy band on the horizon. A few kilometres to your right the houses of the small village of Wissant gleam white against a crescent of pale sand. Close behind you the crisp tan buildings of the Cap Gris-Nez radar station and the high stone tower of its lighthouse crown the headland. The light revolves with the regularity of slow breathing, one flash every five seconds. Except for the breeze, the only sound is the hum of the radar antennas turning in their bearings.

In front of the station the cliff drops steeply to the water's edge, and a tumble of black rocks bounds the left end of the beach below. A rubber boat is pulled up on the sand, and a yellow truck is parked near it. Above the truck a bright red balloon, a sort of miniature blimp, nods and bobs in the breeze. The boat, the truck, and the balloon look as though they have been left there by a giant child. A crowd of people is gathered near the rocks, staring seaward. Gulls wheel over them, and a dog that could be the descendant of the one in Bruegel's painting stands alertly on a wet boulder.

Out in the channel a school of small boats is approaching shore. Ahead of them, just above the water, floats a huge, diaphanous aircraft, more creature than machine. The boats cluster behind it like the attendants of some unimaginable lord of dragonflies as it moves toward the beach. Its silver propeller spins steadily, slow enough to count the turns. It is clear from the faces of the watchers that everything is going as it should, a scene of order and good crafts-manship.

The plane comes closer and closer to the beach. Suddenly it veers northward to clear the last line of rocks, then turns back over the sand, hovers a moment, and gently touches down. A roar of excitement and applause bursts from the watchers. In a world of good craftsmanship, the scene says, one must know what one is doing. Sometimes the workman must wait for the time of his last to come along.

PART ONE

The Gossamer Condor

California Condor (Gymnogyps californianus)
Length: 45–55 inches (114–140 centimetres)
Wingspan: 102–114 inches (259–290 centimetres)
The largest bird in North America.
Voice: Usually silent
Habitat: Found only in Southern California. The last known nesting population is in the mountains of Los Padres National Forest, east of Santa Barbara. The species raises only one young every other year, and the development of the immature is slow. At 10 months the young are still apprentices at flying. Probably fewer than 50 of these birds exist.

•

From *the Audubon Society Field Guide to North American Birds, Western Region,* by Miklos D. F. Udvardy. New York: Alfred A. Knopf, 1977.

1

Stimulus

Forerunners of the Kremer Prize

PARIS, SATURDAY, JULY 9, 1921: At 3:45 A.M. it is cool and still dark at the famed Longchamps racecourse on the western edge of the city. About a hundred people are gathered around the main grandstand as the first light edges the treetops of the Bois de Boulogne. Some are obviously reporters and photographers; others are wearing sporting suits with knickers and high socks; and a few look as though they came straight from a night of merrymaking and a sobering bowl of onion soup at Les Halles. It is a perfect setting for a private *Course des Gentilhommes;* a scene for Degas.

Directly in front of the grandstand, four blue-smocked mechanics are assembling a curious machine. At its center is a racing bicycle with a front wheel larger than its rear wheel, and a frame fitted with unusual brackets. The mechanics are bolting a set of streamlined struts to the brackets; the lettering on their smocks reads *Nieuport.*

At the edge of the track a compact, dark-haired man in a knitted green jersey and shorts stretches his legs unself-consciously and watches the workmen fasten a long horizontal surface to the struts extending up from the front of the bicycle. It is a wing, 20 feet (6 metres) in span by 4 feet (1.2 metres) in chord. In a few minutes, a second wing 13 feet (4 metres) long is attached to the rear brackets on a level with the bicycle seat and just behind it. The wings are connected at mid-span with another pair of streamlined struts. The machine now resembles a small stagger-winged biplane with a bicycle for a fuselage, a sort of aerocycle.

The man in the green jersey comes over to the *Aviette,* as the

crew refers to it, and checks the operation of a lever on the handle-
bars. When he pulls it, both wings tilt up 6 degrees from their
position parallel to the ground and lock into place. The rider seems
satisfied and begins to warm up on another bicycle. His name is
Gabriel Poulain, and he is a 37-year-old pilot and professional
bicycle racer from St. Helier on the Isle of Jersey.

Poulain has been the bicycle sprint-racing champion of France
and the world, but this morning he is warming up for something
more difficult than a bicycle race: He is going to try to take off
and fly under his own power. He is making an official attempt on
the *Prix Peugeot* for a man-powered flight of more than 10 metres
— 32.8 feet. The prize is 10,000 francs, and Poulain has been
trying to win it since it was first offered in February 1912.

Nearly an hour has passed before the rider says he is ready. In
front of the grandstand two pairs of parallel white lines have been
drawn on the surface of the track, the innermost ones 10 metres
apart. Several gendarmes shepherd the spectators into the grandstand seats, showing special deference to the prominent industrialist
and automobile manufacturer, M. Robert Peugeot, who sits in the
front row. The Nieuport constructors move the machine down the
track and steady it while Poulain climbs aboard, then stand tensely
to one side.

Poulain checks the wing incidence lever one more time. At 4:43
A.M. he begins to pedal. The machine accelerates rapidly, rolls
toward the center of the track faster and faster. Before it reaches
the first line Poulain pulls his lever, the wings snap into their
6-degree up position, and — *Merveille!* — the *Aviette* lifts into
the air, climbs to a height of about 5 feet (1.5 metres), and glides
for 39 feet (11.98 metres). Poulain brings the aerocycle to a perfect landing well beyond the farthest line. There is a subdued cheer
from the spectators, followed by a hush of anticipation. The rules
of the *Prix Peugeot* state that the 10-metre flight must be repeated
in the opposite direction within 15 minutes after the first flight, so
as to cancel the effect of a favoring wind.

Four minutes later, at 4:47, Poulain starts in the opposite direction. Once again the aerocycle accelerates in a rush. The wings
angle up, the *Aviette* takes off and, flying a trifle lower this time,
arcs through the air for 38 feet (11.59 metres), easily passing the

10-metre requirement. A cheer goes up, the Nieuport crew are pounding the pilot on the back — but there is a disagreement among the judges. The officials hold a meeting on the track, with much headshaking and discussion. The final verdict is negative: While the distance requirement has been met, the rules require that the takeoff must occur between the first two sets of lines, and Poulain took off before reaching the first line.

There are some surly murmurs from the crowd and the constructors, but Poulain is undismayed. (His response to this setback was to earn him the admiration of all Europe.) He asks for an hour to rest before trying again, and the judges agree. By the time the hour has passed the sun is up, and the air is warmer and less dense; some advantage has been lost. The Nieuport team readies the *Aviette* again, and at 5:54 A.M. Poulain begins his new attempt. Once more the aerocycle accelerates along the track and sails into the air, this time at the proper place. The official distance from the first 10-metre line to the point of touchdown is 10.54 metres, at a maximum height of 1.5 metres. (The aeronautical press was later to note that the true airborne length of this flight from takeoff to landing was 38.5 feet — 11.72 metres.)

The spectators remain quiet as the *Aviette* is turned around. Poulain won his world championship in 1905, and he is not, after all, in the bloom of youth. At 6:03 he starts on the fourth run. Pedaling even harder than before, he confounds the skeptics in the grandstand with a magnificent controlled takeoff and a flight that the judges measure as 11.46 metres, but that is actually the longest of the day at 40.35 feet (12.30 metres). The crowd gives Poulain a standing ovation; the Peugeot Prize for human-powered flight has been well and truly won.

When the *Prix Peugeot* was first announced, on February 1, 1912, Europe and America were in a fever of excitement over aviation. The previous three years had seen a nonstop procession of records and achievements: the first air passenger service, the first seaplane, the first amphibian, the first takeoff and landing from a ship, the first airmail flights, the first night flight, the first flight across the English Channel, the first nonstop flight from London to Paris.

On New Year's Eve, 1912, Sergei Diaghilev's *Ballet Russe* staged a gala performance at the Paris Opéra in honor of French Aviation.

Tamara Karsavina and Vaslav Nijinsky danced *Le Spectre de la Rose,* and perhaps it was Nijinsky's floating leaps, which came closer to natural human flight than anything the French had ever seen, that inspired Robert Peugeot to offer his prize a few weeks later. A total of 198 competitors, including employees of aircraft firms like Farman and Voisin, registered for the first contest, to be held on June 2, 1912. In the event, only 23 machines actually appeared; their designs were weird and wonderful, but despite much huffing and puffing, not one of them was able to leave the ground.

The prize commission — nine aeronautical and engineering authorities — concluded that the task was too difficult and recommended that Peugeot sponsor an easier competition. He accepted their findings, and offered a prize that would make any broad-jumper smile. It was for a "flight" of 3.28 feet (1 metre), at an "altitude" of 4 inches (10 centimetres). It was won on July 4, 1912, by none other than Gabriel Poulain, with jumps of 11.8 and 10.9 feet (3.6 and 3.33 metres). It was probably this success that committed Poulain to a decade of research and development on the *Aviette.*

That decade encompassed World War I, a time of tremendous progress in aviation. The first Peugeot competition resembled a Dada *Tour de France.* It brought out a menagerie of amateur designs that looked like giant birds, butterflies, and rug-beaters. By contrast, Poulain's 1921 machine was built by a major air-craft company — Société Anonyme des Établissements Nieuport — which had produced thousands of 100-mile-per-hour fighter planes and whose founder, Édouard Nieuport, was a famous bicycle racer himself. The *Aviette* was designed by professional engineers, and its wings were pre-tested in a wind tunnel.

Robert Peugeot responded to its success by offering a new prize of 20,000 francs for a more difficult task: a two-way flight over a 164-foot (50-metre) course. That was a respectable goal, a human-powered flight one-third longer than the Wright brothers' first successful flight with an engine. Poulain announced his intention of competing for it with a propeller-driven craft to be built by Nieuport. As far as is known, the plane was never built, and no other competitor ever won the third and largest *Prix Peugeot.*

Prizes like Peugeot's are a symptom of the peculiar niche, half-way between sport and technology, that flying occupies in many people's minds. When Wilbur Wright won the 20,000-franc Michelin Prize by flying 77 miles (124 kilometres) nonstop on December 31, 1908, he was following a well-established tradition, in which the physical courage of the pilot was as important as the abilities of his machine. Peugeot, by offering a substantial reward for human-powered flight, put even more of the responsibility for success on the aviator. His 1912 prize was the first of its kind. Its eventual successor, the Kremer Prize, was to stimulate the first genuine solution to the problems of human-powered flight 65 years later.

During the nine-year tenure of the first *Prix Peugeot,* several other awards for human-powered flights were offered in France. They included the 500-franc *"Decimetre"* Prize, given by George Dubois for a 10-foot (3-metre) flight at a height of 8 inches (20 centimetres), and won by Sigmar Rettig, a German bicycle racer, on October 10, 1912; the *Prix Michelin,* 2000 francs for a flight of 16.4 feet (5 metres), won by Paul Didier on December 21, 1912; the *Prix Dubois* of 700 francs for a flight which reached a height of 32.8 feet (10 metres) — never won; and 100,000 francs offered by the Paris newspaper *La Justice* for a nonstop human-powered flight from Paris to Versailles and back!

Despite the third Peugeot Prize, after Poulain's success in 1921 progress in human-powered flight shifted from France to Germany, a country whose aviation industry was severely restricted. The Treaty of Versailles, signed in June 1919, included terms that were intended to prevent the Germans from developing or maintaining a viable air force. They included a six-month moratorium on the manufacture or importation of any aircraft, aircraft engine, or aircraft component beginning on the signing date of the treaty, and the surrender of all military and naval airplanes, all engines, and all parts for planes and engines.

As is often the case, the restrictions resulted in a focusing of creative energies. During the next decade, Germany became the world leader in gliding and human-powered flight. Most of the progress in these activities centered around a mountain called the Wasserkupe (Water tub) in the Rhön highlands northeast of Frankfurt. The mountain is 3117 feet (950 metres) high, and nearly continuous winds stream over its rounded contours, making it ideal for slope soaring.

The Wasserkupe site had been discovered in 1912 by a group of high school students from Darmstadt. They used it as a hang-gliding hill, patterning their gliders after Otto Lilienthal's bat-shaped designs of the 1890s. The best flight they recorded was one of 2700 feet (823 metres), made by Hans Gutermuth. It lasted 1 minute 52 seconds, a long way from Orville Wright's world duration record of 9 minutes and 45 seconds, made with a biplane glider at Kitty Hawk the previous year.

In the summer of 1920 Oskar Ursinus, an engineer, flying enthusiast, and editor of the aviation magazine *Flugsport,* organized a national gliding meet at the Wasserkupe to encourage the development of motorless flight in Germany. Only twenty-four entries showed up, and their inadequate standards were tragically demonstrated when one glider broke up in flight, killing its young pilot. The situation changed with the arrival of Wolfgang Klemperer, a 27-year-old pilot and aeronautical engineer who had flown for the German Air Force in World War I. He brought with him a cantilever monoplane glider named *Der Schwarzer Teufel* (*The Black Devil*), which he had designed. It had thick, sweptback wings, a slightly reflexed airfoil, and a very low wing loading. (Wing loading is the fraction of the airplane's weight that each unit of wing area must support in the air; it is equal to the weight of the airplane divided by the area of its wing.) Klemperer had also devised a new method of launching, using a long skein of rubber shock cord over a hook on the underside of the glider's fuselage to catapult it into the air.

On his first catapult launch, Klemperer kept *Schwarzer Teufel* in the air for 2 minutes 23 seconds, and flew 6006 feet (1831 metres), a new world's distance record for gliders. This and his subsequent flights in 1920 had an electric effect on young air-minded Germans. The regional technical institutes became bases for design groups striving to outdo each other in advancing motorless flight. At the 1921 Rhön meeting (the same summer that Gabriel Poulain won the *Prix Peugeot* in France), Klemperer beat Orville Wright's duration record by 4 minutes in his new glider, *Die Blaue Maus* (*The Blue Mouse*). He was then beaten himself by Arthur Martens, who flew for 15 minutes 30 seconds in *Vampyr,* a revolutionary machine designed and built at the Hannover Technical Institute. *Vampyr* has been called the first true sailplane, and in one thrilling week during the summer of 1922, it raised the world soaring duration record to one hour, then two hours, and finally to more than three hours.

Three hours without an engine! The news shocked the aeronautical world into recognizing a new regime of flight. The first soaring meet in England was held at Itford Hill in September 1922 and was soon followed by meets in France, Algeria, and the Russian Crimea. Permanent buildings were set up at the Wasserkupe, and another soaring center was established on the sand dunes of Rossiten in East Prussia by the Rhön-Rossiten Gesellschaft, a new organization dedicated to the advancement of motorless flight.

Oskar Ursinus had come up with the right idea at the right time, but even though soaring continued to make dramatic progress during the 1920s, it could not absorb all the creative energy of the repressed German aircraft industry. There was another area of motorless flight to explore: flight by human power. Perhaps inevitably, Ursinus and other soaring enthusiasts soon began to design experimental human-powered airplanes.

As in France, the incentive was a prize. In 1925 the Rhön-Rossiten-Gesellschaft offered an award of 4000 Reichmarks for the first person who could fly a distance of 328 feet (100 metres) in a wind of less than 2.2 miles per hour (3 metres per second) by muscle power alone. The first contest was held at the Wasserkupe in September 1925, and the only competitor to get off the ground was Dr. Martin Brustmann, a Berlin physician who specialized in the physiology of sport. Brustmann flew his bat-winged bicycle about 66 feet (20 metres) — the longest verified man-powered flight in history to that date.

Like Poulain, Brustmann was bitten by the bug. In 1926 he and the distinguished aerodynamicist Dr. Alexander Lippisch began a joint research program on human-powered flight. Brustmann measured the power developed by a number of trained athletes, and concluded that a fit man could produce up to 2 horsepower (1.5 kilowatts) in a short burst, and maintain a steady output of 0.25 hp (0.19 kW). In 1929 he and Lippisch collaborated on the design of a human-powered ornithopter, a flapping-wing airplane

with a wingspan of 32.8 feet (10 metres). Although it was catapult launched, its pilot-actuated wings were able to sustain only
a descending glide.

In the meantime the irrepressible Ursinus, encouraged by Alexander Lippisch, continued to evangelize about motorless flight. One
of the groups he influenced was the Frankfurter Polytechnische
Gesellschaft, which in 1933 offered a 5000-mark prize for a closed-
circuit human-powered flight around two pylons 1640 feet (500
metres) apart. A catapult launch was allowed, provided that the
energy-storage device or an equivalent weight was carried in the
plane during the flight.

The first entry for this competition did not appear until August
1935. The plane was named *Mufli,* a contraction of *Muskel-Flieger*
— Human-Powered Flyer. (The name was doubly appropriate,
since in German a "Flieger" is also a bicycle sprint racer.) It was
designed by Helmut Haessler, a sailplane pilot and engineer at the
Junkers Flugzeuge und Motorenwerke A.G. in Dessau, and built
by Haessler and a fellow Junkers pilot/engineer, Franz Villinger.

Mufli was a streamlined high-wing monoplane, with a T-tail and
a wingspan of 44.3 feet (13.5 metres). It looked like a sailplane,
except for a front-mounted vertical pylon carrying a pusher propeller 5 feet (1.5 metres) in diameter, and a wire-braced wing
to lighten the main spar. Most of its structural components were
made of thin cedar plywood. The pilot sat in a nearly fetal position in a tiny cockpit directly under the wing. He had two open
side ports to look out of, but no direct forward vision.

Mufli's propeller was pedal-driven through a rubber-coated belt-
and-pulley system, and the empty weight of the plane was a remarkably low 75 pounds (34 kilograms). The first tests were made
at Dessau, with Karl Dünnebeil, a 27-year-old glider pilot in the
cockpit. (Dünnebeil added another 143 pounds [65 kilograms] to
the weight of the aircraft.) Haessler's wing incidence control system proved to be marginal, but after 55 short flights, the plane
was moved to Rebstock airfield near Frankfurt for measured trials.

On August 29, 30, and 31, 1935, Dünnebeil made 7 flights on
Mufli that were witnessed by three official observers. All of the
flights began with a rubber-cable–catapulted takeoff to an altitude
of about 10 feet (3 metres), whereupon the pilot began pedaling

to keep the plane in the air as long as possible. The longest flight lasted 24 seconds and covered 771 feet (235 metres).

That was far short of the requirements of the Frankfurt Polytechnic Prize, but everyone concerned with the project was elated nevertheless. The Director of National Sporting Aviation sent a report of the flights to the Minister of Air Forces, Air Marshal Hermann Göring. The judges committee of the Polytechnische Gesellschaft decided that, although the flights did not qualify for the prize, they deserved an award of 3000 marks. Air Marshal Göring personally added another 3000 marks to encourage *Mufli*'s builders, and the Frankfurt Prize was raised to 10,000 marks.

As a result of the Rebstock flights, the builders decided to change *Mufli*'s control system to a conventional rudder and elevator. Haessler was sure that the plane also needed a more powerful pilot if they were to succeed. The man who came to his aid was none other than Oskar Ursinus.

Ursinus's championing of motorless flight was officially recognized by the German government at the end of 1935. With the backing of the Ministry of Aviation, the Polytechnische Gesellschaft set up at Frankfurt the *Muskelflug-Institut* — an Institute of Human-Powered Flight — with Ursinus as its Director. The nominal functions of the institute were to assist experimenters with work on human-powered aircraft and to carry on basic research in the field.

One of Ursinus's first projects was the systematic measurement of human-power output. During 1936 and 1937, he recorded the power developed by a number of athletes in various positions, using arms, legs, and a combination of both. He also compiled data for rotating, oscillating, and reciprocating motion. The results of these experiments were published with admirable promptness, and they are still a valuable reference for physiologists.

One of the athletes that Ursinus tested was a 26-year-old bicycle racer and pilot from Offenbach named Hoffmann. Hoffmann weighed 154 pounds (70 kilograms), and during the tests he produced a momentary output of 1.315 horsepower (100 meter-kilograms) per second, at a frequency of 2 cycles per second, using his legs alone. This was 30 percent higher than the output of any of the *Muskelflug-Institut*'s previous subjects. Ursinus recommended

DR.-ING. HANS SEEHASE'S MD 2 HUMAN-POWERED AIRPLANE. 1937

© JANET GROSSER 4/1980

Hoffmann to Helmut Haessler, and he became *Mufli*'s new pilot/ engine.

On November 17, 1936, in Hamburg, Hoffmann pedaled *Mufli* 1401 feet (427 metres), and on July 4, 1937, at Meiningen, he made his longest recorded flight of 2336 feet (712 metres). Despite Hoffmann's ability and the improvements that Haessler and Villinger made to the plane, *Mufli* was never able to complete the Frankfurt Prize Course. In February 1938 it was retired to the Berlin Air Transport Museum after making about 120 flights.

Considering its shortcomings, it is ironic that *Mufli* became an archetype for subsequent human-powered planes. Its conventional forward-wing and rear-empennage layout, its sailplane-like design, its closely spaced wooden ribs, even its pylon and propeller position, were to be copied many times during the next 40 years, usually with disappointing results. Haessler and Villinger's plane had a wing loading of 2.35 pounds per square foot (11.5 kilograms per square metre). This in turn dictated a relatively high flying speed, which required more power to sustain. Although they seemed logical at the time, most of *Mufli*'s design principles proved to be blind alleys in the search for successful human-powered flight.

In 1937 Dr. Hans Seehase, a German engineer, proposed a radically different solution to the problem in Ursinus's magazine *Flugsport*. Seehase had built several man-carrying kites and two experimental human-powered airplanes. Although his third projected HPA was a high-wing monoplane, it differed in almost every other respect from *Mufli*.

First of all, it was framed with aircraft aluminum tubing instead of wood. Its 43-foot (13-metre)-span wing had a single tubular spar 2 inches (50 millimetres) in diameter, and only a few widely spaced aluminum ribs. The shape of the airfoil was maintained at the leading edge by false ribs, and the rubber-tensioned trailing edge incorporated flexible warping ailerons for roll control. Most of the wing's weight was supported by a pair of lightweight struts and a network of wire bracing rigged to aluminum spreaders.

Seehase's plane was controlled by a very light rudder and sta-

[*opposite*] 1. Dr.-Ing. Hans Seehase's proposed human-powered plane was designed in 1937, and anticipated the structure of the *Gossamer Condor* by nearly 40 years.

bilizer supported at the end of a slim tubular boom on a line with the wing. The pilot sat in a normal cycling position inside a short, streamlined cockpit framed with a vertical truss. A fore-and-aft propeller shaft ran in bearings over his head, on the centerline of the wing and the tail boom. The tractor propeller was 9.38 feet (2.86 metres) in diameter, made of streamlined aluminum tubing, with lightweight wooden blades near its outer ends. The driving force was transmitted from the pilot's pedals to the propeller via an ingenious system of tubular cranks designed by Seehase and built by Deutsche Benzinuhren GmbH of Berlin.

Seehase calculated the wing loading of his plane with a 65-kilogram pilot as 5.6 kilograms per square metre — 1.15 pounds per square foot, less than half of *Mufli*'s wing loading. As far as is known, only a propeller test rig and a few other components of Seehase's third design were actually built. Perhaps, like many such proposals, it deserves to remain buried in the archives of aviation — except that Seehase guessed right.

Anyone familiar with contemporary human-powered planes will experience a shock of recognition on seeing a 3-view drawing of Seehase's HPA: If one reverses the direction of flight, it could be a prototype of Paul MacCready's *Gossamer Condor,* forty years ahead of its time. The proportions, the materials, and the structural design are virtually identical. The tubular aluminum wing spar is even the same diameter in both planes. Seehase's concept was criticized as being too flimsy by his colleagues, but with the advantage of hindsight, we can say that he erred only by not making it flimsy enough. His design is almost a half-scale model of the *Gossamer Condor,* and hence it was probably half as large, and twice as strong, as it needed to be.

One other German constructor perceived that large scale was essential to successful human-powered flight. In 1928 Englebert Zaschka of Berlin built a test chassis to develop an efficient propeller drive, and six years later he completed a large human-powered tractor monoplane with a narrow wing spanning about 66 feet (20 metres). This high aspect ratio wing was wire-braced from a vertical kingpost, a system that has proven very successful in later HPAs. The frame of Zaschka's aircraft was a minimal skeleton of steel tubing, but even with four men accelerating the plane up to its nominal flight speed, it was unable to take off.

During the 1930s many German activities were copied in Italy soon afterward, and in 1936, three years after the Frankfurt Poly-technische Gesellschaft Prize was announced, the Italian government offered a prize of 100,000 lire for a 1-kilometre human-powered flight to be made by an Italian citizen. At that time there was already one Italian-born and -trained aircraft engineer working on an HPA project; the only flaw was that he had emigrated to the United States after World War I and had become an American citizen.

Enea Bossi was born in Milano in 1888 and graduated from the Instituto Technico in nearby Lodi in 1907. Although he specialized in physics and mathematics, he was deeply impressed by the successes of the Wright brothers and decided to devote himself to aviation. In 1908, financed by his father, he designed and built a 46-foot (14-metre)-span biplane patterned after the Wright *Flyer,* and taught himself to fly on it. It became the first Italian airplane to be serially produced (in Bossi's own factory) and won a silver medal at the first international aviation meeting at Reims, France, in 1909. Soon afterward Bossi designed and installed the first aircraft landing-gear brake system and also designed the Italian navy's first seaplane, which proved very successful.

After serving as a bomber pilot and flight instructor for the Italian Navy in World War I, Bossi emigrated to the United States in 1918. In 1928 he founded the American Aeronautical Corporation to build Savoia-Marchetti seaplanes under license, and two years later he supervised the design and construction of the *Pioneer,* the first stainless steel aircraft in the world. This 4-place amphibian was built by the Edward G. Budd Company in Philadelphia, and as a result of its success, Bossi returned to Italy as the European representative of the Budd Company. In 1932 he heard that an airplane powered by a 1-horsepower (¾-kilowatt) engine had flown successfully. The feat prompted him to calculate the minimum power that a man-carrying aircraft needed to fly. He came up with a figure of 0.7 kilowatt — slightly less than 1 horsepower — and this deceptively small-sounding number made him think that human-powered flight was possible.

On one of Bossi's trips back to Philadelphia he made drag tests using a professional bicyclist towing a glider. A spring scale was inserted in the towline, and measurements were made of the speed at which the glider would take off under tow, and the corresponding force exerted by the bicyclist. (This experiment will be all too familiar to anyone who has ever built a human-powered airplane. It was repeated, with variations, many times with both the *Gossamer Condor* and the *Gossamer Albatross*.) Back in Paris, Bossi built a bicycle driven by a pusher propeller of his own design. His test rider reached a speed of 23 miles (37 kilometres) per hour on this machine. It had one drawback: The gyroscopic effect of the propeller made the bicycle unstable, and Bossi concluded (erroneously) that a successful human-powered plane would need two counter-rotating propellers to cancel out the effects of torque. He decided to design an aircraft incorporating this difficult requirement.

While he was working on the design, the Italian government announced its 0.62-mile (1-kilometre) human-powered flight prize. Bossi knew that he could not receive the prize because of his American citizenship, but he decided to try to win it anyway. He took his plans to Vittorio Bonomi, an Italian sailplane manufacturer, and Bonomi agreed to build the airplane under contract. It was to be named *Pedaliante* — "Pedal-Glider."

Pedaliante was a high-winged streamlined monoplane with a wingspan of 58 feet (17.7 metres), and a wing area of 252 square feet (23.4 square metres). The airfoil Bossi used was the American NACA 0012-F1. Control surfaces included a conventional rear rudder and elevator and a pair of wing spoilers, all activated by an ingenious divided-control yoke. The pilot sat semi-upright, and a bicycle chain transmitted the power from his pedals to an overhead transverse shaft that was bevel-geared to large twin propellers extending from the wing on either side of the fuselage.

Bossi designed a wooden airframe of great elegance for *Pedaliante*. His original contract with Bonomi specified an empty weight of 160 pounds (72.6 kilograms), with an overweight contingency of 20 pounds (9.1 kilograms). Bonomi was probably capable of meeting this specification, but the Italian Air Ministry insisted that the plane satisfy the same structural requirements as an engine-powered aircraft. The result was that *Pedaliante* weighed 220 pounds (100 kilograms) without a pilot, a crippling handicap.

Bossi's pilot was Emilio Casco, a major in the Italian army. Casco was a very strong bicyclist, and after a few weeks of trials in early 1936, he took off in *Pedaliante* under his own power and flew 300 feet (91.4 metres). Although subsequent calculations have verified that this flight was physically possible, all sources agree that it was a singular accomplishment, achieved only because of Casco's great physical strength. Bossi decided that the plane's thrust was inadequate, and enlarged the laminated balsa wood propellers in several stages from 6.2 feet (1.9 metres) to 7.4 feet (2.25 metres) in diameter. Each enlargement improved the performance, but the fuselage position prevented any further increase.

Both pilot and designer knew that the plane was greatly overweight and that it couldn't be lightened because of the Italian airworthiness regulations; Bossi decided to borrow a leaf from the Germans' book and try catapult launching. It took several months to develop a launch system that would work for a plane of *Pedaliante*'s size. Late in 1936 Casco flew several hundred metres after a catapult takeoff, and on March 18, 1937, at Cinisello airport in Milano, the plane was launched to a height of 29.5 feet (9 metres), and Casco pedaled it for 0.62 mile (1 kilometre) successfully.

This was a world record for human-powered flight, but there was no catapult launch allowance in the rules of the Italian competition. Like *Mufli, Pedaliante* was retired in 1938 without capturing the prize it had been designed to win. According to the records of its designer it had made 80 flights, 43 of them without the assistance of a catapult launch. At that point *Pedaliante* and *Mufli* were the two most advanced human-powered aircraft ever built. Neither was to survive the impending World War.

2

The Kremer Prize

Human-Powered Flight 1938–1961

A DECADE OF URGENT EXPANSION for the world's aircraft industry began in 1930. No one involved with flying could ignore the thunderheads on the political horizon; all over the globe, air forces began to arm for the coming conflict. The years preceding the war were marked by intense international rivalry in record-breaking and civil aviation, and many of the engineers who were to advance human-powered flight were caught up in these activities.

Between 1930 and 1932 Junkers Flugzeuge und Motorenwerke, where *Mufli* was built, developed the Junkers Ju52 trimotor, one of the world's great transport aircraft. During the first year of the Ju52 program, Junkers had the help of a young Canadian engineer named Beverley Shenstone.

Shenstone was born in 1906, and in 1929 he received the first master's degree in aeronautical engineering awarded by the University of Toronto. Between college terms he learned to fly on a Royal Canadian Air Force Avro 504, and after graduation he took a job at the Junkers Werke in Dessau in order to combine engineering experience with learning German. While working on the Ju52, Shenstone became caught up in the German soaring movement; he used his summer vacation to earn a sailplane pilot's certificate at the Rhön-Rossiten-Gesellschaft. On the Wasserkupe he met Alexander Lippisch, who had just collaborated with Martin Brustmann on a man-powered ornithopter. Shenstone became fascinated with human-powered flight, but within three years he was working on the prototype of the Spitfire fighter. The seed planted on the Wasserkupe was to flower twenty-five years later, when Shenstone, then chief engineer of British European Airways, began the chain of events that led to the Kremer Prize, and eventually to the *Gossamer Condor*.

On March 1, 1935, the existence of the German *Luftwaffe* was announced to an apprehensive world. By that time Shenstone's erstwhile employer was developing the Ju87 *Stuka* dive bomber, but the engine division of Junkers was also trying to make a long-distance record flight with a diesel-powered flying boat. Two years earlier the world distance record had been broken by a small English firm, the Fairey Aviation Company, Ltd. Over February 6–8, 1933, Fairey's Long Range Monoplane flew 5309 miles (8544 kilometres) from Cranwell, Lincolnshire, to Walvis Bay, South Africa. In 1935 the Royal Aeronautical Establishment Resident Technical Officer at Fairey Aviation was a 41-year-old engineer named Robert Graham.

Graham was a mechanical engineer who adopted aviation. Born in Glasgow, he was trained at Darlington Technical College and fought in World War I. (It was only after he was buried by an artillery shell and lost his glasses that an Army oculist decided that his sight was not up to standard and sent him home.) In the 1920s Graham helped develop the Brennan helicopter, becoming one of the world's first helicopter pilots. This project focused his interest on the mechanics of flying and eventually on the most basic form of those mechanics, human-powered flight.

Graham remained at Fairey Aviation through 1939, and during his tenure a new attempt was made on the world distance record halfway around the world: On May 15, 1938, the Japanese *Koken* (Aeronautical Research Institute) long-range monoplane flew 7241 miles (11,651 kilometres) nonstop. One of its principal designers was an engineer named Hidemasa Kimura, whose interests were remarkably similar to those of Robert Graham and Beverley Shenstone.

Kimura was born in Sapporo, Hokkaido, in 1904. He was one of only seven aeronautical engineering students accepted at Tokyo Imperial University in 1924, and after graduation he became a trainee at the university's Aeronautical Research Institute. In 1937 Kimura was appointed to the Institute staff, and after the *Koken*'s successful flight, he was individually decorated by the Emperor of

Japan, an extraordinary honor at the time. Kimura's aeronautical interests included birds, sailplanes, and human-powered flight; but it was only in 1961, after a brilliant career as a designer of transport aircraft, that he started a student team to build a series of human-powered planes. The people responsible for reviving his interest were Beverley Shenstone and Robert Graham.

On September 1, 1939, the German army invaded Poland without prior warning. Two days later Britain and France declared war on Germany, and the second great conflict of the twentieth century had begun. For the next six years, most of the creative minds in aviation were working on war machines. There was little place for human-powered planes in a milieu preoccupied with speed, altitude, and firepower, and it was 1955 before a resurgence of interest in human-powered flight occurred. This time it began in England instead of on the continent, but it followed a historical pattern already established in detail.

Since the *Prix Peugeot* of 1912, all significant advances in human-powered flight had been motivated by prizes. Some were offered by private companies (Michelin, Peugeot); some by non-profit organizations (the Frankfurter Polytechnischen Gesellschaft, the Rhön-Rossiten-Gesellschaft); some by governments (the Italian Air Ministry); and some by individuals (George Dubois). Several competitors for these prizes were subsidized by industrial companies (Poulain/Nieuport; Haessler-Villinger/Junkers).

The designers of successful aircraft had surprisingly similar training and backgrounds. All of the competitions for human-powered flight attracted entries designed by home craftsmen or "intuitive engineers." It is probably safe to say that hundreds of such machines have been built by amateurs in various countries between 1912 and the present. Alas for the dreams of schoolboys — every human-powered plane whose flight has been witnessed by reliable observers was designed and built by professional engineers.

The make-up of the successful teams was also virtually identical. Each group included one or more aeronautical engineers (Nieuport, Lippisch, Haessler, Villinger, Bossi); one or more trained pilots (Poulain, Haessler, Villinger, Dünnebeil, Hoffmann, Bossi, Casco); and one or more bicycle racers (Didier, Rettig, Poulain, Hoffmann, Casco). (Of course some or all of these abilities could overlap in a single individual.) Other points of similarity included experience with sailplanes (Lippisch, Haessler, Villinger, Dünnebeil), and expertise in human physiology (Brustmann, Ursinus). This combination of talents was to be reassembled many times in various countries before the problems of human-powered flight were finally solved.

In 1955 few people were aware that these patterns existed. In fact, to judge by accounts of the attempts at human-powered flight that did take place, the public, the press, and most of the aeronautical establishment still believed that human-powered aircraft were exclusively the province of madmen and quacks. There had been a few constructive postwar contributions to the field. In England, Brian Worley published an article in *Aeronautics* in which he compared the power requirements of *Mufli* and *Pedaliante* with those of a contemporary British sailplane. One of his conclusions — an accurate one — was that research was needed on low-speed, high-lift airfoils. In the United States Dr. August Raspet, an aeronautical engineer working on glider design at Mississippi State College, applied his work on wing-drag reduction to human-powered aircraft and published some (optimistic) design specifications. Both of these studies were concerned with slow flight.

To many aerodynamicists that seemed like an outmoded subject. Since the beginning of World War II, aviation had been revolutionized by the development of enormously powerful reciprocating engines and by the invention and application of the turbojet and turboprop. The high power-to-weight ratio of the jet engine tended to focus attention on the more spectacular frontiers of flight. At the beginning of 1955 the world long-distance flight record, made by a Lockheed P2V-1 Neptune patrol bomber, stood at 11,235.6 miles (18,082 kilometres). The world altitude record was 63,671 feet (19,406 metres), reached by an English Electric Canberra bomber; and the world absolute speed record, then held by a YF-100A Super Sabre fighter, was 755.3 miles (1215.3 kilometres) per hour.

Beverley Shenstone was as involved as anyone in the new developments. As chief engineer of British European Airways he was largely responsible for the introduction of the turboprop-powered Vickers Viscount, and he was deeply committed to the development of a replacement for the ill-fated Comet 1 jet transport. Despite these current professional concerns, in February 1955 he published an article in the *Sunday Times* of London, urging that new research be started on human-powered flight and bird flight.

Perhaps the most important thing about this piece (besides its appearance in a highly respected publication) was the outstanding reputation of its author. No aeronautical engineer could dismiss Beverley Shenstone as a quack, and his article provoked a number of serious replies, including one from Sir Alliott Verdon-Roe, one of the great pioneers of British aviation. In September of the same year Shenstone suggested the building of modern versions of *Mufli* and *Pedaliante* to the Canadian Aeronautical Institute, and on November 12 he presented a paper on human-powered flight to the Low Speed Aerodynamics Research Association in London.

Such technological prompting often only reaches the few enthusiasts who are interested in the same subject. In this case, however, it was a true seminal impulse; many of the subsequent successes in the field can be traced back to Beverley Shenstone's burst of enthusiasm in 1955 and 1956. On January 10, 1957, Shenstone became the nucleus of a committee formed at the College of Aeronautics at Cranfield to encourage the development of human-powered aircraft.

R.A.F. Cranfield can be considered the cradle of British human-powered flight. During World War II it was a Royal Air Force base in a tiny Bedfordshire village, and in 1946 a postgraduate college of aeronautics was founded there to continue the R.A.F.'s wartime progress in aeronautical research. Enrollment was limited to 200 graduate students each year, all of whom were admitted on a full-scholarship basis and by invitation only. (Since 1969 the college has been chartered as Cranfield Institute of Technology and now enrolls some 500 full-time graduate students.)

In January 1957 the following seven men became the founding members of the Cranfield Man-Powered Aircraft Committee (MAPAC):

Dr. J. R. Brown of the London School of Hygiene and Tropical Medicine.

Robert Graham, then just retired (and awarded the CBE) as Director of Aircraft Equipment Research and Development for the Ministry of Supply.

H. B. Irving, President of the Low Speed Aerodynamics Research Association (Committee Chairman).

Thurstan James, Editor of *The Aeroplane*.

A. Newell, Engineering Instructor at the College of Aeronautics, Cranfield.

T. R. F. Nonweiler (now Professor) of the Queen's University of Belfast.

B. S. Shenstone, Chief Engineer of British European Airways.

This group held eight scientific and engineering degrees and many technical society fellowships, but its initial reception by the aeronautical establishment was to give Bev Shenstone several opportunities to indulge his dry sense of humor. When queried by the Scientific Adviser to the Air Ministry about the possible military applications of man-powered aircraft, Shenstone replied, "It has an immediate military value as a more dangerous method of training commandoes." He also asked the Royal Aeronautical Society to designate one of their council as a member of MAPAC, to "indicate that we are not necessarily completely crazy, and that our efforts have some sound technical background."

There was no shortage of enthusiasm among the committee members. Meetings followed closely on each other during 1957, and by February 1958 the membership had more than doubled. The new group included five more aeronautical engineers (including the aforementioned Scientific Adviser to the Air Ministry, now a convert), a physiologist from University College, London, an officer of the National Union of Cyclists, and a well-known wildfowl artist and glider pilot.

A number of review papers and theoretical proposals were presented at MAPAC meetings, but no aircraft was built. At the end of Shenstone's presentation of a design study for a complex, two-man HPA, he commented that successful human-powered flight would result only from design, manufacture, and testing — that is, from hardware. Despite two years of exchanging ideas at Cranfield, little hardware was to be seen. In October 1958, ten members of MAPAC proposed the founding of a man-powered flight committee within the Royal Aeronautical Society, and this was approved the following year. In effect, MAPAC was merged into the Man-Powered Aircraft Group Committee of the Royal Aeronautical Society on October 30, 1959.

One of the original aims of the Cranfield College Committee had been to subsidize the construction of human-powered aircraft. A

modest amount of money was collected for this purpose by members contributing broadcast fees, by gifts from companies, and by
small donations from individuals, but the total was not adequate
to fund an airplane project. Bob Graham (now Chairman of the
Committee) hoped that the official sanction of the Royal Aeronautical Society would improve MAPAC's position for fund-raising. He
was happily surprised by how quickly that happened.

At Farnborough, and later at the Ministry of Supply, Graham
had directed large engineering departments and been responsible
for the development and testing of landing gear, propellers, and
many other mechanical aircraft systems. Despite chronic health
problems, he was very resilient. (Although Graham underwent
many operations, he remained cheerful and productive to an advanced age.) He was obviously far too valuable an engineer to retire
at 62, a fact recognized by the managers of Microcell Limited, the
company that snapped him up as Technical Director immediately
following his retirement from the Ministry of Supply.

The Chairman of Microcell was an engineer and industrialist
named Henry Kremer. Kremer was Graham's junior by thirteen
years — he was born in 1907 in eastern Europe and educated and
trained in Switzerland — but the two men shared a talent for practical, real-world engineering. Kremer's parents had emigrated to
England after World War I and started a small plywood and chip-
board fabrication business. Their son joined the firm in 1927 and
proved to be brilliant at devising new materials and methods of
making them. By the time World War II broke out, Kremer held a
number of patents, including those for the plywood process used
to build the de Havilland *Mosquito* bomber.

Kremer founded Microcell in 1951 and subsequently expanded
it into the Laser group of companies. Bob Graham continued with
him as Technical Director, first of Laser Engineering Ltd., and
then of Laser Engineering (Development) Ltd., a firm specializing
in the design and production of hydraulic systems and components.
By 1959 he and Henry Kremer had become close associates and
friends.

Since working with de Havilland, Kremer had maintained his
interest in aviation, and he was also very interested in physical
fitness. Both subjects were closely connected with Bob Graham's

pet project of developing a human-powered aircraft, and from time to time Graham informed Kremer of the progress of MAPAC and its successor committee of the Royal Aeronautical Society. One day in 1959, Kremer, Graham, H. G. Bennison, Fred East, and Air Commodore Bryan Hatfield stopped for lunch at the Cambridge Hotel in Camberley after touring one of Microcell's factories. The group was in a jovial mood because of a successful merger, and Graham spoke enthusiastically about human-powered flight. "Man *could* fly," he told the other men. "If only someone would put up a prize for it, say about five thousand pounds." (Approximately $14,000 at that time.)

"I'll put up five thousand pounds," Henry Kremer volunteered immediately.

The astonished and delighted Graham turned to his companions and verified that they had heard Kremer's offer. Bennison confirmed it and offered to put a plaque on the lunch table if anything ever came of it. That was the beginning of the Kremer Prize.

The prize was announced in November 1959, and a letter signed by Robert Graham in the Royal Aeronautical Society *Journal* for January 1960 stated that the award would be made for ". . . the first successful flight of a British designed, built, and flown Man-Powered Aircraft, such flight to take place within the British Commonwealth, under conditions laid down by the Royal Aeronautical Society."

The Kremer Prize was heady news for the Man-Powered Aircraft Group Committee. It brought both new responsibilities and some unaccustomed limelight. One effect of the latter was to attract more money. Air Commodore J. G. Weir donated £1000 ($2800) to start a fund for the encouragement of human-powered flight. His gift was followed by others from British Aircraft Corporation, British Petroleum, Hawker Siddeley Aviation, Ltd., Shell Oil, and Westland Aircraft, Ltd. When Henry Kremer learned about this fund, he added an additional £2500 ($7000) to it, to administer his original prize. In some ways this gift was the most important one of all, because it enabled the Royal Aeronautical Society Committee to give a full measure of time and concentration to writing the rules for the Kremer Competition.

A number of optional courses were open to the Kremer rules

committee. The prize requirement could have been a straight-line flight over a specified distance like the *Prix Peugeot*, a combination of distance and height like the *Decimetre* Prize, or a circuit combining distance and controlled maneuvers like the *Frankfurter Polytechnische Gesellschaft* Prize. In the event, the Kremer Circuit was designed most like the Frankfurt Course, but with an added measure of difficulty: Its requirements included distance, turning ability, and altitude.

The rules of the first Kremer Competition were issued by the Royal Aeronautical Society in February 1960 and included some twenty clauses. (The complete set of rules is given in the Appendix.) The main requirements were:

1. That the aircraft be a heavier-than-air machine powered and controlled entirely by its crew.
2. That it must take off from level ground entirely by human power in still air.
3. That it must fly a figure-of-eight course embracing two turning points not less than one-half mile (804.6 metres) apart.
4. That it must fly over a 10-foot (3-metre) height marker at the starting line of the course between the two turn markers, and cross the same altitude marker again at the finish line of the course.

There were also rules banning the use of lighter-than-air gases, jettisonable parts, and energy-storage devices, and clauses dealing with official observers, insurance, and registration. The registration fee was one pound sterling (refundable in the event that a flight was made!), and the competition was open only to citizens of the British Commonwealth. The original announcement also specified that if the prize were not won by February 1962 the rules would be reviewed, and possibly revised.

Seen in retrospect, the Kremer Competition rules are a model of what such requirements should be. They are clear, succinct, free of loopholes, trivia, and ambiguities; and they are written in straightforward jargon-free English. In effect, they turned what could have been treated as a stunt into a serious endeavor. By the time the Figure-of-Eight Competition was won seventeen years later, these rules were accepted worldwide as the definition of human-powered flight.

Their reception was quite different when they were first issued. Given the unimpressive history of human-powered flight, the Kremer Course requirements seemed formidable to most aeronautical engineers, and impossible to many of them. Alexander Lippisch, then living in America, wrote an article criticizing the rules as too difficult and discouraging. Franz Villinger and Beverley Shenstone felt that a straight flight was a more realistic goal, and Thurstan James, a member of MAPAC and editor of *The Aeroplane,* asked in his own column, "Has the prize been put too far out of reach?"

A reassuring answer came quite quickly. G. M. Lilley, a professor of aeronautics at Southampton University, was one of the second group of MAPAC members described earlier. Following a meeting chaired by Lilley in the spring of 1960, three postgraduate students in his department decided to build an aircraft to compete for the Kremer Prize. Their names were Alan Lassière, Anne Marsden, and David Williams, and they called their project *SUMPAC,* for *S*outhampton *U*niversity *M*an-*P*owered *A*ir*C*raft.

With the support of the Southampton Aeronautics Department, Lassière, Marsden, and Williams became the third, fourth, and fifth Kremer Competition registrants to pay their pounds to the Royal Aeronautical Society. (They would have been surprised to know that eventually the list would include 52 competitors from 11 countries.) They began the design of *SUMPAC* in July 1960, working as fast as they could.

Although they had access to new human-power output measurements made by Dr. D. R. Wilkie, the University College physiologist who joined MAPAC, the Southampton group chose to make their own tests. Anne Marsden later described them with wry humor: "We had teams of undergraduates running up and down stairs while we timed them with stopwatches . . . We made a rig to simulate what we thought was a favorable position for the pilot and measured the power output of a number of cyclists. The power was absorbed by electrical resistances from a pedal-driven generator and measured with a wattmeter." The data resulting from this ingenious jury-rig agreed closely with Wilkie's, and also with the wind tunnel drag measurements of cyclists made by T. R. F. Nonweiler, one of the original members of MAPAC.

The *SUMPAC* group had the dedication and enthusiasm of the best student projects, but its resources were limited. However, the reasons that the designers chose to emphasize speed and expediency were not entirely economic. On August 12, 1960, a second Kremer Competition team was formed; from the viewpoint of the Southampton students, it looked like a Goliath to their own David.

The Hatfield Man-Powered Aircraft Club was organized by John C. Wimpenny, then assistant Chief Aerodynamicist of the de Havilland Aircraft Company. The club had the blessings of de Havilland's directors and the support of the company, which was recognized as a world authority on wooden aircraft design and construction. At its peak, the Hatfield club had forty members (most of them professional engineers), a team of apprentices from the de Havilland Aeronautical Technical School, a number of distinguished honorary advisers, and access to all of de Havilland's facilities at Hatfield.

The Hatfield aircraft was named *Puffin,* both for the droll Atlantic seabird and for the state of the pilot while flying; initial financing for the plane came from the founding members of the club. Despite the great difference in resources, for the next fifteen months *Puffin* and *SUMPAC* progressed virtually neck-and-neck in the first race for the Kremer Prize.

By the beginning of 1961, the configuration of *SUMPAC* had emerged as an expanded son-of-*Mufli*. It was a streamlined, cantilever-wing monoplane with a conventional rear empennage and a pylon carrying an 8-foot (2.4-metre) pusher propeller directly over the wing root. It still looked like an auxiliary-powered sailplane, but with a 300-square-foot (27.9-square-metre) wing, 80 feet (24.4 metres) long, it had about twice *Mufli*'s span and triple its wing area. Construction was conventional: The wing used two laminated wood spars and built-up ribs, and the fuselage was a wooden box truss surrounding a sheet aluminum cockpit girder, which carried the mechanical loads and to which the other components were bolted. The main constructional materials were spruce and balsa, and the calculated all-up flying weight was about 264 pounds (120 kilograms).

SUMPAC used a novel drive system: The pilot pedaled a bicycle chainwheel that powered a standard racing bicycle wheel for taxiing. The bicycle wheel was linked to the propeller shaft by a thin tensioned steel band, an arrangement that offered theoretical advantages in weight and efficiency but gave considerable trouble in practice.

The problem of an engine remained. Originally the Southampton group had planned to draft a well-known long-distance runner to fly the plane, but he was not a pilot. A second plan involved all of the designers' learning to fly gliders so they could take turns at piloting. Eventually the team asked Derek Piggott, Chief Instructor of the Lasham Gliding Center, to be *SUMPAC*'s pilot/ engine. Piggott trained dutifully, reaching the level of what Dr. Wilkie classified as an "average fit man." In view of the difficulties of flying *SUMPAC,* the decision turned out to be a wise one.

In January 1961 construction began on *SUMPAC*'s airframe, and the Royal Aeronautical Society responded to a request for financial aid first with £100, and then in February with an additional £1400. In the same month the committee made an identical grant to the Hatfield group.

Puffin's designers had an awesome tradition to uphold. Since 1934, when the D.H. 88 *Comet* won the Robertson England-to-Australia race, de Havilland had produced a series of outstanding stressed-skin wooden aircraft, including the D.H. 91 *Albatross* airliner, and the renowned D.H. 98 *Mosquito* bomber, to which Henry Kremer had contributed so much valuable technology. *Puffin* was designed in that tradition, with little difference from a commercial airplane project in attention to detail. The result was a structural tour-de-force, highly professional and dauntingly complex.

Puffin looked more like *Pedaliante* than like *Mufli*. It was again a streamlined cantilever-wing monoplane, but the pilot was seated at the very front of the aircraft inside a large partly transparent cowling. Behind the wing the short fuselage tapered down and faired into a tall fin and rudder; the 9-foot (2.74-metre)-diameter pusher propeller emerged from a streamlined boss halfway up the fin. *Puffin*'s tapered wing spanned 84 feet (25.6 metres) and had an area of 330 square feet (30.6 square metres). The total projected flying weight was 268 pounds (121.8 kilograms), and the wing loading was 0.81 pound per square foot (3.95 kilograms per square metre). This was slightly lower than *SUMPAC*'s wing loading, and much lower than that of any earlier human-powered aircraft.

Through most of 1961 the two teams worked intensively on their respective airframes. Even with the donation of the huge quantity of balsa wood required for *Puffin,* as well as gifts of many other materials, the Hatfield group needed its RAeS grant-in-aid. There must have been times when the de Havilland apprentices wondered if so much sophistication was necessary. The plans for *Puffin*'s wing specified 124 delicate ribs on 8-inch (20-centimetre) centers, each one built up from many small components. The entire fuselage and the leading edge of the wing were covered with thin balsa sheet, which became a load-bearing surface of the plane.

The apprentices were spared working on the drive system. It was custom-built for *Puffin* by the Aviation Division of the Dunlop Company, and included a 3:1 precision gearbox that drove a bicycle wheel and a bevel-geared magnesium torque-tube to the propeller. The laminated balsa wood airscrew had adjustable pitch blades and was designed and assembled by the propeller division of de Havilland. The first time it was tested in the company wind tunnel it achieved its design efficiency of 89 percent.

SUMPAC was not so lucky. Its propeller, built of ply ribs and balsa infilling on an aluminum tube spar, was tested in Southampton University's wind tunnel and proved to be only 75 percent efficient. The tests showed that the airflow was separating over much of the blade surface, resulting in high profile drag. The fix was in the best student tradition: A serrated paper strip, glued to each blade near the leading edge, produced some boundary layer turbulence, and raised the efficiency to an acceptable 88 percent.

By the autumn of 1961 both airplanes were being covered. Once again Hatfield had an important advantage. *SUMPAC* was covered with parachute nylon, sealed with two coats of glider dope. Unfortunately the only storage available for the airplane was a leaky war surplus Nissen (Quonset) hut at Lasham Airfield. The damp atmosphere slackened the nylon, so that two more coats of dope were needed to tighten and seal it. This added 6 pounds (2.7 kilograms) to the weight of the plane. *Puffin,* by contrast, was covered with a polyester film called Melinex, made by Imperial Chemical Industries, Ltd. It was waterproof, smoother than doped nylon, and very light — the covering of the entire plane weighed about 2 pounds (1 kilogram).

Puffin's plastic skin was still a well-kept secret when *SUMPAC* began its trials at Lasham. Since they had no hangar large enough to hold the assembled HPA, the Southampton students had to drive 25 miles (40 kilometres) to the field, rig the plane — it took three hours — and hope that the wind remained calm enough to fly. The first few tests were small disasters. The undercarriage collapsed, the drive wheel had to be redesigned, even the control directions had to be reversed. By this time rumors were rife that the Hatfield airplane was also ready to fly and was a much more promising candidate for the Kremer Prize than *SUMPAC*.

On the evening of November 9, 1961, with a cameraman filming the trial, Derek Piggott put everything he had into *SUMPAC*. (He said later that it was like pedaling a tandem bicycle up a slope with the other rider not bothering to pedal.) As the plane gathered speed he felt the drive wheel slip, and pedaled harder, and *SUMPAC* lifted awkwardly off the runway, semi-stalled, impossible to steer, but airborne under human power: "Tremendous excitement!" When the plane landed on the grass after its 50-foot (15.2-metre) veering flight, "Anne [Marsden] rushed up to congratulate me, and my reaction was to congratulate her. Their machine had really flown at last, and we had film to prove it!"

That was the first human-powered flight in Britain. Six days later, at 10:15 P.M., *Puffin* was rolled out of its hangar at Hatfield, and John Wimpenny made the first taxi tests. The next morning, November 16, Jimmy Phillips, a de Havilland test pilot, made *Puffin*'s first takeoff and landing. As with *SUMPAC*, retrofits began immediately, and within two days *Puffin* was making flights of one minute's duration. Thanks to Henry Kremer's prize, human-powered flight was off the ground at last.

3

Competition

Kremer Prize Projects 1961–1976

ONLY A FEW PEOPLE in the world have had the thrill that Derek Piggott and Jimmy Phillips did when they lifted off the ground on the first flight of a human-powered airplane. There is a benign exultation that affects the participants in these events, very different from the professional cool of engineers at a prototype aircraft test, or the uproarious celebration of a rocket liftoff.

All human-powered aircraft built thus far must be flown in calm air, so their flights are usually made at dawn or dusk, when the wind is as still as possible. The half-light and the quiet lend an ethereal air to the flight preparations. (In fact, people seldom raise their voices at HPA trials — they behave rather as though they were in a library.) The airplanes are large, silent, and often transparent; they combine delicacy and expanse like the great dirigibles of the 1930s.

The achievement, seen in perspective, is minuscule: the defeat of gravity by human muscles for a short distance, at an insignificant height above the ground. Nevertheless, this small victory usually rewards those who achieve it with a delight and satisfaction out of proportion to the event. It is perhaps the best experience shared by the people who have tried to solve the problem of human-powered flight.

A more frequent common experience is disappointment. For eighteen years after the Kremer Prize was first offered, British teams tried to build planes that could win it; for eight of those years they had competition only from the Commonwealth countries, and yet they did not succeed. *SUMPAC,* the first to fly, was also the first to demonstrate that liftoff was only the beginning of human-powered flight. On Derek Piggott's third attempt, he flew 150 feet (46 metres), and climbed to 5 feet (1.5 metres) above the runway. By that time the list of *SUMPAC*'s defects was already depressingly long: The rudder was too small, the elevator was too sensitive, the ground wheel was blowout-prone and too rigid, the drive belt slipped at high loads (when it was most detrimental), and the propeller thrust was too low.

The Southampton team rebuilt the plane, hoping that gradual improvement would bring them closer to winning the Kremer Prize. Derek Piggott also improved his performance; on November 25, 1961, he flew for 30 seconds, equivalent to a distance of 902 feet (275 metres) in still air. There was, however, a discouraging analogy between Piggott's dedicated training and the upgrading of *SUMPAC*.

All of the physiologists who have tested human-power output have observed a phenomenon that occurs regardless of activity or nationality. The test data divide the subjects into two discontinuous groups: genetically endowed athletes and the rest of the population. It is true that with intense physical training the output of the average person can be raised considerably, to the level of the "average fit person." Thereafter the power curve levels off, and no amount of training can improve his or her output further. Unfortunately the highest output of the "average fit person" is still well below the output of trained athletes who have a genetic predisposition for their activity.

With hard training Derek Piggott had raised his output to the level of the "average fit man." That output was good for a best flight of 2040 feet (622 metres), with a peak altitude of 12 feet (3.65 metres), achieved late in 1962. By that time the Southampton student team had improved virtually everything they could on *SUMPAC*. Although the plane was an admirable effort, it had inherent conceptual limitations, and it too leveled out far below the performance necessary to win the Kremer Prize.

SUMPAC made a total of 40 flights in just over one year. Derek Piggott was the usual pilot, although David Williams, who was responsible for much of the design, also flew a few times. The pedal effort was so high that at times a model aircraft engine was

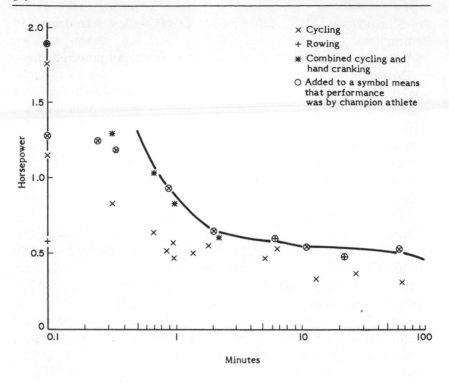

2. Human power output versus time for bicycling and rowing.

fitted to allow the pilot to practice turning without exhausting him-self. With this auxiliary power, *SUMPAC* made a few turns of up to 80°, but nearly all of its flying was straight and level.

In 1963 Alan Lassière, one of the original Southampton student trio, brought the plane up to his new post at Imperial College, London, and started a partial rebuild. The Royal Aeronautical Society underwrote this project with a series of grants, but its progress was very slow. The changes included a new cockpit frame, pylon, and nose fairing, Melinex film covering on the fuselage and tail surfaces, and a toothed belt to replace the steel drive band. After more than two years of work, the modified *SUMPAC* made a few short test flights, but on November 12, 1965, a gust swept it to a height of 29.5 feet (9 metres), where it stalled, dived, and crashed for the last time. (It was later repaired and donated to the Shuttleworth Trust collection at Old Warden Aerodrome in Bedfordshire.)

Although *SUMPAC* had made the first human-powered flight in Britain by a few days, many engineers were sure that *Puffin* was the plane to watch. Certainly, once *Puffin* was airborne it seemed more amenable to improvement than the Southampton craft. The Hatfield club also had an elaborate training rig for their pilots, with a pedal-driven propeller, direct read-out of thrust, and artificial "feel" for control forces. De Havilland's flight simulator was used for practicing roll control.

Slowly, *Puffin*'s flights were extended. The pilots included Jimmy Phillips, J. L. Barnes (also a de Havilland test pilot), and John Wimpenny, all of whom trained with a more luxurious version of the regimen used by Derek Piggott. By May 1962 *Puffin* had made 50 flights and reached a maximum altitude of 14.7 feet (4.5 metres). On May 2, John Wimpenny pedaled it 2989 feet (911 metres) at an average height of 6.5 feet (2 metres), a record for human-powered flight that was to stand for ten years. The Royal Aeronautical Society awarded Wimpenny a prize of £50 from an anonymous donor for being the first man to take off and fly more than one-half mile (0.805 kilometre) solely under human power.

When the Hatfield pilots tried to turn *Puffin,* the best they could do was 83° — about the same as *SUMPAC.* Using a model aircraft engine for auxiliary power, they were able to make one 270° right turn followed by a 90° left turn. This performance couldn't be duplicated with human power because the plane took so much effort to fly. The test program moved with agonizing slowness, and one foggy day the airplane crashed, and nearly 20 feet (6 metres) of its wing was destroyed. Even with their unique resources, it took the Hatfield club 17 months to log 90 flights with *Puffin.*

On April 24, 1963, the plane was being flown by bicycle racer Chris Church when a gust blew it off the runway. Church was unable to turn it back over the paving with the rudder and decided to land. From a height of 5 feet (1.5 metres) he put down in a clay bog, which stopped *Puffin* almost instantaneously. The rapid deceleration caused the wings to fold forward and tear off the fuselage. Church was unhurt, but many components of the plane were badly damaged. The Hatfield club, however, had insured their plane for £4500, and a crash that would have caused the disbanding of many other teams resulted only in the decision to build a new version of *Puffin* — *Puffin II*.

The idea seemed logical: to incorporate in an improved model all the lessons learned in flying the prototype, which was henceforth named *Puffin I*. The logic of the redesign process, however, has been a mystery to many other HPA teams.

As well as being unable to turn under human power, *Puffin I* was difficult to pedal for any great distance. The wingspan of *Puffin II* was raised to 93 feet (28.3 metres), and the wing area increased by 18 percent to 390 square feet (36.2 square metres). This offered the opportunity to lower the wing loading and hence the power necessary to fly significantly. Instead of doing this, the Hatfield team made the new airplane even heavier and more complex than its predecessor. *Puffin I* weighed 117.9 pounds (53.6 kilograms) empty; *Puffin II* weighed 140 pounds (63.6 kilograms). As a result the wing loading dropped by only 8 percent.

The rebuilt plane used the fuselage, tail surfaces, and drive system of *Puffin I*, but its new wing had tip dihedral and a double-tapered outline that was expected to lower the effort of flying in ground effect. It also used a new airfoil designed by Dr. F. X. Wortmann of the Institut für Aerodynamik und Gasdynamik in Stuttgart. *Puffin II* took 2 years and 4 months to build, and by the time it was finished a third British HPA had flown briefly, and another was almost ready to fly in Japan.

The British plane that beat *Puffin II* into the air was a maverick, the product of a single man's obsession. Its designer, builder, and sole financier was Daniel Perkins, a textile engineer employed by the Ministry of Defence at Cardington in Bedfordshire. The locale will immediately provoke a thrill of recognition in anyone familiar with lighter-than-air flight. Cardington is the site of the largest airship hangar in the United Kingdom; it was the hangar in which the dirigible R-101 was built and housed before its tragic demise, and it has remained a center of British lighter-than-air research.

Perkins was in fact working within the airship tradition; beginning in 1959 he built a series of four *inflatable* human-powered planes. All had different configurations, all were unconventional, and the first three were unsuccessful. However, his fourth machine, the *Reluctant Phoenix,* actually took off under human power and made a number of flights inside the 800-foot (244-metre) Cardington airship shed.

Reluctant Phoenix was a delta-shaped flying wing spanning 32.8 feet (10 metres). Its nylon-and-polyurethane envelope was inflated to a pressure of only 0.4 pound per square foot (1.9 kilograms per square metre), and its empty weight was a mere 38 pounds (17.3 kilograms). Both its pedal-driven pusher propeller and the central rudder supporting it were steerable, and the plane could be carried in an automobile trunk when deflated.

Although Perkins was in his fifties when he began his HPA projects, he was the pilot as well as the designer of his first three planes. For the *Phoenix* he enlisted the help of a young racing cyclist named Mike Street, who was able to make four unassisted takeoffs at Cardington. Street's longest flight was 420 feet (128 metres), and his greatest "altitude" was 1.9 feet (0.6 metre). After 96 test flights, Perkins decided that the *Reluctant Phoenix* would not be able to win the Kremer Prize and gave up human-powered flight in favor of starting a new family.

Hidemasa Kimura was, in his own way, just as much of an individualist as Daniel Perkins. During the years since his work on the *Koken* long-distance plane, he had distinguished himself as a designer of transport and long-distance aircraft. Between 1940 and 1944 Kimura designed the SS-1, the first pressurized high-altitude airplane built in Japan, and the Tachikawa A-26, one of the most advanced and least-known planes in the history of aviation.

In 1944 this elegant twin-engined transport flew 10,214 miles (16,435 kilometres) nonstop, and landed with enough fuel to have flown another 1243 miles (2000 kilometres). Its flight exceeded the distance from Tokyo to New York by more than 3315 miles (5000 kilometres). The record was not publicized by the Japanese government, but when the first nonstop flight of the Boeing 747SP from New York to Tokyo was made in November 1975, the guest of honor aboard was Dr. Hidemasa Kimura, the designer of the plane that could have flown the same distance 31 years earlier.

Since 1945, Kimura had been a professor, first at Tokyo University and then at Nihon University, and continued to distinguish himself as an aeronautical engineer. He designed both the first private aircraft (the Okamura N-52) and the first commercial aircraft (the NAMC YS-11 twin turboprop transport) built in Japan after the war. The prototype YS-11 was being assembled when Kimura heard about the successful flights of *SUMPAC* and *Puffin* in 1961.

He was immediately inspired to design a human-powered plane, but the pressure of teaching duties and the development of the YS-11 deferred the project. Also, as he says, "Theses on man-powered aircraft were in short supply even in Britain. No single piece of reference material, such as design data, was available [to us]." In April 1963, he started a program at Nihon University in which the development of a human-powered plane would be the joint graduation thesis project of senior engineering students.

There is a charming modesty and respect for nature in the Nihon program. Kimura expected that the first plane would be able to take off, "but not fly so long." As a result it was named *Linnet,* for a small finch whose flying ability is only moderate. Not until the Nihon student teams had built seven successful human-powered airplanes did Kimura allow them, with some apprehension, to name their next plane *Stork,* after a bird that was a strong flier.

It took the Nihon students three years to evolve the original *Linnet.* During the first year they tested human-power output with a student-designed dynamometer. The second year was used for studies of HPA aerodynamics, aircraft configuration, and optimum dimensions and weight. In the third year the components of the plane were built and assembled.

Linnet was six months from completion when *Puffin II* was rolled out at Hatfield on August 27, 1965, after its long reconstruction. Jimmy Phillips was again the pilot for the maiden flight. His first impression was that the plane needed slightly less power to fly than *Puffin I,* but this was more than offset by control problems. *Puffin II* was, in a word, unsteerable; and test flights were suspended while a larger rudder was designed and installed.

By the time *Puffin II*'s rudder was rebuilt, the Nihon University students had assembled their first human-powered plane at nearby

Chofu Airfield. *Linnet* emerged as a very different bird from any of the European HPAs. It was still a streamlined cantilever monoplane, but from the side it looked almost like a flying wing. The short teardrop fuselage faired into a fin that angled up at 30°, and that supported a high horizontal stabilizer and the pusher propeller. The pilot reclined in a cockpit at the base of the fin, and the drive from his pedals was geared to the propeller via a lightweight torque tube.

The Nihon plane had a span of 73.16 feet (22.3 metres) and a wing area of 279.8 square feet (26 square metres). The flying weight with a 127.6-pound (58-kilogram) pilot was 239 pounds (108.6 kilograms), giving a wing loading of 0.85 pound per square foot (4.18 kilograms per square metre), lower than *SUMPAC* and slightly higher than the *Puffin*s.

Linnet performed exactly as expected. In Professor Kimura's words, "On February 25, 1966, our dear *Linnet,* with Munetaka Okamiya at the controls, lifted wheels off the ground for the first time." The next day the plane flew 49.2 feet (15 metres), making it Japan's first human-powered aircraft. The Tokyo media noted that Okamiya thus became the first Japanese able to walk on the ground, swim in water, and fly in the air under his own power! After some practice, he was able to fly 141 feet (43 metres), *Linnet*'s longest airborne distance.

For the Nihon students, choosing an unpretentious namesake was the right course; they were elated rather than disappointed by *Linnet*'s modest performance. The human-powered aircraft program became a part of the regular university curriculum, and from 1966 on fifteen senior engineering students per year worked on a new design. Each plane took two years to build, and nine different ones were completed in the next decade.

In 1966 *Linnet* was not eligible to compete with *Puffin II* for the Kremer Prize. The Hatfield plane, however, was proving strangely recalcitrant. Even with the enlarged rudder, it was harder to control than its predecessor, and the maximum distance flown with it remained around 0.5 mile (0.8 kilometre) — less than *Puffin I*'s record. It was clear to any objective observer that despite all the time, money, and expertise invested in it, *Puffin II* had little chance of winning the Kremer Figure-of-Eight Competition.

The 1962 deadline for that award had long passed, with considerable disappointment for both the administrators of the prize and Henry Kremer himself. They reluctantly concluded that: (1) the requirements were too difficult for the current state of human-powered flight; and (2) the British Commonwealth represented too small a pool of aeronautical design talent to win the original prize. On March 1, 1967, a set of amended rules was issued by the Royal Aeronautical Society, and a new Kremer Competition was added to the list of aviation prizes.

The original figure-of-eight prize was raised to £10,000, renamed "The £10,000 Kremer Competition," and opened to entrants from anywhere in the world. The new course was called "The £5000 Kremer Competition," and the prize was to be distributed to the first three successful competitors in amounts of £2500, £1500, and £1000, respectively. Like the *Prix Peugeot,* the rules required a pair of flights in opposite directions, to be made within one hour after the first flight began, by the same flight crew.

The new course was a slalom around three posts set ¼ mile (402 metres) apart on a straight line. The aircraft had to start on the line connecting the posts (as near to the outer starting post as the competitor wished), and fly, for example, to the right of the first post, to the left of the second, and to the right of the third, landing again on the center line. In practice this meant a series of three gentle turns over a distance of approximately ¾ mile (1200 metres), followed by a similar flight in the opposite direction within one hour. Henry Kremer wanted to be sure that the course, while easier than the figure-of-eight, would still require a high standard of aircraft design and piloting, so there was also an altitude requirement: The aircraft had to pass the first and third poles at a height of no less than 10 feet (3.05 metres).

Although *Puffin II* had not flown farther than 0.5 mile (800 metres), on one flight of that length it had reached a height of 17 feet (5.2 metres) and had cleared a 10-foot (3.05-metre)-high marker at the end of the flight. In August 1967 it became the first competitor to make an attempt on any of the Kremer courses. John Wimpenny was the pilot, but despite long practice — like Derek Piggott, he had worked hard to achieve the power output of an "average fit man" — he had difficulty in getting the plane to the required altitude. *Puffin II* struggled up to a height of 10.8 feet (3.3 metres), and almost immediately touched one of the poles marking the course. This swung the plane around, and Wimpenny was forced to abort the attempt and land on the grass verge of the runway.

The combination of poor weather, logistics, and fragility limited *Puffin II*'s flights to about 20 a year. In 1968 a glider pilot and bicycle racer named John Wimwell was recruited to fly the plane, but he was not able to stretch the flight distance record. Just after a takeoff on April 6, 1969, *Puffin II* was hit by a gust that yawed it sideways; the pilot touched down at the edge of the runway, but the plane rolled off the paving and across the grass out of control. It was eventually stopped by the concrete base of one of the runway lights, and the entire airframe collapsed. Although some components were salvaged for use in another HPA, the crash proved to be the end of the Hatfield Man-Powered Aircraft Club's activities.

By the time of *Puffin II*'s demise, Professor Kimura's students had completed *Linnet II,* which first flew in February 1967. This was an evolutionary design, and it recorded the best flight of the 4-plane *Linnet* series: an unimposing 298.5 feet (91 metres). As Kimura later wrote, the *Linnet*s "had the most satisfactory educational effects on the students, but did not produce any remarkable progress in the performance of man-powered aircraft . . ." In 1972 a new Nihon student team began work on an HPA named *Egret,* with a configuration closer to *SUMPAC* than to any of the *Linnet*s.

Even without the implied compliment of *Egret*'s design, the early seventies were banner years for British human-powered aircraft. No less than five new HPAs flew in the United Kingdom in 1971 and 1972. *Dumbo,* the first one to take off, had 10,000 man-hours of work put into it over a period of four years before its maiden flight on September 18, 1971.

Like its Walt Disney namesake, *Dumbo* had big ears: two independently controllable wings spanning 123 feet (37.5 metres) — about one and a half times the wingspan of the BAC *Concorde*. *Dumbo* could almost be considered a BAC product itself. It was built by the Weybridge Man-Powered Aircraft Group, which was formed at the British Aircraft Corporation's Weybridge facility in 1967 by Phillip Green, a stress analyst. (*Concorde 01* flew exactly 3 months after *Dumbo;* one can only admire the flexibility of an aircraft company that produces two prototypes with a net weight difference of 407,029 pounds [185,013 kilograms] in a single year!)

Dumbo's Wortmann airfoil wings had an area of 484.3 square feet (45 square metres) and could be rotated about their long axes for turn control. Its frame was made of chemically milled aluminum tubing joined with fiberglass-reinforced resin. The result was a very large plane that weighed only 125.4 pounds (57 kilograms). With a 150-pound (68-kilogram) pilot, *Dumbo* had a wing loading of 0.57 pound per square foot (2.78 kilograms per square metre), by far the lowest of any human-powered aircraft built up to that time.

The propulsion system was similar to *Puffin*'s: a pedal-driven chain coupled to the ground wheel, and a lightweight geared shaft turning a tail-mounted pusher propeller. *Dumbo* incorporated a great deal of aerospace technology, but its performance was very disappointing. The longest of its few flights at Weybridge was 150 feet (45.7 metres) at an altitude of 3.28 feet (1 metre). The plane proved to have even worse yaw control problems than *Puffin II,* and after its discouraging first flights the Weybridge group seemed to lose momentum. Three years later, in 1974, *Dumbo* was moved to Cranwell, renamed *Mercury,* and taken over by a Royal Air Force team led by Squadron Leader John Potter.

Potter was the ideal man for the job; when his group adopted the Weybridge aircraft, he already held the world distance record for human-powered flight. The plane he made it with was the most successful of all British HPAs. Named *Jupiter,* it took eight years to complete and was worked on by more than 100 people.

Jupiter was originally designed by Chris Roper, who started a human-powered aircraft group at Woodford in 1964. Roper tried to combine the best features of *SUMPAC* and *Puffin* in his design. His synthesis was entirely conventional: a streamlined high-wing monoplane with a propeller pylon immediately behind the pilot; spruce-and-balsa construction; rudder, ailerons, and all-moving tailplane flight controls; a chain drive from a normal bicycling position to the ground wheel and the balsa-ribbed pusher propeller.

The result was a plane with a wingspan of 80 feet (24.4 metres), an all-up weight with a 154-pound (70-kilogram) pilot of 299 pounds (136 kilograms), and the rather high wing loading of 1 pound per square foot (4.87 kilograms per square metre). When his colleagues lost interest, Roper worked on *Jupiter* by himself for five years, until it was partially destroyed by a fire in his workshop in 1969.

Enter the Royal Air Force: The remains of *Jupiter* were taken over by a group at the R.A.F. Apprentice Training School at Halton led by then Flight Lieutenant John Potter. The R.A.F. team put approximately 4000 man-hours into reconstructing the plane and completed it late in 1971. One of their improvements was the use of aluminized Melinex as a covering material, which gave *Jupiter* a glistening other-worldly aspect. Meanwhile, John Potter, following in the tire-paths of Derek Piggott and John Wimpenny, had trained himself for the role of HPA pilot/engine, a rating not officially recognized by the R.A.F. On February 13, 1972, he made the first takeoff in *Jupiter*.

From then on, *Jupiter*'s career diverged from that of any previous human-powered plane. During the next 137 days, Potter flew *Jupiter* 64 times. Although his total airborne time was only about one hour, this was the longest stretch of human-powered flight in history. Potter's expertise as a pilot was crucial to the success of these flights, and he made an important discovery: Despite the theoreticians' emphasis on flying in ground effect, *Jupiter* was much easier to fly at an altitude of 19.6 feet (6 metres) than at 3.28 feet (1 metre). On June 29, 1972, Potter's skill and persistence were rewarded with an official flight of 3513 feet (1071 metres) at R.A.F. Benson. This broke John Wimpenny's 1962 record of 2989 feet (911 metres), made with *Puffin*.

Potter made one even longer (unofficial) flight with *Jupiter*, but in 1972 he had to interrupt his work on human-powered flight when he was sent to the University of London for a postgraduate course. Three other British HPAs flew while *Jupiter* was in storage awaiting Potter's return. Two of them were not serious contenders for the Kremer Prize, one because of design flaws and the other by intent.

In mid-1971 a Nottingham design engineer named Peter Wright began building an ultralight plane for the Kremer Competition. Like other one-man HPA projects, this one progressed almost to final assembly in the builder's own home. Wright decided that minimum weight was the most important requirement for success, and he built his airframe from expanded polystyrene and balsa wood, reinforced with a carbon-fiber/epoxy matrix. Carbon fiber has extraordinary strength and stiffness for its weight, and it was not widely available at the time that Wright began using it. (It is now used for many jet aircraft components and is a major structural element of the *Gossamer Albatross*.)

Wright's midwing monoplane had a short fuselage, a cruciform tail, and a wingspan of 71 feet (21.6 metres). Its empty weight of 90 pounds (41 kilograms) was less than that of any contemporary HPA except the inflatable *Reluctant Phoenix,* but it had the same generous wing area as *Dumbo:* 484.3 square feet (45 square metres). The result was a wing loading of only 0.5 pound per square foot (2.44 kilograms per square metre), the lowest yet. Wright also designed the plane to be transportable in sections. In February 1972 its components were loaded into a moving van and taken to Langer Field near Nottingham. Wright assembled the plane, and on his first attempt took off and flew 600 feet (183 metres) at an altitude of 1 foot (0.3 metre). It was a brave beginning, but Wright made only a few more flights (the longest one about 900 feet [274 metres]) before he lost his space at the airfield and gave up the project.

The next human-powered plane to leave the ground in 1972 had an even shorter airborne career: one flight of 60 feet (18.3 metres), barely above the runway. Happily, this was not an attempt on the Kremer Prize, but the outcome of an educational program similar to those at Nihon University. The pilot was Dr. Keith Sherwin, an avid proponent of human-powered flight and current member of MAPAGC. Sherwin has been a lecturer in mechanical engineering at Liverpool University since 1968, and in 1969 he started a course similar to Professor Kimura's, in which engineering students would design and build a human-powered plane.

When the members of the dormant Hatfield Man-Powered Aircraft Group heard about this project, they donated to it the re-

mains of *Puffin II*. A surprising number of components, including
the propeller, pilot frame, and tail surfaces, had survived the con-
frontation with the runway marker; Sherwin's students combined
these with a pod-and-boom fuselage and a balsa-and-polystyrene-
foam wing spanning 64 feet (19.5 metres). The resulting hybrid
weighed a robust 140 pounds (63.6 kilograms), and was christened *Liverpuffin*.

On December 17, 1971, the 68th anniversary of the Wright
brothers' first flight, *Liverpuffin* was rolled out for trials at Wood-
vale Airfield. Before any flights could be made, a gust of wind
snatched the plane from its crew and flipped it over, breaking the
propeller and the outer wing sections, and demolishing the tail
plane. Two months later the damage was repaired, and on March
18, 1972, *Liverpuffin* made its one and only flight at a ground
clearance of 9 inches (0.23 metre) before being permanently
retired.

Liverpuffin's brief career was overlapped at both ends by that
of the first twin-engined human-powered plane. *Toucan*'s name
was a contraction of its builders' thesis: *Two can fly if one cannot.*
The rationale was that of Martyn Pressnell, who organized the
Hertfordshire Pedal Aeronauts in September 1965, at the Radlett
Airfield facility of the Handley Page Aircraft Company. The Hertfordshire group had no academic aims; they were after the Kremer
Prize, and they spent their first fifteen months of collaboration on
a detailed design study. Their plans were submitted to the Royal
Aeronautical Society in December 1966, with an application for
a construction grant. The RAeS responded with £500, and *Toucan* seemed to be well begun.

Toucan resembled a well-fed offspring of *Puffin*. It was again
a cantilever monoplane, with a cruciform tail and a rear-mounted
pusher propeller. The provision for two crewmen, one behind the
other, resulted in a straight-lined, slab-sided fuselage, and the wing
was mounted at mid-height rather than at the fuselage top. What
is still impressive about *Toucan* is its size. The original wingspan
was 123 feet (37.5 metres), but it was later extended to 142.7
feet (43.5 metres). This is more than twice the span of *Liverpuffin* and exactly equal to the span of an intercontinental Boeing
707-320.

Pressnell's team designed a straightforward structure of spruce and balsa for *Toucan,* but the support frame for the crew was riveted up from thin aluminum alloy and looked like part of a giant Meccano set. The drive system was identical to *Dumbo*'s: pedals coupled via bicycle chain to the ground wheel and by gears to the torque-tube drive for the propeller. The main difference is that *Toucan* has two sets of pedals. The front set is for the "power man," who is essentially all engine. The pilot sits above and behind, and both pedals and flies the plane.

Control of such a large aircraft was a challenge from the start. Since the fuselage is short, the designers felt that a rudder would have an inadequate moment arm to turn the plane. They chose instead to use an all-flying tail plane for pitch control, and a pair of slot-lip ailerons (a Handley Page patent) for turning forces. The huge wingspan and the need to make the plane transportable in sections did not make the control surface design any easier.

The original completion date for *Toucan* was postponed by several years because of the failure of the Handley Page Company in March 1970. (The company had been founded by Frederick Handley Page in 1909 and was noteworthy for its independent house style and the production of many British airliners, especially during the 1930s.) Since most of the *Toucan* team members were Handley Page employees, work on the airplane stopped until the builders found new jobs and in many cases new homes.

Toucan was finally completed in the summer of 1972, seven years after the team was founded. The first taxiing trials revealed that the plane would take off momentarily without the propeller, but refused to fly with it. After the propeller was redesigned, *Toucan* made three flights on December 23, 1972, with Derek May as the main engine, and Bryan Bowman as the pilot/booster engine. Its longest airborne distance that day was 204 feet (62 metres) at a height of 2 feet (0.6 metre). *Toucan* made no more significant flights until July 1973, and by that time an important change had occurred in the prize it was meant to win.

None of the human-powered aircraft built since 1959 had come close to finishing either of the Kremer Courses. In June 1973 Henry Kremer, perhaps despairing of ever seeing his prizes won, made a magnificent gesture: He raised the award for the Figure-of-Eight Competition from £10,000 to £50,000 (about $129,000 at that date), thus making it the largest prize in the history of aviation.

The first response to the Royal Aeronautical Society's announcement of the quintupled prize was *Toucan*'s longest flight to date: 2100 feet (640 metres) at a height of 15 feet (4.5 metres), on July 3, 1973. Unfortunately, on the same day one wing failed, and the airplane crashed and was badly damaged. The team decided to increase the wingspan as mentioned earlier, but like its predecessors, *Toucan* never proved to be a successful challenger for the Kremer Prizes. It was eventually retired to the Shuttleworth Trust collection at Old Warden Aerodrome, and hung next to *SUMPAC*.

A number of new human-powered aircraft were completed during the next three years, some stimulated by the larger Kremer Prize, and others that finally flew after the long gestation period typical of the breed. In Paris, M. Maurice Hurel, an authority on the aerodynamics of narrow wings — wings of high aspect ratio — designed an original HPA which flew at Le Bourget Airport in 1974.

Hurel resurrected the nostalgic name *Aviette* for his plane, perhaps in honor of Gabriel Poulain and the other aerocycle riders of the early twentieth century. The slender, wire-braced wing of the *Hurel Aviette* spanned 132 feet (40.2 metres), and was mounted high above the fuselage like a parasol. J. Pierre Thierrard, a pilot and bicycle racer, powered the 10-foot (3-metre)-diameter tractor propeller at the very front of the aircraft. The wing loading of the *Hurel Aviette* was only 0.51 lb/ft² (2.49 kg/m²), but although it made one straight flight of 3281 feet (1000 metres), it proved too fragile and unwieldy to fly either of the Kremer Courses.

Between 1973 and 1976 Professor Kimura's student teams continued to design and build human-powered planes whose performance improved slowly but steadily. In 1973 *Egret II* raised the Nihon University flight distance record to 505.2 feet (154 metres), and the following year *Egret III* flew 666 feet (203 metres). On June 2, 1976, *Stork,* the plane that Professor Kimura finally allowed his students to name after a strong flier, justified its name and flew 1952.2 feet (595 metres) at Shimofusa Naval Air Station, with Takashi Kato as pilot. Two days later Kazuhiko Churei, another student pilot, piloted *Stork* through a 180° turn, but banked too

sharply to recover. The plane spiraled in on its left wingtip, breaking both the wing and the fuselage. In a short time it was rebuilt
as the world record-breaking *Stork B,* but months passed before
any Western HPA teams learned of Churei's turn or the outstanding performance of *Stork B.*

At the time of *Stork*'s crash, human-powered flight experience
in the United States was far behind that in Japan and the United
Kingdom. In 1970 a single letter to *Aviation Week* tried to stimulate U.S. interest in the Kremer Prize. Soon afterward Dr. John
McMasters, an aerodynamicist at the Boeing Company, began a
campaign similar to Beverley Shenstone's in England. During the
early 1970s McMasters published a series of provocative papers in
aeronautical journals and magazines, urging the American aviation
community to attack the problems of human-powered flight. Like
Shenstone's, his campaign had some tangible results.

At the Massachusetts Institute of Technology in 1973 a group
of students led by Professor Eugene E. Covert built a two-man
biplane HPA named *Burd.* *Burd* spanned 62 feet (18.9 metres)
and had a projected flying weight of 405 pounds (184 kilograms).
On its first takeoff attempt, the wings suffered a major structural
failure and the plane had to be completely rebuilt. A second version, *Burd II,* also had a star-crossed history, being severely damaged by an accident in the workshop where it was being assembled
before it could fly.

In 1976 the credit for the first human-powered flight in the
United States went to Joseph A. Zinno, a retired Air Force lieutenant colonel from Centredale, Rhode Island. Zinno started the
design of his *Olympian ZB-1* in 1972, and the plane took him 7000
man-hours, over a period of 4½ years, to build. *Olympian* was a
midwing pusher monoplane spanning 78.7 feet (24 metres) and
weighed 291 pounds (132 kilograms) with Zinno aboard. It was
built of spruce and balsa around a steel cockpit frame and used
a tubular aluminum boom to support the tail surfaces. The external covering was transparent Du Pont Mylar film.

On April 21, 1976, at 8:10 A.M., Zinno lifted off the runway at
Quonset Point Airport, North Kingstown, Rhode Island. His flight
lasted 5 seconds, and covered 77 feet (23.5 metres) at a ground
clearance of 1 foot (0.3 metre). As far as is known, this was the

Olympian's only successful human-powered flight. In September 1976 the plane crashed while being towed and was destroyed.

Although there were other American HPA projects under way, Zinno's plane represented the state of human-powered flight in the United States in August of 1976. At that point, the authorities on the subject would have been incredulous if they had been told that the Kremer Prize would be won within a year by an American airplane that was not yet begun and for which no plans existed. As it happened, the man who was going to surprise them believed that he had just figured out how to do it. He fitted the historical profile of a successful HPA designer perfectly: He was a skilled pilot, an aeronautical engineer, and had been the soaring champion of both the United States and the world. His name was Paul MacCready Jr.

4

Ground School

Paul MacCready Jr.

PAUL MACCREADY JR. was born in New Haven, Connecticut, a city not famous for good flying weather. His father, Paul Beattie Mac-Cready, received his bachelor's degree from Princeton University and his M.D. from Johns Hopkins. At Johns Hopkins, MacCready Sr. met a winsome nurse, Edith Margaret Hollingsworth, the daughter of a Quaker-Presbyterian minister, and promptly married her. The couple settled in New Haven, where Dr. MacCready established a successful practice in otolaryngology. Paul Jr. was their third and last child; when he arrived on September 29, 1925, he had a sister Anne, six years old, and a sister Isabelle, five. Pediatricians would classify Paul as a functional only child, and that definition is justified by the care and attention lavished on him. To put it plainly, he was the apple of his parents' eye.

Paul says that he "can't remember not being interested in airplanes." Many years ago his mother noted in her diary that his fascination with model planes began when he was seven years old. At that time the MacCreadys were living on East Rock Road in New Haven, but it is clear from the children's reminiscences that the place that shaped most of their memories was the summer cottage that Dr. MacCready built in Branford, Connecticut, in 1929.

The MacCready cottage was at Johnson's Point, on Long Island Sound, and Paul was four years old the first summer they spent there. He wasn't yet able to swim, though he would paddle around wearing water wings. One day his sisters took him for a ride in the family's new rowboat; Anne was rowing, Isabelle sat in the stern, and Paul straddled the bow with both feet in the water. The two girls decided to change places, and as the boat rocked, Paul suddenly fell off and sank out of sight. Isabelle leaned over the side, groping wildly beneath the surface, and caught his hair. She and Anne were just able to drag him back into the boat.

The baptism was appropriate for a childhood whose conditioning was not aeronautical, but marine. Both sisters agree on the lack of any parental urge toward aviation. "Father wasn't air-minded at all. He loved fishing and boating — he started with a rowboat, and ended with a professional swordfishing boat." The summer after he fell overboard Paul was swimming (he learned by forgetting his water wings during a game of King of the Raft) and rowing a little green scow around Johnson's Point.

Dr. MacCready had meanwhile started the escalation of his navy. By 1933 he was on his third motorboat and well up into the cruiser class. Paul knew all about powerboats by that time; he could steer and throttle like an old salt, but he wanted a sailboat, as did his sisters. Despite the wry complaints about expenses in his memoirs, MacCready Sr. was an easy mark for his children. A few weeks after the campaign started ("Paul was very persistent until I got the boat"), he came home with a 10-foot (3-metre) sailing dinghy. It was late, and he was too tired to give the three excited children their first sailing lesson on the spot. To stop Paul's pestering he promised that they could sail the next day: "You can sail the boat by yourself. You can go over to Long Island if you want to."

In the morning he discovered that Paul had taken him literally. When the family came down to breakfast, the new sailboat was a speck in the distance, three miles out toward Long Island under the command of its 8-year-old skipper. They watched transfixed as he tacked around and headed back, running before a brisk easterly breeze.

Everything went well until he was close to home. Paul had watched his father bring a motorboat smartly into the cove, reverse the throttle to slow it down, and slide gently up to the dock. He assumed that sailboats worked the same way. The new boat skimmed into the cove at top speed — but sans engine and throttle. Paul sailed it straight into the dock. Later he said that it never entered his head that you couldn't slow it down the same way you could a powerboat. Dr. MacCready took a philosophical Spock-

and-Gesell view: "Fortunately we were able to fix up the sailboat and everything was fine."

The summers of the mid-1930s at Johnson's Point sound idyllic. The days were full of swimming, fishing, and that most delightful of waterside occupations, messing about in boats. The three children spent hours exploring the little creek that emptied into the cove, hunting for fiddler crabs at low tide, and catching jellyfish. Anne still remembers the eerie feeling of stirring the bucket of jellyfish at night and watching the cold phosphorescence grow and swirl in the water.

"There were insects around," she says bluntly. Amen, anyone will add who has spent a summer swatting mosquitoes on the Eastern shore. The insects were the first indicators of Paul's future preference for wings over fins. He was fascinated with butterflies, and began going out at night to collect moths. Before long the cottage and the house in New Haven had drawers filled with beautifully mounted and labeled specimens. Around 1935 the Lepidoptera began to be supplanted by manmade flying machines; the airplane phase had begun in earnest.

Paul's first models were built from the kits he brought home from the ten-cent store. They actually did cost ten cents: long flat boxes labeled Comet, Megow, Peerless, Scientific, a complete Sopwith Camel or Caudron Racer for a dime. For twenty-five cents you could buy a plane that spanned as many inches, and an opulent half-dollar took you into the big time: a Comet *Gull* or Scientific *Victory,* "Guaranteed to Fly One Mile."

Inside the box would be a plan the full size of the model; a thin sheet of balsa wood with the patterns of the wing ribs and body formers printed on it; another balsa sheet slit into narrow strips; turned hardwood wheels, a hardwood thrust button, a sawed balsa blank for the propeller, a wire propeller shaft and rubber hook, wire landing gear, two diminutive brass thrust washers, a long strip of rubber, a couple of sheets of brilliantly colored Japanese tissue, and a little tube of cellulose cement — airplane glue. All that for a dime!

Many 1930s neophytes would hoard this collection of goodies greedily, but when they tried to convert it into a three-dimensional flying machine, most could only echo Dylan Thomas's plaint at

Christmas: *Oh, easy for Leonardo.* Paul MacCready was one of the naturals. The models fell together under his hands, they came out looking like the picture on the box, and, best of all, they flew.

This genre of model airplanes has a charm and character that is quite different from the gas-engined and radio-controlled models prevalent today. They are very light — a small rubber-powered model that weighs more than one ounce has little chance of flying long or well. They are also very strong for their weight. (It is common for one to fly into a tree or wall and bounce off undamaged, an ability that would be welcomed by the users of full-sized aircraft.) They are silent and nonpolluting, and they fly freely, with no attachments to the ground. Their colored tissue covering has the delicate translucency of a butterfly wing seen against the sun.

Such models are also remarkably easy to repair. It is only a matter of slitting the tissue with a sharp razor blade, cutting out the damaged part, and gluing in a new piece of balsa. It can be done on the field in the middle of a flying session, and often is. At East Rock Road the MacCreadys had a Ping-Pong table in the basement. After Paul discovered model airplanes the table was never used for Ping-Pong again. He and his friend Lee Nettleton appropriated it, and by 1937 its surface was completely covered with balsa wood, glue, airplane dope, and Japanese tissue.

In the meantime Dr. MacCready had acquired a flagship, the 38-foot (11.6-metre) swordfishing boat *Mohawk*. The *Mohawk* had a tall braced mainmast with a crow's nest at its head for spotting fish. For several summers the crow's nest became one of Paul's favorite places, and he would ride there for hours as a lookout for his father's fishing cronies. In 1938 three changes occurred in his lifestyle. First, he graduated from the Worthington Hooker School and was enrolled at Hopkins Grammar School, a private preparatory school of august lineage. Second, instead of building kits, he began to design his own model planes and enter them in contests. And third, Dr. MacCready finally caught a swordfish and soon afterward sold the *Mohawk*. From then on he gave up owning boats and became the enthusiastic ground crew for his son's aeronautical pursuits.

Paul's early model designs were all gliders or rubber-powered. A look through the family scrapbooks turns up something peculiar.

Many of his planes were what are termed in modeling circles "unorthodox." That usually means pushers, ornithopters, autogyros, and similar craft. Paul did indeed build all of these — models that were designed only to fly and that did not even pretend to resemble full-sized aircraft — but many of his planes were also designed with the stabilizer forward of the wing. Aircraft with a stabilizing surface in this position were common in the early days of aviation. They were nicknamed *canard* in French, both for their fancied resemblance to a duck in flight and for the comment that is out of place with the rest of a conversation. "Oh, it flies backwards!" is the charmingly ingenuous remark that fliers of canards become used to hearing from non-aeronautical observers.

Paul built — and his family photographed — sheet-balsa canards, tissue-covered canards, glider and duration model canards. He joined the Academy of Model Aeronautics and began entering his planes in sanctioned meets. Soon MacCready began collecting trophies, and in 1939, at age 14, he set a world record for model autogyros with a canard design that stayed aloft for 12.7 minutes in front of a crowd of 5000 spectators. He was awarded a junior record because of his age; his flight time was higher than the senior record for which he was not yet eligible.

Heady stuff, but when Paul is questioned about these years the first thing he mentions is not aeronautical but medical: an emergency appendectomy when he was eleven years old. He is still convinced that he provoked it by gorging on sugar and powdered Ovaltine. A picture from that period shows a pudgy, round-faced boy who bears little resemblance to today's Paul MacCready, but who looks exactly like someone who has just cleaned out the sugar and powdered Ovaltine. At the top of the picture, held up by a sturdy arm, is a large, beautifully built model airplane. It is a conventional tractor layout, not a canard, and it is powered by a Brown Jr. gasoline engine.

Dr. MacCready doubtless meant it as a creative bribe: progress, the spirit of the age, and so forth. He told Paul that when he built an airplane big enough to need an engine, Dad would supply the engine. It was not an insignificant bribe; in the 1930s model airplane engines were relatively scarce and expensive. Paul soon built an appropriate plane and received his Brown Jr. Perhaps as Dr. MacCready hoped, the first gas model was followed by more and

larger ones. Although Paul enjoyed them, the excursion into powered aircraft was a psychological detour away from the areas of
silent and gliding flight that interested him most. He wasn't to return to it until 1945.

The transition was made with a bang. In September 1941 Paul
went to the National Model Airplane Championships in Chicago.
He was 15 years old, and he brought with him a trunkful of his
original designs. He had already established six national junior
records: Outdoor Autogyro, Helicopter, and Ornithopter; Indoor
Autogyro, Class D Stick, and R.O.W. (Rise-Off-Water). At the
Nationals he won Junior Outdoor Stick, Flying Scale, and several
indoor events, and was named Junior National Champion. On
September 29 he turned 16, and one month later he soloed in a
Piper Cub at New Haven Airport. Five weeks after that the United
States declared war on Japan.

Suddenly everything was different. Pearl Harbor inflamed the
country with a sense of outraged patriotism. Fathers and older
brothers began leaving for military service, and schools and colleges
speeded up their classes to supply men to the officer training programs. Paul MacCready was accelerated a half-year at Hopkins,
with a scheduled graduation in February of 1943. But airplanes
were in, airplanes were suddenly important as never before, and
because of that there was time during the dark days of 1942 for
one of the most important meetings of Paul's life.

After Pearl Harbor, pilot training became an urgent priority.
Everything needed for it was in short supply: planes, engines, in-
structors. A few American aviators knew about the pioneering days
of the Wasserkupe, and it was recalled that the German *Luftwaffe*
had trained many of its ace pilots during the 1930s on gliders —
aircraft that could be built of wood instead of essential aluminum,
and that didn't require engines. A development program for a two-
place training glider was begun at the Ludington-Griswold Company in Old Saybrook, Connecticut. (Griswold, the president of
the company, was the brother of the president of Yale University,
and his hobby was aviation.) The plane was designed, and a firm
with long experience in wood construction was given a government
contract to build 75 of them: the Pratt-Read Piano Company of
Deep River, Connecticut.

One of the designers of the Pratt-Read glider was Henry Struck, a nationally famous airplane modeler. Dr. MacCready heard of Struck's presence at Old Saybrook from a patient, and early in 1942 he took Paul, with one of his original models, to meet Struck. Struck enjoyed the 16-year-old MacCready immensely, and introduced him in turn to his colleague, Parker Leonard. Leonard also worked at Ludington-Griswold; he was a pilot, a sailplane instructor, and a builder of boats and full-sized gliders. He was to become Paul MacCready's friend, role-model, teacher, and eventual father-in-law.

During his senior year at Hopkins Paul was still able to find enough scarce aviation gasoline for a little pleasure flying. (He used some of it to take his mother for a ride in the Piper Cub he had soloed on.) He visited Parker Leonard's home in Essex, Connecticut, and became friends with Parker's wife, Tippy, and their 14-year-old son, Kirke. The Leonards also had a 10-year-old daughter named Judy, who followed the boys around and asked a lot of questions.

February 1943: The word was Grow Up Fast. In one month Paul graduated from Hopkins, entered Yale University, and joined the U.S. Navy flight-training program. He was a physics major, and between Newton's laws and Planck's constant the Navy sent him to Peru, Indiana; Athens, Georgia; and Memphis, Tennessee; to learn to fly bigger airplanes than Piper Cubs. In the scrapbooks the change is instantaneous: *Shazam!* From the clean-cut kid playing with model airplanes on East Rock Road to the Navy flyboy jock leaning nonchalantly against the wheel of a Yellow Peril — a Stearman PT-17 — with a big black Continental radial engine looming over his shoulder. Another picture looks like a still from a World War II movie: A gag shot, handsome smiling young pilot in helmet and goggles, white scarf around his neck, cigar in hand, posed beside a clutch of garbage cans with a scruffy mop for a date. It's the tearjerker, the picture that turns out to be held by a pretty young matron standing in front of a white cross in a military cemetery when they pull the zoom lens back.

This time they pulled the zoom lens back in 1945, and the war was over. It was halfway through college, halfway through the Navy, and a new ball game, with the country hell-bent for tranquility and a good profit. Almost everything that could shoot, fly, or float was declared war surplus. The Ping-Pong table at East Rock Road was soon covered with used airplane instruments. Celt will out; Dr. MacCready noted that "It was carefully pointed out to me how much these instruments were worth, and how little they had been bought for."

In the fall of 1945, Paul, Parker Leonard, and Henry Struck visited the Wasserkupe of American soaring, Elmira, New York. Paul met the legendary Schweizer brothers and took his first sailplane lesson from the equally legendary champion soaring pilot, Johnny Robinson. It was a return to the right hangar for Mac-Cready. Soon afterward, he, his cousin Norman Hollingsworth, and Lee Nettleton drove to Americus, Georgia, and bought a war surplus sailplane. It cost them $500, and it was none other than their old friend, the Pratt-Read training glider. Was it a bargain? The government had paid $17,000 to build each one, but like Grandfather's bassoon in *Peter and the Wolf,* Dr. MacCready could be heard rumbling in the background about "The speculator who had obtained these gliders for $200 each from the War Assets Administration."

The Pratt-Read was moved to Brainard Field in Hartford, Connecticut, and Parker Leonard became Paul's regular instructor. Brainard Field was full of new pilots learning to handle their war-surplus Pipers and Stinsons. One of the planes in the traffic with Paul and Parker was a Piper L-4 flown by a man in his forties and his cute teenage daughter, a jeans-clad tomboy with curly dark hair. Like some other young ladies from Connecticut, she was going to turn up again in Paul's future.

In a remarkably short time — his parents were mystified by its brevity — MacCready acquired his "C" sailplane pilot's rating, and registered for the 1946 National Soaring Championships at Elmira. His ground crew were Dr. and Mrs. MacCready. Several preconceptions were shattered during the meet. The first one was that the rugged Pratt-Read could double as a competition sailplane. Its workmanship was excellent, and there was no skimping of material (it took four men to lift each wing). It was simply built too much like a piano.

The second one was that soaring was an inexpensive sport. After all, Paul had assured his parents, there was no engine and no fuel to buy; the air was free. Unfortunately the Pratt-Read's trailer was as substantial as the glider. Paul finished 11th in the championships, a creditable showing in his first competition with a heavy ship, but the MacCready family car finished last as a tow vehicle. It barely made it back to New Haven, and had to be replaced.

Lightness was clearly the answer. The sailplane that finished second in the Nationals in 1946 was a lightweight homebuilt with a wingspan of only 35 feet (10.7 metres). (Standard Class sailplanes have a wingspan of 49.2 feet [15 metres] and unlimited designs can exceed 69 feet [21 metres].) The plane had several other peculiarities: Its fuselage was unusually short and fat, and it whistled when it flew. These characteristics were commemorated in its name, the *Screamin' Wiener*. After taking second place with it, its owner, movie stunt flier Paul Tuntland, decided to sell it. In fact it was already an old plane that had been rebuilt twice, but it was light! It weighed only 250 pounds (113.4 kilograms), and it could be handled by two ordinary mortals and towed behind something smaller than a Mack truck. Since the ground crew and the financial vice-presidents of the MacCready soaring team were identical, lightness carried the day. In January 1947 the *Screamin' Wiener* came home to New Haven as a belated Christmas present.

It fitted perfectly with the other member of the MacCready squadron. In 1946 Paul had sold his interest in the Pratt-Read and bought his first powered plane, a Buhl LA-1 Bull Pup. No one could have called it a hot rod. It had been built in the 1930s, and it was powered by a three-cylinder Szekely radial engine that produced 45 horsepower — less than that of a Volkswagen. The Bull Pup was a strange combination of modern and antiquated design. Its oval metal monocoque fuselage was far more advanced than the fabric-covered frame of a Piper Cub, but its wooden wing was braced with external wires attached to a kingpost, à la World War I. Still, it was pretty, it was relatively inexpensive, and it appealed to Paul's taste for the unorthodox.

In June 1947 MacCready graduated from Yale in physics, and entered the *Screamin' Wiener* in the 1947 Nationals at Wichita Falls, Texas. He and his friend Gordon Neiswanger towed the glider in its trailer 1800 miles (2897 kilometres) behind Paul's father's own newly reconditioned car. When Dr. MacCready followed them a week later he found that his car was leaking water, oil, and gas; but the pressure of the contest made the MacCready team forget everything else. It was a rite of passage for Paul, and he was given no quarter by the seasoned and mostly much older competitors. (From Dr. MacCready's diary: "How professionals hate a new-comer to their bailiwick!") The weather was ferociously hot; they lived on ice water, iced tea, salt tablets, and sodas, with no lasting satisfaction in any of them. On the fourth day Paul made a flight of 208 miles (335 kilometres) and became the first pilot in the meet to win his Golden C rating. From then on the competition became worse — short-tempered, punctuated with protest meetings and flights in which the pilots took too many chances. When the meet ended Paul MacCready was runner-up, a phenomenal per-formance for the youngest pilot flying in his second national contest.

During his senior year at Yale, MacCready had been accepted to graduate school at the California Institute of Technology. In September of 1947 he drove out to Pasadena, where he has lived ever since, and moved in with Glenn Bowlus of the Bowlus sail-plane family. Soon afterward Paul joined the Southern California Soaring Association and met its founder, a world-famous glider pilot and aeronautical engineer who was to become the West Coast surrogate for Parker Leonard. Wheels within wheels: The new mentor was none other than Dr. Wolfgang Klemperer, the hero of the Wasserkupe and the designer of *Schwarzer Teufel* and *Blaue Maus*.

After his success at the Aachen Aerodynamische Institut, Klem-perer had moved to the Luftschiffbau-Zeppelin GmbH at Fried-richshafen. The Zeppelin company was then building the airship LZ 126, which was to become the U.S.S. *Los Angeles*. In 1925 the company sent a team of aerodynamic experts to the newly founded Goodyear-Zeppelin Company in Akron, Ohio, and Wolfgang Klem-perer was one of them. Klemperer liked the United States very much, and after a stay in Europe during which he met and married a Viennese girl named Mia Engelman, he returned to Los Angeles in 1932 as an engineer for the Douglas Aircraft Company.

Mia and Wolfgang Klemperer quickly "adopted" Paul Mac-Cready, and appointed themselves his social and cultural tutors. Both of them were related to the conductor Otto Klemperer, and

Paul found that his education was rapidly expanded from aerodynamics to piano recitals and chamber music concerts. He also found
himself the idol of another ten-year-old girl. Eleanor Klemperer
remembers that even among her parents' well-educated friends, Paul
seemed very intelligent. "He could communicate with my father
intellectually, which not many people could do, especially young
people. I admired him for that, but I also had a crush on him."

Later that year Paul emulated his father's ways with boats and
bought a larger, more beautiful, and more competitive sailplane.
It had been built in Poland for the 1939 Olympic Sailplane Design
Competition and was then exhibited at the New York World's Fair.
The *Orlik* ("Eaglet" in Polish) was as different from the *Screamin'
Wiener* as an eagle from a sausage. It had graceful gull wings, a
slender, streamlined fuselage, and a sweeping red-and-white paint
scheme. It looked like a winner, and it was. In the summer of 1948
MacCready received his M.S. in physics from Cal Tech, took the
Orlik to the 15th National Soaring Championships at Elmira, and
became National Soaring Champion. He came home with the Richard C. Du Pont Memorial Trophy and a lot of valuable experience.

Some of the experience came in handy that winter. Paul and
Johnny Robinson, then three-time U.S. soaring champion, brought
their planes to Bishop, California, to try to soar the giant waves
of air that crest over the eastern slope of the Sierra Nevada. On
December 31, Paul was towed up behind a PT-13 biplane (the
ancestor of his first Navy flight trainer) and rode the Sierra wave
to an unprecedented 29,500 feet (8991 metres). He had prepared
for the flight by taking high-altitude conditioning in a Lockheed
pressure chamber and learning to parachute jump. During the
flight he was on oxygen most of the time, and despite a thick layer
of fiberglass insulation in *Orlik*'s cockpit, the temperature at Mac-
Cready's head was 65°F (18.3°C), and at his feet, 40 degrees
below zero. One foot was still numb from frostbite three weeks
after the record-breaking flight.

The preoccupation with wings that had dominated Paul's recre-
ational life now took over his academic career as well. Although
his first two degrees were in physics, he registered as a Ph.D. candidate in aeronautics at Cal Tech. "I was really more interested
in meteorology," he says, "but Cal Tech didn't have a course in it,

and this was as close as I could get." His practical expertise in gauging weather had reached a point where he and *Orlik* were invincible. He won a second national championship in 1949, and in 1950 he became a member of the U.S. international soaring team. Two years later he received his doctorate, *cum laude;* his thesis was on atmospheric turbulence, an area where aeronautics and meteorology meet, and the one that has interested him most in his professional life.

It wasn't all hard work and Air Scouts. Paul was dating sporadically, especially two girls, Nancy Copeland and Jackie Horner. One day in 1954 at a friend's house, he discovered that the ten-year-old girl from Essex, Connecticut, who asked so many questions had grown up and was living in Los Angeles. Judy Leonard was working as a medical technician at California Hospital, but she was planning to move to Denver shortly ("I was chasing a boy from the University of Oklahoma").

Sure enough, Paul found, Kirke's little sister had become a full-fledged blonde with a dynamite smile and a great deal of other equipment to go with it. When Tippy Leonard suggested that Paul stop off and see Judy in Denver on his trips across the country, Paul quickly agreed. A year later he was trying to run his own business — Meteorology Research, Inc., which he had founded in 1951 — and missing planes out of Denver regularly. Judy was sure it was the real thing. "Every time he left I would get these stomach aches. That's what they called him around the lab — the stomach ache." In 1956 she moved to Pasadena, but the romance was interrupted by one more trip: the World Soaring Championships at St. Yan, France.

Paul had won his third U.S. championship in 1953 and was again on the international team. In France he flew a borrowed Breguet 901 sailplane, and on the next-to-last day of the contest he was well ahead of all the other entrants. The last task was a 190-mile (306-kilometre) goal flight to St. Auban in the Alpes Maritimes. MacCready left St. Yan, heading for the ridge along the west edge of the Hautes Alpes, and somehow became trapped in a high mountain bowl with fifty-mile-an-hour downdrafts and the worst turbulence he had ever experienced in his life. He held on, completely out of control, and by what he still views as luck

and Providence, the plane was swept across the bare face of the
rock on a thin curtain of updraft and escaped. It was a hair-raising
flight, but he was one of only four contestants to reach the goal.
He became, by a wide margin, the first American International
Soaring Champion.

A few weeks after Paul returned from France, he described
Judy to his friend Peter Lissaman, in order of priority: "I've met
this neat girl — she likes airplanes, she's pretty, she's smart, and
she wants to marry me." He made a joke out of it to his old crew-
mate Gordon Neiswanger, who was now working at the Jet Propulsion Laboratory in Pasadena: "I've figured out a way to get a
Volkswagen for two dollars."

"How?"

"I'm getting married."

Gordon was nonplused. Paul and Judy were married on May
18, 1957. A photograph of them sitting together on the cliff at
Torrey Pines was published in the newspapers with the caption,
"Mr. and Mrs. World Soaring Champion." It was more ironic
than the paper knew, because on his last flight in France, Paul
had had a *crise de conscience*. He decided that competition was
tempting him to take chances with his life that he shouldn't be
taking. He decided on that flight — if he came down alive — to
give up competitive soaring forever.

There was more than enough to do. MacCready was already
consulting for the President's Advisory Commission on Weather
Control, and for the Munitalp Foundation. In 1958 he became
president of the Atmospheric Research Group. The next year he
and Judy had a son, named for Parker Leonard, and three years
later another son, Tyler. The sixties were business years, crowded
with contracts and consulting, and in the middle of them Paul
turned forty and his third son, Marshall, was born. In 1966 a
company named Cohu Electronics bought Meteorology Research,
and Paul became a director of Cohu.

It should have been a decade of splendid financial success, the
material consolidation of all the promise that had gone before.
That didn't happen. People of less intellect, less achievement, and
yes, less integrity, were getting startlingly rich — that is hard to
avoid in Los Angeles. It irked Paul; he envied it, he talked about
money quite a lot, and his friends noticed some of his father's

attitudes beginning to show around the edges. Not that there was any real hardship. MacCready's companies went along all right; they just didn't climb like rockets.

Paul still kept up with aviation, flying powered planes, sailplanes, and occasionally balloons in meteorological research flights. By that time he had instrument and twin-engine ratings, and he had owned five lightplanes and four sailplanes. Parker and Tyler were beginning to build models, and one upstairs bedroom was turned into a workshop. In 1969 Paul had his first ride on a hang glider. He enjoyed it, despite the shortcomings of the primitive design. Hang gliders had too high a sink rate and too little control, but he kept flying them intermittently. As a hang glider pilot, he says, "I was . . . safe, but not brilliant."

He also was aware of the sporadic progress in human-powered flight. The structures of the British and Japanese contenders for the Kremer Prize were like syntheses of MacCready's own past experience, crosses between giant airplane models and ultralight sailplanes. All of them took years to build — far too much time to take away from a business — and they were terribly fragile. Still, Paul couldn't fail to be impressed by the announcement that the Kremer Prize had been raised to £50,000. It was a princely sum, the largest prize in the history of aviation. Henry Kremer, he thought, must have been a very successful businessman.

In September 1970 Paul decided that although Meteorology Research was going along satisfactorily, the corporate arrangement meant that he would still be doing the same thing in five or ten years. He resigned from the board of Cohu Electronics, and hence from his own original company. The major business success still hadn't come, and his investments seemed to have the same problems as hang gliders. He felt that he needed a new start.

Kirke Leonard, Judy's older brother, had reached the same conclusion a few months earlier. Kirke had taken his bachelor's degree in mechanical engineering at Worcester Polytechnic Institute, come out to Los Angeles, and earned an M.B.A. from the University of Southern California. For the past 18 years he had been working as an engineer for various Southern California aerospace firms. In 1970 he came to Paul with a proposition that wasn't aeronautical, but marine: Together they could buy a small company named Gen-Mar that made fiberglass sailing catamarans, a competitor of Hobie. They would build a better boat that would fill a gap in the growing market for small sailing cats.

Gen-Mar was named after *Genie* and *Marlin,* two boats designed by Alan Arnold. Kirke wanted to build the company's third design, a 15-foot (4.6-metre) catamaran called *Sea Spray.* It was an idea with resonances deep in both Paul's and Kirke's pasts. Kirke had helped his father, Parker, build boats and was an expert craftsman himself. Paul had been sailing since he was eight. *À la recherche du Johnson's Point:* Paul agreed to be a backer and director of Gen-Mar and to raise some of its principal from his associates. The initial capitalization was $130,000: $40,000 from MacCready, $25,000 invested by friends, and $65,000 from a bank loan. (Kirke and his mother later provided other loans.) They bought the company in February of 1970 and started building boats in Hermosa Beach with great enthusiasm.

Paul also decided to start a new company of his own. Between the mis-timed investments and the commitment to Gen-Mar, his assets were precariously low. He put most of them into incorporating Aerovironment in the summer of 1971. The company's objective was to solve energy and environmental problems in the areas of MacCready's expertise. Paul recruited two vice-presidents: his old friend Dr. Peter Lissaman, a specialist in low-speed airflow and fluid mechanics, and Ivar Tombach, a Cal Tech Ph.D. in aeronautics who was an authority on meteorological and air-quality instrumentation. At the end of 1971 the California Portland Cement Company made Aerovironment a partially owned subsidiary, and its staff began to scramble for contracts.

It seemed like a pair of bright beginnings. Both companies had technical talent and willingness to work. Aerovironment soon began to make a reputation for itself with excellent studies of air quality and plume dispersion. Gen-Mar began to produce the *Sea Spray,* and it was indeed a competitive boat. But both companies were short of a vital asset: marketing skill. The low capitalization of Gen-Mar didn't allow for the sales force needed to penetrate the highly competitive small boat market. Kirke eventually signed an agreement with the marketing manager of Alcort, builders of the successful *Sunfish* and *Sailfish.*

For the next five years Aerovironment prospered modestly, doing consistently good work and slowly expanding to 60 employees. Gen-Mar went gently downhill, selling a few hundred boats, but not making a profit. In 1976 Paul and Kirke sold the rights and tooling for Gen-Mar's designs to Sea Spray Canada, Ltd. The residual debt was $90,000, a large percentage of the original capitalization. Gen-Mar carried the loss on its books as a tax credit, and Paul took over the worry of paying off the debt. None of his friends pressed him for their investment.

It seemed unreasonable, almost like 1970 all over again. Mac-Cready had broken many records, won drawersful of medals and trophies, risked his life a number of times, worked hard, made valuable contributions to science and engineering, written more than a hundred papers, married, raised a family, and lived a life of clean-cut respectability. It is true that soaring is a solitary pursuit that does not suffer fools gladly, and business is otherwise, but Paul believed that he had made major concessions to social behavior. It also seemed to him that he had done nothing but worry about business for as long as he could remember. In the summer of 1976 he decided to take a real vacation, no matter what.

5

Genesis

The Origins of the *Gossamer Condor*

TRACING THE BEGINNINGS of the *Gossamer Condor* is like spiraling down through a thermal, diving against the current of air and time to the small circle of warm sand where a minimal twist of wind started the whole rising cloud of success.

For Paul MacCready the circle of sand was probably on a beach in the town of Nokomis, Florida, in July 1976. The MacCreadys took a family vacation that summer, driving to the east coast of the United States and back in a blue-and-white GMC van. Their route from Pasadena went through White Sands and Carlsbad, New Mexico, and across the southern part of the country. It was the first time in many years that Paul felt relaxed enough to forget his business problems and let his mind float.

One of the subjects that floated up repeatedly was ultralight aircraft. In the spring of 1976 Doug Lamont, the editor of *Soaring* magazine, had asked MacCready to write an article on hang gliding. It was a diplomatic gesture, because the directors of the Soaring Society of America were quite negative about this new renegade sport. Each time Lamont tried to report on its progress he had his wrist slapped. He hoped that MacCready, as an outstanding member of the soaring establishment, could put hang gliding in perspective for other sailplane pilots. Paul's article, titled "Developments in Ultralight Gliding," appeared in June 1976, just as the MacCreadys were starting their vacation; one of the most interesting parts of it compared the performance of hang gliders to that of gliding parachutes and soaring birds.

It was hardly surprising that soon after the trip began Paul became fascinated with watching large soaring birds through the van's windshield. Anyone who has seen the curving flight of great hawks and vultures across the skies of the American Southwest can understand his interest. Stop the car to scan with binoculars? Most bird watchers do that, but there was also something else motivating Paul. In 1949 he had read Alfred Woodcock's classic paper on soaring sea birds, and that *tour de force* (in which Woodcock confirmed a laboratory discovery in fluid mechanics simply by watching birds) had made a deep and lasting impression.

On this trip Paul became convinced that he could make a similar discovery by observation; it might not be an inductive leap into another field of science like Woodcock's, but perhaps he could reveal something new about the birds themselves. Watching circling birds became first a diversion, then a compulsion, then almost a focus of the trip. By the time the MacCreadys reached Florida, Paul was stopping the van and getting out to clock the circles of turkey vultures and frigate birds. He also tried to enlist his sons as fellow observers.

Parker MacCready was 16 that July. Three years later he remembered Paul's obsession vividly: "We thought he was nuts. He kept forcing us to watch birds and estimate their bank angle, and count how long it took for them to do a three-sixty [degree turn]. It seemed pretty nuts."

At his mother-in-law's house on the west coast of Florida, Paul had more time to observe circling birds and to sharpen the equations he had been writing in his head. He found that by estimating a bird's angle of bank and timing its circles, he could calculate three parameters of its flight: (1) the radius of the circle, (2) the flight speed, and (3) the equivalent straight-line flight speed at the same angle of attack (the angle at which the air meets a wing traveling through it). If he also knew the bird's wing loading — its weight per unit of wing area — he could estimate its coefficient of lift (C_L), the quantity that indicates how efficient any flying object is at flying. The average lift coefficient he arrived at for soaring birds was 0.9 — a considerably lower figure than those reported for birds earlier. When he compared this value to the lift coefficients of the hang gliders he had flown and written about, he found them surprisingly close.

On July 14 the MacCreadys visited Kitty Hawk, North Carolina, the site of the Wright brothers' first flights. The next day, en route to Williamsburg, Virginia, Paul found himself meditating first on bird flight, then on hang gliders, and wondering whether ". . . there was . . . some little hunk of aviation that hadn't been touched yet, something like a super hang glider."

He knew that a typical hang glider uses about 1.45 horsepower (1.08 kilowatts) while gliding. That may sound paradoxical for a plane without an engine, but there are no free rides in terms of energy. The "engine" of a glider is the force of gravity. Impelled by that force, all gliders fall through the air around them when they are flying, and their fall is converted, in part, to forward and lateral motion by the aerodynamic surfaces of the plane. (Of course, the air may be rising faster than the plane is falling, as in the case of a thermal updraft.) The sinking speed can be measured, for example, in feet per second; when it is multiplied by the weight of the aircraft in pounds, the product is in foot-pounds per second, one of the units of horsepower. (One horsepower equals 550 foot-pounds per second, or 746 watts.)

MacCready calculated that a reasonably efficient hang glider carrying an average-size pilot weighs about 200 pounds (90.7 kilograms) and has a sinking speed of approximately 4 feet (1.2 metres) per second when flying in still air. Under these conditions, the glider is converting potential energy to motion at the rate of $4 \times 200 = 800$ foot-pounds per second, or 1.45 horsepower (1.08 kilowatts).

The same energy balance is valid for any kind of aircraft, powered by any kind of engine. The power necessary to fly (P) is simply equal to the weight of the aircraft (W) times its sinking speed (w):

$$P = W \times w$$

It would not be surprising to find that the sinking speed of an airplane is also related to its wing area. Allowing a little simplification, if two airplanes weigh the same amount and have wings of quite different sizes, the one with a much bigger wing is likely to be a "floater," and the one with a very small wing will probably be a "sinker." That is, an airplane falls slower if each unit of wing area has less weight to support, and faster if it has more. The amount of weight that each unit of area supports is called the wing loading (L). As we have seen earlier, it is simply equal to the weight of the plane (W), divided by the area of the wing (A), and it is a very useful quantity in aircraft design. In fact, the minimum sinking speed of an airplane (w) is proportional to the square root of its wing loading:

$$w \sim \sqrt{W/A}$$

Given these relationships between power and wing loading, MacCready reasoned that if you could triple all of a hang glider's dimensions and keep its weight about the same by using very light structural materials and external wire bracing, then the wing area would increase, and the wing loading would decrease, by a factor of 3^2, or 9. Then, from the formula above, the sinking speed would be decreased to one-third of its former value, and consequently, so would the power necessary to fly:

$$W \times w/3 = P/3$$

That meant that such a giant hang glider would fly on only a third of the power used by a standard hang glider: 1.45 hp (1080 W)/3, or 0.48 horsepower (360 watts), within the range of human capability.

Tyler MacCready remembers the ride to Williamsburg as "hot and buggy." His father remembers it as "pleasant," even including the interminable Beatles tapes and Monty Python skits. By the end of the day the crucial connections had come together: Paul was sure that it was possible to build a human-powered airplane by using hang-glider technology. He didn't think the visit to Kitty Hawk had anything to do with it.

If every inventor in history who thought of building a human-powered airplane had actually built one, we would probably have run out of airport space long ago. In Paul MacCready's case, the motive for converting his private hypothesis into a major project was financial gain. He is not embarrassed by that idea, and given the circumstances it could hardly be called cupidity. He knew that the £50,000 Kremer Prize was worth about $86,000 at the current rate of exchange. The Gen-Mar debt was approximately

$90,000, in two levels of obligation, and even in the unlikely case that a prize-winning aircraft could be built for nothing, the Kremer Prize would not pay off the entire debt. MacCready had also been involved in business and aviation long enough to know that building a human-powered airplane was not a realistic way of getting rich quickly. Still, it was a chance to tackle a difficult and fascinating problem, and possibly pay off some of the Gen-Mar debt at the same time. The combination was irresistible.

The next stop on the loop home was New Haven. Paul looked up the wing loadings of birds at the Peabody Museum and the Yale Library and sketched out an article that would compare the aerodynamics of soaring birds and hang gliders. In Elmira, New York, he talked to his old friends Paul and Ernie Schweizer about the human-powered airplane concept. With each interaction his confidence in the idea of a scaled-up hang glider grew. Stan Taylor, now executive vice-president of Aerovironment, was general manager of Searle & Company's laboratory instrument division when the MacCreadys spent a weekend at his home in Winnetka, Illinois. The two families had been neighbors in Pasadena for seven years, and Stan remembers that by the time of this visit Paul was already convinced that he could build an airplane that would win the Kremer Prize.

On July 29 the MacCreadys arrived at Fort Collins, Colorado, to send Tyler to the Waverly West Soaring School. The last stop was Pasadena, and soon after he arrived home Paul built what might be called a nestling: an 8-foot-span, thread-braced, balsa-wood-and-tissue model of the airplane that would become the *Gossamer Condor*.

To understand MacCready's concept, it is necessary to know how a hang glider is built. In 1976, the majority of hang gliders flying were "standard kites." That is, they were versions of the triangular, flexible-wing glider patented by California engineer Francis M. Rogallo and his wife, Gertrude, in 1948. Because of the shape of the fabric sail, the visual impression of a Rogallo kite is that of a broad triangular arrowhead flying point-forward. Only when the covering is removed does the fundamental shape of the frame become clear. It is really a three-dimensional cross, like a child's jack.

Color plate 2 shows a typical Rogallo hang glider. The keel tube runs fore-and-aft, parallel to the direction of flight. The crossbar runs spanwise, at right angles to the keel, and is joined to it where the two members cross. Standing straight up out of this central main joint, perpendicular to both of the other frame components, is the kingpost, and directly below the main joint is the yoke or control bar, which can be considered a divided downward extension of the kingpost. Bracing wires connect the tips of these members, and if the wires are rigged tight a rigid structure results. A model of the frame looks like a diamond crystal, or two pyramids joined base to base.

The two leading edge spars that form the characteristic A-shape of a Rogallo wing are superimposed on this basic frame. They are joined at the front of the keel and fastened to the ends of the crossbar, which serves as a transverse brace. Stripped of its skin, a Rogallo airframe looks more like a structural art project than the skeleton of a flying machine. It is unrecognizable as a relative of the elegant and highly developed sailplane.

The frame of a quality contemporary hang glider is made of strong, lightweight aircraft aluminum tubing. The fittings that connect the tubes are also aircraft-grade aluminum. The bracing and flying wires are high-tensile steel, and the sail is tightly woven (and usually flamboyantly colored) Dacron.

That wasn't always the case. Paul MacCready's first hang glider flight was made in 1969 on one of Richard Miller's "Bamboo Butterflies." The frame tubes were bamboo poles lashed together, and the covering was black polyethylene of the best hardware-store grade. Total material cost was about $10 — but it flew. On May 23, 1971, Paul was towed up on Taras Kiceniuk Jr.'s *Batso* — another bamboo bomber — at the first Lilienthal hang glider meet near Newport Beach, California. (Taras was 17 at the time, and this encounter began an association with Paul that was to last through the construction of the *Gossamer Albatross*.) Paul was quite enchanted with the flight, which he found both easy and fun. Two years later the MacCreadys built a ¾-size replica of Taras's kite, on which Parker and Tyler learned to fly.

During the past few years the shapes of hang gliders have changed and diversified in a search for lower sink rates and better

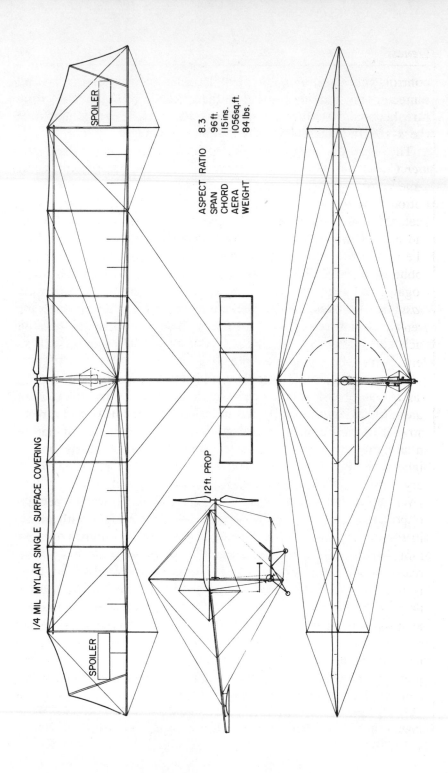

1/4 MIL MYLAR SINGLE SURFACE COVERING

SPOILER

SPOILER

12ft. PROP

ASPECT RATIO	8.3
SPAN	96 ft.
CHORD	115 ins.
AERA	1056 sq.ft.
WEIGHT	84 lbs.

control. MacCready predicted this evolution in a paper he presented to the Soaring Society of America in 1975, but the structure he visualized for his human-powered airplane was based on the x-y-z frame of the classic Rogallo kite.

The relationship can easily be seen in the drawing of the *Gossamer Condor 1* on page 72. The main airframe joint is still in the same central position, with the kingpost extending above it and a bottom post replacing the hang glider's control bar below it. The keel, as before, lies along the line of flight, but its drooped forward end has become a bowsprit to support a stabilizing control surface. The most dramatic change is in the crossbar; from a modest brace, about 16 feet (4.8 metres) long in a standard 24-foot (7.3-metre) Rogallo, it has grown to the 96-foot (29-metre) main spar of the *Gossamer Condor*'s wing. Although the *Condor*'s frame members aren't truly orthogonal — the plane's wings were eventually swept back 9° to adjust its center of gravity — a child's jack is still evident at the center of its skeleton.

The decision to use this structure for a human-powered plane was an inspiration, but a lightweight structure by itself was not a guarantee of success, as the Perkins and Wright HPAs had already shown. Like any object that must conform to the laws of nature, an airplane is a set of interlocking compromises. Some have a higher priority than others, and Paul determined early on that a very large wing was one of them.

Why must it be so large? A typical hang glider weighs perhaps 40 pounds (18 kilograms), so that its all-up weight with an arbitrary 165-pound (75-kilogram) pilot is 205 pounds (93 kilograms). A 24-foot (7.3-metre)-span standard Rogallo has a wing area of about 196 square feet (18.2 square metres). Its wing loading is therefore 93/18.2, or just over 1 pound per square foot (5 kilograms per square metre). MacCready had calculated that for the same pilot to fly his hypothetical human-powered airplane any great distance, the wing loading would have to be a quarter of that value: only ¼ pound per square foot (1.25 kilograms per square metre). Allowing some realistic increased weight for the much larger structure — say 79 pounds (36 kilograms) — meant

[*opposite*] 3. The *Gossamer Condor 1,* as built and flown at Mojave Airport.

that the projected HPA would need about $36 + 75 = 111/1.25 = 88.8$ square metres (956 square feet) of wing area to provide an adequately low sinking speed.

Long narrow wings (wings of high aspect ratio, like those used by Maurice Hurel on his *Aviette*) are more efficient in most flight regimes than short wide ones. The area and aspect ratio requirements predicted a wingspan of nearly 100 feet (30.5 metres) for MacCready's airplane. Paul knew that such long wings would require an intricate web of external bracing, hundreds of feet of exposed drag-producing wire. It was a prospect that would make a conventional airplane designer shudder, because in order for a plane to fly it must sustain a balance between the paired forces that act on any flying object: Its lift must be equal to the pull of gravity, and its thrust must be equal to its drag. There is not much thrust to spare in a human-powered aircraft.

Aerodynamicists divide drag into two kinds: *parasite drag,* which is caused by the frictional resistance of air to things moving through it, and *induced drag,* which is the energy price the wing pays for generating lift. Since airplanes must generate lift in order to fly, designers usually try to reduce parasite drag to a minimum by streamlining and eliminating friction-producing structures. Their aim is an aerodynamically "clean" plane. In this case that seemed impossible to achieve. The only option was to fly very slowly, so that parasite drag would be low, and to depend on the big wing to provide enough lift.

It is unlikely that Paul realized at the time how much his own background had conditioned him to accept a wire-braced airframe. He attributed it to hang-glider design, but the designers of other Kremer Prize contenders were also aware of hang gliders. Almost all of them, in different parts of the world, chose to build streamlined, cantilever-wing monoplanes — aircraft that looked like propeller-driven sailplanes (and in many cases like the Haessler-Villinger *Mufli* of 1935). It is a safe bet that if the designers of *Jupiter* or *Linnet* had been offered plans for the *Gossamer Condor,* they would have rejected them with a mixture of amusement and disdain — that primitive thing with all the wires?

Paul's sister Anne has a theory about his liking for wire-braced structures. She remembers his fascination with the crow's nest on the *Mohawk.* "Paul used to love to ride up there for hours — he

1. Paris, July 9, 1921: Gabriel Poulain and his *Aviette* at Longchamps racecourse, on the morning that he won the 10,000-franc *Prix Peugeot,* the first prize for human-powered flight.

2. *Mufli,* the human-powered plane built by Junkers engineers Helmut Haessler and Franz Villinger, flying at Rebstock airfield near Frankfurt in August 1935.

3. Enea Bossi's twin-propellered *Pedaliante,* piloted by Emilio Casco; on March 18, 1937, at Cinisello Airport in Milano, Casco pedaled it 1 kilometre after a catapult launch.

4. Henry Kremer (left) and Robert Graham, the two British engineers whose friendship resulted in Kremer's offering in 1959 the first of the prizes for human-powered flight that bear his name.

5. *SUMPAC* — for *S*outhampton *U*niversity *M*an-*P*owered *A*ir*C*raft — was built by a team of postgraduate students in response to the original Kremer Prize. In November 1961 it made the first human-powered flight in Great Britain.

6. *Puffin*, designed by a team of engineers at the de Havilland Aircraft Company, flew 6 days after *SUMPAC* but was no more successful in the Kremer Competition. This is *Puffin II,* with a larger wing and rudder than the original version.

7. *Linnet I* was the first of a series of human-powered planes built by Nihon University students under the direction of Professor Hidemasa Kimura. On February 25, 1966, Munetaka Okamiya piloted it on the first human-powered flight in Japan.

8. *Jupiter,* the most successful HPA ever built in Britain. Flight Lieutenant John Potter pedaled it to a world distance record of 3513 feet (1071 metres) at R.A.F. Benson on June 29, 1972; the record stood for nearly 5 years.

9. *Toucan* ("Two can fly if one cannot") was built by the Hertfordshire Pedal Aeronauts at the Handley Page Aircraft Company. In final form it had the wingspan of a Boeing 707-320, but its longest flight was only 2100 feet (640 metres).

10. As the twig is bent: Dr. Paul
Beattie MacCready and 15-year-old
Paul MacCready Jr. warm up a
Comet *Zipper* gas model. New
Haven, Connecticut, 1940.

11. The future Dr. Paul MacCready
Jr., aeronautical engineer and designer of the *Gossamer Condor*,
tries an engine-powered experiment . . .

12. . . . And the future bicycle racer
and human-powered aircraft pilot
checks the ground handling of a
basic prototype. Bryan Allen, Tulare,
California, 1956.

13. "The foundation of all success must be laid in doing things well." Vern Oldershaw, California State Champion, and Maude Oldershaw, en route to the National Model Airplane Championships, 1946.

14. Vern Oldershaw, building a wing rib of the *Gossamer Condor 2*. Shafter Airport, Shafter, California, 1977.

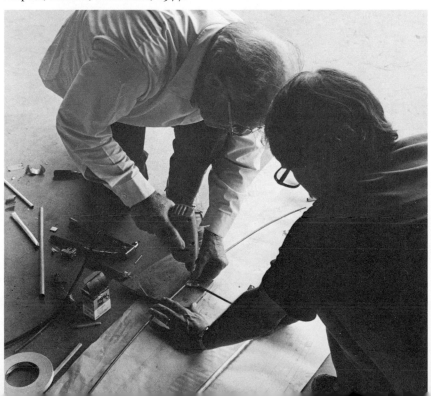

15. The final version of the *Gossamer Condor* takes shape. Jim Burke working on the fuselage in the Shafter hangar, March 1977.

16. Competition for the *Condor:* On January 2, 1977, Professor Kimura's *Stork B* flew 6869.75 feet (2093.9 metres) in 4 minutes, 27.8 seconds at Shimofusa Naval Air Base, nearly doubling John Potter's 1972 world record with *Jupiter.*

17. The *Gossamer Condor* team after the successful Kremer Figure-of-Eight flight. Standing, left to right: Pete Plumb, Tyler MacCready, Paul MacCready Jr., Parker MacCready, John Lake, Kirke Leonard, Joseph Mastropaolo, Jim Burke, Peter Lissaman. In foreground, from left: Phil Esdaile, Vern Oldershaw, Jack Lambie, Jack Franklin, Bill Beuby, Sam Durán, Bryan Allen.

18. Human-Powered Aircraft Factory, I. At Shafter Airport a wing and fuselage frame of the *Gossamer Condor* are suspended above Taras Kiceniuk Jr.'s *Icarus* HPA and the parts of the *Gossamer Albatross*. July 1978.

19. Human-Powered Aircraft Factory, II. At Hangar 522 on Terminal Island, Long Beach, California, Dave Saks builds the fuselage of *Gossamer Albatross 2,* while other team members assemble its wing and stabilizer panels around the fuselage of *Albatross 1.* March 1979.

20. Part of the *Gossamer Albatross* team at the American Embassy in London, May 16, 1979. Standing, from left: Blaine Rawdon, Morton Grosser, Ted Ancona, Kirk Giboney, Bill Watson, Sam Durán, Kirke Leonard, Sterling Stoll, Paul MacCready Jr. Kneeling, from left: Steve Elliott, Taras Kiceniuk Jr., Bryan Allen.

21. Waiting for the weather. Team members with the components of the *Gossamer Albatross 1,* stored in a warehouse on the Warren, Folkestone, Kent. June 1979.

22. The cockpit of the *Gossamer Albatross 1* immediately before the Channel flight. R.A.F. Manston, Kent, England, June 1979.

[*opposite, top*] 23. The voyage begins: Bryan Allen starting across the English Channel in the *Gossamer Albatross I,* on the morning of June 12, 1979. [*opposite, bottom*] 24. An hour into the flight, turbulent air, coupled to the increasingly rough water, drains Bryan's stamina; and the *Albatross* dips to within a few inches of the surface. [*above*] 25. Both of Bryan's legs are cramped, but with victory in sight, he brings the *Albatross* past the line of rocks bounding the beach at Cap Gris-Nez, France.

26. The reward. Members and affiliates of the Royal Aeronautical Society
Man-Powered Aircraft Group Committee after the awarding of the Kremer
Cross-Channel Prize, December 18, 1979. Standing, from left: R. G. Moul-
ton, K. W. Clark, M. J. Brennan, C. F. Joy, G. M. Lilley, H. C. N. Goodhart,
A. Welch, L. Welch, H. Kremer, F. W. Vann, P. MacCready Jr., J. C. Wim-
penny, K. Sherwin, D. R. Wilkie, M. S. Pressnell. Kneeling: B. Allen, T.
Kiceniuk Jr., F. Irving.

was excellent at spotting fish and markers." She recalls that on a number of occasions he explained to her that it was not only fun, it was also perfectly safe because the mast was braced with wire stays.

In 1941 Paul established junior indoor model airplane records in several classes. Indoor model airplanes are extremely delicate and specialized; they use ultralight tissue or transparent microfilm-covered wings braced with hair-thin Nichrome wire. And though MacCready's first full-sized powered plane looked outdated to many people in 1946 when he bought it, it looked perfectly all right to him. Its wing was braced with exposed wire stays radiating from a kingpost, just like the mast of the *Mohawk,* the wing of an indoor airplane model — and the frame of the *Gossamer Condor*.

Ironically, at least some of MacCready's open-mindedness toward the *Condor*'s arcane structure can be attributed to his isolation from current airplane design. Since taking his Ph.D. in 1952, he has had almost no direct involvement with aeronautical structural engineering; his main professional activity has been in meteorology. Unlike other HPA designers, he was able to concentrate on the problems of human-powered flight without the need to produce a "modern" human-powered vehicle. Certainly the sketches for the original *Gossamer Condor* contained more of MacCready's past than of aviation's present.

In the beginning there was little more to the plane than the huge wing and its bracing booms. Paul wanted to use as few components as possible to keep the airframe light. He hoped to stabilize the plane in pitch — fore-and-aft rotation about the wingspan axis — by placing the pilot well below the wing where his weight would act as a pendulum stabilizer, a technique still used to control some flying scale models.

Paul built two balsa models of his design between August 10 and 20, 1976. A block of wood and some modeling clay represented the weight of a pilot at the foot of the bottom post, and the wing was covered only on its upper side, again like an indoor model or a hang glider. The models had bowsprits carrying small stabilizers, and the very low wing loading that MacCready's theory specified, but the first test glides showed that they were unstable in pitch.

"I'll get by with a little help from my friends," the John Lennon–

Paul McCartney lyric goes. Both its sentiment and its English origin make it an appropriate theme song for the Gossamer aircraft projects. At this point Paul asked his friend and colleague Dr. Peter Lissaman for some advice about stabilizer size, and the nucleus of the Gossamer Squadron was formed. A number of observers have commented that the apparently casual process by which the multi-talented team was built up, changed, and adapted to the requirements of several different prize-winning aircraft was as remarkable as the airplanes themselves. Certainly there were times when it appeared to have the inevitability of natural selection.

Peter Lissaman believes that it has a great deal to do with the sociology of California. Lissaman is currently Aerosciences Vice-President of Paul's company, a tall, handsome South African expatriate with formidable scientific credentials and quite devastating charm. He is a classic example of a California life-change: from the proper scholarship student at Natal University and Trinity College, Cambridge, to a divorced, open-shirted Ph.D. in aeronautics at Cal Tech and a metallic blue four-wheel-drive; but the Commonwealth loyalty is still well stuck in under the suntan. Peter came to Cal Tech in 1954 to take his M.Sc. in aeronautics. He met Paul MacCready, married a girl that Paul introduced him to, and took her back to England, where he worked first for the Bristol Aeroplane Company and then for Handley Page, the company that later spawned *Toucan*. While at Handley Page, Lissaman became friends with a young Irish test pilot named Sean Roberts who had attended the Cranfield College of Aeronautics and who knew many of the original members of MAPAC. Roberts was to emigrate to California a few years after Peter returned there in 1958.

During the next few years Lissaman earned his pilot's license, taught at the U.S. Naval Postgraduate School at Monterey and at Cal Tech, consulted for the Jet Propulsion Laboratory, and directed the Continuum Mechanics Laboratory for the Northrop Corporation. Although most of his work was concerned with large aircraft and fluid mechanics, he knew all about the Kremer Prize. When Paul broached the giant hang glider idea, Peter was skeptical: "Lots of people have tried lots of technology." Still, it took him only a few moments to calculate, on the back of the proverbial envelope, that the pendulum effect of a pilot's weight would not provide enough stability in pitch; one had to use a fair-sized external stabilizer.

The second model was soon fitted with a larger canard stabilizer, and test-glided successfully. That too must have looked very familiar to Paul. (Voices from the past: "Oh, it flies backwards!" the *Condor* and *Albatross* teams would become used to hearing from charming non-aeronautical observers.) Like so many of the models built at 156 East Rock Road in the 1930s, this one had quite legitimately developed into a canard. It even flew. "Not a brilliant model," MacCready says, "but good enough to convince me that it was . . . worthwhile to go ahead."

He had already telephoned Lloyd Licher, Secretary of the Soaring Society of America, to verify that the Kremer Prize actually existed. He had also asked Robert Laidlaw of Flight Systems to find out if there was any hangar space available at Mojave Airport. Now he was encouraged enough to tell Tyler MacCready to start training to be the pilot of a human-powered aircraft.

At 6'1" (185.4 cm), Tyler is the tallest and lankiest of Paul and Judy MacCready's three sons. In August 1976 he was 14 years old and attending the Chandler School in Pasadena. He was moderately interested in rock climbing and running cross country, and very interested in "basically building anything that flies." At that point he wasn't particularly interested in training to be the pilot of a human-powered aircraft that didn't exist yet. Tyler did raise his output considerably, but decided that "Training was too much work — I started quitting training pretty soon."

Unaware of this defection, Paul called his brother-in-law Kirke Leonard and announced, "I'd like to build a human-powered airplane — how much space do you have in the barn?" (The barn was Gen-Mar's erstwhile final assembly building in Hermosa Beach.) Kirke allowed as how there was some space, thus adding his years of engineering experience and craftsmanship to the project. Within a few days he and Paul were drawing templates and building the first wing ribs. The prototype model that Paul sketched in his notebook had a wingspan of 88 feet (26.8 metres) — one foot less than a DC-9 Series 10 airliner. It took only a few measurements to show that the plane would have to be assembled in some space larger than the Gen-Mar shop. While aluminum tubing began to be shaped into frame members, a search for a nearby hangar began, and Paul recruited a fourth teammate.

Jack Lambie is another immigrant to California, with a lifestyle that would raise eyebrows in his home town of Elmhurst, Illinois. Trained as a science educator, he is before anything else air-minded. He holds the highest badge in soaring, the Diamond C, and his pilot's logbooks show thousands of hours in dozens of different aircraft. Lambie was a principal organizer of the original Lilienthal hang glider meet in May 1971, the meet at which Paul MacCready flew Taras Kiceniuk Jr.'s *Batso* and became interested in hang gliding. He has been director of education for the Los Angeles Museum of Science and Industry, but what people remember about him are his flamboyance, his verbal adroitness, his ability to look a decade younger than his fifty-one years, and his mercurial sense of humor. Jack is flexible about time, and he has boundless energy for short-term exciting projects. When Paul asked him to have lunch in August 1976, Jack had just returned from a honeymoon, during which he rode a tandem bicycle 15,800 miles (25,428 kilometres) around the world with his new 23-year-old wife, Karen.

Like Peter Lissaman, Jack was skeptical about the hang glider concept at first. It is ironic that even the enthusiasm of a hang gliding pioneer should have been dampened by the many unsuccessful attempts to win the Kremer Prize, but that is how Jack felt until Paul won him over. The combination of low speed and low wing loading convinced him, and he became a full-time member of the team. Paul agreed to pay him $5000 if they won the prize, and an hourly rate for his time if they didn't.

The hangar search turned up a temporary assembly site: the Rosemont Pavilion, a large building used during the construction of the mobile floral displays for Pasadena's annual Tournament of Roses. It was close to the MacCreadys' home, and since Peter Lissaman lived only a few doors from Paul and had a spare bedroom, Jack moved into Peter's house while he worked on the plane. The one drawback was limited time; the building would be needed in a few weeks to begin preparations for the Rose Bowl Parade. Paul decided to try it anyway. The materials were moved in on September 2, and for the next ten days Jack, Kirke, and Paul sawed and drilled aluminum tubing, while Peter verified calculations and nine-year-old Marshall MacCready acted as official mascot, acrobat, and clown.

Most of the plane's components were lofted full-size on the floor, using chalk, tape, and paper templates (a method still used three years later on the *Gossamer Albatross*). The wing spar was assembled from eight lengths of 2-inch (50-mm)-diameter aluminum alloy tubing. There were only seven thin aluminum tubing ribs, and they were weighted with water bags to simulate flying loads while the bracing wires were rigged. The covering was Du Pont Mylar, a transparent polyester film similar to Melinex.

The plane went together so simply that Paul began to worry; it was too easy to copy, and there was a flow of casual visitors through the building. Lambie's acting ability came in handy as he fended off questioners with three different straight-faced fictions: (1) They were building a water-bag holder; (2) they were building a sculpture for the Pasadena Museum of Modern Art; (3) they were building a float for the Rose Bowl Parade that symbolized government meddling in private affairs.

Anyone who has worked in the aerospace industry can only smile at the thought of four men proposing to build an 88-foot-span airplane in ten days. It is too funny to even argue about. There were several conditioning factors that allowed the builders to take this improbable idea seriously. The first was a shared background as model airplane builders. (In fact, that is probably the greatest single commonality for the *Gossamer Condor* and *Albatross* teams. One teammate observed that if we were to add up the balsa wood consumed by all of us since childhood, we would probably be sued by the Sierra Club.) Airplane model builders are used to finishing things in a short time; a number of national championships have been won with a plane built overnight by a bleary-eyed flier who had crashed his best ship the day before. This HPA prototype even looked like a strange sort of giant model.

The second factor is Paul's habitual optimism about the length of time a job will take. It has nothing to do with experience or rational estimates; it is simply constitutional, like having freckles. It became formalized during the Gossamer airplane projects as the

"MacCready Factor." The MacCready Factor, or M.F. if you like, is the number that one must multiply Paul's estimate by to arrive at the actual time a job will take. On the *Albatross* project, according to the team member consulted, it varied between 3.5 and 6. One can determine it more closely for the *Condor*. When Paul started the project, he believed that it was possible to design and build an airplane that would win the Kremer Prize in six weeks. Since then he has been twitted repeatedly by businessmen for spending so much time on such a bizarre effort. "I thought it would take about six weeks," he replied. "Wouldn't you take six weeks to win $86,000?"

In the event it took 52 weeks, almost to the day. The MacCready Factor for the whole *Gossamer Condor* project was therefore 52/6, or 8.6. But for the first prototype, it was, astonishingly, 1.0. Ten days after the team started assembling the trial plane upside down on the floor of the Rosemont Pavilion, it was ready for glide tests. It even had a name. The California Condor (*Gymnogyps californianus*) emerged as the prime candidate for a namesake in several MacCready family conferences because of its rarity, its ungainliness, and its great wingspan. *Gossamer* was added because of the plane's fragility and lightness, and also, as Parker said, "Because it sounded right."

Paul was away on a business trip on September 14. When he returned at 8:30 that evening, it was to the news that the project had to be fitted into a single storage bay of the Rosemont Pavilion by the next morning, and out of the building completely by the afternoon. He decided that they should finish the plane and fly it that night.

It took three hours to cover the wingtip rudders with Mylar, connect their rubber-band centering controls, and attach the last few wing wires. Just after midnight Paul, Kirke Leonard, Tyler MacCready, Jack Lambie and his son Tom, Paul's neighbors Easy and Nancy Sloman, their son Chris, and his cousin Scotty eased the huge plane out to the Rose Bowl parking lot and turned it right side up. There had been heavy ground fog all evening, and now the fog turned to a fine drizzle. The crew lined up a few cars and turned their headlights on. It is tempting to imagine what a passer-by might have thought of this fragile dragon with its aluminum skeleton and plastic skin shimmering in the lights: the embryo of an airplane.

The first job was to weigh the plane. Paul had calculated its empty weight as 42 pounds (19 kilograms), but rainwater was already building up on the wing surface, and the first weight was 58 pounds (26.3 kilograms). While the team watched, the one-inch (25mm)-diameter kingpost bowed more and more under the weight of the water, and then buckled. They hurriedly replaced it with a 1.5-inch (38mm)-diameter tube and rerigged the stays. Paul decided to try glide tests in a grass parking field for the Rose Bowl, and the now-sodden group trundled the plane on a dolly across Seco Street to the field.

For the next two hours the team slogged back and forth on their makeshift runway. Crew members steadied the *Condor*'s wingtips and bowsprit while Paul held up the bottom post and tried to control the pitch angle with a clothesline attached to the stabilizer. By 1 A.M. the plane weighed 80 pounds (36.3 kilograms), and all the participants agreed that an hour later its original weight had doubled.

Finding agreement on what else happened that night is more difficult, an aeronautical *Rashomon*. Kirke Leonard was the most disparaging: "It was a very foggy night, and the fog turned to rain and condensed on the wings. There wasn't any headwind, but when we tried to run it wouldn't fly at all. It never got off the ground."

Jack Lambie saw only the good parts: "Although the rain added a lot of weight, it was apparent that the craft was more like a balloon than an airplane. We walked with it at five miles per hour and it lifted easily, straining at the ropes we attached to the corners. Nothing broke in the flight tests."

For Paul, despite the problems, the test was a confirmation of his theories: "The plane was soggy . . . droopy, and the wires were not as short as they should have been." Without the weight of a pilot, the center of gravity was too far forward, and Paul had Jack pull down with a force of about 30 pounds (14 kilograms) on the rear of the plane. "Then the pitch seemed okay, and I was able to 'fly' it with the bowsprit above Kirke. I . . . mainly wanted to see whether the structure would work, and . . . if the canard stabilizer would control the pitch. It did that, maybe not perfectly, but enough so that it was . . . worthwhile to go on. When the wing lifted, I hung on and became convinced that the design was what we had hoped for."

By 2 A.M. they had made ten test runs. In his notes on these "flights" Paul referred to the wing as a sail; the design was still an ultralight hang glider in his mind. On their way back to the Rosemont Pavilion the team discovered one of the drawbacks of an ultralight hang glider. As they crossed Seco Street, headed northeast, a gusty tailwind hit the plane. The trailing edge of the wing bent down sharply, the right wing snapped at the inboard joint, and then at others. A few moments later several ribs buckled, the right wingtip broke off, and tears began to spread across the Mylar covering. It was ludicrously similar to the old films of human-powered flight attempts that are shown as real-life cartoons.

The team dragged the remains into the pavilion, disassembled them, and moved them into a storage bay. At 2:20 A.M. the prototype *Gossamer Condor* was a pile of bent aluminum tubing, wire, and bedraggled Mylar that, in fact, had never flown at all. The next morning it was trucked up to Mojave Airport, to be made into a human-powered aircraft that could win the Kremer Prize.

6

Eyrie

Mojave Airport

IF A CALIFORNIA CONDOR were to take off from the Rose Bowl in Pasadena, which has an altitude of 860 feet (262 metres) above mean sea level, and fly a course of 0° true — due north — meanwhile climbing to an altitude of 2787 feet (849 metres), in exactly 61 miles (98 kilometres) it would find itself over the main runway of Mojave Airport. *Key 122.8 five times in five seconds for runway lights,* the pilot instructions say.

Runway lights are unnecessary frills for a condor, and from the air one's impression is that a desert-loving bird would be more at home here than an airplane. Mojave looks like an Ozymandias of airports. The runway is almost 10,000 feet (3000 metres) long, big enough for military jets, but the only sign of concentrated settlement is the town of Mojave, 2600 souls and a strip of low buildings in the middle distance. Otherwise the horizon is bounded in all directions by a vast western geology whose features have names out of a cowboy film: *Antelope Valley, Horned Toad Hills, Jawbone Canyon, Sierra Nevada.*

There is a flight operations office with Unicom but no active tower at Mojave. The double-takes begin as soon as you turn off the runway and taxi in. Instead of the usual Cessna 150s, the aprons are crowded with F-86 jet fighters, painted a slick civilian blue and white and missing their military flashes. A pair of giant C-133 transports brood at the end of a taxiway in peeling MATS insignia. One can only blink in disbelief at a glimpse between hangars: a World War I de Havilland D.H.-2? An aviation junkyard, perhaps — but the next plane is a sleek, unfamiliar bizjet, as shiny as a new toy, with the four blades of a turboprop emerging from its silver nosecone. This is clearly a peculiar place.

When one drives into town, the car leaves a tan cloud behind it, a kind of dusty sigh. Mojave is that way; it has expanded and contracted over the years like an old concertina, and it knows what it is, more or less. It was first settled in the mid-nineteenth century as a borax station on the western edge of the Mojave Desert. Then gold was found nearby. The town boomed, gold-bearing ore replaced the borax, and in 1876 the Southern Pacific Railroad arrived and steam locomotives replaced the 20-mule teams. Eventually the gold ran out, as gold will. The miners straggled away, and Mojave became an isolated rail-switching center with a dwindling population. After World War II the U.S. Marines built the airfield and the town swelled again, this time with government money. Then the Marines moved out. Sigh. "We're really growing," the nice bespectacled lady in the chamber of commerce office says.

In 1972 Kern County established a 3000-acre (1214-hectare) airport district at Mojave and appointed an ingenious pilot named Dan Sabovich as its general manager. Sabovich recognized the special character of the place, and under his direction Mojave has become a center of aeronautical invention and development. It is a haven for people who have more time and ingenuity than money to spend on new ideas, and it seemed like a logical nest for the *Gossamer Condor*.

When Paul called his old friend Robert Laidlaw, whose Flight Systems, Inc., owns the blue-and-white air force at Mojave, Laidlaw's hangars were full. But the next one up the line, Hangar 61, was leased by Dr. Sean Roberts, the ex–Handley Page test pilot whom Peter Lissaman had met in England, and who now ran a school for military test pilots at Mojave Airport. His heavily instrumented de Havilland *Dove* took up only half of the blue wooden building, and he agreed to sublet the other half to MacCready for $300 per month. The hangar was one foot too short for the 96-foot (29.26-metre) wingspan that Paul had now decided on. The *Condor*'s wing spars were each clipped 6 inches (15.2 centimetres), and the forlorn-looking pile of parts for the human-powered plane was moved in next to Sean Roberts's twin-engined *Dove*. It seemed like a perfectly ordinary arrangement for Mojave.

All Values in Percent Chord		
x	upper surface	lower surface
0	0	0
1.25	2.25	-1.64
2.5	3.34	-2.01
5.0	4.96	-2.30
7.5	6.15	-2.30
10	7.06	-2.16
15	8.40	-1.70
20	9.26	-1.38
30	9.92	-1.06
40	8.97	-0.91
50	6.96	-0.75
60	4.86	-0.60
70	3.16	-0.45
80	1.81	-0.30
90	0.84	-0.16
95	0.41	-0.08
100	0	0

Nose radius 1.84, center of nose circle (1.84, 0.14)

Trailing edge angle from chord line
Upper surface 4.5°, Lower surface -0.9°

4. The Lissaman 7769 Airfoil, which was used on the *Gossamer Condor,* both *Gossamer Albatrosses,* and the *Gossamer Penguin.*

At this stage the most important shapes on MacCready's airplane were its wing and stabilizer airfoils and its propeller blade contours. A propeller is simply a rotating wing mounted so that its lift is applied as thrust, and at the low flying speeds envisioned for the *Condor,* the curves were not unrelated. Peter Lissaman was becoming more and more intrigued with the project; he decided to design these crucial curves from scratch rather than use existing airfoils. Aerovironment owned a Hewlett-Packard 9820 desktop computer and a connected 9862A x-y plotter. Peter devised a program that enabled the computer to generate and draw the airfoils needed for the *Condor*'s strange flight regime.

Children relate intuitively to the outlines that the plotter produced for the Lissaman low-speed airfoils. They have a kindergarten follow-the-dots look, and a delightful apparent simplicity. The high lift conditions that they had to satisfy were not simple at all, especially in the first single-surface wing. Only when Jack and Kirke began to form the wing ribs from thin aluminum tubing did their extreme slenderness and great length — 11¾ feet (3.58 metres) — become apparent. The propeller that Peter designed for the *Condor* had the same disconcerting scale. It was assembled from balsa ribs spaced along a hollow aluminum spar, and covered with Monokote. An easy project for model builders — but it was 12½ feet (3.8 metres) long!

Any aircraft of this size, however basic it looks, has hundreds of joints and components. During September 1976 designs for these began to evolve from the sketches in Paul's and Kirke Leonard's notebooks. The general design concepts were few and straightforward:

1. Use a big, single-surface wing for high lift and light wing loading at a low flying speed.
2. Brace the wing spar with wire stays from the ends of a kingpost, a bottom post, a keel tube, and a bowsprit, like a hang glider.
3. Mount the canard stabilizer at the forward tip of the bowsprit, thus giving it maximum pitch control moment with the least additional structure.
4. Position the propeller high up behind the wing, to give it adequate ground clearance and a clean slipstream.
5. Locate the pilot directly under the center of lift so that his weight would provide some pendulum stability.
6. Make every part as light as possible.
7. Try the easiest solution to each problem first.

There was also an eighth commandment, which Paul insisted on from the beginning. He believes that it was still in force in 1979 when the second *Albatross* was being built, but anyone reviewing the history of the project must regard it as a diminishing variable, rather than a constant precept. It was: *Do only what you have to, and build quick and dirty*. It may have been followed during the building of the first *Condor*. Jack Lambie clearly favors that school of construction, Kirke Leonard less so. But while the Gossamer planes remained easy to repair throughout their development (at least compared with most earlier HPAs), they also became more refined, and less "dirty." One has only to compare the elegant ribs of the *Gossamer Albatross* with the flimsy airfoils of *Condor No. 1* to see how far the standard of expediency was diluted in three years.

Two important principles in the design of the *Condor* were negative ones — factors observed by previous HPA designers that MacCready chose to ignore. One was ground effect, the lower induced drag and apparently greater lift of a wing that flies close to the ground. Paul figured that the structural and maneuvering advantages of the high wing outweighed the possible benefits of ground effect. The other was takeoff assistance in the form of large-diameter driven wheels. His reasoning in this case was that if such a slow plane could fly at all, it would be able to take off with propeller thrust alone.

From *Model Airplane News,* September 1942:

> This young man is by far the most versatile model flier ever to come to our attention. Apparently he doesn't go out with the sole objective of winning prizes, but he is also interested in models for the purpose of experiment and developing new ideas. Construction is secondary as long as he can demonstrate a new principle or an efficient way to handle an old one.

A structural hypothesis, however brilliant, is still only a hypothesis. Soon after the giant hang glider concept occurred to Paul he began worrying about suitable materials for it. His first productive lead was a magazine article in *Sport Aviation* on composite material technology. He called the author, Hans Neubert, expecting to get some advice about plastics and carbon fiber. To his surprise, Neubert suggested that the frame of the *Condor* be made of aircraft aluminum tubing, chemically milled to reduce its weight. MacCready quickly agreed that aluminum had some convincing advantages, including well-known mechanical properties, ready availability, and relatively low cost.

Lee Griswold, the manufacturer of Sea Cat catamarans, recom-

mended Aerochem of Orange, California, to Paul as a reliable
company for chemical milling. (In fact, although most of Aerochem's business consists of large orders from the aerospace industry, the company went out of its way to expedite the *Condor*'s
components throughout the project.)

Paul's aim was to make the *Condor*'s skeleton as light as possible, and to rely on wire bracing for strength in tension. As a
result he used 6061-T6 heat-treated aluminum tubing 2 inches
(50.8 millimetres) in diameter for the wing spar. It came in 12-
foot (3.66-metre) lengths and had a wall thickness of 35 thou-
sandths of an inch (0.89mm). After milling, each half of the
assembled spar had a wall thickness decreasing in 4 sections from
.020" (0.5mm) at the center joint to only .015" (0.38mm) at
the wingtip — about the thickness of an office staple. A 95-foot
(29-metre)-long aluminum beer can would be a close approxi-
mation to the size, shape, strength, and weight of the complete
spar. It could be buckled between your thumb and index finger,
and it was, more than once.

The other frame tubes were etched to a wall thickness of 20 thou-
sandths of an inch (0.5mm); they varied from 2 inches (50.8mm)
down to ¼-inch (6.35mm) in diameter. The tubes were connected with sheet aluminum gussets and braces, pop-riveted in
place. At butt joints, wooden plugs were inserted into the ends
of the tubes to provide a surface for epoxy cement, and some
joints were reinforced with Mylar, glass filament, and duct tape
(the latter was also invaluable for repairs). The bracing wires
were steel, ranging from .022" (0.56mm) to .035" (0.89mm)
in diameter.

While Paul's sketches and the Rose Bowl model provided guidelines for the *Condor*'s lift and control surfaces, there was as yet
no place for the pilot/engine to sit. Kirke and Jack were by this
time putting hundreds of hours into building what Jack described
as "the first snazzy version" of the plane. They knew that the
length of the bottom post was determined by the required bracing
angle of the lift wires attached to its lower end. They eventually
mounted the pilot's saddle tube at junior bicycle height, 22"
(56cm) above the bottom end of a post 9.3 feet (2.8 metres)
tall. The pilot straddled the tube and was supported in a semi-

reclining position by a red canvas backrest laced across a light-weight frame. A transverse tube under his seat allowed two helpers to boost the airplane during takeoffs.

The pilot's recumbent position was a compromise between efficient power generation and low wind resistance. Paul's aerodynamic calculations for the plane had converged on a probable flight speed of about 8 miles (12.8 kilometres) per hour. Although the drag of an exposed pilot is relatively low at this speed, it is still lower with a horizontal pilot than with a vertical one. At that point the drag component was almost a token quantity, since with respect to parasite drag the plane approximated a flying bedspring. (The *Condor*'s drag regime provoked a theological discussion during one of the *Albatross* team's bull sessions. The main point was that according to our flight tests, harp-carrying angels had high drag and must fly very slowly in air; therefore either angels operated in a vacuum, or heaven must be quite small, or else things take a long time to happen there.)

Power transmission provided another requirement for the pilot's position. The propeller was above and behind the pilot; its drive shaft ran parallel to the keel, over his head, and a chain transmitted his pedal effort to a sprocket on the shaft. The forces developed in the chain continued to surprise the team for the next three years, but it was obvious that the closer the chain ran to the bottom post, the better the post would be able to absorb the compression loads on it. This meant that ideally the pedal sprocket should be mounted directly on the post. A semi-recumbent flying position kept the pilot's body clear of the post, and also allowed him reasonable visibility and arm movement.

Visiting bicycle racers recognized most of the *Condor*'s running gear at a glance: TA cranks and drive sprocket, Lambert shaft sprocket and toe clips, Sheffield Sprints pedals, Christophe straps, and a Mavis sealed bearing. That wasn't true of the chain. "What's that stuff?" That stuff was translucent red-orange urethane timing chain, with two thin steel cables molded into it. It is made by the Winfred M. Berg Company and is often used in food conveyors and packaging equipment. It had been tried on earlier human-powered planes because of its light weight (1.2 ounces per foot or 111.6 grams per metre) compared with standard bicycle chain, but on the *Condor* it seemed to have a persona of its own. The team developed an almost superstitious belief in the strength and reliability of one batch of chain as opposed to another. "Good chain" that was free of visible molding voids was saved for record attempts, and "practice chain" was used more or less recklessly in daily flights.

Two pairs of aluminum tubing legs angled down forward and aft from the saddle tube and joined a horizontal brace to form the cockpit frame and landing gear. The *Condor*'s molded black plastic ground wheels were bought in quantity from a local toy store. They were filled with plastic foam for rigidity and equipped with ball bearings. During both the *Condor* and *Albatross* projects Paul took special delight in telling people about these wheels: "We buy toy fire trucks, take off the wheels, and throw the trucks away. They're the best toy fire truck wheels that money can buy."

Toy wheels were an appropriate choice for the first version of the *Condor*. Its stabilizer control was a horizontal shaft extending back toward the pilot with a miniature steering wheel on the end of it. From a distance the cockpit with its bright red seat and little steering wheel looked like a small bicycle attached to a large television antenna.

The resemblance was not coincidental. Advanced bicycle technology has been an invaluable source of ideas for the transmission systems and training regimes of all the Gossamer aircraft. Paul once remarked that many parts of his background seemed to fall into place in an almost predetermined way during the airplane projects. That was certainly true of his interest in high-speed bicycles, an interest fostered by Jack Lambie and Professor Chester Kyle of California State University at Long Beach.

Lambie and Chet Kyle met at an American Institute of Aeronautics and Astronautics streamlining symposium held in Los Angeles in 1974. They found that they were both building nearly identical streamlined bicycles. Their friendship and mutual enthusiasm led to the founding in 1976 of an organization with one of the least streamlined titles in history: The International Human-Powered Vehicle Association. IHPVA holds annual competitions for absolute speed, and distance at speed, in human-powered vehicles. To date its members have produced the fastest forms of human propulsion extant, including the fastest bicycles in the world.

(In 1979, three teams won coveted complimentary speeding tickets from the California Highway Patrol for the first human-powered vehicles to exceed 55 miles [88.5 kilometres] per hour over a level timed course.) Many members of the Gossamer aircraft teams are also members of the IHPVA. Its current international president and chief timer is Paul MacCready Jr.

Paul met Chet Kyle in June 1974, when Jack Lambie invited him to watch the tests of Chet's streamlined bike in a hall of the engineering department at Cal State Long Beach. Kyle and Mac-Cready hit it off immediately. They both combine a solid technical background with a high action potential and a liberal sprinkling of engaging eccentricities. Kyle holds a B.S. in mechanical engineering from the University of Arizona and an M.S. and Ph.D. in fluid mechanics from the University of California at Los Angeles. He is a capable architect and guitarist, among other things, and he has been racing bicycles since 1943. At age 51 he was seeded 8th in California and 21st in the United States in the veteran racing class.

The bicycle that Chet was testing was unlike any that Paul had ridden or bought for his sons. A streamlined transparent shell fitted over the frame and enveloped both bicycle and rider almost to the ground. Although the test course was only ⅛ mile (201 metres) long, MacCready became an immediate convert to Kyle's work. He examined the experimental bicycle carefully and agreed to be the timer for the first streamlined bicycle competition, planned for April 1975. In September 1976, when Kirke Leonard and Jack Lambie built the pilot's support frame for the *Gossamer Condor*, its dimensions were those of a reclining-position bicycle that Chet Kyle had designed and built that summer.

While the framework of the *Condor* was taking shape, Paul began to think about the engine. He knew that Kyle had published a paper on the horsepower requirements of bicycles, so he called him to ask for advice. Chet arranged a meeting with a colleague who knew even more about the horsepower of bicycle riders than he did: Dr. Joseph Mastropaolo, professor of exercise physiology at California State University at Long Beach, who was to become the chief engine tuner of both the *Gossamer Condor* and *Gossamer Albatross*.

Joe Mastropaolo doesn't jump to conclusions. He is 52 years

old, a lean 6'2" (188cm), and a superb physical specimen. His eyes, behind gold-rimmed glasses, often have a solemnly amused expression. He is likely to give a slow, considered look at an apple he is about to bite, as if it held some great philosophical secret. He has seven children, and one would search a long time to find a kinder man under a more laconic exterior.

Dr. Mastropaolo — he prefers Joe — has the usual impressive list of academic credentials consonant with his position, the last one being a Ph.D. in physiology from the University of Iowa. But one of his five diplomas is a little rarer than the average university degree: It is the Diplomate of a fencing master from the oldest and most exclusive academy of swordmanship in the world, the École Supérieure d'Escrime in Paris. In 1951 Joe was the only American accepted to the school; in 1953 he graduated first in his class, with championship-level performance in épée.

At the meeting in September 1976 Paul MacCready was surprised to learn that this gentle musketeer had been interested in human-powered flight since 1960. In 1967, when he was a research physiologist for the Douglas Aircraft Company at Huntington Beach, California, Joe organized a team to design a contender for the Kremer Prize. Though the team grew to 20 members, it never built a plane, and when Joe left to teach at Long Beach State the group drifted apart.

Mastropaolo and Kyle were both interested in the *Gossamer Condor,* but both were also skeptical. (When Chet first explained Paul's concept to Joe, he said he was afraid that the plane "isn't gonna make it.") Joe soon changed his position; he was greatly influenced by Paul's open-mindedness toward physical training. "I told him about the ergometer, and he said, 'Great, let's get it.' " In this way a machine that various team members regarded as anything from an invaluable asset to a medieval torture device became a permanent part of the project.

An ergometer looks like another kind of odd bicycle. It has a bicycle seat, pedals, cranks, a chain, and a large wheel that spins rapidly, but it never goes anywhere no matter how fast it is pedaled. It is mounted on a strong frame, and its purpose is to calibrate and enhance physical output (the invaluable asset version), or to reduce otherwise healthy people to sodden, trembling wrecks (the medieval torture school). Its name comes from the Greek *ergon,* work, and *metron,* a measure or rule. It is basically a stationary bicycle that can be adjusted to make the work of pedaling more or less difficult, and can also measure the torque produced on a continuous and quantitative basis.

An ergometer is only as effective as the person programming and calibrating it, and Joe Mastropaolo proved to be a wizard at both. On September 24 he loaned MacCready an ergometer, and three days later he followed it with a detailed training program. It was divided into aerobic, anaerobic, and test flight practice sections; and it was designed to raise Paul's physical output to the level of an average college athlete (or, once again, the "average fit man"). MacCready turned 51 at the end of September, and although he did not regard himself as being in spectacular physical condition, he started working out on the machine at a much more strenuous level than the program prescribed. He quickly "turned green and sweaty and flimsyed out." On October 4 he had his heart checked, and a few days later he recorded a treadmill electrocardiogram at Huntington Hospital. Both examinations gave him a clean slate, and after a week's rest he started on Mastropaolo's regimen, this time as directed. Joe also wrote ergometer programs for Mac-Cready's sons, and Paul applied to the Royal Aeronautical Society for Kremer Competition licenses for himself, Parker, and Tyler. His application was the 48th one received; the 45th was that of Professor Hidemasa Kimura.

While the MacCready males pedaled their way through October, the frame of the *Condor* began to look more and more like an airplane, albeit a strange one. In the meantime, another crew member recruited himself. When Jim Burke heard about the project, "I collared Paul and told him I wanted to get on board." It was a characteristic announcement for an ex-Navy pilot, and a competitive sailor since age 10. Jim first met Paul at Cal Tech, where he took his bachelor's degree in mechanical engineering, an M.S. in aeronautics, and an aeronautical engineer's degree. He has worked at the Jet Propulsion Laboratory for years, was a director of the *Ranger* space probe program that placed the first American satellite on the moon, and is on the advanced planning staff for solar physics and astrophysics.

Dry sounding credits — and misleading. Jim Burke is really an aeronautical Shackleton, the kind of man you could trust to get you home from Elephant Island or Phobos. He has very clear blue eyes — sailor's eyes — set in the classic Steve Canyon square-jawed face. He is fascinated by deep space, but his face crinkles with pleasure when he talks about flying boats. He flew PBY *Catalina* patrol bombers in the Navy, and he has definite esthetic opinions about the dwindling family of seaplanes: "The Grumman *Mallard* is the prettiest airplane ever designed." In 1976 he was happy to suppress his esthetics and drive up to Mojave Airport on weekends for a chance to work on MacCready's ugly duckling.

Burke completed the core of the *Gossamer Condor* team, which in addition to him included Paul MacCready Jr., the three Mac-Cready boys, Peter Lissaman, Kirke Leonard, Jack Lambie, and Joe Mastropaolo. (Chet Kyle came up to Mojave many times, but he considered himself an adviser rather than a member of the project.) In October 1976, excluding the MacCready sons, the average age of the men was 48.3 years — the youngest was 45 and the oldest was 51. They had between them 3 doctorates, 15 other university degrees, and a formidable array of talents. None of them realized at the time that what had started as an aeronautical lark was going to test their maturity, strain their interrelationships, exhaust their patience, and require more dogged and persistent practicality than all of their credentials could guarantee.

By November 3 the plane was ready for its first outdoor test. Dawn was crisp and breezy at Mojave, but at 8 A.M. the wind died to nearly zero, and they started push flights with Tyler Mac-Cready in the pilot's seat. Anyone who has built big model sailplanes knows the feeling of those first flights. There are the balance tests that should ostensibly trim the plane perfectly, the last-minute adjustments, and then the first running launch. If you are lucky and have built without warps, the plane leaves your hand and floats away in a long, slow glide, more graceful than any bird. It is indescribably beautiful; it holds you poised with one foot off the ground like Eros until the model touches down many yards away. The feeling of buoyancy, the way the plane rides the air, its suitability for its destined element, are all implicit in that first long glide. If it is good, it leaves you high, incredibly elated, with a lump in your throat.

The *Gossamer Condor* was not good. Despite its phenomenally low wing loading, Tyler could keep it airborne for only a few seconds at a time: "The Mojave plane didn't fly very well. I never thought it would work. It would barely get off the ground. I could never make a minute — no way. I basically thought it would never work." For now at least he was right; a few minutes into the test the bottom post buckled at the pilot's seat tube. Two days later Kirke had made a new post and they were ready to try again with Paul in the pilot's seat. On his third short push flight the wing broke in two without any warning. They dragged the plane into the hangar; it felt like Pasadena again.

This was not a matter of turns, just straight sustained flight. Paul's original estimate of six weeks was already long past. Suddenly the brilliant idea didn't look so brilliant, the skeptics looked smart, and the MacCready Factor went up sharply. What was wrong?

First of all, flexibility. The long slender ribs were indeed very light — too light to maintain their shape under flight loads. The wing bent and twisted in any wind at all; it behaved more like a strip of ribbon than Peter Lissaman's carefully designed airfoil. The tubular spar formed the leading edge of the wing, and the team tightened the guy wires to it in an attempt to make the structure rigid. The wing still twisted, and when the wires were tightened further the spar buckled under the compressive stress. Paul reluctantly gave up his principle of minimum structure, and a rear spar was added near the wing's trailing edge.

Now it was the ribs' turn to carry a compression load, locked between the leading and trailing edge spars. Another weekend test showed that they couldn't; they flexed and buckled maddeningly, so that only one short section of the wing at a time maintained its original curvature. The weather began to turn cold at Mojave, and gloves appeared in the hangar. By late November the wing had acquired spreaders like a sailboat's mast, and more wire bracing on the top surface of the airfoil to keep the ribs from distorting. The flights were still measured in seconds.

Everyone who worked in Hangar 61 that winter complained about the cold. The plane was so wind-sensitive that it could be flown only in absolutely dead air. Somehow, everyone had overlooked the warning about Mojave in the *Pilot's Guide to California*

Airports: "Pilots should tie aircraft securely due to possibility of high winds." The winds came, and they kept the plane on the ground and howled vindictively through the hangar as well. "Mojave was a bitch," Kirke remembers. "Your fingers were always cold, the plane wouldn't do anything. New England all came back to me."

Still, they persisted. On November 24, Paul, Parker, Tyler, and Marshall MacCready retested themselves on the ergometer and telephoned the results to Joe Mastropaolo. They had improved tremendously: Paul produced 0.34 horsepower (253.5 watts) for 7 minutes, and Parker developed 0.26 horsepower (194 watts). It sounded encouraging, even though Paul's output was only about half of what a professional bicycle racer could produce in the same interval. By this time Jim Burke had developed the team obsession with the *Condor*: "We had no concerns except making it fly." Piece by piece, they whittled away at it. For the time being aerodynamic theory went by the board. Burke again: "It wasn't a matter of ingenious design, it wasn't exotic materials, it wasn't hotshot aerodynamics, it was just a single-minded insistence on doing only what you have to do."

Externally, Paul still agreed with that, but the plane's unsatisfactory performance had also convinced him that the aerodynamic theory was either incomplete or incorrect. On December 11 he called his old friend, sounding board, and aerodynamic authority, Henry Jex. Jex is a principal research engineer at Systems Technology, Inc., in Hawthorne, California, and a highly successful aircraft designer. Like MacCready, he is also a lifelong aeromodeler and a sailplane pilot. Paul asked Jex to study the stability and control problems of the *Gossamer Condor,* and Henry agreed to work on them as soon as he could, although he was very busy.

Meanwhile, in the few calm moments at dawn or dusk, the tests continued. The plane's optimum flying speed with pilots weighing between 110 and 140 pounds (50–63.6 kilograms) was now 7 to 8 miles (11.2–12.8 kilometres) per hour, and it stalled below 6 miles (9.6 kilometres) per hour. On the day after Christmas, 1976, Parker MacCready used all the energy and flying skill he had and made a straight flight of 40 seconds. It covered 469 feet (143 metres) — six times the distance of Joe Zinno's solitary flight —

at an altitude of more than 3 feet (1 metre), and it was the first flight that the crew could call "long."

Unfortunately, at 8 miles per hour the mile-long Kremer Prize course would take seven and a half minutes — 450 seconds — to fly. The *Condor* couldn't remain airborne for one tenth of that time in a straight line, let alone turn. It was obvious that many changes had to be made, and the cost of materials was beginning to mount up alarmingly. So far, Paul MacCready had put $15,000 into the project. Five months had passed since he started out to win $86,000 in six weeks. On December 14 Bob Graham, who had received the original prize grant from Henry Kremer 17 years before, died without having seen the prize won.

7

Fledgling

Mojave/Shafter

ON DECEMBER 19, a week before Parker MacCready's 40-second flight, Paul MacCready wrote in his logbook: "Vehicle now nicely rigid." Considering the structural failures that were yet to occur, his comment was an indication of how incredibly flimsy the original *Gossamer Condor* was. Paul still felt that the *Condor* could win the Kremer Prize reasonably soon, but here are the changes that he wanted to make in January 1977: *Remove bowsprit tip. Make king-post tip smaller. Make bottom post tip smaller. Make new 3rd rib. Lighten rear spars. Streamline tubes. Reduce drag on bike. Install smaller wires. Make lighter weight fittings. Install better bearing wheels. Repair Mylar and trim wing. Check prop efficiency and improve its airfoil. Brace pilot's seat.*

Much work for many hands. By this time Peter Lissaman and Jim Burke were coming up to Mojave every weekend to work on the plane. Soon the families of team members were also recruited, and the hangar began to look like a coed school. Paul prized this development; when the expected weeks of work on the *Condor* lengthened into months, he had been worried and guilt-ridden about spending so much time away from home. After the families became involved with the plane the guilt was absolved, more work was done, the children had a real and challenging project to contribute to, and a valuable spirit of play was added to the team.

One result of this is that the Gossamer teams have built many more model airplanes than full-size airplanes over the past few years. Visitors to the *Condor* and *Albatross* hangars often found the scene a cross between a playground and a hobby shop, and more than one reporter expecting to meet a group of cliché technologists talking in equations has had to dodge a Ph.D. towing a ten-year-old around the hangar on a skateboard. Paul hoped to have this whimsical aspect of the project, as well as the scientific parts, recorded for posterity. An accurate visual record and potentially useful publicity were two of the reasons why he agreed to allow film maker Ben Shedd to make a documentary on the building of the *Gossamer Condor*. He first discussed the film with Shedd in August 1976, before construction of the *Condor* prototype had started, and as December numbed the team's fingers at Mojave, Shedd began to film the evolution of the fledgling airplane.

From the log of the *Gossamer Condor:*

January 5, 1977: *Rent 2 propane heaters.*
January 6, 1977: *Learned of Japanese competition.*
January 7, 1977: *Cold.*
January 8, 1977: *Cold!*

There is no doubt that the chill of apprehension on January 6 was as piercing as Mojave's frigid winds. Paul scribbled a terse note to himself: "Win final prize as quickly as possible, ignoring fanfare, if Japanese competition turns out to be severe."

It was more severe than he or any of the other team members realized. Professor Kimura's years of patient development with the *Linnet* and *Egret* series of human-powered planes at Nihon University had culminated in the *Stork,* a marvel of ultralight craftsmanship. *Stork* first took off on March 12, 1976, and during the next two months it made a series of well-controlled flights up to a distance of 595 metres — more than a third of a mile. Then, as described earlier, it crashed on June 2 in the process of making a 180° turn.

The phoenix is a potent symbol in Japan. Within a few months the Nihon craft was rebuilt as the even more elegant *Stork B*. The new plane was airborne on November 24, 1976, with Nihon's top pilot, Takashi Kato, aboard. Six weeks later the rumors drifted to California: On January 2, 1977, *Stork B* had flown for 4 minutes, 27.8 seconds, at Shimofusa Naval Air Base. The flight was confirmed by the *Fédération Aéronautique International* as a new world record of 6869.75 feet (2093.9 metres), nearly doubling John Potter's 1972 record of 3514 feet (1071 metres) with *Jupiter*. *Stork B*'s flight was almost exactly equal to the airborne distance that Paul MacCready had calculated was necessary to complete the Kremer Figure-of-Eight Course.

That was worrisome news to the *Condor* team, but there was one consoling thought. The Kremer Course required an airplane that could turn, and like all the other human-powered record flights thus far, *Stork B*'s was a straight line. The Californians still did not know that on the final flights of *Stork A*, Kazuhiko Churei had completed his 180° banked turn at a height of 10 feet (3 metres). At the last moment Churei overcontrolled and spun in, but Professor Kimura was sure that his students could learn to turn *Stork B*.

Each of the Nihon University HPA fliers had to be both a licensed pilot and a trained athlete in top physical condition. Although Joe Mastropaolo's training program had doubled Paul MacCready's physical output in three months, his curve had leveled off well below the elite athlete level. Paul had to concede that the *Condor* was going to need the best pilot-athletes available to win the Kremer Prize. Late in December he asked Chet Kyle for the names of some possible candidates. Kyle suggested Ron Skarin, ten-time national bicycling champion, who lived in Van Nuys; and Greg Miller, an 18-year-old bike racer from Seal Beach that Kyle felt had great promise. Skarin was exceedingly busy, but Paul took out a license for him to fly in the Kremer Competition anyway. Miller was an unknown quantity.

"I had never heard anything about it." Greg Miller turned out to be a compact, powerfully muscled young man with deep-set eyes, dark brown hair, and an easy smile. "One day in January '77 Chet Kyle called up and said, 'Why don't you come out and try this human-powered airplane?' " Greg was open-minded, if slightly baffled by the idea. Between running track and cross-country at Los Alamitos High School, he had built handlaunch and towline gliders. Just as long as it didn't have an engine: "I hate planes with engines." He says it with some force, and he has reason to hate other vehicles with engines. He started bicycle racing in 1973, and in 1976, while he was bicycling across the United States, he was hit by a truck. Six of his vertebrae and five ribs were broken in the accident. He was still recuperating when Chet called him.

Greg arrived at Mojave on January 9. When the *Condor* was turned upright late that morning it had some but not all of the many changes that Paul had decided to make after Parker's 40-second flight of December 26. At about 2 P.M. Tyler flew a short test hop, and then Greg made a first flight of 30 seconds. He was surprised that it was so hard, and of course, "It was so *cold*." As the flights continued the wind increased, and the plane's performance deteriorated steadily. They quit at 6 P.M.; despite Greg's extra power, none of his flights had equaled Parker's 40 seconds. It was a long way from *Stork B*.

Two days later Paul glumly concluded that the tests on December 26 had been more promising than those on January 9. The changes had been, if not steps backward, only steps in a wrong direction. A new set of modifications was begun, and test flights started again on the 12th. Tyler needed 4 pounds of ballast at the tip of the boom to correct the center of gravity when he flew, and he was chagrined to find that he couldn't take off with the ballast (a plastic bag of water) in place. But Greg's interest had now been aroused, and he began coming up to Mojave to fly regularly. His confidence increased with each flight, and on January 15 he demonstrated that, even without pilot training, muscle counted for something.

The day didn't begin auspiciously. In the small hours of the night Paul had installed a cuff around the leading edge of the left wing to widen it and make the drag bucket (low drag range) less critical. Parker, Tyler, and Greg each flew short hops in the morning. Their flights were not impressive, and Greg, unfamiliar with the new wing behavior, stalled the plane while pedaling very hard. One of the propeller brace wires snapped, the left wingtip spar buckled at the outboard rib, and a seat support broke.

The team spent the afternoon repairing the damage and extending the cuff along the entire leading edge. Late in the day the wind died to nearly zero. Tyler and Parker timed the propeller revolutions while Greg tried again. This time there was an immediate improvement; the first flight went 250 yards (228.6 metres). They turned the plane around, facing into a breath of headwind. Greg started pedaling, and suddenly, as Burke the seaplane pilot said, the *Condor* "got up on the step," and began to float along. With the wing runners puffing to keep abreast, Greg flew 1300 feet (396

metres) in 135 seconds, and made two gentle turn corrections to
boot. The first half of the flight was made at an altitude of 12 feet
(3.6 metres) and a speed of about 8.5 miles (13.6 kilometres) per
hour. There was a noticeable decline in the second half, to a speed
of 6.5 mph (10.4 kph) and an altitude of 8 feet (2.4 metres). Still,
it was triple Parker's previous record, and a magical morale booster.
The hanger almost felt warm.

Not as warm as Tulsa, the newest member of the team might
have said. In August, when he was at a high pitch of excitement
about the "short-term" airplane project, Paul had called his old
friend and one-time co-member of the American international soaring team, Bill Beuby, in Tulsa, Oklahoma. Bill was retired, he was
another expert craftsman, and on January 18 he arrived at Mojave
with a nascent case of *Condoritis*. He brought with him the longest
aviation pedigree of anyone who worked on the Gossamer aircraft.

Beuby remembers seeing his first airplane overhead when he was
five years old. The plane was a Thomas-Morse scout, and the year
was 1917. His earliest plane rides were in a de Havilland D.H.4
flown by Lieutenant Lowell H. Smith, later the deputy commander
of the first successful round-the-world flight in 1924, and Lieutenant — later Lieutenant General — James H. Doolittle. After that
Beuby never got the smell of airplane dope out of his nostrils. When
he won a San Diego model-building contest with a scale S.E.5, his
prize was presented to him by Captain Charles A. Lindbergh, recently returned from Paris. Bill was taught to fly by Hawley Bowlus,
designer and builder of the Bowlus sailplanes. He later became a
champion soaring pilot, and he has had a hand in the design and
production of Douglas aircraft ranging from the World War II A-20
attack bomber to the DC-8 jet transport. He was to spend much of
1977 working on the *Gossamer Condor*.

Bill's maturity and aeronautical history were complemented by
another Mojave recruit, Jack Franklin. Jack was a soft-spoken 28-
year-old pilot for Sunbird hang gliders. Like Beuby, he was fascinated by airplanes, and in 1969 he graduated at the top of his
class from the U.S. Navy Aircraft Mechanics School. Jack met
Tyler and Parker MacCready through hang gliding, and after his
first visit to Hangar 61 Paul hired him to build parts of the *Condor*.
Between Jack's shoulder-length locks and Bill's sparse tonsure they

had, as one team member noted, "plenty of hair for two men —
just distributed wrong." The challenge of making the *Condor* fly
was enough to insure that these very different pilots worked together
smoothly.

The day that Bill Beuby arrived, Paul was trying to find out why
the plane took so much effort to pedal. He used the same test that
Enea Bossi had 45 years earlier, measuring the *Condor*'s towing
force with a spring scale. He found that the force required to move
the 70-pound plane in still air was about 12 pounds (5.4 kilograms), but as soon as there was any wind, the drag increased to a
prohibitive 25 pounds (11.3 kilograms).

They continued the tests over the next few days, towing and then
pedaling. The conclusion was inescapable: The slightest turbulence
made the plane almost impossible to fly. The wing covering was
tightened, and tufts of yarn were fastened to it to indicate airflow
patterns. Test flights were made with the stabilizer at different
angles of attack, but the resistance was still too high. Finding flying time in Mojave's incessant winds was becoming more and more
difficult. On many days the wind never died at all; it only shifted
from daytime gusts to the evening's cold drainage flow off the
Sierra.

Paul was still optimistic. One flight of January 19 seemed to
offer a clue. Greg took off strongly, keeping the nose down, and his
pedaling felt easier than before. After about 90 seconds, when he
began to tire and pedaled harder to compensate, the flight speed
decreased, even though the angle of attack was still low. They tried
one unassisted takeoff that day, and Greg succeeded in getting the
Condor over a 10.5-foot (3.2-metre) T-bar for the first time. The
poor results from hard pedaling, and the small difference between
Tyler's and Greg's flight times, despite Greg's higher power, pointed
to an inefficient propeller.

In three hectic days a new propeller was designed, built, and installed. The first flight with it, on a foggy January 23, began well;
then the propeller shaft connection and one blade spar broke. Paul
was undeterred; he felt so sure that this propeller would be the
answer that while it was being repaired he called Ben Shedd and an
official observer for the Kremer Prize to the airfield. The prop was
fixed by midafternoon, and late in the day the wind dropped to 2

miles (3.2 kilometres) per hour. The Kremer Course pylons were set up, but Tyler, who flew first, could make only a short straight flight. Greg was also unable to equal his previous best. Paul ended the disappointing day with another list of modifications, and the observers went home.

The official observers for the Kremer Prize had to be certified by the British Aircraft Owners' and Pilots' Association, after nomination by the contestant. The first four observers that MacCready nominated were Lloyd Licher, Secretary of the Soaring Society of America; Manny W. Phillips, Chairman of the Technical Committee of the National Aeronautic Association; Alden De Witt, Vice-Chairman of the same committee; and Albert E. Taylor, Chief Timer of the U.S. Air Racing Association. All were approved by the AOPA. Unfortunately, they had to contend with a situation out of the fable *Condor! Condor!* Paul recognized that a successful flight was unlikely, but each time it seemed that he had solved the airplane's problems, he would call out an observer for a record attempt. There was a need to test the observation procedure, but every attempt at Mojave was premature and anticlimactic, and the novelty soon wore off. It isn't surprising that the observers began to get disillusioned.

Some of the builders were starting to feel the same way. MacCready's response was to get more help. He called another soaring colleague, John Lake. Lake was writing a book on aerodynamics for pilots, but he was willing to play hooky from his own project to help build the *Gossamer Condor*. He worked full time on the airplane for the next six months.

Lake's background was particularly appropriate for the *Condor* project. His flying experience was similar to MacCready's: solo in 1944 at age 16, stick time in many civil and ex-military aircraft, some Goodyear air racing adventures, Commercial, Instrument, and Multi-Engine ratings, a Commercial Glider ticket. But while Paul had only dabbled in hang gliding, John had become deeply involved with it. He is a board member and Flight Director of the United States Hang Gliding Association, the inventor of a Rogallo wing stabilizer that has been credited with saving a number of lives, and the builder of the first successful auxiliary-powered hang glider in the United States. In hang-gliding circles Lake is regarded as an authority on downwind turns. He was surprised to find that the plane he was coming to work on couldn't turn even in still air.

Up to this point the team had been so intent on achieving long straight flights that they had paid only cursory attention to the *Condor*'s lack of lateral stability. In retrospect Paul says that the shortcoming was understandable, because the plane had no vertical surfaces. Kirke Leonard was less philosophical about it: "The plane wasn't controllable at all. You would start a turn, or sometimes you wouldn't, and it would slide off until it hit." They made many attempts to remedy this awkward trait with rudders and fins. The triangular area between the kingpost and the keel brace above the wing was filled in with Mylar, and wingtip rudders and inboard vertical stabilizers of various shapes were fitted. None of them worked.

After the unsuccessful test of January 23, Paul decided to try a more dynamic approach to turn control, and let the stabilizer roll laterally. At first the canard surface was controlled directly by wires; later it was made to tilt by small balsa servo tabs, much like ailerons, attached to the trailing edge. This turned out to be the first constructive step toward steerability.

By the end of January the winds at Mojave were blowing a minimum of 12 miles (19.3 kilometres) per hour most days. When the plane was taken out on the 29th in a bravado attempt to fly, the left wing spar broke almost immediately, and the right wing was badly distorted. Repairs seemed to take forever in the drafty hangar, and the morale of the team was low. MacCready considers himself a congenital optimist, but at this point his own fatigue and preoccupation began to show through.

One Sunday night he and another team member worked on the plane until the early hours of the morning. The temperature was bitter cold, and the wind howled through the building. They finished the repair, and Paul made a list of the materials they needed. Then he turned, obviously deep in thought, and walked out of the hangar. The teammate listened in surprise as he heard MacCready start his car and drive off. There was no other transportation back to Pasadena, the airport was completely shut down, and there was not even a sleeping bag in the hangar. "It was unbelievably thoughtless," the teammate comments ruefully. He spent a frigid night alone with the plane, and though he continued to work on the project, he didn't forget the incident.

The relationships of the original *Condor* team have for the most part survived such episodes. The group is connected by a web of social and educational bonds that would be unusual in anything but a family project. When Peter Lissaman came to Cal Tech in 1954, Paul MacCready had recently received his Ph.D. in aeronautics there, and was dating a pretty blonde girl named Nancy Copeland. In 1955 Nancy married Peter Lissaman. Her sister Caroline was already married to Paul's friend Jim Burke, who had taken his aeronautical engineer's degree at Cal Tech while MacCready was working on his doctorate. In 1957 Paul married Judy Leonard, whose father, Parker, had been his teacher years earlier, and whose brother, Kirke, had also moved to Los Angeles and was working for AiResearch Manufacturing Company.

When Kirke Leonard bought Gen-Mar in 1970, Paul MacCready became one of its directors. Paul founded Aerovironment one year later; Peter Lissaman was his third employee, and Jim Burke became one of his directors. A short time later, when Aerovironment began its research program on aerodynamic vehicles, Jack Lambie became the company's consultant.

More than one of these team members felt discouraged when the *Gossamer Condor* seemed no closer to winning the Kremer Prize in 1977 than it had in 1976. The progress they had made from the Rosemont Pavilion was not enough; it was clear that some significant breakthrough was needed. In an attempt to simulate the topsy-turvy relationship between the *Condor* and its flight medium, MacCready built a 5-foot (1.5-metre)-span balsa model that he "flew" underwater in his swimming pool. The hang glider–based airframe was so large and light that the air mass affected by it had more inertia than the plane itself. One of the hunches that Paul confirmed with the swimming pool model was that the *Condor* was almost impossible to roll as one would an ordinary airplane. There was simply inadequate force to bank the huge wing against the mass of air above and below it.

At the end of January, Paul called a meeting and proposed to Peter Lissaman and Jim Burke that they redesign the plane from the ground up. Peter remembers that they were sitting in Mac-

Cready's living room when he came out with a more surprising statement: "Well, guys, I guess we have to move."

"I don't know why, but it seemed like an incredibly brave decision at the time. Paul was completely casual about uprooting the project, but of course he was absolutely right. Mojave just wasn't working at all." The only question was, where? They needed an airfield without high winds or heavy traffic, and with an empty hangar that could hold a 95-foot (29-metre)-span airplane. The answer was to come from the Getty Oil Company, via a chain of coincidences.

Getty is the second largest producer of crude oil in California, and one of its major sources is the Kern River field near Bakersfield. Kern River crude is as thick as syrup; it has to be urged to the surface with injections of high-pressure steam. The generators that supply the steam also eject sulfur dioxide and other gases into the air, and in 1976, Getty hired Paul MacCready's company to study the dispersion of these gases in the Bakersfield area. One of Aerovironment's experts on plume dispersion is Ivar Tombach, and Getty assigned a young environmental engineer named Sam Durán to work with Tombach on the Bakersfield study.

Samuel Navarette Durán is a good example of what American industry stands to gain from affirmative action. He was born to Spanish-speaking parents in Whites City, New Mexico, population 50. His father was a caretaker at Carlsbad Caverns. After an intermittent, upward-mobile education, Sam received a bachelor of science in chemistry from California State University at Bakersfield, and a master of science in environmental engineering from the University of Southern California. His training was interrupted by the U.S. Army, which drafted him, discovered his engineering talent, and sent him to Vietnam as a fire controller for 105mm howitzers.

Sam is a gentle man, and Vietnam was not gentle. When he returned to California in 1971 he was suffering from moderate battle shock: "I was really looking for someplace peaceful and quiet." He enrolled at Cal State Bakersfield and was assigned to a dormitory room occupied by two biology majors, Mike Flanders and Bryan Allen. Bryan was involved in bicycle racing and hang gliding, and before Sam knew it, he was the owner of a 10-speed bike and a one-third owner of a bargain hang glider. The glider proved to be a poor copy of an Eipper 17. "It was a death machine if you ask me," Sam says with a smile — he has an altogether winning smile — but he was soon an enthusiastic convert to hang gliding.

When Ivar Tombach learned of Sam's involvement he asked if Sam had read Paul MacCready's articles on hang gliding. Sam had, but he said it was probably a different MacCready. (Bryan Allen later assured him that it was the same one he was working with, and Sam's reaction was, "No way, it can't be; this guy's *fifty*.") Paul heard about Sam's and Bryan's interest and invited them to Mojave to see the *Gossamer Condor*. The three visits that they planned were jinxed with bad weather or crashes, and they never made it.

One day in January 1977 Ivar mentioned the *Condor* team's frustration with the weather at Mojave to Sam. "Why not move to the San Joaquin Valley?" Durán asked. Ivar said that sounded like a good idea, but it wasn't so easy; they needed a low-traffic airport within reasonable driving distance of Pasadena, and an empty hangar that could hold a 95-foot wingspan airplane. On January 27 Sam called Paul and told him about Shafter Airport. It was an uncontrolled field about 15 miles northwest of Bakersfield, used mostly by agricultural crop dusters. It had a 4550-foot (1387-metre) lighted runway, a big available hangar with a wide apron in front of it, and many periods of stagnation during which there was little or no air movement. Ivar seconded Sam's suggestion.

Jack Lambie flew up to inspect Shafter on February 12 and reported back, "Boy, this place is perfect." MacCready promptly arranged to sublease part of the hangar for $100 per month. Four days later Jack, Kirke, Bill Beuby, and John Lake packed the parts of the *Gossamer Condor* into a rented semi-trailer, drove it to Shafter Airport, and unloaded their pile of aluminum tubing, Mylar, and tools into a corner of the big yellow hangar. It looked like the Rosemont Pavilion again, except that the pile of parts was larger. The next time they were assembled the result would be very different.

On January 13 Henry Jex had started to recalculate the flight equations for the *Condor* in response to Paul's request. He included the gust gradient terms and noticed that there was something unusual about the plane's theoretical apparent mass. He didn't have time to work on the problem again until February 22, when Peter

Lissaman telephoned with new derivatives for the *Condor* that he had calculated with Aerovironment's computer. For the next four nights Henry worked on the problem nonstop. "Superseded" scrawls impatiently across pages of calculations made on the 22nd; on the 23rd the apparent mass is attacked with heavy artillery, followed by the roll equations.

By that night Jex had succumbed to the lure of the *Condor*. The next computer printout (bootlegged on Systems Technology's proprietary aircraft dynamics program) is time-stamped 21:54 hours. At midnight an aeronautical *Eureka!* appears circled in red under a graph of roll angle versus time: "No *wonder* ailerons NG in normal use!" The gist of the discovery was that although a right wing down aileron normally rolls a plane to the left, the *Condor*'s roll moment was so high that after a few ineffective seconds, the adverse yaw of the aileron swung the plane to the *right*. The turn was unstable, as the team had already found repeatedly.

The next night STI's computer produced a new set of flight equation derivatives for the *Condor,* based on Jex's findings. They showed that the plane's dynamics were very different from those of conventional aircraft. The results went off to Peter Lissaman with Jex's suggestion that because of the *Condor*'s nearly infinite roll moment, the team should use the yaw effect to turn the plane in the opposite sense from a normal aileron turn. Jex also confirmed that the turn could be initiated by wing warping as well as by letting the canard surface roll.

By the time this analysis reached Paul, his notebooks were full of drawings for a new airframe. The meeting with Peter Lissaman and Jim Burke at which they decided to move the project had also produced the decision to reduce the *Condor*'s wing chord at the tips. They hoped by this to lower the plane's roll moment, but that one small-sounding change initiated a whole series of interlocked revisions. The narrower wingtips resulted in a tapered wing, and hence less wing area. Less wing area meant that the plane would have a higher flying speed and higher drag, which in turn prompted the design of a double-surface, lower drag wing, and a streamlined cockpit enclosure for the pilot. Paul decided to sweep the wings back to put the center of gravity in the right place, and also, "because it looked right."

Although MacCready claims it was simply an evolution, the plan view of the new plane looks like a quantum jump. A sketch of the original *Gossamer Condor* could easily be mistaken for a child's kite. The new design with its swept, tapered wings has a sense of purposefulness and balance. It is clearly an airplane, and there is no longer any doubt about which direction it is meant to fly; one senses it intuitively. It was a whole new beginning.

8

Adolescence

Shafter Airport

THE LAST SURVIVING CALIFORNIA CONDORS nest in the inaccessible mountain canyons of the Los Padres National Forest, east of Santa Barbara. It is back country in the true sense of the word. On a pilot's chart a flight line from Los Padres to Mojave Airport lies on a course of 79° — east by north — and measures about 80 miles (128.7 kilometres). If you visualize that line as the base of a shallow triangle, half as high as it is long, Shafter Airport lies at the vertex, 40 miles (64.3 kilometres) north. Its original name was Minter Field, and in its own way it is as insular and atypical a flying base as the other two points of the triangle. It is almost as if the *Gossamer Condor* needed as much seclusion as its namesake.

Shafter's isolation isn't obvious from a map; the little airplane silhouette that marks its location looks only a short distance from the bright red artery of route 99 bisecting the Central Valley of California. The pilot's manual tells another story: *No tower. No food service at field. No easy transportation. Motel does not pick up at airport.* As you drive down the dusty, bumpy road off the Lerdo Highway wondering who flies here? the car roof suddenly vibrates around your ears with the roar of a 600-horsepower (447-kilowatt) Pratt & Whitney radial engine. You clutch the wheel and duck as a big yellow Grumman Ag-Cat heads straight at you and climbs out over the car as if someone upstairs is pulling it on a string. *In light or calm wind conditions, ag aircraft may be operating from any runway or taxiway.* Yes indeed.

The fields around Shafter are planted with acres and acres of beautiful Acala cotton. "Not as long staple as Egyptian," the farmer says candidly, "but consistent as hell." Constant staple, they call it, and the textile mills pay a premium for it, knowing that it will spin and weave the same way it did last year. It makes a lot of money for the cotton farmers. There are also many residents of the San Joaquin Valley who think that it makes an excellent gourmet dinner. Straw hat pushed back on the head, brim hand scratching the sunburned pate in a timeless rural gesture: "We got some of everything, I guess. Mites, bollworm, loopers, Lygus bugs, you name it." All of those acres must be sprayed to prevent insects from destroying the cotton crop.

The planes that do the spraying are the bulldozers of aviation, tough professional machines that sustain day after day of heavy loads and high-G turns. Many are converted from ex-Army or Navy biplanes. Grumman's Super Ag-Cat is typical of postwar designs. It weighs more than 3 tons all up, and the air over the runway sings for a long while after a fully loaded one takes off.

Only a conditioning at Mojave can prepare the visitor for a more unusual sight at Shafter. It is a small hangar with its own apron, set back from the main flight line. Parked beside it are a Douglas B-26 bomber, a de Havilland Vampire jet trainer, and a de Havilland Tiger Moth. They are the property of Dwight Reimer, a used-airplane broker, who also flies them on the equivalent of state occasions at Shafter Airport. (The *Gossamer Condor* was later responsible for one of these occasions. During the dedication of the *Condor*'s California state historical marker we watched the Vampire whine overhead and learned afterward that the short tribute to human-powered flight by this distant relative of *Puffin* had consumed 306 gallons of jet aircraft fuel.)

Psychologically, Shafter was almost as eccentric as Mojave, if less glamorous, and that made it a comfortable home for a human-powered airplane. Physically, it was better in every way: The hangar was larger, the field altitude was 425 feet (129.5 metres) as opposed to Mojave's thin 2787 feet (849 metres), and the all-important calm weather was there as predicted. For the Pasadena crew members it was farther away. The 120-mile (193-kilometre) drive was long enough to discourage casual trips, and the change of base led to a slow change of personnel on the team.

Soon after the *Condor* moved to Shafter Airport, Paul made sure that they would have a measured course to fly. He calibrated the odometer of his GMC van against the highway mileposts near Shafter, and then used the car to mark off a half-mile section of north–south runway 34. He allowed a little extra distance for a safety factor and put down two silver duct tape crosses on the runway approximately 2650 feet (807.6 metres) apart to mark the pylon positions. The turn pylons were fluorescent plastic cones used for traffic control — "Dayglo Duncecaps" to the crew — with 10-foot (3-metre) bamboo poles topped with silver Mylar streamers projecting out of them.

As soon as the tools were sorted out, Jack Lambie and Bill Beuby started work on the new canard, and John Lake and Jack Franklin began building ribs for the double-surfaced swept wing. In the meantime Kirke Leonard invited a Bakersfield resident that Lambie recommended as a possible team member out to Shafter. Vern Oldershaw arrived on February 19; he looked like Bill Beuby's sturdy brother, and after his first visit to the hangar, he says, "I never left."

If the United States adopted the Japanese government's system of awards, the Oldershaw family would probably be subsidized as a living national treasure. Vern was born in 1915, the next-to-last of his parents' eleven children. He was building rubber-powered airplane models in 1926 (Paul MacCready was still in diapers), and he has been modeling ever since. In 1936 he met a very pretty girl from Richmond, Virginia, on a tennis court at Bakersfield College. Her name was Maude, she liked airplanes as well as tennis, and one year later they were married. In 1946 they both learned to fly, and Vern won the California Model Airplane Championships with a plane of his own design, the *Glory Bee*.

The year that Vern learned to fly sailplanes, the president of the Soaring Society of America was Parker Leonard, Paul MacCready's teacher. In 1952 Paul and Vern met at a Soaring Association meeting. They already knew quite a lot about each other. Paul was then two-time National Soaring Champion, and he was familiar with Vern's contest-winning model designs, which had been published in several national magazines. From then on they kept in intermittent contact. In 1959 Paul asked Vern to build the prototype models for Meteorology Research's sampling aircraft, and in 1965 Vern became president of the Southern California Soaring Association, of which Paul was a member.

Given the Oldershaw family background, it was inevitable that they would become interested in human-powered flight. Soon after the Kremer Prize was raised to £50,000, Vern and his son Paul each did a set of design calculations for a human-powered airplane. (By this time Oldershaw had begun building full-sized aircraft as well as models.) In December 1976 Vern heard that the *Condor* project was going to move to Shafter Airport. Six weeks later he became a member of the team, and Maude, *pari passu,* became the irreplaceable Hangar Mother of the *Gossamer Condor.*

With many skilled hands working on it, the new *Condor* began to take shape rapidly. MacCready had studied Henry Jex's calculations, and he was worried that even the major changes they were making wouldn't solve the turn problem. In two weeks the plane was almost complete, but Paul was still sketching revisions in his notebook: turned-down wingtips to lower the roll moment, even a tractor propeller. In the event, the version of the plane that was finished on March 2 turned out to be in all but detail modifications the final configuration.

Perhaps this is the place for a note about design evolution. It was hard to tell when one "version" of the *Condor* (or the *Albatross*) evolved into another one. The process of test and change was almost continuous, going on week after week. It would be easier for an observer outside the project to identify the important design changes than for a crew member working in a steady blur of alterations. If a number is needed, 12 is probably a valid one; that is, there were 12 more-or-less discernible "marks" of the airplane between the first crude prototype and the successful final version. If you had asked the team members to label them along the way they would have been stymied. Even in this case, when there was a whole new airplane, it was to be altered away from that configuration and back to it again before the prize was won.

How would it fly? After the disappointing debut of the Mojave *Condor,* no one could be sure. The first chance to test the Shafter plane came on the night of March 4. The wind veered between one and four miles per hour, and there was a bright moon. Tyler MacCready was the pilot; the crew included his father, Bill Beuby, John Lake, Vern Oldershaw, and Sam Durán and his roommate, a thin, glasses-wearing young man whose name Paul noted as "Keith Allen."

Here is Allen's description of the first flight: "Tyler got in and started pedaling, and within about six steps it took off and was floating along, and it was so big and easy — every one of my ideas about human-powered flight popped just like that." He still snaps his fingers when he says it. "It's easy now!" Tyler called. "Your grandmother could fly it now!" He made six short flights, and once past the takeoff it was indeed easy compared to the Mojave version — until a turning force was applied. The old bugaboo was still there. Paul hoped that a full tilting stabilizer would solve the problem, and after the test flights the crew rigged the canard to tilt and put the plane to bed.

The next morning at 7:30 they had the *Condor* out on the apron again. Tyler made twelve flights, three of them close to a minute long. He was able to initiate a slow turn, though not quickly or positively enough to fly the Kremer Course. The power estimate was 0.30 horsepower (0.22 kilowatt) for straight flight — right on target. Now what they needed was Greg Miller to provide the extra muscle.

Greg came up to Shafter early the following day. At 7:30 A.M. Tyler made a first flight of 2 minutes, 9 seconds. Greg biked around the apron, warming up, and the crew watched expectantly as he climbed into the cockpit. To everyone's surprise, he could only make several short flights, much shorter than Tyler's. Paul patiently tried to check Greg's instinct — common to most novice pilots — to keep the pitch angle high and try to climb too soon. The windy afternoon was spent on detail changes and tuning the controls. Tufts of wool were attached to the stabilizer as stall warning indicators. That evening the wind calmed to about 3 miles (4.8 kilometres) per hour. At dusk Paul set up the pylons for the Kremer Course, and the plane was walked down to the south pylon, facing into the wind. Two vans were parked beside the runway with their headlights illuminating the course.

Ben Shedd walked over to Greg, juggled his camera from one shoulder to the other so he could reach his wallet, and said, "I'll give you fifty bucks if you can make it all the way to the hangar."

Paul said, "How about twenty feet?"

Greg nodded, and started pedaling as hard as he could. He flew all the way to the hangar, into a 4-mile (6.4-kilometre) per hour headwind: 5 minutes and 5 seconds, the longest human-powered flight in history!

That was March 6, 1977, an important day in the great race of manmade birds; The *Condor* had caught up with and passed the *Stork*. Not a word was breathed to anyone outside the team about this new world record, but MacCready began to worry about publicity again, and about protecting his idea. He alerted the film crew, he called Lloyd Licher as official observer, and he called a patent attorney. He didn't realize that the same persistent problems that bedeviled Professor Kimura's plane would obstruct the *Condor*, at the same stage of its development.

On the morning of the 7th Paul decided to fly the plane himself. He took off and cleared the 10.5-foot (3.2-metre) T-bar that marked the height requirement for the beginning and end of the Kremer Course, but it took so much effort that he had to land after only a hundred yards. On the next flight a gust of wind caught the left wing, banking the plane to the right. Paul tried to turn into the wind, but there was no response. He applied full left stabilizer, the plane kept banking steeply to the right, and two wing wires broke. As the *Condor* veered drunkenly toward the ground Tyler caught the nose and swung it into the wind, saving the wing spar. When they took the plane into the hangar, they found that a third of the Mylar covering and the leading edge of the left wing had failed.

It was an important lesson in several respects. First, they were a long way from solving the control problem. Second, it was the hang glider pilots who made the best ground handlers. They were used to yawing their kites into the wind — it is often difficult or foolish to attempt to control them any other way — and they instinctively moved the wind-sensitive *Condor* in the right direction. At Shafter they were helped by the use of a diminutive wheeled dolly, lighter, smaller, and more flexible than the toy wagon that had been used to move the plane at Mojave.

By this time the crew could repair the airplane in their sleep, and in a few hours it was as good as new. That is, not good enough. It had everything that they thought it should have: a more rigid, double-surfaced wing using the new Lissaman 7769 airfoil; a proven propeller with the same airfoil; an enclosed, reasonably streamlined cockpit with a Velcro-fastened access panel; an airspeed indicator adapted from an Erisman wind-velocity meter; stabilizer controls that should have made it turn and bank. In fact, it looked essentially as it would for the rest of its existence. It just didn't turn.

Unraveling the individual contributions to making the *Condor* turn is almost impossible. During the first few months at Shafter the problem was discussed, argued, and passed from one teammate to another again and again, like an intellectual taffy-pull. Henry Jex's analysis and suggestion of wing-warping made sense; one by one the various team members contributed bits of aeronautical experience and advice to bolster it, trying to work out a practical solution. There is a picture of Paul MacCready, Peter Lissaman, and Jim Burke sitting outside the Shafter hangar in aluminum lawn chairs, unshaven, with floppy sun hats over their eyes. They look resigned, weary, and utterly sick of talking about something. It was undoubtedly turning the *Gossamer Condor*.

Of the 16 people in the official photograph of the *Condor* team, seven in the picture and one who was absent remember making *the* crucial suggestion that led to solving the problem of turning. They are all sure of it, they are all fliers, and probably they all did what they believe they did. But in the middle of March Paul was still skeptical about the need for wing twist, and they were back to trying a rudder the way they had at Mojave. This time John Lake built a beautiful double-surfaced one, with a smoothly radiused leading edge like a real airplane control surface. It didn't work any better at Shafter than it had at Mojave.

The flight logs were full of frustration as the end of March approached. Each time the team failed to solve the turn problem, their attention would switch to other shortcomings of the plane. The work list for March 17 is terse and uncompromising: *Lighten to 60 lbs. Streamline everything. Better covering, more ribs, better leading edge.*

Jack Lambie had an idea for improving the covering. The Mylar was usually loose and full of wrinkles, even after they stretched it meticulously while taping it on. It was transparent, it was plastic, and it reminded Jack of the plastic monofilm coverings used on large model airplanes. Those are applied with moderate tension, and then shrunk to a smooth taut surface with an electric

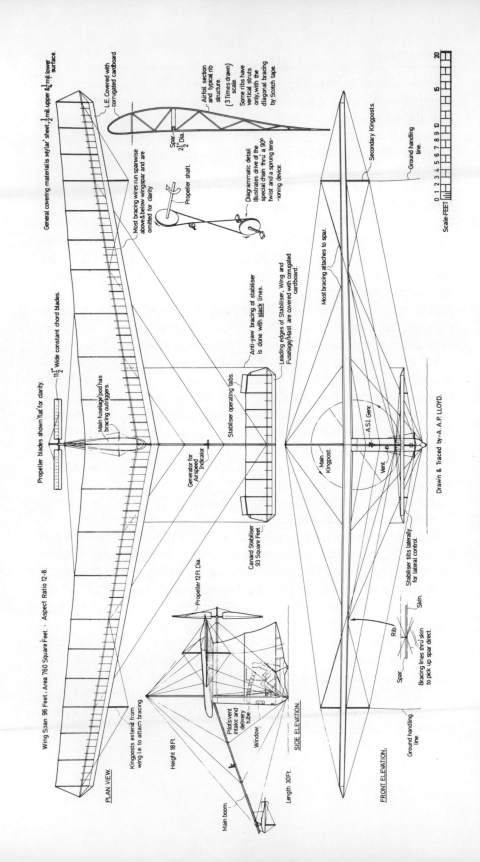

PLAN VIEW.

Wing Span 96 Feet : Area 760 Square Feet : Aspect Ratio 12·8.

Propeller blades shown 'flat' for clarity.

General covering material is Mylar' sheet. ½ mil upper &¼ mil lower surface.

L.E. Covered with corrugated cardboard

Most bracing wires run spanwise above&below wingspar and are omitted for clarity.

Airfoil section and typical rib structure.

(3 Times drawn scale.)

Some ribs have vertical struts only, with the diagonal bracing by Scotch tape.

Spar 2½ Dia.

Propeller shaft.

Diagrammatic detail illustrates drive of the special chain thru a 90° twist and a sprung tensioning device.

11½" Wide constant chord blades.

Main fuselage pod has bracing outriggers.

Kingposts extend from wing l.e. to attach bracing.

Height 18 Ft.

Propeller 12 Ft. Dia.

Pilot's vent intake and delivery tube.

Window.

Length 30 Ft.

Main boom.

Generator for Airspeed Indicator.

Stabiliser operating tabs.

Canard Stabiliser 93 Square Feet.

Anti-yaw bracing of stabiliser is done with slack lines.

Leading edges of Stabiliser, Wing and Fuselage/Mast are covered with corrugated cardboard

SIDE ELEVATION.

Most bracing attaches to spar.

Secondary Kingposts.

Ground handling line.

Main Kingpost.

Vent.

A.S.I. Genr.

Stabiliser tilts laterally for lateral control.

Skin.

Rib.

Spar.

Bracing lines thru skin to pick up spar direct.

Ground handling line.

FRONT ELEVATION.

Drawn & Traced by· A. P. LLOYD.

Scale·FEET
0 1 2 3 4 5 6 7 8 9 0   5   10   20

iron or a hot-air gun. Perhaps Mylar would work the same way. Lambie tried it, and it worked perfectly — the Mylar shrunk smooth and tight. Although some of his early demonstrations were enthusiastic to the point of warping the framework, heat-shrinking the covering soon became a standard procedure for all the Gossamer aircraft.

John Lake suggested what seemed like a throwback material to improve the contour of the wing leading edge. It was one-sided corrugated cardboard, like the kind used to line candy boxes. It proved to be perfect for the job: flexible across the grain and strong longitudinally, lightweight, cheap, readily available, and easy to work with. After a successful trial, it became the material of choice for the front of the airfoil.

Between the smoother covering and the other refinements, the *Condor* kept looking better, but the original observers were not impressed. They had seen too many failed attempts at the Kremer Course, and the drive up to the San Joaquin Valley was another deterrent to their enthusiasm. Paul decided to enlist a new set of observers based closer to Shafter. As before, each one had to be approved by the British Aircraft Owners' and Pilots' Association. He nominated four officers of the Kern County Department of Airports, all of them skilled pilots. They included Alfred Eaton, Aviation Assistant; Everett Julkowski, Operations Supervisor; William Richardson, Maintenance Supervisor; and Stephen P. Schmitt, Director of Aviation. General Brook Allen of the National Aeronautic Association acted as a preliminary judge and intermediary for the British AOPA. All of these observers were approved, and one of them, Bill Richardson, developed an interest in the *Gossamer Condor* that was to prove indispensable.

Richardson was born in Porterville, California, in 1917, the year that Bill Beuby saw his first airplane, and two years after Vern Oldershaw was born. Like them, he has logged thousands of hours as a pilot, with an awesome percentage of them as a flight instructor (he is still teaching today). He had his first cockpit ride in a Ford Trimotor in 1932, soloed in 1935, and taught Army pilots all

[*opposite*] 5. The *Gossamer Condor 2*, built at Shafter Airport, in the form in which it won the Kremer Figure-of-Eight Competition.

through World War II. Bill has survived some hair-raising student errors, as well as a desperate low-level jump — without a parachute — from a flaming Stinson Reliant. He is easily mistaken for a squire rancher, complete with handsome white mustache and broad-brim hat. Not surprisingly, he can look anyone straight in the eye, and he is an accurate and unflappable observer. He came out to observe the *Gossamer Condor* practice and fly more than a hundred times.

Bill's observer's application was submitted on March 25, a cloudy Friday with intermittent showers at Shafter. The weather predictions for that weekend are logged in great detail in Paul MacCready's notebooks. Immediately underneath them are the forecasts for the Tokyo area, in equal detail. Greg Miller's license for the Kremer Competition had been activated on January 14, and now Paul decided to activate Ron Skarin's, even though Skarin had only minimal contact with the project. Despite the five-minute flight, there was still concern about Greg's flying skills.

Jim Burke decided that he needed practical instruction, and took Greg up in a Piper Cherokee to teach him basic piloting. John Lake took him up in an Aeronca Champion, and let him fly repeated figure-eight courses, using only the elevator and ailerons, while John controlled the rudder and throttle. During one of these flights Greg dropped a bombshell; he said that he had decided to leave California and go to Belgium to compete as a professional bicycle racer. John tried to explain to him that as a bicycle racer he would be one of thousands, competing against European professionals who had spent their lives in the sport. If, on the other hand, he stayed with the project (which Lake felt was certain to succeed), he would probably become famous both as a human-powered aircraft pilot and as a cyclist.

Greg was adamant. He told Paul that he was planning to compete in the European Bicycle Criteriums as part of a three-man United States team, and that they would have to leave for Belgium on April 19. His announcement pitched the team into a kind of limbo. As if to echo the mood of indecision, the weather around Bakersfield stayed changeable, windy, and wet. (The weather in Japan, still noted in the log, was quite similar over the next few weeks.) Some of the team members became disheartened at the

prospect of a team with a human-powered airplane, but no pilot/
engine. Kirke Leonard had worked on the project patiently for
seven months. Now, he says, "I was burned out. I didn't want to go
back to Shafter much, and I didn't." The MacCreadys went to
watch Ron Skarin race, perhaps hoping to enliven his interest in the
Condor, but he was clearly too busy and successful to want to interrupt his athletic career.

As at other times when progress seemed to be blocked, Paul di-
verted his creative energy, and spent a week working on a design
for a windmill-powered land sailer. Then the abominable turning
problem crept back to the surface of the team's mind again, interspersed with ideas for a new, thicker airfoil. On March 29 the first
version of a control designed to warp the wings differentially by 2°
was fitted to the plane. Greg tried to test it the next day, but complained that the effort required to fly the plane was much higher
than before Paul's crash three weeks earlier. (Tyler had made the
same comment during a short test flight.) The new warp control
jammed on Greg's first flight; after it was freed neither he nor the
observers could tell whether it actually produced any twist in
the wing. The turns were just as mushy and indefinite as ever,
and the flying horsepower seemed discouragingly high.

"Make more efficient," was MacCready's curt order to himself:
*New wing spar, mill more. New wing ribs, mill ¼" tubing. New
LE* [leading edge] *made with heated foam sheet. Twist added to
turn control. Use non-stretch wing covering.* The last was a sore
point. Vern Oldershaw had measured the various thicknesses of
Mylar sheet used on the plane, and found that most of it was more
than double its nominal gauge, and hence more than twice as heavy
as it was supposed to be. On April 3 the crew worked on the stabilizer and a new version of the wing twist controls, and then everyone drove down to Greg Miller's home in Seal Beach for a farewell
party.

Greg really was leaving; the team really didn't have a pilot. In
retrospect it seems incredible that the situation could have occurred, and that it was an eventuality that hadn't been planned for.
The day after the party Paul casually asked Sam Durán if he knew
anyone who rode bicycles competitively and who could also fly.
Sam had a short affirmative answer: "My roommate." His room-

mate was Bryan Allen, who had been wing running the airplane with Sam for several months. Paul jotted down the specifications of the possible new engine: "Brian Allen — a category I & II [bicycle racer]. Hp/Out is good. Tall (6′), 145–155. Is unemployed. Also is good at building stuff. Responsible. Hi I.Q. Could get in shape quickly. Some small bonus." He telephoned Bryan's parents in Tulare and left a message for Bryan to call.

"I found a note from my father when I came home: Call Paul MacCready. I did, and he wasn't there. Eventually Paul called and asked if I wanted to fly the plane." Bryan nearly jumped through the telephone: "Everyone who was a wing runner just *had* to fly the plane — here, take my car." They arranged for Bryan to try the *Condor* on April 7.

In the meantime the balky wing twist controls had been overhauled and improved, and the stabilizer pitch control rerigged. On April 5 Paul had to go to Las Vegas on business. The flight crew that morning was Kirke Leonard (still hanging in there) and his son Kirke Jr., John Lake, Jack Lambie, and Tyler MacCready. The wind was down to ½ mile (0.8 kilometre) an hour when they towed the plane out on its diminutive dolly. Tyler made a short flight and tried a 90° turn using only the stabilizer to roll the plane. He made it out of the turn, but not by much. On the next flight he tried using the wing warp control. The crew watched in ecstatic disbelief while the *Gossamer Condor,* as graceful as its namesake, banked around in a beautiful stable turn — which it entered with its wing twisted the opposite way from every airplane any of them had ever flown!

John Lake was overjoyed. "As soon as we had the wing warping, I knew we were going to get the prize." The secret was reverse warp: using the twisted trailing edge of the wing as a drag-inducing yaw brake rather than as a roll-inducing aileron. The result was an airplane that turned in an opposite sense to the normal aileron settings. The only drawback was that Tyler had to guess how much twist to use, and the small warp control lever didn't give him enough sensitivity. Jack Lambie made a detent — a positive click stop — in the warp quadrant, so the lever would have a repeatable fixed setting. By the time he finished the wind had come up, and there was no more flying that day. Paul heard about the successful turn from John Lake that afternoon. "Worked *PERFECTLY!*" is scribbled in his notebook, with an exclamation point twice as high as the words.

High wind kept the plane in the hangar the next day, but Thursday, April 7, was another major milestone in the *Condor*'s short life. The air was calm, but not dead still when Tyler tried to repeat his success. After a short straight flight to test the controls, he took off and made a sweeping 200° shallow turn, straightened the plane out, and landed. "All *perfect!*" the log exults. There was some discussion about using the canard to make fine banking adjustments, and then it was the turn of the unknown quantity, Bryan Allen, to fly. Somehow, delivering the plane into the hands of a novice carried more emotional tension now that the team was sure it was a winner. At 6:30 A.M. Bryan made a first test flight, 15 seconds long, straight ahead. "All OK," the flight log notes. Then, pedaling harder, he took off with a boost from the crew and flew for nearly a minute with fine pitch control, made two slight course corrections, and landed gently and straight. "Get new license application for Allen," Paul wrote.

How did it feel? "It didn't really feel like flying — it was like pedaling some strange kind of bicycle. It wasn't easy — like pedaling a house. It was hard to get used to the idea that you pedal harder to go up rather than mess with the pitch control." There is only one note in Bryan's own logbok for that flight: "Neat!"

When Bryan Allen stepped out of the plane's cockpit, it was as a new pilot of the *Condor* team. Two more people became team members the same day. One was a tall, slim young man named Peter Plumb, who had been watching the airplane since it arrived at Shafter. Pete was 20 years old — four years younger than Bryan — and had been flying since he was 16. He held private pilot and glider licenses, and had built his own hang glider. In 1977 he was working in a wing shop at the airport, rebuilding the wooden wings of ex-military biplanes to agplane standards, and he was another expert model builder. On the night of Tyler's first flight at Shafter, Pete and his girlfriend (now wife), Robin Avery, were flying over the airport in a Cessna 172 and saw mysterious lights on the runway. They came to the hangar later and found Tyler and the *Condor*. "We flew it tonight," was all Tyler said, but it was enough.

From the time of Bryan's first flight, Pete took every opportunity he could to help with building or flying the airplane.

The second addition to the team was more unlikely. Phil Esdaile was born in 1955 in Lumsden, South Island, New Zealand, the son of a World War II Spitfire pilot. He studied surveying at Otigo Polytech for two years, joined the New Zealand Forest Service for a time, and eventually went to work in a Western Australian iron ore plant where he suffered a serious hand injury.

In June 1976, Esdaile used his accident benefits to fly to San Francisco for a friend's wedding, bought a motorcycle, and began touring around California. His savings gradually disappeared, and one night in January 1977 he found himself broke, freezing cold, and lost in Kern Canyon. The next morning he rode down toward Bakersfield and was stopped short by the sight of three Grumman Avenger torpedo bombers at an ag spray company. On impulse, he walked into the office and asked for a job. He was sent to Ag-viation Inc., which needed a mechanic at Shafter Airport. For the next three months he read engine maintenance textbooks at night and watched other mechanics like a hawk during the day. In March 1977 he was laid off. Phil had been coming over to the *Condor* hangar during his lunch hours for quite a while, and now he began spending more time there. One day John Lake walked up to him and asked, "Are you a craftsman?"

"Of course I'm a craftsman," Phil said. John told Paul Mac-Cready, and Paul asked Phil if he'd like to help on the *Condor*. Phil said he sure would, and when Paul mentioned payment, Esdaile said he'd start helping first, and they could talk about money if they won the prize. Paul accepted this *prima facie*. "Will work for free," he wrote in his notebook, although that was not quite what was meant. Phil started working on the airplane full time in April 1977, and the final crew of the *Gossamer Condor* was complete.

9

Practice

The Turning Point

ON APRIL 8, 1977, Paul MacCready agreed to pay Bryan Allen $3.00 per hour to pilot and work on the *Gossamer Condor*. For Bryan, it was a 9-cent-an-hour reduction from his last job. For Paul, it turned out to be one of the great bargains of a lifetime, and it must have made the canny MacCready ancestors smile.

Whom exactly had he hired? Bryan Lewis Allen was born on October 13, 1952, in Visalia, California. He is the eldest of three children, and one only has to meet his parents — in Peter Lissaman's words, "The principal designers, manufacturers, and distributors of engines for the *Gossamer Condor* and *Gossamer Albatross*" — to understand Bryan's unique endowments.

Marvin and Beverly Allen were born within twenty miles of Tulare, California, where they now live. They are atypical residents of the second richest agricultural county in the United States. Marvin is slim and soft-spoken, with curly gray hair and gold-rimmed glasses. He majored in biology at Fresno State College, and after graduation was posted to the more grisly segments of the New Guinea campaign in World War II. He came back somewhat the worse for wear, started a teaching career, married Beverly, and was redrafted for the Korean War. Since his second discharge he has taught school in a low-income district of Tulare, and, not surprisingly, he has small tolerance for officialdom. He has a pilot's license, is regarded as an excellent teacher, and carries considerable intellectual tension under a quiet exterior.

Beverly Allen can only be called an original. The source of Bryan's infectious smile, she is thin, wears glasses, and simmers with

nervous energy; it rarely takes her more than one sentence to dis-
arm anyone she meets. She has an aversion to cities, but she is an
au courant intellectual and a compulsive reader and joiner of book
clubs. Beverly went to the College of the Sequoias in Visalia; she
does crochet and needlepoint, but she also works full time as an
accountant and is currently studying photography. She is aware
that there are some drawbacks to the rural environment: "I guess
the people around here think we're kooks. Sometimes I have to call
up Bryan [in Bakersfield] just to have someone to talk to about a
book or an idea."

Bryan has inherited it all: He grew up surrounded by books, with
a mother who was a one-woman literary salon, and a father who
flew airplanes, disliked regulations, and could use his hands as well
as teach. In high school he showed that he also had the family impatience with apparently silly requirements. "I knew I could get
A's in anything I wanted, but I wasn't willing to put in that extra
little bit of work, except in English. I couldn't help getting A's in
English." His high school English teacher was dumfounded when
he refused to parse sentences because he thought it was stupid. Here
are his grades for senior English: A–A–A–A–D–A–A–A.

In 1970 Bryan went to the College of the Sequoias, studying
mostly biology. Two years later he received an associate of arts
degree, entered California State University at Bakersfield as a junior,
and was assigned to the same dormitory room as Sam Durán, who
has since become his closest friend. In 1974 Allen received a
bachelor of science in biology, and suddenly it was time to work.

What to do with all that energy? Since the eighth grade much of
it had gone into bicycling. Bryan's first 10-speed bike had, by mistake, front gears with a difference of only three teeth. Since he
didn't know about alpine gears, he rode up hundreds of steep grades
with the close gears, which has given him outstanding hill-climbing
ability ever since. At Tulare High School he ran cross-country in
his junior and senior years, was a miler on the track team in his
senior year, and won the annual bike race three times in a row.

Airplane models were the first outlets for Allen's urge to fly; he
taught himself to pilot U-Control planes with his own unorthodox
method, flat wristed, palm down. He flew lightplanes with his father,
and he desperately wanted to fly sailplanes. There were a few seduc-

tive glider rides at Tehachapi Airport, but he found that soaring was a rich man's sport. In 1974 he went to the Southern California School of Hang Gliding, where he met John Lake. Even on the miserable first kite that he bought with Tom Armstrong and Sam Durán, his natural flying skill was evident.

Talent for hang gliding and bicycle racing were not much help in making a living. Between college terms Bryan worked as an irrigator for Superior Farms, and after graduation the company offered him a job supervising a fruit dehydrator. Before long he was doing lab tests and assisting Superior's senior horticulturist. It wasn't bike riding, it wasn't flying, and it had many regulations. In the spring of 1975 Superior had a cutback, and Allen was laid off. He began to make a discovery that many free-spirited college graduates make: Work that pays well almost always requires submission to rules, and some of the rules can seem silly.

During the summer of 1975 Bryan took a job as a loader and later a salesman for the Wickes Lumber Company, at $3.09 per hour. In a few months he found that low-powered work was even less satisfying and more rule-bound than high-powered work. He grew disaffected, quit, and found himself in a kind of limbo. At age 23 he was able to win bicycle races and fly a hang glider superbly, but he wasn't able to find satisfying work. For a troubled year he supported himself by doing odd jobs, working at a subsistence level. When Paul MacCready asked him if he wanted to fly the *Gossamer Condor,* it was more than an apt request; it was as if the work that Bryan had been unable to find had sought him out of its own accord.

Like Joe Mastropaolo, Allen knew quite a bit about human-powered flight. He told Paul that he had read everything in print in the United States on the subject, including articles on the *Condor,* but Clyde Goering's HPA was the only one he had seen before watching Tyler fly at Shafter. Goering's plane weighed 200 pounds (91 kilograms), spanned 43 feet (13.1 metres), and had a short, wide-bladed propeller. Bryan wasn't impressed by it, and thought that it was typical of the breed. He changed his mind abruptly when he saw the *Condor* fly.

From the first time that Bryan piloted the airplane, it had his complete commitment. He and Sam started training together, riding their bikes about 200 miles (322 kilometres) a week. Joe

Mastropaolo developed an ergometer exercise program to fit Allen's build and physiology, which were very different from Greg Miller's. The program was designed to improve Bryan's ability to pedal the *Condor* at 90 revolutions per minute. The 62-tooth drive sprocket and 52-tooth shaft sprocket resulted in a step-up ratio of 1:19, and a propeller rpm of 107.3 for the 90-rpm pilot rate.

On April 11, four days after his first trial, Bryan made eight flights, five of them with unassisted takeoffs. On the fourth flight that day he completed a perfect 180° left turn. Most of these flights were only about a minute long, but they were logged with comments that display an acute intuition about the plane's behavior. One of them resulted in reversing the direction of the all-important warping lever: "It's the other way now, which is less logical."

By April 16, Bryan's flight duration had more than doubled, and the building crew was full of enthusiasm again: *Fuselage rebuilt; leading edge of main wing strengthened; rear part of driveshaft modified* (which reduced weight and made power transmission easier). Allen's flight time went up to 2 minutes, 30 seconds. On April 25, Ron Skarin came up to Shafter and flew the plane several times. He was very strong, but the difference in piloting skill was evident to everyone on the crew. The next morning Bryan was making a left turn when the seat back snapped without warning. The *Condor* slewed into one of its slow-motion crashes, breaking the rear wheel and the left wing tensioner. MacCready's easy-fix philosophy shows up in the construction log a few hours later. There is only one word after the damage report: *Repaired*. The next day the flights were up to 2 minutes again, and the last one was terminated only because the plane ran out of runway.

By this time the life of the *Gossamer Condor* had settled into a mature routine, with two overlapping rhythms: daily and weekly. The daily routine was controlled by the same wind and weather that affected the birds. A typical weekday cycle would begin in the evening, with the crew finishing up the latest changes in the plane and checking the weather forecast for the following day. During the spring and summer the night wind at Shafter is from the southeast. The day wind is from the northwest, and at dawn and dusk there are often periods of calm air when the winds change over; the right time to fly.

Many nights Vern and Maude Oldershaw would bring their GMC motor home out to the hangar, and the crew would sleep in it or in pop tents and sleeping bags pitched on the apron. There was automatic reveille at Shafter if the weather was fair: the coughing roar of the ag planes' big radial engines firing up at 4 A.M. Rise and shine; check the wind (Sam Durán standing out on the apron sleepy-eyed, peering at a Dwyer wind gauge). If it was calm enough the wing runners would slowly roll open the heavy sliding doors of the *Condor*'s hangar. (Inside the hangar, in the dark, the plane would nod and rustle like a great sleeping bird.)

For Phil Esdaile those mornings were like dreams. In the foggy half-light three men would float the huge wing out on to the apron, often without a word or a visible signal to each other. Then would come the hardest job: waking Bryan. Despite his early morning activities, Allen is probably a night person. He is as possessive of his sleeping bag as a limpet, and getting him out of it is like trying to pull an impacted tooth with a pair of mittens. There are team members who would bet that Bryan could sleep through an ag plane revving up right next to his bedroll.

With Allen over his violent phase, the crew would give the plane a preflight inspection. Bryan usually checked the canard and wing warp controls himself, first on the ground, and then in a short airborne test. Then the flights began, with the crew trying to evaluate the changes made the night before. Often Bill Richardson would come out to watch and time the trials. The ag pilots were wonderful to the fragile *Condor,* trying to use distant parts of the runway, and keeping their prop blast away from the plane. If nothing broke, flying would go on until the wind came up, and the pilot or crew chief for the day called a halt. The airplane would be trundled into the hangar, and everyone's notes would be compared to see what could be improved.

By the time flight testing was finished the crew would be ravenous. Like homing pigeons, they headed for Maude's motor home, from which wafted the smell of what Paul MacCready calls "the best pancakes in the world." On the mornings when the Oldershaws couldn't make it the team would drive to Hutch's Coffee Shop in Shafter. (Sample breakfast for a *Gossamer Condor* crew member: A large glass of orange juice, a bowl of peaches, two scrambled eggs with biscuits and gravy, a side order of bacon, and two glasses of milk.) After breakfast the crew would go back to the hangar, and Sam Durán would go off to his job at Getty Oil.

The afternoons would be spent making modifications or repairing damage. One of the drawbacks of a craft built so close to the limits of minimum weight and strength is that things wear out quickly. Fatigue loads that wouldn't have affected unmilled aluminum tubing for months caused the *Condor*'s ribs and spars to buckle in a few weeks. Sometimes it seemed that the plane couldn't make a single flight without needing some part replaced. As time went on, Vern Oldershaw began making more and more of the detail design changes at Shafter.

On clear days work was suspended just before sunset for a Druidical ritual: watching for the "green flash" at the instant the sun dipped below the horizon. (Mostly, people missed it.) At dusk there would often be another calm period with more test flights squeezed into it. The quiet air could also bring out one of Pete Plumb's radio control models, or a flock of hand-launched gliders.

Refueling and debriefing the *Condor* team frequently took place simultaneously at Hodel's in Bakersfield. This Mennonite buffet restaurant provided an informal atmosphere and huge quantities of wholesome food at reasonable prices. "Huge" is used advisedly. On a typical night there would be thirty different dishes offered at Hodel's, and the team sampled most of them. Bryan was keeping track of his intake during this period, and one evening at Hodel's he consumed 3.15 pounds (1.43 kilograms) of food for dinner. The other crew members acquired similar appetites by osmosis. Dinner was often followed by another work period at the hangar to prepare the plane for the next morning's flights, and the cycle would begin again.

By April 26, the *Gossamer Condor* had made 300 flights, more than all other Kremer Prize contenders combined. It had evolved into a very different craft from Paul MacCready's original design, and had been improved in many ways — but it still couldn't fly the Kremer Course. Paul still believed that 180° turns could be made by coordinating yaw and roll in a series of "mini-turns," which would add up to the desired change of direction. Even after the first successful turns with wing warping, that didn't prove to be the case.

The turn capability was hampered by the persistence of high drag and by an apparently random variation in flying effort. In retrospect Peter Lissaman and Paul agree that solutions were staring them in the face, but the *Condor*'s behavior was so strange compared to their past experience that they were unwilling to accept the evidence. By May 2, the plane's performance had deteriorated so much that they decided to build a new, thicker wing. The original wing had a maximum thickness equal to 11 percent of its chord; the new airfoil thickness was increased to 13.7 percent in an attempt to provide higher lift and lower drag.

Twelve days later the original Shafter wing had been removed and hung on the wall of the hangar, and the new version was ready for testing. On the first few flights Bryan could tell only that the warp control needed tuning. Many adjustments followed, including a change of dihedral, but there didn't seem to be any reduction in drag or flying effort. On May 20, the team took off the propeller and made tow tests to try to measure the drag and the sink rate. The first test, an auto tow, nearly resulted in a high-speed crash. Hand towing to an altitude of 30 feet (9.1 metres) gave only inconclusive results.

The next morning, Bryan tried an all-out takeoff attempt with the new wing. He had to pedal very hard, and the crank bearing pulled out of its mount, derailing the chain. On the 23rd, MacCready directed a detailed comparison of the old and new wings, with tufts of wool attached to the surfaces to indicate airflow. The results were surprising: Both wings improved significantly when their covering was re-ironed and shrunk, but the old wing seemed better in almost every respect, especially profile drag. At the end of the month, concluding that the thick wing experiment was yet another blind alley, they decided to change back to the original configuration.

By this time the Central Valley was warming up — Bryan recorded an oral temperature of 102°F (38.9°C) after one strenuous test flight — and the tempers of some of the crew members were beginning to fray. The tensions that developed during this period of apparent stagnation split the team in several directions.

John Lake and Bill Beuby had been working full time on the *Condor* for about five months. Both of them had made important contributions to the project, and both had strong opinions about

the way things should be done. When Jack Lambie flew in on occasional visits and altered their work with his cheerfully slapdash
techniques, they were incensed. Lake, a perfectionist who candidly
admits that he has trouble being tactful, was particularly outspoken.
He had already crossed swords with Vern Oldershaw ("I never
argued with John Lake — no point in that"), and he decided to
leave the project early in June. Bill Beuby made the same decision
and left for Tulsa on May 29.

The strongest polarity of the *Gossamer Condor* project, and one
that was kept submerged for the most part, was the weekly rivalry
that developed between the Shafter crew and the Pasadena group.
Although the concept and the airplane had originated with Paul
MacCready and his Cal Tech friends, the location of the plane at
Shafter forced a weekend commute schedule on the Southern California contingent. The Bakersfield team, working with the *Condor*
every day, soon developed a strong sense of possessiveness and
identification. To them, it seemed as though they were the principal
testers and builders of the airplane, and the Pasadena people were
the interlopers.

Phil Esdaile: "We were the everyday people, and they were the
weekenders. We'd take it out every morning and get it on the runway without even talking to each other in two minutes. Then they'd
come up on the weekend and yell and carry on and take twice as
long to do everything. It felt like we were going 'round in circles.
I'd get so I'd hate to see them come up." Bryan Allen: "We had
the 'Weekend Effect.' We'd take five steps forward during the week,
and they'd come up on the weekend and take seven confident (but
wrong) steps back. I'd be sitting in a blue funk, and Phil would be
ready to kill someone, and Vern and Maude were the rock that
held it all together." Sam Durán: "We had almost a personal relationship with the plane. The weekenders would come up and do
something, and we'd think, 'Oh, no!' But we'd just keep quiet and
let them so we wouldn't hurt their feelings. We got to know the
Condor pretty well."

That was an understatement if anything. Certainly no one developed a more intimate relationship with the plane than Bryan.
The first time he made a 180° turn away from the sun, "I saw the
shadow of the plane on the ground, and the shadow of the propeller

going around — before that I had just been pedaling something — and my own shadow, and wow, that was the first time I felt like I was *flying*." By the beginning of June, Vern Oldershaw was in much the same position as constructor.

Each time a part broke or was modified, Vern would fix or redesign it. At first he was frustrated by MacCready's ambivalence. "Paul didn't want any clean engineering. Then after I did it he would say 'Isn't this beautiful?' " Maude finally told Vern, "Do it your way," and from then on he did. Since Vern is an expert craftsman in wood, and partial to it, more spruce and balsa began to be blended with the *Condor*'s aluminum skeleton.

There was plenty for Vern to do. The *Gossamer Condor* is very different in execution as well as concept from the jetliners whose wingspan it matches. Most air travelers have been on a plane with missing bolts and loose panels. On a human-powered plane, every part and connection is crucial: If a single wire isn't fastened in the casual-looking but correct way to a stress point, the plane will crash. Paul MacCready regards the terminal design of the *Condor*'s bracing and flying wires as one of the most important contributions to its success. It looks ludicrously simple, a leftover from Scout camp. The stainless steel wire, which varies from .022" (0.56mm) to .035" (0.89mm) in diameter, is formed over a lightweight thimble to make a dependable eye. The free end of the wire is then wrapped tightly around the standing part 8 times, doubled back on itself, and broken off. The wires are intentionally made a little too short, and they are fastened to the airframe with a loop of 200-pound (91-kilogram)-test braided polyester cord that has a bowline at one end and a quick-disconnect knot at the other. This light, cheap, and adjustable connection allowed the plane to be rigged and tuned quickly and easily. It was developed by Paul McKibben, another of MacCready's engineer friends. Like many good ideas, it seems obvious after the fact, but it took much thought and experiment to devise.

As June progressed the confidence level of the team began to rise again. Bryan's flight times were up to 3 minutes, and the plane seemed tractable in 90° turns. A few days into the month the Shafter group received some remarkable news: The *Condor* was about to be joined in the hangar by another human-powered aircraft. This was Taras Kiceniuk Jr.'s *Icarus,* which had been test-flying at El Mirage Dry Lake. Pete Plumb could hardly contain his excitement: "Taras, my hero — I'm really gonna get to meet him!"

Pete was 20 years old when he made that exclamation. Kiceniuk had just turned 23, but he was already a legend in ultralight aviation. Taras had soloed his first plane in India at age 14, and in 1971 he and three friends at Pasadena's John Muir High School designed and built *Batso,* the bamboo-framed Rogallo wing on which Paul MacCready had an eye-opening ride at the first Lilienthal Hang Glider Meet. *Batso* was followed by *Icarus I* and *II,* rigid-wing biplane hang gliders that soon became famous for their outstanding performance. In 1972 Kiceniuk entered Cal Tech and asked Mac-Cready's help with a design for a swept-wing monoplane that no one could dismiss as a mere ground skimmer. MacCready encouraged him and introduced him to Peter Lissaman, who was generous with aerodynamic advice and calculations. The result of this interaction was *Icarus V,* a world landmark in ultralight gliders. Although foot-launched like a Rogallo, it can gain altitude like a sailplane and stay aloft for hours in winds too light for standard kites.

In January 1974 Kiceniuk took a leave from Cal Tech to work on a human-powered airplane that would fly only in ground effect. Named? Of course, *Icarus.* Peter Lissaman helped design its footthick (0.3 metre), humpbacked airfoil, and in 1974 Taras met Bill Watson, the perfect construction partner. Watson is an expert airplane craftsman and model prototype designer from Van Nuys, California, who built his own *Icarus V* hang glider. Taras also needed a high power-to-weight ratio athlete to fly the plane. Watson had a friend named Dave Saks, who not only filled the bill physically, but was also a glider pilot, and had experience in precision wood and sheet metal work.

Taras, Dave, and Bill were, respectively, 20, 22, and 24 years old at this point. They were used to building things quickly, but they underestimated the time needed for so complex a machine. It was November 1975 before the plane was ready to test, and the first attempts to fly it were unsuccessful. Finally, in September 1976 at El Mirage Dry Lake, Dave Saks made two unassisted takeoffs and short flights in the *Icarus* HPA — the second and third unassisted human-powered flights in the United States.

MacCready's reaction to these flights was to call Taras, congratulate him, and ask him to join the *Condor* project. Soon after Taras graduated from Cal Tech in June 1977, he, Bill Watson, Dave Saks, and Ted Ancona brought the *Icarus* HPA to Shafter, and "slid sideways into the hangar beside the *Condor*." It would have taken a talented seer to know that this quartet would form the second nucleus of the *Gossamer Albatross* team a year later.

On June 14 the original 11-percent-thickness wing, now rebuilt and improved, was installed on the *Condor*. On its first test flight, Bryan made an unassisted takeoff and flew for 3 minutes and 30 seconds. Although the wing shape and the turn control needed tuning, the flying effort was very low. Just as the plane came in to land, a sharp crosswind gust caught the ground crew by surprise. The left wing spreader post hit the ground, the spar failed, and several ribs and the brand-new leading edge crumpled. "Very unnecessary," was Allen's peeved comment in the log.

It took a week to repair the wing, but the next trial, on June 24, was even more successful: a 4-minute flight, with a complete 190° left turn and a 100° right turn. The flight path diagram suddenly becomes recognizable as a long loop — half of the Kremer Course! By the end of June Bryan had completed an S-turn, and the flight durations were regularly exceeding 4 minutes. At last the prize began to look accessible.

The beginning of July was hot and gusty. The crews of the *Condor* and the *Icarus* worked on each other's planes in the hangar, suggested improvements, and traded turns piloting. Bryan made a flight of about 800 feet (244 metres) in the *Icarus,* the longest to date, but it was clear that Kiceniuk's design had some fundamental problems. One weekend Paul MacCready and Peter Lissaman helped do a tuft test on the *Icarus*'s wing and found that the flow was separating on the top surface of the airfoil, a crucial disability, and one not easily changed because of the wing's ingenious but inflexible solid foam construction.

The *Condor* was also having some airflow problems. As earlier, after the flight times crept up, there was a sudden relapse. "Duration 2½ minutes. Unable to maintain altitude. Wire to front of canard tube broke, and tube crumpled." "Duration 30 sec. Canard banking cable broke." "Prop pitch too coarse. Duration 1½ min."

This time the design team accepted the evidence. Every time the Mylar covering became slack enough to quiver in the wind, the *Condor*'s drag climbed prohibitively high. The covering *had* to be tight, and the plane's structure had to be strong enough to support it when it was tightened.

On the morning of July 16 there were eighteen people at Shafter to help with the airplane and watch Bryan fly. The sky was partly cloudy, but the wind was below one mile per hour (1.6 kilometres per hour). All of the *Condor*'s broken parts were repaired, and the covering was taut. Paul set out the Kremer Course pylons for a practice run.

Bryan waited for five minutes after the last crop duster left the runway, and then took off, flying strongly and easily. He started at the center of the course, flew down to the south end, made a perfect sweeping right turn, passed the center point on the way back, and was preparing to turn left at the north pylon when the left wing suddenly broke in midair. The *Condor* was about 4 feet (1.2 metres) off the ground, and even with 22 feet (6.7 metres) of the wing folded over backward, Allen was able to bring the plane to a gentle landing.

The spar was snapped completely in half, as if it had been broken by a giant hand, but not a single bracing wire had failed. It took a few minutes to solve the mystery. The last crop duster, a Stearman, had taken off on a course parallel to the *Condor*'s northbound flight leg, and turned left across the runway. The invisible but powerful vortex from its wingtips was still propagating in the still air when the *Condor* flew into it. The force was enough to buckle the hollow aluminum spar in an instant. It was another sobering reminder of the human-powered plane's fragility, and it meant yet another depressing delay. Paul was still as optimistic as ever, but some of the *Gossamer Condor* team members were beginning to wonder if they would ever have an unjinxed chance at the Kremer Prize.

10

Triumph

Winning the Kremer Prize

IF MAUDE OLDERSHAW FELT ANY APPREHENSION about the *Condor*'s chances of winning the Kremer Prize, she didn't show it. On the morning of the vortex crash she provided her usual cheery breakfast to the outsize crowd watching the airplane. (MacCready's notebook: "Fabulous!")

Behind the scenes things were rather different. Vern was sure that most of the *Condor*'s repeated stumbles were due to Paul's insistence on quick and dirty construction. Maude kept urging him to do his own work on the plane, without reference to MacCready's standards. The component that Vern felt most dissatisfied with was the fusclage, which he had covered himself after Paul decided that it should be streamlined to reduce pilot drag. He regarded its frame as a makeshift adaptation from the original exposed cockpit, and not a proper redesign. When he suggested to MacCready that they build a lighter and more aerodynamic fuselage, Paul said there was no need to. With Maude's encouragement, Vern quietly began building the components for a new one at home, in his own workshop.

Meanwhile, he was still directing the daily repairs on the plane. On Tuesday, July 19, the broken left wing was rebuilt again, and Bryan took the plane up on a one-minute test flight for wing tuning. "No tuning needed!" his log exults. This time there was no crowd watching, only the usual weekday crew when Bryan took off for a second flight. Starting midway between the two pylons, he flew the south leg of the Kremer Course, made a 200° left turn around the south pylon, flew all the way back to the north pylon, and landed.

Nothing had broken, he wasn't tired, and the flight duration was
5 minutes and 15 seconds. It was a new record, the first time that
Allen had beaten Greg Miller's flight of March 6, 1977. That afternoon Vern telephoned Paul MacCready in Pasadena and told him
that they were ready to try for the Kremer Prize.

Paul had been anticipating Vern's message. Since mid-May, the
entries in his notebooks about publicity had grown more and more
frequent. There were lists of magazines, reminders to get plenty
of glossy photographs, names of reporters and media contacts. On
the day that Vern called the reminders are succinct: "3 TV, 3 News
service, including Reuters." Underneath them is another kind of
reminder, the original goal of the *Gossamer Condor* project re-
asserting itself. It is simply the number *$86,000* surrounded by
wiggly ovals of increasing size, and framed in a baroque double
figure-eight.

The official observers were notified that the attempt was on,
and Paul compiled a long list of contributors to the project and
potential spectators for the record flight. On the morning of July
20, Bryan tried to fly the course in a 4-mile-per-hour (6.4-kilo-
metre-per-hour) wind. He made it halfway around the second pylon, and then landed. From his log: "Duration 6 min. 0 sec. Pooped
out (unable to maintain altitude during turn). Wind made altitude
gain on downwind leg impossible." The aborted circuit was followed by a couple of short demonstration flights for photographers
from *Newsweek*. The next day they tried again. Bryan was not
confident — he felt that they were trying to luck out on conditions.
His apprehensions proved correct when the canard roll control cable
broke after four flights with a total duration of only 5 minutes.

During the next week the *Condor* made 13 flights, none of them
longer than 3½ minutes. On many of the starts when Allen was
able to clear the height marker, it seemed to the observers that the
initial spurt exhausted him completely. ("Superhuman effort, then
sank quickly," Paul wrote.) It looked like the old oscillating jinx
was at work again.

On July 29, Vern tried to break it with a new stabilizer. It still
used the same Lissaman airfoil as the wing, but its ribs were framed
with elegant lightweight wooden channel sections, and it weighed
1 pound (0.45 kilogram) less than the old one. The first time

Bryan flew with it, he went 4 minutes, the second time, 6 minutes and 20 seconds, and by August 4 he was up to 7 minutes. That flight was an official attempt, with Al Eaton observing. On the takeoff Maude held up the 10.5-foot (3.2-metre) aluminum T-bar used to mark the official height, and Bryan skimmed it, hooking the *Condor*'s wheel on the crossbar. The crew yelled for him to abort, and he stopped pedaling and descended to 2 feet (0.6 metre), then changed his mind, and continued around the course. "*Almost* made it," he wrote. "Would have had I not hit obstacle and aborted and lost altitude. An exciting flight."

There was another exciting one the following day. Bryan flew for 7 minutes again, but part way around the course the plane was hit by a downdraft and the nosewheel grazed the ground, disqualifying the attempt. "Not completely blown out," the log reports. The diagrams in the logbooks are unmistakable figure-eights now; the prize flight couldn't be far off.

On Saturday, August 6, the weekend crowd was back in force, augmented by reporters and television cameramen. In the early morning there was a brisk north-northeast breeze, estimated by various crew members as about 10 miles (16 kilometres) per hour. It was too windy to try the Kremer Course, but they took the plane out and Bryan made four short flights over the T-bar for various photographers. Later in the day there was a lull in the wind, and Paul decided to make an official attempt on the prize. The pylons were set up; Bill Richardson was the official observer.

Tyler MacCready flew the plane down to the takeoff point, and found the effort low. Bryan noted that although the wind was calm, there was strong air convection over the runway. He took off, cleared the T-bar, and completed the first left turn, controlling the plane assertively in air that Paul described as "squirrelly." When the *Condor* was about halfway down the course toward the center point, a pulley in the stabilizer pitch control circuit broke loose. The pitch control failed, and the plane porpoised violently and whipstalled into the ground. The bowsprit shattered, the left wing bent, the center wing ribs crumpled, and the fuselage collapsed. Bryan was slammed on to the runway and climbed out of the wreckage with bloody abrasions on his left arm and leg. "Bummer," he wrote in the log.

There were plenty of hands to carry the mangled craft back to the hangar. Paul MacCready recalls the accident through the rose-colored filter of the eternal optimist: "Not really bad." Maude Oldershaw says, "He was discouraged in a way that I hadn't ever seen before." When they were standing around contemplating the damage, Vern said, "Come on Paul, let's start rebuilding it." He led Paul over to Maude's motor home, dispensary of unlimited encouragement and the best pancakes in the world, and began to take out the prefabricated parts of the new fuselage. Paul was delighted; recovery was almost instantaneous.

The new fuselage frame was assembled by August 9, and its finished weight was only 7 pounds (3.2 kilograms) — 6 pounds (2.7 kilograms) less than the structure it replaced. "Not really bad," however, translated into 11 days of painstaking reconstruction before the *Condor* was ready to fly again. On the 15th Bryan made a few short test hops and found that the plane's center of gravity was shifted to the rear, the fuselage angle of attack was higher, and the airspeed indicator calibration had changed. The 16th was devoted to adjusting the new parts and retuning the plane. Bryan made 7 flights that day, the longest about 2½ minutes, and when he was finished flying the crew had another set of retrofits to work on.

Several of the most important changes concerned cooling the cockpit and supplying air to the pilot. As the ambient temperatures at Shafter rose to their normal summer levels in the low 100s (38°C), keeping the *Condor*'s pilot and engine cool became more and more of a problem. Joe Mastropaolo had already sent memos to Paul and Bryan insisting that Bryan drink plenty of chilled water — more water than he was comfortable drinking — before each flight. The flights of August 16 led to the decision to provide a face air tube and a cooling vent in the front of the fuselage.

Four days later the plane was ready to fly again. During the beginning of August the reminders about various forms of publicity in Paul MacCready's notebooks reached record levels, and on August 20 (a Saturday) there were, as Bryan put it, "spectators galore." The wind velocity was 3 miles (4.8 kilometres) per hour, with gusts from the north and east. After a short warm-up and a couple of trim tests, Allen took off and flew the entire length of the Kremer Course, but without the height requirement. His flight time was estimated by various observers at about 8 minutes, his maximum altitude was 7 feet (2.1 metres), and the plane touched the runway three times during the circuit when it encountered downdrafts. Despite the flaws, this was, as far as anyone knew, the first time that the complete figure-eight course had ever been flown, and the longest human-powered flight to date.

Bill Richardson observed that circuit, even though it wasn't an official attempt. Al Eaton was also at the field, and now that the prize seemed so close, he began to worry about Paul's method of measuring the course. He suggested that they have it accurately surveyed. Paul was sure that the distance he had run off with his car was conservative, but agreed that a survey would be a worthwhile check. Vern Oldershaw called a local civil engineering firm and made an appointment for the following Monday, the earliest time they could do the job.

Despite Al's worry about the course, Paul was so excited by Saturday's flight that he decided to stay at Shafter overnight and try for the prize the next morning. The rest of Saturday was abandoned to a mini-celebration and general release of tension. Paul, Peter Lissaman, Taras Kiceniuk, and Bill Watson drove over to Hart Memorial Park and spent the afternoon drifting down the Kern River on inner tubes. Some of the crew ate dinner at Hodel's and went to see the movie *MacArthur* in Bakersfield. As with a theater company, the team had reached a point where they felt most comfortable in each other's company around the hangar, and that is where most of them drifted back to late in the evening.

Sunday dawned clear but windy, much to the disappointment of the NBC *Weekend* television crew and the other media representatives who had hoped for a record flight. Bryan made a few short trim tests and gave interviews for the press, but the wind stayed too gusty to fly the course. That night Paul went back to Pasadena, along with many of the Southern California group. He told Vern and Bryan to try for the record whenever they could.

Monday morning, August 22, was the next opportunity. At 7:30 the wind was only 1 mile (1.6 kilometres) per hour from the south. The TV crews were up and waiting, and Vern decided to go for it. Bryan took off at 8 A.M., flying northbound, and crossed the

T-bar easily. He turned the first pylon to the left, and as he flew down toward the center point the wind reversed direction and increased to about 2 miles (3.2 kilometres) per hour from the north. This made the second turn very large — "wastefully large," Bryan said later, even though he made it all the way around. As he headed north again he started the climb to clear the final crossbar, but between the headwind, the effort expended on the wide turn, and his difficulty in locating the slender aluminum pole, he was 2 feet (0.6 metre) too low at the finish line. His flying time was 7 minutes and 22 seconds.

Bill Richardson had seen washouts before: "When Sam asked me for the NBC tapes if they made it, I had to say 'Not quite.' " Bryan was chagrined, but he made a couple of short flights with a camera mounted on the downpost and on his helmet. On the second flight the lower seat-back bolt broke on takeoff, and they quit for the day. For Sam Durán the flight of August 22 was a moral victory: "The 22nd was actually the day we did it psychologically — knowing that we could do it was all Bryan needed." Vern agreed with Sam; he called Paul MacCready in Pasadena and told him to come back up to Shafter, because they were going to make the record flight the next day.

In the meantime, the surveyor that Vern had called arrived at the airport. He set two metal spindles into the runway paving spaced exactly 2640.0 feet (804.6 metres) apart on a north–south line, and checked their separation twice with a Hewlett-Packard electronic distance meter. MacCready's duct tape crosses fell well outside these points, so his original odometer reading had indeed been conservative. To make sure that the course would still be conservative, new yellow crosses to mark the pylon positions were painted on the runway 4 feet (1.2 metres) north and south of the spikes, at a total separation of 2648 feet (807 metres).

When Paul received Vern's call, he telephoned a number of friends and invited them to come up and watch the prize flight. Then he left for Shafter with Parker, Marshall, and a pile of sleeping bags. By this time Parker had come to hate the long drive: "The last forty minutes of the San Joaquin Valley were hell." At about 4 A.M. Judy MacCready arrived at the airport with Tyler and a group of his hang gliding buddies. Altogether some thirty-five people stayed around the hangar that night, and six more slept out on the apron in sleeping bags.

The team was up by 6 A.M. Tuesday morning. When the sun rose at 6:20, the wind was blowing 5 to 6 miles (8 to 9.6 kilometres) per hour, veering from east to northeast; too windy to fly. It was also clear that the day was going to be a scorcher. As far as Sam was concerned, the weather outlook was poor: "It didn't look like a good day, but all the TV and camera crews were there." (Maude Oldershaw estimated that about 100 people came to watch the *Condor* that morning.) The crew rolled the plane out at 6:30. Vern had fixed the seat back, and Bryan had taped a battery-powered strobe light to the top of the T-bar to help him see it. Paul felt that they had to fly by 7 A.M., before the turbulence and convection cells became too strong.

Seven o'clock came and went, and they still waited. Marvin and Beverly Allen had driven down from Tulare to watch Bryan make the flight, and now Beverly had to leave for work. Some of the other spectators made the same decision. The temperature rose steadily. At 7:25 the wind died to 2 miles (3.2 kilometres) per hour, and Paul decided that they should try the course. Sitting on the runway, he cut extra ventilation holes in the front and rear of the *Condor*'s fuselage to try to cool Bryan's legs during the flight.

A start–finish line had been marked on the runway 248 feet 8 inches (75.78 metres) south of the north pylon. Tyler MacCready, barefooted, picked up the T-bar and walked out to the line, and the *Gossamer Condor* was dollied into position 500 feet (152.3 metres) south of him, pointing north. Sam Durán and Phil Esdaile were the bicycle-mounted outriders. Bryan, wearing bike racing shoes, black bicycling shorts, and a red-and-white T-shirt, was taped into the cockpit. At exactly 7:30 A.M. he took off, pedaling strongly, and immediately climbed on the elevator to 11 feet (3.35 metres). He cleared the height bar at 12 feet (3.65 metres) with room to spare, and headed up the north leg of the course clockwise, the opposite sense from the day before. Sam and Phil rode on either side of the plane, acting as audible altimeters, telling Bryan where to start turns, coaching and encouraging. The *Condor* flew a steady right turn 430 feet (131 metres) in diameter around the north pylon, but it came out of the turn with only 2 feet (0.6 metre) of altitude, which Bryan gradually pulled up to 3 feet (0.9 metre) on the half-mile southbound leg.

The big red-and-yellow propeller spun rhythmically and silently. Phil and Sam were shouting now, coaching Bryan into the second turn. Phil remembers the strangeness and the contrasts, everyone calling, pedaling, running after the huge, diaphanous airplane as it banked slowly into the south loop of the Kremer Course. Bryan made a beautiful, sweeping 425-foot (129.5-metre) left turn around the south pylon, and held his altitude at 3 feet (0.9 metre) as he leveled off for the final northbound leg. "It wasn't until I got to the last pylon that I knew I was going to finish." This time there seemed to be no shortage of energy for the final sprint.

Suddenly Vern Oldershaw felt a breeze on his cheek. He remembered the shift of wind that had thwarted the flight two days before, and started calling to Bryan, "Climb! Climb!" Bryan didn't hear him, but Sam Durán did. Riding beside the plane, Sam shouted it to Bryan, and Bryan recognized the urgency in his voice. He poured on the power and the plane started to climb, but the effort swung the course to the left of the runway, over the unpaved border. The *Condor* had crossed the starting line 221 feet 11 inches (67.6 metres) west of the center line between the pylons; now it was headed for a point 65 feet (19.8 metres) west of that. Tyler Mac-Cready, still barefoot, ran to head off the airplane at the line, but stopped short at the prickly scrub edging the runway. Chuck Weissenberg, the Oldershaws' 17-year-old grandson, was running right beside him, and Tyler passed the T-bar to him like a relay racer. Chuck stood on the finish line holding the bar unwaveringly upright and bent his head backward to watch as the *Gossamer Condor* soared over him, over the bar, and over the barriers to one of man's oldest aspirations.

Bryan cleared the 10.5-foot (3.2-metre) bar by more than 2 feet (0.6 metre), still climbing, and if the plane had been powered by applause, he could have flown the course a second time on the cheers of the spectators. As it was, he kept flying and made another half right turn, landing the *Condor* gently 282 feet (85.9 metres) north of the north pylon, right on the center line of the Kremer Course. It was, finally, a complete triumph.

The *Gossamer Condor*'s prize-winning flight took 7 minutes, 27.5 seconds, and Paul MacCready calculated the total length of the flight path as 1.35 miles (2.172 kilometres). Bill Richardson followed the plane in a pickup truck driven by Eugene Oldershaw, and carrying the NBC television camera crew in the back. He had the official time: 6 minutes, 22.5 seconds, between the clearance of the start and finish T-bar. The distance flown on the Kremer Circuit itself was 1.15 miles (1.85 kilometres), the average speed, 10.82 miles (17.4 kilometres) per hour. The airplane weighed 70 pounds (31.8 kilograms), the pilot's weight was 137 pounds (62.27 kilograms), and his pulse rate was 120 per minute, one minute after completing the flight.

When the plane landed, the scene on the runway was riotous, with everyone shouting, laughing, slapping each other on the back. "Wow, we did it!" was Bryan's first comment. Bill Richardson, famous for his even disposition, was as giddy as the rest. "Oh, boy!" he remembers; "Were we excited!" Vern and Maude were prepared, as usual. For three months they had been carrying a half-dozen bottles of chilled champagne in the refrigerator of the magic motor home. Now they began opening it and passing cups around to the delirious team. Paul headed for the nearest telephone to report the news, only to find all the phones completely tied up by an NBC representative and a freelance writer. Somehow a message was gotten through to Beverly Allen's employer in Tulare, and as soon as she reached the office she turned around and drove the 52 miles (83.6 kilometres) back to Shafter.

Even with all the excitement, the celebration still seemed like a family party. It took Bryan only a few minutes to recover his usual levelheaded demeanor. "I don't think I'm excited," he told a reporter from Tulare. "Mainly, it's a very satisfied feeling." What the team didn't know was that as soon as the first wire service sent out the news, the Bakersfield telephone switchboards were flooded with incoming calls asking for the number of Shafter Airport. "There is no telephone number for Shafter Airport," the operators told callers repeatedly, and then, as the calls became more insistent, they began to give out the numbers for the agricultural aviation companies headquartered at Shafter. Soon the offices of Ag-viation, Larry Klassen Enterprises, and Inland Crop Dusters, Inc., had become message-handling centers for the *Gossamer Condor*.

The origins of the calls amazed the crew. "I took the one from the BBC myself," Vern recalls. He was interviewed by a London correspondent for fifteen minutes, and other members of the team had similar experiences. "Up to then we still thought it was just local news. When all the calls began coming in from overseas we began to realize what we had done."

Peter Lissaman realized it when he walked into Aerovironment at 8:30 that morning. "There was this general air of jubilation around the place. Someone said 'They did it!'

" 'Who did what?'

" 'They flew the Kremer Course!' "

Peter was astonished not to have heard about the attempt in advance. After he had sorted out some of the details his first re-action was to call Jack Lambie. As he recalls it, the time was about 9:30 A.M., and Jack took a while to answer the phone. "Are you doing anything?" Peter asked.

"Yes, I'm making love. It's okay, what did you want?"

"Do you remember that group, the one that was making the funny airplane that you pedal?"

"Oh, them. Sure, I remember them. Why?"

"Well, they did it."

"Did what?"

"They flew the Kremer Course."

"The hell they did."

"No, they did it this morning."

"Really? Why didn't they call us?"

"I guess they didn't have time. But anyway, they did it."

"Well I'll be damned. Listen, I'll talk to you later."

When Paul had telephoned a number of friends to come up to Shafter and watch the *Condor*'s prize flight, he unaccountably for-got two of the earliest members of the team. At first Peter and Jack assumed that the attempt had been so spontaneous that there wasn't time to phone anyone. When they learned that many people un-connected with the project had been called, and that they had been overlooked, they were both annoyed and disappointed. It took quite a while for their feelings of unfair treatment to subside.

For three days after the successful Kremer Competition flight, Shafter Airport and the *Gossamer Condor* team were besieged by representatives of the world's media. It was heady attention for

Shafter, a quiet town of 6000 whose main occupation is growing cotton and potatoes. Every major American television network reported on the flight, as well as the Canadian Broadcasting Company, the BBC, and French National Television. On the 24th and 25th Bryan flew demonstration flights for the network camera crews: takeoffs and landings, flights over the T-bar, flights with a helmet camera, and one turbulent trip past a crane-mounted cameraman that nearly ended in a high-level crash. ("Hairy!" the log notes.)

Paul tabulated the newspaper articles and gave many patient interviews. The team members weren't surprised to meet reporters from the AOPA *Pilot, Glider Rider, Hang Gliding,* and *Flight International*; these were specialist publications that many of them read as a matter of course. But their queries were interspersed with others from *Sports Illustrated, National Geographic, Scientific American, U.S. News & World Report,* and even *The Wall Street Journal.* Vern's realization that they might have done something of more than local interest slowly began to dawn on everyone connected with the project.

On August 26, Bill Richardson sent his official observer's report to General Brook Allen of the National Aeronautic Association, and requested him to forward it to Kenneth Clark, the Secretary of the Man-Powered Aircraft Group Committee of the Royal Aeronautical Society. The report included Bill's response to each of the Kremer Competition requirements; his account of the flight; an affirmation of his, Paul's, and Bryan's credentials, and of the required insurance coverage; the surveyor's report on the course; two copies of Polaroid photographs showing the *Condor* clearing the start and finish height bar, and an aerial photograph of the Shafter runway with the path of the flight shown on it. Paul appended a letter to the report in which he invited Mr. Henry Kremer to come to California and fly the *Gossamer Condor,* if he liked.

The same invitation was extended to many members of the team the next day. Tyler MacCready warmed up the plane with a short flight, and then Bryan flew several demonstration flights for French National Television. One of these was almost another complete Kremer Circuit. He was followed by Paul MacCready, who noted that even though the wind was getting a bit strong,

Bryan made the flying look easy. Drs. Chet Kyle and Joe Mastropaolo had driven up from Long Beach, and they both took turns flying the plane they had helped to make successful.

Paul had also invited Jack Lambie and Peter Lissaman to have a belated try at piloting the *Condor*. Both of them were considerably heavier than any of the pilots who had flown the plane before. Jack was given a boosted takeoff and made a short flight. Then it was Peter's turn. Peter is 6'2" (188cm) and now cuts a very svelte figure, but at that time he weighed 207 pounds (94 kilograms), exactly 70 pounds (31.8 kilograms) more than Bryan Allen. He was shoehorned into the cockpit, and as he started pedaling, two crew members ran alongside and heaved the plane into the air.

The *Condor*, still defiantly Gossamer, stood up to the load for a few seconds, until Peter tried to make a turn correction. Then the left wing buckled in flight and the left inboard spar broke in several places; the right spar, now subjected to a negative G overload, snapped at two points, followed by a three-part failure of the left center wing section. The *Condor* descended slowly but definitely to the ground, where the fuselage, impelled by Peter's irresistible bulk, fell over and collapsed, the left wing sprit parted company with the wing, and one blade of the propeller broke off. "What a mess!" Bryan wrote in the log.

It was a magnificent crash, worthy of a Roadrunner cartoon, and since the French Television crew was on the spot, it was also filmed in full color. When the pilot emerged, however, it was not with the élan of the irrepressible Coyote. Peter was unhurt, but his ego was sorely wounded. "I was," he says, "absolutely mortified." (He has long since recovered to the point where he shows the film of the crash to lecture audiences as a joke on himself.)

Vern's new canard was miraculously undamaged. It is a significant commentary on the rest of the *Condor*'s structure that the major aluminum frame components were all either repaired or replaced on the day of the crash, early enough for the crew to continue celebrating at a hangar barbecue put on by Dwight Reimer (the owner of the Shafter Air Force) that afternoon.

There was only a slight letup in the parties and the press coverage during the next few weeks. Between the need for many of the team members to catch up on their sleep, their jobs, and their family life, it was September 18 before the *Gossamer Condor* was covered with new Mylar and ready to fly again. Bryan flew most of the figure-eight course in 6 minutes to check trim and effort. During a photo flight past a hot air balloon, he experienced a new phenomenon: flight at zero power. For more than 30 seconds, the *Condor* coasted through a thermal, holding its altitude like a sailplane without any effort from the pilot. On the same day Taras made a 20-second flight in the *Icarus* HPA — his longest to date.

Four days later, on Thursday, September 22, an event occurred which many members of the team had been waiting for, and which was to change the class initials of the *Gossamer Condor* and all of its subsequent kin. Bryan made two short flights to tune the plane, and then Vern and Maude Oldershaw were asked to fly it. Vern flew for 30 seconds and had plenty of pep left for more, but it was Maude that everyone was watching. Maude was due to have her sixtieth birthday in a few days; she was a pilot, a civil service examination administrator, and a grandmother ten times, and she had endeared herself to every person on the project. She was installed ceremoniously in the *Condor*'s cockpit, and with the aplomb that she knew the team expected, she took off and flew, laughing for most of the flight, and landed beautifully. As she later told Lin Burke when her turn to fly the airplane came, "Go on, you can do it — it's easy!"

The flight was duly witnessed, and as far as is known, was the first woman-powered flight in history. In 1957, when the Cranfield College of Aeronautics group was founded, its members named it MAPAC — the Man-Powered Aircraft Committee. As a result, the machines that competed for the Kremer Prize before the *Gossamer Condor* were known as MPAs. After Maude Oldershaw's flight twenty years later, they became, irrevocably, HPAs — Human-Powered Aircraft. The team gave Maude a unique commemoration of her part in the project. It is a stainless steel pancake turner, engraved as follows; "Maude Oldershaw, Gossamer Condor Hangar Mother — 1st Woman-Powered Flight, September 22, 1977."

On the day of Maude's flight Paul received a communication from the Royal Aeronautical Society. The rules of the Kremer Competition stipulated that all entrants had to submit a registration fee of £1 sterling, and that if an attempt actually took place, the fee would be refunded. Enclosed with a letter from Kenneth Clark, the Secretary of the Man-Powered Aircraft Group Committee, was a £1 note, made over to Dr. Paul B. MacCready and Bryan Allen, and autographed by the members of the committee. The letter noted that the award of the prize was the responsibility of the Council of the RAeS, which met on September 29.

Paul had wanted to organize a team celebration since the flight, and had half-settled on Pasadena as the location for it. Maude suggested to him that they give a hangar party at Shafter instead, and let anyone who wanted to fly the plane. The date was set for October 8, and in addition to having the *Condor* to fly and a catered party, they covered the hangar windows with black plastic and held a slide and movie orgy, during which everyone showed pictures and made speeches to his and her heart's content.

Before that party and the intervening celebrations were over, the *Gossamer Condor* had been flown by more people than any human-powered plane in history, including men, women, and children of both sexes and a wide range of ages. Several of the people who flew it couldn't even ride a bicycle. Bryan discounted his expert instruction: "It only takes thirty seconds of ground school, and it flies so slowly that you can walk alongside and tell the pilot what to do. Besides, almost everyone has the same reaction the first time."

Part of the reaction was to expect to exert a great deal of effort at takeoff — more effort than the plane required. As a result, most first-time pilots were flying before they realized it. Their facial expressions were as unguarded as those of a person jumping, and their first cautious glimpse to either side said transparently, "It's so *big*." The second expression was invariably the realization that they were actually *flying* this huge machine themselves. Then a broad grin would spread across their faces — and they would forget to pedal. The plane, of course, would stop flying and glide gently to the ground, where the handlers, who had seen it all before, were waiting for it.

There is a photograph of Lin Burke in a transport of excitement just after flying the *Condor* that sums up the feeling of those days following the prize flight. It was a kind of ingenuous and irrational delight. At that point Paul MacCready had spent about $50,000 on the project and there were still many unpaid bills, so he had not achieved his goal of paying off the Gen-Mar debt. Yet, like most of the others on the team, he seemed amply repaid by the satisfaction of making the airplane fly.

At the hangar party on October 8 Paul had two pieces of paper to show everyone who had worked on the plane. One was a telegram from Kenneth Clark dated September 30, 1977: THE ROYAL AERONAUTICAL SOCIETY LONDON ANNOUNCES YOU WINNER OF THE 50,000 POUNDS KREMER PRIZE HEARTIEST CONGRATULATIONS. The other was a letter from Donald S. Lopez, Assistant Director of Aeronautics for the Smithsonian Institution. In it he confirmed that the Director and Deputy Director of the National Air and Space Museum had approved the acquisition of the *Gossamer Condor* for display in the museum's new building in Washington, D.C. This time the *Condor* would not be reduced to a forlorn pile of parts. Instead it would be suspended permanently in a place of honor, in the element to which it had earned the right: the air.

PART TWO

The Gossamer Albatross

Wandering Albatross (Diomedea exulans)
Length: 44 inches (112 centimetres)
Wingspan: 144 inches (366 centimetres)
The albatross has the largest wingspan of any living bird. Its wings are long and narrow and, despite their size, seem perfect instruments of flight. The bird may soar hour after hour on fixed wings, descending rapidly to the waves, ascending steeply and tacking again. The young of the albatross stays aground until its wings are very long — a matter of 229 to 251 days. Of the birds that have learned to live over the ocean, none is more self-sufficient than the albatross.

•

From *Living Birds of the World,* by E. Thomas Gilliard. Garden City, New York: Doubleday & Company, Inc., 1958.

11

Sequel

The Cross-Channel Prize

I have been interested in the problem of mechanical and human flight ever since as a boy I constructed a number of bats of various sizes after the style of Cayley's and Penaud's machines. My observations since have only convinced me more firmly that human flight is possible and practicable . . . I believe that simple flight at least is possible to man, and that the experiments and investigations of a large number of independent workers will result in the accumulation of information and knowledge and skill which will finally lead to accomplished flight.

From Wilbur Wright's first letter to the Smithsonian Institution, written at Dayton, Ohio, May 30, 1899

SEVENTY-EIGHT YEARS after Wilbur Wright wrote the letter that began his and Orville's experiments with flying, and sixty-five years after Robert Peugeot offered the first prize for human-powered flight, the *Gossamer Condor* finally redeemed their convictions. Ironically, the solution had only taken one year, but it was a year unmatched in intensity by any previous HPA project. In 1881 Louis-Pierre Mouillard, the author of a pioneering book on the flight of soaring birds titled *L'Empire de l'Air,* wrote that solving the problem of human flight was a haunting, all-consuming thought that preempted every other idea once it occurred. He could not have known that the obsession persisted, even after one had solved the problem.

During the weeks following the Kremer Course flight, the *Gossamer Condor* team was slightly dazed by the publicity and celebrations. There were parties, telegrams and letters of congratulation,

requests for interviews, autographs, T-shirts, and pieces of the airplane; all of the puzzling and (for this mostly ingenuous group)
unforeseen accompaniments of success. One of the most surprising
communications that Paul MacCready received in September 1977
was a congratulatory letter from Dipl. Ing. Franz Villinger of Bört-
lingen, West Germany. This was the same Franz Villinger who
had been the co-designer of *Mufli* in 1935, and he informed Paul
wistfully that he was "a member of a loser competitive crew for
the Kremer-Competition."

Some of the American boosters of human-powered flight also
felt wistful about the *Gossamer Condor*'s success. In October 1977
Dr. John McMasters, who had been a principal HPA prophet for
more than a decade, wrote, "The final winning of the prize seems
a little sad. The rules stood as a magnificent challenge always just
beyond reach." He need not have worried. The seed of another
magnificent challenge had already taken root in a number of aeronautical minds.

It is fitting that pride of place for the appearance of the idea in
print should go to Rear Admiral Nicholas Goodhart (retd.), of
Newbury, Berkshire, England. Since 1975 Goodhart had been
working on a new challenger for the Kremer Prize. His *Newbury
Manflier* was in several ways the most startling HPA yet: Not only
was it a huge twin-propellered plane with a wingspan of 137.8
feet (42 metres) and an airframe weight of 160 pounds (72.6
kilograms), but its two pilots were housed in separate nacelles 70
feet (21.3 metres) apart.

There was no doubt among the various British companies that
donated the materials for the *Manflier* that Goodhart had the credentials to make this audacious design work. He was a distinguished
naval aviator in the Second World War, the inventor of the mir-
ror landing system for aircraft carriers, a designer of sailplanes,
and (in 1977, at age 57) the holder of the United Kingdom gliding distance record of 360 miles (580 kilometres). He was also
an old friend and soaring rival of Paul MacCready.

On August 28, 1977, five days after the *Gossamer Condor*'s
successful completion of the Kremer Figure-of-Eight Course, the
Sunday Times of London published an illustrated interview with
Admiral Goodhart. The article noted that Goodhart's disappoint-

ment at being beaten to the £50,000 prize was short-lived. At that time the *Newbury Manflier* had not yet flown, but the Admiral was already looking forward to his next project. It was particularly appropriate for a flag officer in the Royal Navy: a human-powered flight across the English Channel.

For this extraordinary venture, Goodhart proposed to add a 63-foot (19.2-metre) center section to his airplane, carrying another pilot/engine nacelle. This would have brought the *Manflier*'s total wingspan to 210 feet (64 metres) — slightly larger than a Boeing 747 — and made it the first human-powered trimotor in the world. Goodhart was sure that if a sponsor provided attractive prize money there would be many contenders, and the Channel crossing would be turned into an international race. "And what better than to stage such a race in 1979, the seventieth anniversary of Bleriot's first flight across the Channel in an engine-powered aircraft?" he asked.

Even the more enthusiastic advocates of human-powered flight were left a bit breathless by this proposal. When Goodhart first broached it to the Man-Powered Aircraft Group Committee of the Royal Aeronautical Society, its secretary, Kenneth Clark, responded cautiously: "We are still at the teething stage of man-powered flight, and it is quite early to predict how it will progress." Goodhart remained optimistic: "It may sound like pie in the sky, but there seems no logical reason why greater distances even than the Channel could not be achieved — depending largely, of course, on the stamina of the pilots."

However skeptically these views were received at the offices of the RAeS, they struck an immediate responsive chord in two other places. When Paul MacCready received Admiral Goodhart's *Times* interview, he had it copied and bound into the booklets then being made up to commemorate the flight of the *Gossamer Condor*. A few days later, only two weeks after the *Condor*'s successful flight, Henry Kremer offered two new aviation awards to the Royal Aeronautical Society. One was a prize of £10,000, for the next human-powered flight around the figure-of-eight course by anyone other than a citizen of the United States. The other one was ten times larger: £100,000 sterling, for the first successful human-powered flight across the English Channel. The RAeS promptly set up a committee to write the rules for the competition. They realized from the outset that while the prize was magnificent, the task was potentially much more difficult and dangerous than the one Paul MacCready's team had just accomplished.

MacCready had already received Henry Kremer's congratulations for "a brilliant design," but on September 27 he was prodding himself to improve it: "Let's build ultimate." By mid-October he had begun making notes for a human-powered Channel crossing: "Fly 12 mph. HP 0.2. Takes 2.7 hrs. (say 2 hrs. with light helping wind)." A few days later Admiral Goodhart's kindred spirit emerges in Paul MacCready's notebook with two more visionary proposals: "Fly to Catalina [Island]; [Fly] London to Paris."

As it happened, the *Condor* team's next flight was neither of these, but from Los Angeles to London; and although Bryan Allen was aboard, the plane was propelled by ordinary jet engines. On November 25, Bryan, Marvin, and Beverly Allen, Bill Beuby, Jim and Lin Burke, Sam Durán, Phil Esdaile, Jack Lambie, Peter Lissaman, Paul and Judy MacCready, Greg Miller, Vern and Maude Oldershaw, and Bill Richardson flew to London to receive the Kremer Prize. It was a first trip to the United Kingdom for many of them, and the Royal Aeronautical Society went out of its way to make their visit not only pleasant but stimulating. Among the guests that were invited for the team to meet were Derek Piggott, the pilot of *SUMPAC,* Rear Admiral Goodhart, and — flown from Japan at the expense of the RAeS — Professor Hidemasa Kimura.

The parties preceding the prize ceremony brought together some of the members of the original Cranfield Man-Powered Aircraft Committee, and those of the current Royal Aeronautical Society Committee as well. They included Professor Geoffrey Lilley, now Head of the Department of Aeronautics and Astronautics at Southampton University, who began the *SUMPAC* project; John Wimpenny, designer and pilot of *Puffin;* Dr. Keith Sherwin, the designer of *Liverpuffin;* Squadron Leader John Potter, the pilot of *Jupiter;* Martyn Pressnell, the progenitor of *Toucan,* and of course Beverley Shenstone, who in a sense had started the whole thing.

The California model builders were especially delighted to meet Ron Moulton, whose name they knew from dozens of model aviation articles, and who was both a Director of Model & Allied

Publications and a member of the RAeS Man-Powered Aircraft Committee. Moulton had also been appointed Chairman of the rules committee for the Channel crossing competition, and at one reception, he had a quiet chat about the regulations with Paul MacCready. In another part of the same room Sam Durán, Vern Oldershaw, and Professor Kimura could be found huddled over a pocket calculator, comparing the lift coefficients of *Stork B* and the *Gossamer Condor*.

Between parties the team members steeped themselves in the tourist attractions of London. For this group the required sights included not only Piccadilly Circus and Big Ben, but the airplane gallery of the Science Museum and the Royal Air Force Museum at Hendon. Paul and Judy MacCready and Peter Lissaman went to a performance of Shaw's *Candida* that filled Peter with nostalgia for his student acting days at Cambridge, and Nick and Molly Goodhart invited the crew members out to Newbury to see the *Manflier*.

One of the first things that the Americans learned about from their new British friends was a ribald coincidence. In California, the crew had several nicknames for the *Gossamer Condor,* depending on their mood and its performance. One that they used when the plane was particularly intractable demoted its aerial namesake to a lowly contraceptive. In England they were informed that this was a redundant pun, because the plane's *first* name meant exactly the same thing in U.K. slang. ("What a name," one London reporter groaned. "How are we going to print that?")

On Wednesday, November 30, the most rarefied guild of human-powered flight experts ever convened in one place assembled at the Royal Automobile Club on Pall Mall. The Kremer Competition award was incorporated in the Royal Aero Club's annual prize meeting, and the prizes were to be presented by His Royal Highness, The Prince of Wales.

None of the *Gossamer Condor* team members will forget that evening. Dressed in suits and ties that would have made them unrecognizable at Shafter Airport, they were wined and fed, and then applauded by a large audience of distinguished and appreciative aviators. On behalf of the Royal Aeronautical Society, Prince Charles presented Paul MacCready with a handsome bronze sculpture commissioned from the Royal College of Art, and Henry Kremer presented him with a handsome cheque for £50,000 sterling.

After the ceremony the team members were introduced to the prince, and found him witty, charming, and — best of all — a knowledgeable airman. It was especially rewarding to receive the Kremer Prize from someone who could appreciate the intense and specialized work that had gone into winning it. No one on the *Condor* crew was particularly surprised when Prince Charles had the longest conversation with Maude Oldershaw.

At the Royal Aeronautical Society reception following the ceremony, the Americans had an opportunity to talk with the soft-spoken donor of the Kremer prizes, and with members of his family. One would have thought that Henry Kremer had already made an adequate contribution to the advancement of human-powered flight, but he too showed that Louis-Pierre Mouillard had been right. On the back of a photograph of Henry Kremer, Paul Mac-Cready, Bryan Allen, and Ron Moulton taken at the RAeS reception, Moulton noted that they were ". . . discussing the Channel challenge." It was to take his committee many months to write and refine the rules for the cross-Channel competition; when they were published a year later, they would prove to be an appropriately rigorous set of guidelines for Henry Kremer's newest prize.

Although the *Gossamer Condor* crew had a wonderful reception from their aeronautical colleagues in London, they returned to California with mixed feelings about the reaction of the British press to their victory. Many U.K. newspapers persisted in calling the *Condor* "a simple, unsophisticated design." Several of them implied that the team had simply been lucky to stumble on a combination that could win the Kremer Prize quickly. "They really thought we were a bunch of Yahoos that just bolted together some tubing and covered it with plastic," one team member observed. Already thinking about a human-powered plane that could fly the English Channel — or from London to Paris — MacCready decided that the next time there would be no holds barred on advanced technology.

"Breathe in, breathe out," is Sylvia Ashton-Warner's timeless advice to students. During the past twelve months the *Condor* team had been breathing out in a nonstop crescendo of work and innovation. For the moment their headlong momentum had run down. During the Thanksgiving and Christmas holidays there was time at last to breathe in, to celebrate what had been accomplished, and to think about the future. Taras Kiceniuk's notes describe this period as a footnote to Shakespeare's *When icicles hang by the wall:* "Winter comes and Shafter is at a standstill. *Icarus* and the *Condor* and the spare *Condor* pieces sit in the hangar."

By the end of December the Smithsonian Institution was ready to install the *Gossamer Condor* in the National Air and Space Museum. Before sending the plane to Washington the team decided to have one more flying session at Shafter, and on December 31 the *Condor* was cleaned, tightened, and tuned up for its last flights. Of the original crew, Paul, Parker, and Tyler MacCready, Bryan Allen, Jim Burke, Sam Durán, and John Lake came out to fly that day. They were joined by Ted Ancona and Bill Watson, both of whom were to help develop MacCready's next airplane, and by one happy guest from England, Professor Geoffrey Lilley of Southampton University, the birthplace of *SUMPAC*.

Christmas had been cold and windy at Shafter, but the last day of the year was calm, and the *Condor* was flown ten times. Professor Lilley was surprised by the sensitivity of the pitch control, but nevertheless pedaled the plane 200 yards (182.8 metres), 12 times farther than *SUMPAC*'s maiden flight. Like most novice HPA pilots, he was thrilled with the experience. For Paul MacCready, one of the greatest satisfactions that day was knowing that when the *Condor* was dollied into the hangar, it had completed more than 430 human-powered flights during its short and hectic life.

On January 4, the *Gossamer Condor* was disassembled, and its sections were suspended on nylon lines inside a 40-foot (12.2-metre) van. The van was hauled by a huge diesel tractor with a sleeper cab; the combined weight of the tractor and trailer was more than 25,000 pounds (11,500 kilograms). While the *Condor*'s parts filled the van from end to end, they weighed only 70 pounds (31.8 kilograms), making the shipment one of the lightest payloads in trucking history.

Jack and Karen Lambie drove this not-so-gossamer rig across the United States in one week, arriving in Washington on Wednesday, January 11. In the meantime, Bryan Allen and Vern and

Maude Oldershaw had flown to the capital to help rebuild the airplane. A roped-off work area was set up for them on the mezzanine of the Air and Space Museum, and during the next five days they reassembled and covered the *Condor* under the curious eyes of thousands of visitors. The museum staff helped them hang the plane in a place of honor above the Wright *Flyer* and near Lindbergh's *Spirit of St. Louis* for the official dedication on March 3.

When the Oldershaws left the museum to fly home to Bakersfield it was snowing, and Maude was careful not to look back. ". . . If I did, I knew there would be tears mingling with the snowflakes on my cheeks. This was the end of an incredible year. I thought, how ridiculous to become emotionally attached to a mere armload of aluminum tubing, piano wire, and Mylar!" The surrender of the coolheaded pilot to the warmhearted grandmother only assured Maude of an even firmer place in the affections of the other team members.

For them, a new beginning was already under way. By November 1977 Paul had established the proportions of a second-generation human-powered airplane. In mid-December he met with Peter Lissaman and Jim Burke to determine its specific design elements. They decided to use the same airfoil as the *Gossamer Condor,* a similar but narrower-bladed propeller, and a horizontal bowsprit to lower the parasite drag. MacCready also suggested a name for the plane which most of the other team members found silly and inappropriate: the *Gossamer Penguin.* Paul had no convincing reason for wanting to name his advanced human-powered aircraft after a flightless bird except that Judy MacCready liked penguins very much. He received plenty of kidding about it from the building crew ("*Gossamer Ostrich* here." "The *Gossamer Kiwi,* did you say?"), and his only explanation is that he thought the names were getting too serious. In this case, he was to be outvoted before long.

Another decision the design group made was to use carbon-fiber–reinforced spars instead of aluminum tubing for the airframe. This meant that much of the technology would have to be invented, because it was impossible to buy such exotic components off the shelf. Kirke Leonard took on the job of developing the carbon-fiber frame, and as a result became the structural engineer of the new plane in the same sense that Vern Oldershaw had been the detail designer for the *Gossamer Condor*.

On February 1 Kirke received a shipment of 6-inch (15-centimetre)-wide carbon-fiber sheet at the Gen-Mar assembly building in Hermosa Beach and began to experiment with it. At about the same time, Paul Jankowski of Du Pont sent Paul MacCready some samples of a new differentially tensilized Mylar used as the base material for audio tapes, with the suggestion that it might make a superior covering material for the new plane. This exchange marked the beginning of a closer relationship between Du Pont and the Gossamer team. The Mylar was stored at Gen-Mar while Kirke worked out a way to make carbon-fiber–reinforced frame tubes.

The material that Kirke was experimenting with is called Fiber-Rite. It consists of thousands of minute carbon filaments held side by side in a matrix of uncured epoxy resin. It has the sheen of well-brushed black hair, a slightly sticky feel, and the disconcerting limpness of a thin sheet of licorice. To make a load-bearing member from carbon-fiber sheet, one must form it around a matrix or inside a mold, hold it in place, and heat the assembly until the epoxy resin melts and then cures into a rigid structure. It would all seem to be a great nuisance, except that carbon fibers have astonishing rigidity and tensile strength for their weight.

A comparison of average values shows that a unidirectional CFRP (*C*arbon-*F*iber–*R*einforced *P*lastic) has a density of .055 pound per cubic inch (1.52 grams per cubic centimetre), a little more than half that of a typical aircraft aluminum alloy. It has an ultimate tensile strength of 200,000 pounds per square inch (14,061 kilograms per square centimetre), which is 3.225 times higher than that of the same alloy. This means that its specific strength (ultimate strength divided by density) is 5.86 times that of the material that the *Gossamer Condor* airframe was built of. Simply put, the carbon-fiber structure offers almost six times more tensile strength per unit of weight than aircraft aluminum. It is perhaps even more impressive to learn that CFRP has a specific strength 5.76 times greater than cold-rolled *steel*.

Because of this remarkable strength-to-weight ratio, CFRP ap-

peared to be a particularly appropriate material for a human-powered plane. (As described earlier, Peter Wright had come to the
same conclusion in England in 1971.) One of the major obstacles
to using it was size. Kirke knew that commercially produced CFRP
tubes for golf club shafts and fishing rods were wound on tapered
steel mandrels, heated to cure, and slipped off the mandrels. Since
MacCready's new HPA needed wing spar sections at least 24 feet
(7.3 metres) long with a constant diameter of 2 inches (5 centimetres), the use of steel forms seemed impractical.

During February 1978, Leonard developed an ingenious technique for forming tubular CFRP spars of the required size. Bryan
Allen worked with him, Taras Kiceniuk volunteered a few hours
a week, and at the end of the month Bill Watson, who had met
the *Condor* crew at Shafter when he was helping Taras with his
Icarus HPA, was hired to work on the project full time. At that
point the tubes were cured for three days, but eventually the process was refined to the point where a complete new spar could be
produced in four hours.

After making some laminating tests, Kirke's crew built a Rube
Goldberg (or Heath Robinson) tube-winding machine. It is about
15 feet (4.5 metres) long, powered by a small, low-speed electric
motor, and its exposed belts and pulleys have the same kind of
quaint charm for engineers as Victorian doll houses have for new
mothers. To form a spar, a 12-foot (3.6-metre) length of aircraft
aluminum tubing of the appropriate diameter is inserted in the
machine and clamped between its centers. The epoxy-impregnated
carbon-fiber sheet — "prepreg" is its generic name — is fastened
to the mandrel at one end and wrapped on the slowly rotating
tube in a tight spiral. Kirke's machine allows the operator to control three variables simultaneously: tension, wrapping angle (usually 16°), and amount of overlap. Each layer of prepreg is 0.007"
(0.17mm) thick, and several layers are wrapped diagonally over
each other, until the tube looks like a long section of bicycle han-
dlebar. A combination of computer analysis and cottage industry
allows the placement of handmade but optimal reinforcements at
areas of high stress. These include elliptical pads at the points
where brace wires are attached, and graded cuffs at the ends where
the spar sections will join.

After the carbon-fiber sheet is fastened firmly at both ends, the entire tube is bound with transparent shrink tape that locks the prepreg tightly in place and forms a glass-smooth surface mold for the epoxy resin. To cure the resin the taped assembly is placed in one of the team's most disreputable-looking appliances, an oven improvised from a 15-foot (4.5-metre) length of large-bore aluminum tubing left over from one of Gen-Mar's catamarans. The tubing is wound with a sandwich of fiberglass tape and Nichrome resistance wire, and that in turn is surrounded with fiberglass and aluminum foil roofing batts held in place with string. A Variac runs the resistance heating element at approximately 40 volts.

The shrink-taped spar is baked at 290°F (143.3°C), as measured by two candy thermometers in the end plugs of the heating tube. In one hour the epoxy has melted and cured to a beautiful mirror-black finish, fusing the layers of fiber-impregnated sheet into a rigid structure. After the assembly has been removed from the oven and cooled down, the shrink tape is stripped off and the spar is slid into a capped length of PVC plastic sewer pipe. The pipe is filled with a 10 percent hydrochloric acid solution (bought in bulk from swimming pool cleaning services), and the aluminum mandrel is dissolved out from the inside of the spar.

Although the production equipment looks crude, the result of this process is a superb structural element that can be tailored exactly to the job it must perform. Depending on the part of the plane a tube was destined for, it could have different numbers of carbon-fiber layers — 3 to 5 was the most common range — and different reinforcements. To complete the wing spars, the 12-foot (3.6-metre) tube sections are spliced together with short aluminum inner sleeves and carbon-fiber wrap, and heat-fused into 24-foot (7.3-metre) lengths. Epoxy-coated Styrofoam plugs are spaced at approximately 10″ (25cm) intervals inside the large-diameter tubes. The plugs weigh very little, but they greatly increase the tube's resistance to buckling.

The propeller shaft gives a good indication of the CFRP tubing's performance. It is close to a wing spar module in size: 10 feet (3.6 metres) long by 2 inches (5 centimetres) in diameter. When Bryan is pedaling hard at takeoff, the shaft must transmit a peak shear force of approximately 5000 pounds (2268 kilograms)

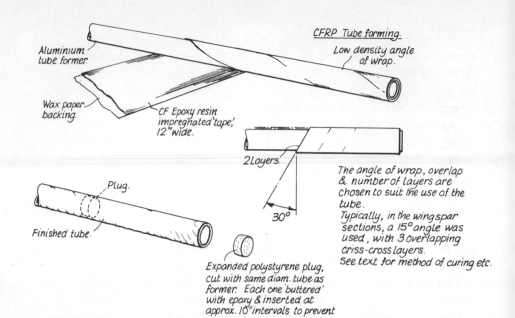

CFRP Tube forming.

Aluminium tube former.

Low density angle of wrap.

Wax paper backing.

CF Epoxy resin impregnated 'tape', 12" wide.

2 Layers.

30°

Plug.

Finished tube.

Expanded polystyrene plug, cut with same diam. tube as former. Each one 'buttered' with epoxy & inserted at approx. 10" intervals to prevent ovality of tubes under strain.

The angle of wrap, overlap & number of layers are chosen to suit the use of the tube.
Typically, in the wing spar sections, a 15° angle was used, with 3 overlapping criss-cross layers.
See text for method of curing etc.

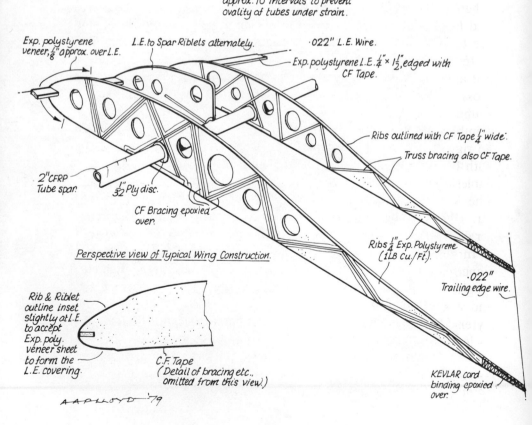

Exp. polystyrene veneer, $\frac{1}{8}$" approx. over L.E.

L.E. to Spar Riblets alternately.

·022" L.E. Wire.

Exp. polystyrene L.E. $\frac{1}{4}$" × $1\frac{1}{2}$", edged with CF Tape.

Ribs outlined with CF Tape $\frac{1}{4}$" wide.

Truss bracing also CF Tape.

2" CFRP Tube spar.

$\frac{1}{32}$" Ply disc.

CF Bracing epoxied over.

Ribs $\frac{1}{4}$" Exp. Polystyrene (1LB Cu./Ft.).

·022" Trailing edge wire.

Perspective view of Typical Wing Construction.

Rib & Riblet outline inset slightly at L.E. to accept Exp. poly. veneer sheet to form the L.E. covering.

C.F. Tape (Detail of bracing etc., omitted from this view.)

KEVLAR cord binding epoxied over.

A.A. PLLOYD '79

from the chain sprocket to the propeller. It does so most of the time (Bryan did break it twice), and its total weight is 475 grams — just over one pound. It can easily be balanced on one's little finger.

At the beginning of March 1978, 11 members of the *Condor* team, including the entire MacCready family, flew back to Washington for the official dedication at the National Air and Space Museum. By the time they returned it was clear that Kirke Leonard's carbon-fiber engineering was a success. Bill Watson was already testing the bonding systems for the frame tubes, based on his experience with building fiberglass racing bicycles. Watson is 29 years old, a natural craftsman, and a born inventor; in addition to his expertise with synthetic materials, he has designed and built prize-winning electric aircraft and radio-controlled blimps, as well as RC airplane models kitted by several manufacturers. His inherent ingenuity, kindhearted disposition, formidable dexterity, and large appetite blended perfectly with the team that was beginning to re-form around the new airplane.

In April the Gen-Mar crew, including Bill Beuby, who had come out again from Tulsa, made carbon-fiber spars with D and triangle cross sections, but the choice eventually went back to the simpler round tubes. That same month Paul McKibben designed a revised thimble-and-wire termination that would allow the new plane to be rigged and unrigged quickly. Kirke Leonard was experimenting with Kevlar, an extremely strong Du Pont aramid fiber, for control cables, bracing wire connections, and component reinforcement. The Kevlar was supplied in many different forms by Du Pont's Dr. Halvar Loken; before long the construction crew found uses for it that its manufacturer had never dreamed of.

In keeping with the new technology, Kirke and Bill Watson designed all-plastic ribs for the new wing. Assembling them was like magic. The blank for a center rib was 5.5 feet (1.6 metres) long, and was cut from a ¼-inch (6mm)-thick sheet of expanded polystyrene foam with a hot wire. It weighed 0.7 ounce (20 grams) — less than a first-class letter — and it was as fragile as a giant

---

[*opposite*] 6. The technique of forming the carbon-fiber frame tubes of the *Gossamer Albatross,* and the basic wing structure.

piece of meringue. On the side of this pristine white airfoil, thin black lines of carbon-fiber tape were contact-cemented in the shape of a diagonal truss. It looked like a truss drawn on a blackboard to illustrate a lecture in statics. The difference was that in this case the truss was actually functional. When the rib was capped with the same narrow carbon-fiber strips, fitted with a thin plywood spar ring, and bound with Kevlar cord at its trailing edge, it weighed about 1.7 ounces (50 grams) complete — less than two first-class letters — but it was a full-fledged load-bearing member of remarkable strength.

Bryan Allen could be described in the same way. While the parts of MacCready's new plane were taking shape in Hermosa Beach, the chief pilot was improving his training regimen in Bakersfield with Joe Mastropaolo's help. By June 1978 Bryan was putting out 0.31 horsepower (0.23 kilowatt) for two and a half hours continuously. That was more than enough, by MacCready's reckoning, to fly the English Channel.

Although the Kremer Cross-Channel Competition rules had not yet been published, Paul expected to make an attempt on the Channel in the fall of 1978. He never volunteered an estimated completion date for the new airplane, so the MacCready Factor for its first flight must remain problematic. Certainly the structure went together with only a small fraction of the travail and frustration that accompanied the birth of the *Gossamer Condor*. That is still quite remarkable, considering that all of the technology was new except the bicycle pedals. In May 1978 Paul sold the first set of *Gossamer Condor* plans (the price was $80). To people who questioned him about building a copy of the *Condor* at that time, he said that any moderately skilled craftsman could do it in one year, with an outlay of about $600 for materials. That could not be said of the new plane. Not only had the construction crew made virtually every piece of it by hand, they had designed and built most of the tools necessary to make the pieces as well.

Another difference between the old plane and the new one was fame. The story of the *Condor* had appeared in many magazines and technical journals, and the emotion it seemed to inspire in most engineers was envy (of the project, not the prize). After Paul MacCready won the first Kremer Competition, many highly trained people were eager to volunteer valuable time and uncommon skills to associate themselves with his next plan.

One of these was Edwin Shenk, a senior principal electronics engineer with Polaroid Corporation. Soon after the introduction of the Polaroid One-Step Sonar camera in the spring of 1978, MacCready called Polaroid and asked whether the Sonar focusing technology could be used in a low-level altimeter for the cross-Channel flight. Ed Shenk had designed the electronics for many Polaroid cameras, as well as the new Sonar system, and he spent an hour talking over the problem with Paul. Two weeks later he produced the first working breadboard circuit (on time donated by the Polaroid Corporation and at no cost to MacCready), and in two months he had a complete prototype Sonar altimeter ready to test.

A goal that Paul had been pursuing without success since the beginning of the *Condor* project was documentation. He wanted to have a written history of the airplane, but while he had been contacted by a number of journalists and freelance writers, none seemed satisfactory to him. He was not easy to satisfy; he wanted an author who could make his human-powered flight projects understandable to a wide audience, but who also had engineering and aviation experience and could work well with the rest of the team.

The problem was solved in June 1978 at Parker MacCready's graduation from the Thacher School in Ojai, California, when Paul met the parents of a girl that Parker had been dating. The couple had heard about the *Condor,* and during their conversation MacCready mentioned his search for an author/engineer. The husband replied that he knew the person that MacCready was looking for, and supplied his phone number. In a short while Paul and I had traded résumés and publications. I was committed to a major consulting project at that time, but several months later I agreed to join the team; a few weeks after that my wife, Janet, and I began commuting to Southern California to collect data and work on MacCready's new airplane.

Early in July most of the parts for the first model of the craft that Paul (but no one else) called the *Gossamer Penguin* were completed. On Saturday, July 15, he drove the components up to

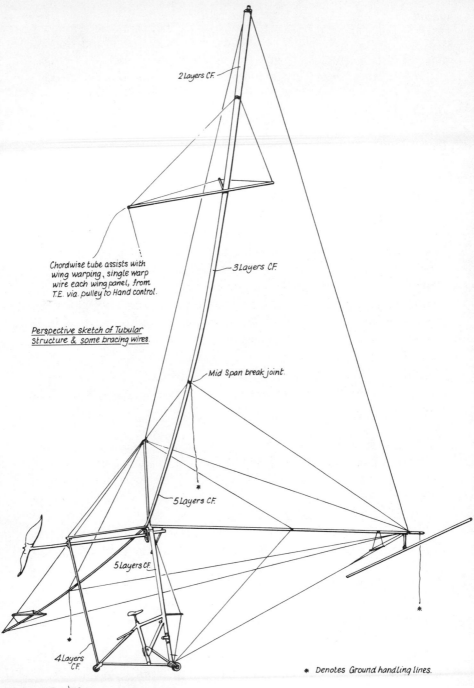

2 Layers C.F.

Chordwise tube assists with
wing warping, single warp
wire each wing panel, from
T.E. via. pulley to Hand control.

Perspective sketch of Tubular
Structure & some bracing wires.

3 Layers C.F.

Mid Span break joint.

5 Layers C.F.

5 Layers C.F.

4 Layers
C.F.

✳ Denotes Ground handling lines.

A.A.P LLOYD '79.

Shafter Airport in a rented truck. The team that day included Bryan Allen, Ted Ancona, Sam Durán, Taras Kiceniuk Jr., Kirke Leonard and his son Kirke Jr., Paul and Parker MacCready, Dave Saks, and Bill Watson. It was almost a year since the *Condor*'s successful flight, and the crew treated it as a ritual anniversary: Between work sessions on the plane they ate at Hutch's Coffee Shop twice, and had huge dinners at Hodel's.

The next day the team held an inaugural meeting. Peter Lissaman has paraphrased a set of rules for the Gossamer teams' daily hangar meetings:

1. All meetings are held standing up in a circle.
2. All participants are heard in turn.
3. All meetings must arrive at some definite decision.
4. All decisions must be acted on immediately.

The July 16 meeting was no exception to the usual pattern of democratic, definite, and short. First, MacCready's *Penguin* namesake was vigorously criticized: "It can't fly." "It sits on its tail." "It swims underwater." "It's short and stubby." In the face of nearly unanimous rejection Paul surrendered. Bryan and Sam were the principal advocates for the name that the team eventually decided on, the *Gossamer Albatross*. (Even this name met with some criticism because of its associations with Coleridge's *The Rime of the Ancient Mariner*.) Second, Taras Kiceniuk Jr. was appointed head of construction. Third, Ted Ancona and Dave Saks became members of the *Albatross* team.

Once again what Ron Moulton calls "MacCready's biblical connections" resulted in apparently casual but invaluable additions to his working group. Ted Ancona is another California *wunderkind* disguised as a slender, quiet-spoken young man with curly dark hair. The only clues that a stranger might notice are his intense alertness and the occasional unguarded laugh that can start the whole team roaring. Ancona was a music and science major at Hollywood High School and the first-chair bassoon of its unusually talented orchestra. At the University of Southern California he began as a music performance major, and then switched to elec-

[*opposite*] 7. The skeleton of the *Gossamer Albatross*.

tronic and film media technology. (He comes by that field honestly; his father is an Emmy-winning audio engineer and TV color consultant.)

Like the other team members, Ancona is an expert craftsman and an airplane enthusiast. In 1974, at age 22, he built his own Rogallo hang glider, and in 1975 he built an *Icarus V*. His graduation thesis project at U.S.C. was a color documentary film (accompanied by his own original music and sound track) of the plane's construction and maiden flight. The following year he received his private pilot's license on a Cessna 150, and soon afterward converted his *Icarus* to a motorized ultralight glider. When Ted joined the *Albatross* team he was a lecturer in the Electronic Music Department at U.S.C. and first-chair bassoon of both the Burbank and Highland Park symphony orchestras.

Dave Saks was born four months after Ted Ancona, and he is the *Albatross* team's analog to Phil Esdaile. Peripatetic, multi-talented, warmhearted and skeptical at the same time, Saks has a difficult time getting along with authority. As a child he was bounced around like a pinball between sets of divorced parents. As a young adult he has done the same thing with professions, accumulating a fascinating backlog of skills. A pathological airplane fan and model builder, he worked as a line boy to pay for his glider lessons. (He originally met Bill Watson at a model airplane meet in Sepulveda Basin.) He is an expert machinist, has several years of precision sheet-metalworking experience, equal time in cabinetmaking, and, improbably, a year as a breakout tongs floor hand on oil rigs.

Saks looks down on automobiles as wasteful and effete; he only rides motorcycles. Although he never finished college, most of the degree holders on the team learned to listen to him when he questioned a procedure on the airplane. Dave is not very tall; he affects a surface gruffness, but when the *Albatross* went to England, he was almost lost to the team because the couple that owned his bed & breakfast threatened to adopt him.

After the morning meeting on July 16, the team spent the rest of the day assembling and rigging the new airplane. At 8 P.M., just as the sun was setting, the *Gossamer Albatross* took off for its first tuning tests at Shafter Airport. Even though some of the parts were jury-rigged substitutes and the fuselage was uncovered, the plane flew right off the board, a much more encouraging debut than that of the *Gossamer Condor*. Parker MacCready was the pilot, and he said it was very easy to fly. (Soon after this flight Parker coined his permanent Anglophile nickname for the new plane, the *Albert Ross*.)

Paul was surprised that the *Albatross* flew so slowly. After six short hops to determine the optimum wing incidence (6°) and rigging angles, the plane was weighed in at 60 pounds (27.2 kilograms). MacCready, disappointed with this figure, noted that part of it was due to the use of an old, large stabilizer that was 5 pounds (2.2 kilograms) overweight, and also to "miscellaneous crummy fittings & wires & ropes," which added about 2 pounds. That night the *Albatross* was housed in the *Condor*'s old hangar at Shafter; the plan was to replace the temporary parts during the next few days and tighten up the plane for its first extended flights the following weekend.

12

Evolution

The *Gossamer Albatross*

ALTHOUGH THE PLANE that Paul MacCready's team assembled at Shafter Airport in July 1978 had the same general layout as the *Gossamer Condor,* it was a radically different aircraft. A good analogy for it would be the Boeing 720, which most laymen regarded as a modified 707, but which was in reality a major redesign.

First of all, the *Gossamer Albatross* is virtually an all-plastic machine. The only metal parts in it are the pedals, cranks, and chain sprockets, the post for the Stella Italia bicycle seat, the thin cables molded into the drive chain, the stainless steel bracing wires, and a few fittings. Its skeleton is carbon-fiber–reinforced plastic tubing. The leading edges of the wing and stabilizer are heat-formed from expanded polystyrene foam sheet, and the ribs are made of the same material braced with carbon fiber and Kevlar. The final version of the propeller uses a carbon-fiber spar inside a core of dense blue polystyrene foam; the blades are skinned with Kevlar cloth. The control lines are braided Kevlar, the wheels and the canard anti-yaw cords are nylon, and the drive chain is molded polyurethane. Even the aluminum control-cable fairleads and pulleys used on the *Condor* were redesigned in Du Pont Teflon and low-friction Delrin acetal resin for the *Albatross.* The pilot's windshield is transparent vinyl, and the plane is covered with various thicknesses of Du Pont Mylar polyester film.

Given the plans or the aerodynamic knowledge, it is conceivable that the Wright brothers could have built a flying version of the *Gossamer Condor* using materials that were available in 1903, the year of their first successful powered flight. It would have been impossible to reproduce the *Gossamer Albatross* as recently as ten years ago, because some of its materials did not even exist, and nothing else offered the same properties.

In addition to materials there were many detail changes in configuration between the two airplanes. Perhaps the most obvious one was pilot position. The *Albatross* has a fully enclosed streamlined cockpit 10 feet (3 metres) high and 8 feet (2.4 metres) long, which allows the pilot to pedal in a normal upright cycling position. The decision to change from the supine posture was confirmed by ergometer tests in which Bryan Allen's power output and oxygen consumption were compared in both attitudes. His peak short-period output pedaling upright was 1.6 horsepower (1.19 kilowatts) for 6 seconds, as opposed to 1.3 horsepower (0.97 kilowatt) for the same period supine.

Although the Lissaman 7769 airfoil was used on both airplanes, the wings of the *Albatross* have only two thirds of the area, and much less taper than those of the *Condor*. They are swept back 7.5° instead of 9°, and they are covered with biaxially tensilized Mylar that shrinks more lengthwise than crosswise when it is heated. The Mylar is applied with the higher shrink direction aligned along the wingspan. This allows the film to be tightened to provide a smooth boundary layer surface, and also maintains the airfoil contour more accurately than before by preventing dips between the ribs. The ribs are connected at their rear tips by a 0.022″ (0.55 mm) transverse wire that forms the trailing edge of the wing. When the Mylar covering is tightened, the flexible trailing edge is drawn into shallow curves between the ribs (the familiar "bird wing" look of World War I aircraft), and the spar and the leading edge are pulled back in a slightly convex line.

The stronger and lighter carbon-fiber spars of the *Albatross* allowed the substitution of internal Kevlar cord braces for the *Condor*'s external wing bracing spreaders and the use of a longer, less drooped, nose boom to support the canard. All these changes meant that despite the experience of crewmen from the *Condor* team, there were still many lessons to learn about the new airplane.

In July 1978, while the *Albatross* was being set up for its first real flights, Paul MacCready began to worry about sponsorship. It was one thing to reimburse the team members for driving 120

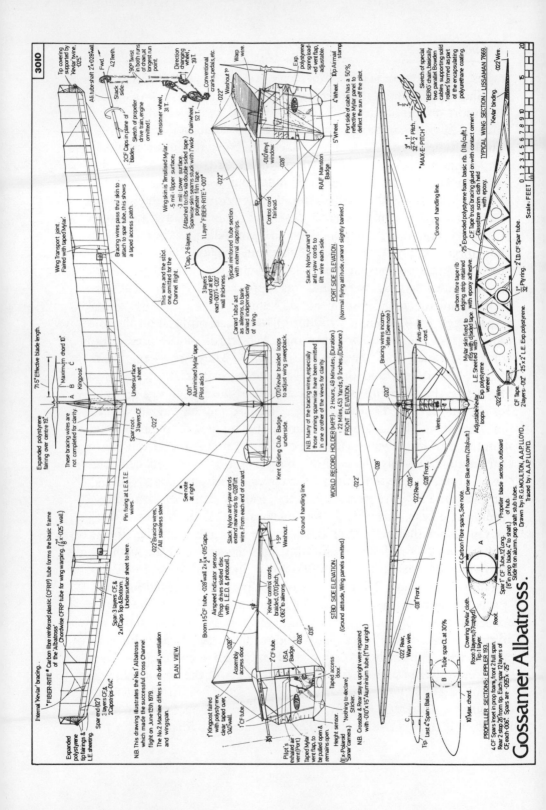

Gossamer Albatross.

miles (193 kilometres) from Pasadena to fly a supervised course at Shafter Airport. It was quite a different matter to finance the transport of a large aircraft and its support crew and spares 6200 miles (10,000 kilometres) to England and maintain a base there until it was possible to make an attempt on the English Channel. On July 18 Paul received a call from Samuel Waltz Jr., who had just become Product Information Supervisor for Du Pont Mylar. Waltz was very enthusiastic about Du Pont's association with the Gossamer aircraft, and after talking with him MacCready began to think about Du Pont as a potential sponsor. He was also thinking about IBM and the Polaroid Corporation as possible donors for the $150,000 that he then felt would be required to mount the English Channel expedition.

Without sponsorship the MacCready Factor for the first Channel crossing attempt with the *Gossamer Albatross* went up significantly. Paul had originally planned to try a flight in August or September of 1978; now he reluctantly concluded that it was "probably too late" to make the autumn weather window. He was also sobered by the final accounting for the *Gossamer Condor*. The dollar value of the £50,000 Kremer Prize at the time of exchange was $94,700; the expenses of the *Condor* project had reached the unexpected total of $68,500. This left a profit of $26,200, less $3000 in California state taxes. Even though most team members had been paid at previously agreed rates, Paul noted that some of the profit should be paid to Sam Durán, Bryan Allen, and Vern Oldershaw, whose remuneration he felt had been unfairly low.

On Saturday, July 22, the *Albatross* team regrouped for test flying. There were still some flaws that the crew hadn't had time to fix during the week: The lower rear section of the fuselage was missing its covering, and there was a slight bend in the aluminum propeller hub shaft. (Paul suspected that the tubing hadn't been checked to make sure that it was 6061–T6 and not a softer alloy.) At 7:45 P.M. Bryan made a short flight to check the controls and found that the cords needed tightening and balancing. The lines were adjusted, and fifteen minutes later Allen took off again and

[*opposite*] 8. The *Gossamer Albatross*, in the form in which it was flown across the English Channel on June 12, 1979.

flew for more than a minute at a height of 5 feet (1.5 metres) in a series of S-turns. The crew estimated the plane's speed as 12 miles (19.3 kilometres) per hour. "First true flight. Very easy," the pilot's log notes. To Paul, Bryan reported that he "could have flown an hour." Kirke Leonard was, of course, delighted when what was very much his baby flew easily right from the beginning.

The next evening the crew attached tufts of yarn to the rear section of the fuselage to study the airflow around it. At 8:50 the wind was still gusting slightly, and when Bryan took off into it the hub section of the propeller shaft failed, confirming Paul's suspicion. The team made several push flights without the propeller that showed that the airflow was smooth around the fuselage, and then hangared the plane until a replacement shaft could be made and sent up to Shafter.

MacCready's decision to postpone the Channel attempt removed much of the feeling of urgency from the project. The construction crew took the unusually long time of ten days to make a new carbon-fiber propeller shaft, bring it up to Shafter from Hermosa Beach, and install it on the *Albatross*. During that time Paul was preoccupied with one problem: Money. Day after day he made notes of possible sponsors, trying to identify a company that would be willing to put up the substantial sum that was needed to get the team and the airplane to England. His public relations consultants felt that, based on their level of advertising support, liquor and tobacco companies would be good candidates. MacCready vetoed these prospects out of hand; he had a moral objection to anything other than what he regarded as "clean" money. Since not one person on either the *Condor* or the *Albatross* team smoked, and their alcohol consumption was limited to an occasional beer or glass of wine, Paul's feelings were strongly supported by the rest of the team.

"Clean" is, of course, a relative term. A list of potential sponsors that MacCready compiled on July 31 included Adidas, AMF-Voit, Arco, Eastman Kodak, Eaton Fastener, Exxon, Fluor, Flying Tigers, Geigy, Getty Oil, Gulf Oil, IBM, *The Los Angeles Times*, Mobil, Perrier, Rockwell International, Schweppes, Sony, Texas Instruments, Union Oil, U.S. Steel, Wilson, and Xerox. This is a subjective portfolio, heavy on petrochemicals and more arbitrary than balanced. Oddly, the list does not correlate with either aviation interest or corporate performance for the preceding year. Even more surprising, it omits the major U.S. plastics manufacturers, including Du Pont.

On the day that Paul wrote this list, he learned that an Italian appliance manufacturer named Zanussi had invested $285,000 in the unsuccessful attempt of the British balloonists Donald Cameron and Major Christopher Davey to fly the Atlantic from west to east. On July 29 their balloon, named for its sponsor, had come down in the ocean 110 miles (177 kilometres) off the coast of France after a 96-hour flight from Newfoundland. Zanussi, far from being disillusioned by the failure, was reportedly delighted with the publicity the event had received. Even though MacCready preferred to have an American backer for the Channel attempt, he decided to find out more about Zanussi.

He also decided to find out more about the Kremer Cross-Channel Competition. On August 1, he called Kenneth Clark at the Royal Aeronautical Society. Clark explained that while the prize would definitely be offered, the rules would not be ready for several months. He outlined some of the stipulations that Ron Moulton's committee had decided on, including the provision of insurance and the requirement that the competitor supply his own boats to follow the aircraft. While these rules were meant to increase the pilot's margin of safety, they also meant that the steep expenses for a non-British competitor would be higher still.

This was discouraging news to a team without a sponsor, but Paul realized that worries about boats were premature until the airplane had been proven. While the broken propeller shaft was being rebuilt, he and other members of the team analyzed the teething problems of the *Albatross*. A rerun of the speed calculations showed that the plane actually flew at about 10 miles (16 kilometres) per hour, which was slower than expected. "If anything, felt slower than GC [*Gossamer Condor*]," MacCready noted. Bryan also felt that the controls were imprecise and sticky. Paul outlined a major redesign program for them, but postponed any hardware changes until after the next test flights.

On August 4, Parker MacCready made two brief flights with the new prop shaft and a new drive chain. He reported that the plane was easy to pedal. Paul flew a short S-turn, and also found the effort low, at least for that distance. Five days later he tried to fly again, but when he took off in a stiff crosswind a brace wire to the right wing broke, and the flight was aborted. MacCready was determined to push up the plane's flying times and try for some duration records.

On Friday, August 11, Parker made a one-minute warmup flight, and on his second try took off over a 6.5-foot (2-metre) T-bar and flew for 3 minutes and 44 seconds, most of it at an altitude of 20 feet (6 metres). In the middle of the flight he made a complete 360° turn, but when he landed, he reported that the pitch control was out of balance. Bryan Allen then took off like a human-powered rocket, going up on the elevator to 25 feet (7.6 metres), and flew for 4 minutes and 40 seconds. He cut the flight short because of the pitch control adjustment, and noted in his log that while the pedal effort was easy, the canard tended to overbank. (The normal angle of bank is 9° to either side. The adjustment of the *Albatross*'s stabilizer had to be determined empirically, because unlike most canard control surfaces, it operates at a lower coefficient of lift and a lower angle of attack than the main wing.) Bryan made several shorter flights, trying S-turns in both directions, but still found the controls unsatisfactory for a longer flight.

The next morning Sam Durán tried a takeoff and stalled out when the canard overcontrolled in pitch. He made a short second flight, and like everyone else, reported that the pedaling effort was low. Bryan then took off strongly, climbing to 20 feet (6 metres) and cruised at that altitude for 2 minutes. As he started to make a left downwind turn the warp control jammed, and the canard locked in the left roll position. The *Albatross* went into a steep left spin and dove into the runway at full speed.

The flight crew was on top of the situation in a few seconds. Bryan clambered out of the wreckage with bloody bruises on his left ankle, knee, and hip. The fuselage was totally destroyed; the vertical post was broken, as was the wing spar, the kingpost, and the bowsprit in two places. The canard was damaged, the wing leading edge was crumpled, a number of ribs were smashed, and one propeller blade was broken. It was the worst crash in the history of the *Condor* and *Albatross* teams.

The crew's first worry was the pilot. Bryan quickly showed the advantages of being in superb physical condition. A few minutes after the accident he was ignoring his injuries, and the next day he was well enough to make a 2-hour hang glider flight on his Wills Alpha 185. The *Albatross* was not so lucky. Instant repairs had been a specialty of the Gossamer teams from the beginning, but this crash seemed to sap the morale and energy of the project. It took three weeks for the fuselage to be rebuilt, and the rest of the repairs stalled at that point. No one who knew the crew's reputation would have predicted that the *Gossamer Albatross* would not fly again for five months.

At that point the team had no airplane, no sponsor, and, it soon developed, no hangar. The Shafter hangar was taken over by new lessees in September, and in Taras Kiceniuk's laconic phrase, "HPAs kicked out." The *Albatross* was disassembled and moved back to Gen-Mar. Taras's *Icarus* was taken first to the California State Fair in Sacramento, and then to the San Diego Air and Space Museum. With the airplane project in limbo, Paul felt that he needed someone to manage its public relations even more than he needed a hangar, so that he could pay more attention to Aerovironment. (In fact, some of Aerovironment's managers were becoming quite restive at the prospect of MacCready spending another year working on a successor to the *Gossamer Condor.*)

Early in September Paul was contacted by Tom Horton, the Director of Marketing of an advanced technology company named Xonics, Inc. He and MacCready had met at an American Meteorological Society conference in Boulder, Colorado, a year before, and MacCready suggested that Horton contact him if he changed jobs. Before working for Xonics, Horton was Vice-President of Jacques Cousteau's Thalassa Corporation and Director of Special Projects for the Cousteau Society, and had been responsible for many of Cousteau's films and television productions over a period of seven years. He had excellent references, an empathetic personality, and considerable experience with boats and aircraft. Horton could also appreciate the physical training aspects of human-powered flight because he had been a member of the United States Olympic kayak team in 1948 and 1952. As of October 1, Paul hired him to be the public relations manager of the *Albatross* project. By this time MacCready had raised his cost estimate of the Channel expedition to a more realistic $200,000. Horton's first priority was an intensive search for a sponsor.

The rest of the team was looking for a hangar. Their search covered an area from Buttonwillow to Long Beach, and it was in the latter city that Jim Burke turned up a lead in mid-September. Burke felt that overwater practice was essential before a Channel attempt, and he remembered a large unoccupied seaplane hangar on Terminal Island, between Long Beach and San Pedro, that could serve as a test base. The hangar had been part of the U.S. Navy's Reeves Field during World War II, and for years a derelict Navy PB2Y *Coronado* flying boat slated for the scrap heap had been parked in front of it. Hangar 522 was located in a gerrymandered section of Terminal Island, between the still-active Navy Base and the Los Angeles Police Driver Training Course. It was more than adequate in size: 160 feet by 166 feet (48.7 by 50.6 metres), and it was equipped with electricity and suspended gas heaters. Burke learned that its demolition schedule was hazy, and with help from his friend Jim Kilroy, he received permission from Fred Crawford, the General Manager of the Port of Los Angeles, to use it for the *Albatross*. Late in November Paul arranged to rent it for $200 per month.

Although there was now the prospect of a new nest, the *Gossamer Albatross* was still an orphan. During his first weeks with the project Tom Horton had approached many companies and organizations for sponsorship. The prospects ranged from Union Oil to The National Geographic Society, and from the Shaklee Corporation to Emery Air Freight; all but two of them saw the *Albatross* as only a large ugly duckling. The two cautious exceptions were Du Pont and Zanussi.

On October 30 Horton met with Du Pont's Sam Waltz, who had been helping MacCready with Mylar samples and contacts. Waltz was very enthusiastic and started to urge the idea of sponsorship within Du Pont. Horton flooded him with data, and on November 30, after many telephone calls, Waltz reported that he thought the proposal was moving along well. On the same day, Zanussi wrote to say that they were very interested in sponsoring the Channel attempt, but preferred that it be an international event, either as a race or with a tri-national crew. After thinking about this, Mac-

Cready rejected the idea. Zanussi wrote back to say that they were still interested on his terms.

Paul was in a quandary. He couldn't afford to make an attempt on the Channel without a sponsor, but he very much wanted to have an American sponsor. Tom Horton tried an end run: He called his friend Dick Welsh, who was a Media Vice-President of Batten, Barton, Durstine, and Osborn, and in charge of the Du Pont account. Welsh recommended that Horton call Ray Alfano, the Manager of the Du Pont Corporate Advertising Group. Alfano said he would think about it and would talk to Dick Woodward, Du Pont's Associate Director of Public Affairs.

A few days later Sam Waltz reported to Tom Horton that the proposal had reached Richard J. Woodward. There was some implication of weight in his tone, but it was hard to know from outside Du Pont that Woodward was the man who would say yes or no. On December 12, Woodward called to say that the answer was probably no, but that the door was not shut. One week later, Zanussi called to say that they had decided yes, but that they wanted to come to California on January 22 to see the *Albatross*. MacCready was ambivalent; Horton was depressed. On December 22, Dick Woodward called to say that on reflection, "We are intrigued with the idea of the flight, and with the technical challenge." He arranged to visit Pasadena on January 11.

Tom Horton all but threw his hat in the air at this crest of what had become an emotional roller coaster. His intuition was right on target. The January meeting was held at Aerovironment; the *Albatross* team participants were Jim Burke, Tom Horton, Peter Lissaman, and Paul MacCready. Lissaman was in top form, and Tom later felt that Peter had "charmed the spats off of Woodward."

It is no slight to Peter's formidable panache to doubt that anyone could charm so much as a shoelace off of Dick Woodward if he didn't want them to. That affable but acute gentleman had, as usual, done his homework; the Aerovironment meeting was more a case of confirming his expectations than of discovering anything new. He emphasized three of Du Pont's major interests in the project: First, *Safety,* which has long been a matter of corporate pride within Du Pont. Second, *Weight Reduction* through the use of new materials. Third, *Energy Conservation,* which could be dramatically demonstrated by an airplane that could cross the English Channel on human power. Toward the end of the meeting Woodward did a little charming of his own. He noted that in a company the size of Du Pont, it is difficult to find a project with a sense of fun. He felt that the *Gossamer Albatross* could provide a healthy focus for corporate excitement and identification. When he left, Paul MacCready was very much impressed, and Tom Horton was sure they had a sponsor. On January 19, 1979, Woodward called and confirmed it.

During Horton and MacCready's tortuous search for funding, several other problems had also been solved. The crew had built a closed plywood trailer to British road standards to transport the disassembled *Albatross,* and Hangar 522 on Terminal Island had been made available. On December 18, the trailer and a few worktables were moved into it. The building was huge and cold, and the concrete floor was still wet from being hosed down. The only source of warmth was a single electric hair dryer: it was used alternately to shrink the covering on the plane, and to thaw the team's frigid hands and feet.

The construction crew that day was Bryan Allen, Janet and Morton Grosser, Taras Kiceniuk, and Kirke Leonard and his son Kirke Jr. Their first priority was to repair the damage still remaining from the crash of August 12. The atmosphere was one of gelid disorganization, with tools and adhesives scrambled together in soggy cartons. While the crew epoxied fuselage tubes, installed a new propeller shaft, and re-covered the outboard port wing, Paul's new project manager improvised an office in one of the bays along the side of the hangar.

Sterling Stoll was a typical choice for the *Albatross* team. He was 34 years old and had been a personnel analyst for the city of Pasadena. He had an A.A. in physics, a B.S. in psychology from the University of Southern California, and a pilot's license. Stoll had been a ski instructor for two years, but when MacCready met him he was working as a designer and test pilot for Seagull Hang Gliders, and had just finished third in the National Hang Gliding Championships. Sterling is also very handsome — in England he was a scourge of the Kent pubs — and had flown the hang gliding sequences in several national TV series. As usual, Paul followed his instincts rather than convention in evaluating Stoll's unusual credentials for a business manager, and in a short time Sterling developed into a first-rate manager.

After moving to Terminal Island, the team slowly began to regain its momentum. Kirke Leonard's tubing machine and spar oven were installed in the hangar, a rib shop was set up in one side bay, and Sterling's office began to look semi-official. By January 17 the original *Albatross* was mostly repaired and reassembled, and Mac-Cready was drawing sketches for two more airplanes using the same technology. The first was a back-up *Albatross,* with a number of small refinements. The second was a plane that the crew referred to as "the sports car." It was to have a wingspan of 72 feet (22 metres), instead of the *Albatross's* 96 feet (29.2 metres); and it was designed to fly somewhat faster — about 14 miles (22.5 kilometres) per hour. The ink was hardly dry on the sketches before Paul began referring to it (again!) as the *Gossamer Penguin.* General derision in the hangar; one crew member cracked that MacCready had missed his calling as an Antarctic explorer.

On January 18, Paul's youngest son, Marshall, made three short test hops with the *Albatross* on the police training course behind Hangar 522. These were assisted takeoffs, and although the plane flew, it was difficult to tell much about its behavior. The unobstructed area at Terminal Island was extremely small for an aircraft that was supposed to fly 23 miles (37 kilometres) nonstop. The limiting dimension was less than ¼ mile (0.4 kilometre) from north to south, and Paul calculated that the largest safe circle they could fly was only about 755 feet (230 metres) in diameter. The flying area was also used by the Los Angeles Police for high-speed chase training, and for helicopter surveillance and control exercises.

On January 20, Bryan checked the plane out in a series of short flights totaling less than six minutes. The aim of these tests was to measure the tension in the brace wires and to calibrate the speedometer, but they also turned up a number of flaws. The most important discovery was that the new fuselage envelope had been designed incorrectly; it was too narrow at the pilot's feet, and it needed better formers and access hatches. These retrofits were begun at the same time that construction of parts started for the two airplanes that MacCready wanted to have for back-up. Several more crew members were recruited to help with this work. Like most of their predecessors, they were recommended by people already on the team.

The first was Steve Elliott, a 25-year-old mechanical engineering student who was a long-time friend of Taras Kiceniuk. Steve was one of the John Muir High School quartet who built the first *Batso* hang glider in 1971, and he and Taras achieved a certain notoriety a year later, when they collaborated on a two-man, high-speed wooden railroad handcar named *The Midnight Flyer*. They operated it nocturnally and (of course) illegally on the Santa Fe Railway line between Pasadena and Cucamonga for quite a while before getting caught by the police.

Steve helped build *Icarus I*, but he is more of a traditionalist than the other members of the crew. His boyhood model building centered as much around clipper ships as airplanes, and during the *Albatross* expedition he became enamored of eighteenth-century English bracket clocks. Elliott is small, blond, mustached, and almost as softhearted as Bill Watson. Anyone watching him play fiddle to Taras's harmonica accompaniment would take him for a stray Country and Western musician. He is also the team's artist and silk-screen expert, which in this context translates as ad lib manufacturer of *Gossamer Albatross* T-shirts.

At the same time that Steve began working in Hangar 522, Blaine Rawdon started helping on the *Albatross* two days a week, a schedule that soon evolved into full team membership. Rawdon was born in 1951; he has a bachelor's degree in physics from Amherst, and another one in architecture from U.S.C. His major diversions are 35mm photography and designing and building radio control gliders, and his picture is familiar to the readers of modeling magazines as a frequent soaring contest winner. Blaine has Clark Kent looks and an addiction to outrageous puns. Like many of the team members he is also a certified scuba diver and looked perfectly at home burbling around the Wellington Dock at Dover in a wet suit. It was his friendship with Bill Watson that brought him first to Mojave Airport to see the *Gossamer Condor,* then to Shafter to see Taras's *Icarus* HPA, and eventually to Terminal Island and the *Albatross.*

With the addition of more skilled hands, work at the hangar began to speed up, though not enough to maintain the workload that MacCready wanted. Paul had an increasing sense of urgency about the Channel attempt, but the feelings he projected to the crew at this point were primarily those of fragmentation and lack of direction. Neither Sterling nor Taras had a clear understanding of their authority, and Paul's instructions to them seemed vague and impulsive. Bryan felt that the impromptu experimental changes that MacCready was suggesting, like an extended thin canard boom, were not well analyzed, and because of his frequent absence from the hangar, not well understood by the building crew.

On January 22, MacCready called Ed Shenk at Polaroid and asked him to send the Sonar altimeter out to California; Shenk replied that he would bring it himself early in February. Unfortunately Paul and Judy were planning to go to England for several weeks on January 28 to lay the groundwork for the Channel expedition. MacCready arranged for Shenk to contact Sterling Stoll at the hangar, but on the 24th the first major disagreement between Paul and Bryan Allen erupted.

Allen felt that the project was being mismanaged, that his own contribution was undervalued, and that some of the other team members were overworked and underpaid. He communicated his feelings to MacCready in a long and intense telephone call. Paul was able to reach agreement with Bryan on only one point, the payment of temporary help who were not part of the team. In his own summary of the talk, MacCready made a misjudgment that he was to retract, with interest, much later; he tried to convince Bryan that the Channel attempt did "not need super strength, but a team guy."

Above all, the dispute revealed that the two men had strongly divergent views about work and compensation. After their talk Paul felt that there was no way to resolve the philosophical differences between himself and Bryan; they would simply have to work together on a professional basis, and try to keep everyone on the team pulling for the main goal, which was to succeed in the cross-Channel flight.

While the construction crew reworked the *Albatross,* Paul and Judy MacCready flew to England for ten hectic days of research. Paul met first with members of the Royal Aeronautical Society, and then with officers of the British Army, Navy, Air Force, and Coast Guard. He and Judy took photographs of Kent beaches in the Dover–Dungeness area and tried to locate nearby airfields where they could establish a headquarters for the team. They contacted inflatable boat and outboard motor suppliers, met with aircraft underwriters and trucking companies. Paul collected weather records from the U.K. Meteorological Service (the "London Mets") and from Oceanroutes, Inc., a California weather-prediction company that had offices in Scotland and Gravesend and generously offered to help the project.

The rules for the £100,000 Kremer Cross-Channel Competition had been issued by Ron Moulton's committee at the end of October, and the official Royal Aeronautical Society press release was dated 15 November 1978. When MacCready arrived in London, he had a chance to discuss the rules in detail with the people who had written them.

The course was simple: "From the mainland of the UK to the mainland of France." The aircraft was to take off from a location in the United Kingdom approved by the U.K. Aircraft Owners' and Pilots' Association, not more than 98.4 feet (30 metres) above Ordnance Datum (astronomical mean low water level, fixed for the U.K. in 1936). That is, a takeoff from the top of the White Cliffs of Dover, or any other cliffs, was prohibited. A starting ramp of less than 6-foot (1.8-metre) height was allowed, as was takeoff from a ship or the water, provided that the aircraft circled back over England, and an official observer, before heading for France. The lowest part of the aircraft was not permitted to exceed a height of 164 feet (50 metres) above the sea for any period of three minutes; i.e., no thermal gliding was permitted. To complete the flight, the aircraft had to land on a part of the French mainland that was uncovered by the sea at that time; tidal sands were allowed. The flight had to be continuously observed from takeoff to landing by one or more observers approved by the AOPA.

The aircraft had to be heavier-than-air and could carry no energy storage devices, hot air, or lighter-than-air gases. It had to be powered and controlled entirely by its crew over the entire flight, receive no aerodynamic assistance from any outside vehicle, and jettison neither parts nor persons during the flight. Three ground crewmen were permitted to stabilize the plane during takeoff (but not to accelerate it). There was no limit to the number of flying crew, as long as they used no drugs or stimulants, and stayed aboard for the entire flight.

The first clause under 4.2, *Safety,* stipulated that "Prior to any competition attempt, the machine must have made an officially observed flight of at least two minutes' duration or 400m (437 yds) distance and landed without damage." The trial flight had to be made over level ground and reach a height of 6.5 feet (2 metres). That, Paul thought, would be a piece of cake for the *Albatross.* The rest of the safety requirements were more complicated, including "adequate arrangements . . . to ensure the safety of the crew following a forced landing on water," and "at least one suitable vessel, vehicle, or aircraft, capable of rescuing the crew." The rescue vehicle had to be operable in shallow water, and was to be provided by the entrant.

In case these measures failed, the entrant also had to indemnify the Royal Aeronautical Society against all claims that might arise out of the Channel-crossing attempt. The registration fee for the contest was £10, and as with the other Kremer Competitions, the fee was refunded if an attempt took place. (The RAeS received a total of eight entries for the Cross-Channel Competition: two from the United Kingdom, three from the United States, and one each from Australia, Belgium, and New Zealand.)

While meeting with the Channel Competition Rules Committee, MacCready also learned the origin of Henry Kremer's concern with physical fitness. Twenty years earlier Kremer had suffered a collapsed lung and been hospitalized for several weeks. When he left the hospital, determined to regain his health, he began jogging. Since that time he had been running 5 miles (8 kilometres) a day, taking approximately 45 minutes, and also playing badminton daily.

Back in California, Bryan Allen was also keeping fit, bicycling 50 miles (80 kilometres) a day — "the easy part" — and working out on the ergometer for an hour — "the hard part." On February 6, while Paul was still in England, Bryan test flew the *Albatross* with the new extended canard boom. The test lasted ten seconds, reached a height of 4 feet (1.2 metres), and was a total disaster. The boom broke off in flight as Bryan was pedaling hard to gain altitude. The crash damaged the canard, the two central wing joint boxes, the fuselage down tube, and the pilot. Bryan had cuts on his chin, thigh, knee, and both arms. He was not happy with the experiment, and neither was the crew.

It took a week to repair the damage and replace the 1″ (25mm)-

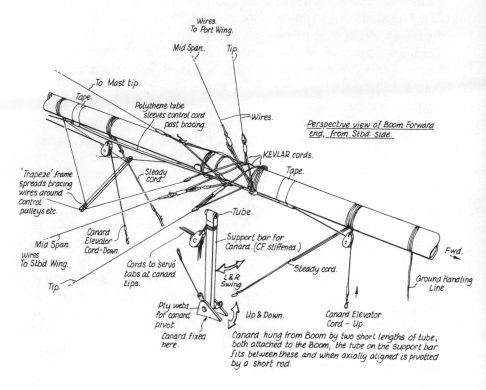

Wires.
To Port Wing.

Mid Span.

Tip.

To Mast tip.

Tape.

Polythene tube
sleeves control cord
past bracing.

Wires.

*Perspective view of Boom Forward
end, from Stbd. side.*

KEVLAR cords.

Tape.

'Trapeze' frame
spreads bracing
wires around
control
pulleys etc.

Steady
cord.

Canard
Elevator
Cord-Down.

Mid Span.

Wires
To Stbd Wing.

Tip.

Tube.

Support bar for
Canard. (CF stiffened.)

Cords to servo
tabs at canard
tips.

L&R
Swing.

Ply webs
for canard
pivot.

Canard fixed
here.

Up & Down.

Steady cord.

Canard Elevator
Cord – Up.

Fwd.

Ground Handling
Line.

Canard hung from Boom by two short lengths of tube,
both attached to the Boom, the tube on the support bar
fits between these and when axially aligned is pivotted
by a short rod.

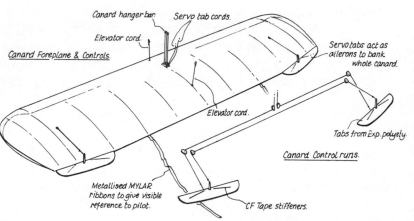

Canard hanger bar.

Servo tab cords.

Elevator cord.

Canard Foreplane & Controls.

Servo tabs act as
ailerons to bank
whole canard.

Elevator cord.

Tabs from Exp. polysty.

Canard Control runs.

Metallised MYLAR
ribbons to give visible
reference to pilot.

CF Tape stiffeners.

diameter boom with 1.5″ (38mm) tubing. During that week Paul flew from London to New York on the *Concorde,* and attended meetings at Du Pont and in Washington, D.C. He came out to Terminal Island while the plane was being rebuilt, but missed the next test flight on February 13. The plane flew for only one minute that day; "Horrible control" is the comment in the pilot's log. The next morning the canard was moved farther out on the boom, and the performance stayed poor: "Control sluggish, power high." On the 15th, Ed Shenk's Sonar altimeter was installed in the fuselage for the first time. It worked perfectly, but the *Albatross* made another poor showing, flying for only two minutes. The sweep angle of the wings was decreased slightly, which took some flight load off the canard and improved the control to "mediocre," but partway through the third flight the plastic sheathing stripped off the drive chain and the cable broke. This incident reinforced the crew's belief in the special quality of certain batches of chain.

Bryan made four short flights the following day, and found that the plane was slightly easier to control with the reduced sweep, but that the power was up to about 0.4 horsepower (0.29 kilowatt), far too high for any duration flying. The crew had already concluded that it would be impossible to make long flights at Terminal Island anyway — Allen estimated the maximum to be about three minutes. The next day, February 17, was clear but gusty, with an offshore breeze of about 4 miles (6.4 kilometres) per hour. On the fifth test the left forward flying wire pulled out of its mount, buckling the spar in flight. The *Albatross* crashed again, and Bryan jumped through the covering on the left side of the fuselage (not the normal entrance side) to save the structure from his weight.

This was the third major crash in the wonder plane's short career. Thus far it had not equaled the longest flight time of the "primitive" *Gossamer Condor;* in fact it had never flown as long as five minutes. There were only ten weeks remaining before the May-June weather window that the British meteorologists felt would be the optimum time for an attempted cross-Channel flight.

[*opposite*] 9. The canard stabilizer of the *Gossamer Albatross* and its rigging.

13

Endurance

The First Long Flights

ON FEBRUARY 20, 1979, Paul MacCready was happy to learn that Ben Shedd's film, "The Flight of the *Gossamer Condor*," had been nominated for an Academy Award in the short documentary class. Unfortunately, at about the same time the flight program of the *Condor*'s immediate descendant reached an impasse, and the temper of its pilot reached the boiling point. On February 21, Bryan Allen sent Paul a carefully worded but scorching four-page letter, accusing him of mismanagement, lack of direction, poor communication, refusal to delegate authority, and capricious design changes. Copies of the letter were also sent to certain other team members.

Despite Bryan's impassioned tone, he backed up every charge with evidence that was difficult — the crew would have said impossible — to refute. One section began,

> The Gossamer Albatross . . . has crashed three times in the last ½ hour of flight testing. On two of these occasions I have suffered minor injuries . . . I think that you possibly have not realized that the philosophy of "fly, crash, repair, and fly again" which was used in the early stages of the *Condor* project is no longer a valid method. The pilot . . . is going to be maimed or killed if this philosophy is used on an aircraft which can so easily be popped up to 30 or 50 ft. We *should* have an obligation to our sponsor and to ourselves that we do *everything,* whether it be design, construction, flight testing, promotion, or repairing, *to the absolute peak of our abilities*.

Ironically, Paul's own philosophy agreed completely with the last statement. To himself, it seemed as though he was struggling to do a conscientious job in several places at once. Perhaps that fragmentation was what provoked Bryan's criticism. MacCready's notebooks for this period have the harried tone of a man trying to manage too many different aspects of the project. Even though Tom Horton was responsible for public relations, Paul's concern with publicity also had a way of distracting his attention from technical problems.

In the end, the team's community of high standards prevailed over the transient flaws of direction. Bryan Allen was then 26, a relatively unknown bicyclist from Tulare who was still having his name misspelled and his college education omitted in articles about the *Gossamer Condor*. Paul MacCready was 53, the holder of a doctorate in aeronautics, a world-famous glider pilot, and the president of his own corporation. His reaction to Allen's indictment was to treat it as a well-deserved reproof. He took every charge in the letter seriously, and on February 24 he drafted a new management plan for the *Albatross* project.

One line in this document would have astonished Paul's old crony Jack Lambie. It said: "GA1 [*Gossamer Albatross 1*] clean & neat." Other instructions included, "Get all checks out now," "Get more people so [we] can operate in parallel," and "Write up safety plan (a) For land test flying; (b) For water test flying, ditch recovery." By coincidence, on the same day that he wrote these notes MacCready had an opportunity to make amends to a number of teammates in front of a large audience.

In September 1978, a little more than a year after the *Gossamer Condor*'s prize-winning flight, Vern Oldershaw called Paul to tell him that the California State Historical Landmarks Commission had approved Shafter Airport as the site for a marker commemorating the flight. This was to be the first state historical landmark placed in more than a decade, and the first one ever placed less than fifty years after the event it commemorated took place. The dedication was set for February 24, 1979.

About 150 people assembled at Shafter Airport that day for the unveiling of California Registered Historical Landmark No. 923. The quintessentially American scene could have been taken from Eugene O'Neill's *Ah Wilderness!* There was warm hazy sunshine, a uniformed oompah band riding on an antique fire engine, and punch and cookies served by the Kern County Historical Society.

All of the Central Valley *Condor* team were present: Bryan, Beverly, and Marvin Allen; Sam Durán; Phil Esdaile and his girlfriend (now wife), Kathy Bond; Vern and Maude Oldershaw; Pete Plumb and his fiancée (now wife), Robin Avery; and Bill Richardson. Jim and Lin Burke and Jack and Karen Lambie flew lightplanes up from Southern California, and Peter Lissaman stepped out of his 4-wheel drive wearing a black cowboy hat, and squiring a handsome lady dressed for 5th Avenue or New Bond Street.

Paul and Judy MacCready brought Marshall with them, and Bill Richardson brought most of his family. As the master of ceremonies began the program, Bill's tenth grandchild, then two years old, wandered out in front of the lectern. The M.C. stopped and asked him if he would like to try the microphone. Mike said yes, and when he was held up, chirped "Hello, everybody," to thunderous applause. That set the tone for most of the speeches. Stephen Schmitt, the Director of the Kern County Department of Airports, noted that the *Gossamer Condor* had been welcome to fly free at Shafter as an experimental aircraft, but that after it won the Kremer Prize, it had become a revenue-earning carrier and therefore owed Kern County a landing fee. The fee was computed at the rate of 43 cents per 1000 pounds, so that counting Bryan's weight the project owed 9 cents. At that point Paul MacCready came up to the lectern and handed Schmitt a dime; the extra penny was to pay the interest accrued since the flight.

When Paul's turn came to speak, he did his best to make up for any previous stinting of credit for the Bakersfield team members. Each person on the crew was mentioned by name and praised generously. Paul and Bryan lifted the California flag off the handsome bronze plaque commemorating the Kremer Prize flight (and bearing both their names), Dwight Reimer flew his de Havilland Vampire jet overhead in a deafening aerial salute, and Bryan had his picture taken with another local pilot, Christopher Reeves, who had just played Superman in the film of the same name. (The newspapers published the photo with the title, "The *Real* Superman.") That evening Bryan and Sam treated the entire gang to a huge Chinese dinner, and it was obvious that the tension on the team was eased.

MacCready started expanding the construction crew and improving their living conditions as soon as he returned to Southern California. Dave Saks had been commuting a 130-mile (209-kilometre) round trip to Terminal Island from Van Nuys every day on his Honda 400/4 motorcycle. Bill Watson had been driving the same distance, and Sam and Bryan had been coming down from Bakersfield. Paul rented a new 6-man apartment for the team in nearby San Pedro; it was immediately christened "Albatross Heights," and soon filled up with sleeping bags, computers, stereo systems, and racing bicycles. Sam Durán, who was famous for his fiery and delicious Mexican *salsa,* became House Father over his own protests, and tried to organize alternative kitchen crews with small success.

The first new construction assistant that Sterling hired was Scott Strom, a cheerful contemporary of Bryan Allen's who had a Jaguar, a pilot's license, and extensive experience in metal and plastic fabrication. Scott was followed by a group of eight more temporary helpers, including Mike Bame, Gary Cox, Ken Hamlyn, Norm Kozma, Mike Reagan, Mark Schwinge, Jeff Stephenson, and John Volk.

Although these young men were hired on a short-term basis, all of them had enough talent to become members of the team. Bame and Hamlyn were friends of Bill Watson's, and Reagan was Dave Saks's brother-in-law. Bame has an aircraft engineering degree, and Hamlyn and Reagan were expert fiberglass fabricators at Walt Disney Productions, which was then on strike. Kozma, Schwinge, and Volk were friends of Sterling Stoll's from Seagull Hang Gliders. All were advanced hang glider pilots (Volk was National Champion in 1975), and Volk and Kozma had been officers of Eco-Flight Systems. Schwinge was an assembler and test pilot for Seagull; he had a bachelor's degree in English literature from U.C.L.A., but at 23 he also had Private, Instrument, Multi-Engine, and Commercial Pilot's ratings. Jeff Stephenson was another hang gliding expert from Porterville, who was starting a company to manufacture flying harnesses.

On weekends the crew was augmented by a clean-cut high school student named Larry McNay. Larry was brought out to Terminal Island by his father, Dave, an engineer with McDonnell Douglas and sometime *Albatross* helper. At 16 Larry was an Eagle Scout, an avid model builder, and a student glider pilot, and he got along well with the older crew members. After a few weekends he became more and more involved with the team, and eventually joined it in England.

In retrospect John Lake and Peter Lissaman have attributed much of the success of the Gossamer Squadron to the extraordinary bank of talent that Paul MacCready was able to draw on. John and Peter are immigrants to California, and they both feel that there is probably no other place in the world where one can recruit so many versatile and highly skilled people on such short notice.

The enlarged crew speeded up the pace of building tremendously. Replacement wing ribs were made for those that had been damaged in the *Albatross*'s last crash, at the same time that new ones were being built for *Albatross 2*. The etch tank was kept busy continuously; it had to be cooled with a garden hose when a fresh batch of acid was added, and it slurped and gurgled as if it were harboring a small dragon inside. When the weather warmed up the distractions at Long Beach became as colorful as they had been at Mojave or Shafter. Grumman *Mallard* and PBY *Catalina* seaplanes landed in the Terminal Island estuary, water bikes raced in the shadow of the *Queen Mary,* and the Los Angeles Police staged hair-raising duels between squad cars and helicopters right behind Hangar 522.

Toward the end of February the problem of sticking control lines was solved at last. Ernie Franzgrote, a chemical engineer at the Jet Propulsion Laboratory, persuaded William McCown, Dave Miller, and Humphrey Price, all JPL mechanical engineers, to redesign the control line pulleys for the *Gossamer Albatross.* The Delrin-and-aluminum version they came up with weighed only 0.15 ounce (4.5 grams), and the lines slid through it like silk. "Perfect pulley finally!" Paul exulted in his notebook.

At about the same time, the construction crew learned that they were performing beyond their ability. The third Man-Powered Aircraft Group Symposium had been held at the Royal Aeronautical Society on February 6, 1979. Some weeks later, Paul MacCready received copies of the papers presented, including one on "Structural Materials for Man Powered Aircraft" by F. W. Vann, the

Deputy Chief Structural Engineer of British Aerospace Corporation. Vann reviewed the mechanical properties of balsa, spruce, aluminum alloy, steel, fiberglass, and carbon fiber, and concluded that wood was still the easiest material to shape, join, and repair. Metal was described as considerably more difficult to work with, although Vann gave full credit to the successful structural design of the *Gossamer Condor*. His reservations about fabricating carbon-fiber–reinforced plastic were much more stringent. Standing around their homemade tube machine and spar oven, the *Albatross* builders read with (1) puzzlement and (2) mirth, that "It is not easy to form hollow CFRP profiles with sufficient accuracy to ensure local stability . . . Hot bonding of carbon fibre pre-pregs is obviously beyond the capacity of the home constructor."

Notwithstanding this fiat, MacCready's band of home constructors continued to form and bond carbon-fiber tubes at a rapid rate. By the third week in March they had completed about half the frame of *Albatross 2* and had started on the parts of the irrepressible *Gossamer Penguin*. Their progress was reported to the media on March 19, when the Du Pont Company held a press conference at Hangar 522 and announced its sponsorship of the cross-Channel attempt.

The conference was organized by Jack Conmy, a Du Pont Public Affairs Manager who was assigned to the *Albatross* project, and it was supplied with press handouts of a lavishness hitherto unknown to human-powered flight. Some newsmen took this as a sign of Du Pont's hand on the controls, but nothing could have been further from the truth. Apart from Dick Woodward's valuable insistence on safety, Du Pont offered technical help, advanced materials, and indispensable financial backing — all with good humor and without any strings attached.

During the month of March, the *Gossamer Albatross* made only a few short test flights at Terminal Island, none of them longer than 80 seconds. As part of the new contingency plan, MacCready decided that the team should have some back-up pilots. Dave Saks was an obvious candidate. He was light, strong, and well-coordinated, and he had been the pilot of Taras's *Icarus* HPA; on March 10 he began flying the *Albatross*. Joe Mastropaolo was another potential flyer; although he was nearly twice Dave and Bryan's age, he was in superb physical condition and had a very high power-to-weight ratio. (In fact Joe broke Bryan's absolute power output record on the ergometer a few days before the attempt on the English Channel.) Bryan also scouted his bicycle racing friends for reserve pilots and recommended a young Bakersfield college student named Kirk Giboney to Paul.

On March 12, Sam Durán took a leave of absence from Getty Oil to become the flight director of the *Albatross* project. By the end of the month he convinced Paul that for duration flying the team needed more space and better weather than they had at Terminal Island. On March 30 the *Albatross* was disassembled, packed into its white-and-blue trailer, and test-towed at freeway speed on the police training course with the MacCreadys' GMC van. The van sported a new California license plate: G CONDOR, a present to Paul from Judy. That afternoon the plane was driven up to Shafter Airport to practice flying on familiar and less circumscribed terrain.

The Terminal Island crew were surprised to see the trailer roll back into the hangar late the next day. On its fifth tuning flight at Shafter that morning the plane had crashed again, this time because of a genuine error. Despite the tightened-up safety program, one flying wire end fitting, about the size and shape of a paper clip, had been missed when the plane was checked over. The fitting opened in flight, the wire slipped off its anchor on the outboard starboard wing spar, and the spar broke. The right wing folded up, crumpling the leading edge and three ribs. The fuselage frame and one propeller blade were also broken when the plane hit the runway. This time, however, there were no injuries, and, more important, the team's response was aggressively upbeat. *Fix it and get flying again* was the mood; it felt like the old days.

It took 51 minutes for the crew to assemble the airplane at Shafter, but the trailer was hardly back in the Terminal Island hangar before Ted Ancona and Steve Elliott had the damaged wing panel out and were stripping the covering off the broken section. Bryan and Blaine Rawdon worked on the fuselage, Taras and Janet Grosser rebuilt the canard suspension, and Bill Watson and Dave Saks made a new propeller blade.

The propeller was one component that Paul felt needed improvement. On April 2, while it was being repaired, he mentioned his disenchantment with it to Hewitt Phillips, a modeling and gliding friend, at a soaring symposium. Phillips referred him to Professor Eugene Larrabee, an aerodynamicist at the Massachusetts Institute of Technology who had directed several student human-powered flight projects. When MacCready spoke to him, Larrabee offered to have his students design a computer-optimized cruise propeller for the *Gossamer Albatross*. Paul accepted the offer gratefully. During the next week Hyong Bang, Bob Parks, and Harold Youngren stayed up nights to run some 150 solutions of an algorithm for HPA propeller chord and twist. Their computer time was donated by the M.I.T. Student Information Processing Board. The most promising blade shape they arrived at was 88 percent efficient, and the specifications for it and 30 other related designs were hand-carried to California within a few days. Hewitt Phillips suggested that MacCready use the Eppler 193 model airfoil on the new propeller, because of its proven performance at low Reynolds numbers.

There was still no evidence that the *Gossamer Albatross* could cross San Pedro Harbor, let alone the English Channel, but the mood of the project had switched back to aviation manic. As usual, Paul was worrying several steps ahead; his new preoccupation was, How do we get the planes to England? The airline freight price was $38,000, and Du Pont was reluctant to pay so large a bill. At first there seemed to be several possibilities of free transportation, but they disappeared one by one as various team members called their erstwhile aerospace employers and friends without results. (Boeing's reaction was typical. They listened interestedly when told that the parts of the two *Gossamer Albatross*es and the *Penguin* were large enough to fill the hold of a 747 freighter. Then they asked how much the shipment weighed. "Well, about 200 pounds." There was a long pause. "You mean the three airplanes weigh the same as *one passenger?*" The rest of the call, including much nervous laughter, was used mostly to establish the sobriety of the caller.)

At that point things began to move in a way that made the team feel that the *Albatross* was in tune with the universe; it was like those occasional early flights when the *Condor* would suddenly get up on the step. On April 3, Paul MacCready received a call from Fred Hoerner, the Chairman of the Society of Experimental Test Pilots and Assistant Technical Director of the Naval Flight Test Center. Some weeks earlier Hoerner had asked MacCready to give a speech to the SETP. Paul was too busy at the time, but offered to trade a talk for some help with the transportation problem. Hoerner said he would have a shot at it. After mentioning it at a meeting in Washington, he was approached by the British Air Attaché, R.A.F. Group Captain Tony Woodford. Now Hoerner was calling to say that Woodford had the answer: The Royal Air Force was sending a Lockheed C-130 *Hercules* transport to Nellis Air Force Base in Nevada on May 10, and it would probably have room in it to take the Gossamer aircraft back to England — free.

As if responding to the news, the crew had the *Albatross* repaired and ready to fly again two days later. They also installed a skeletonized two-way radio with a push-to-talk switch for the pilot. The added weight of the radio had been anticipated, but the plane was also getting heavier each time a spar was spliced or a frame tube replaced. It is doubtful that the *Gossamer Albatross* maintained its design weight of 55 pounds (25 kilograms) for more than a few days during its youth; by the time it reached England it was a middle-aged airplane, and like many middle-aged individuals it had gained a significant amount of weight. It had also decreased in size. The redesign of the wing into four detachable sections resulted in a shortening of span from the original 96 feet (29.2 metres) to 93 feet 10 inches (28.6 metres).

On the morning of April 5, the plane was back at Shafter Airport, and the crew took 62 minutes to assemble it and check every single wire and connection. Bryan made three short tuning flights, and on the last one two feet of the drive chain stripped out near the idler wheel. The crew continued testing it with four more push flights, and stopped when the wind came up at 8:17. It took 42 minutes to take the *Albatross* apart and store it in the trailer.

That evening was a reenactment of the *Condor* days at Shafter: At 6 P.M. Taras splices a new chain two pitches longer than the old one, and it is installed with a larger 40-tooth idler sprocket to ease the turning stress. Everyone watches for the green flash at sunset (no luck), and then Ted gives Taras a ride in the Cessna he flew up from Santa Monica. The blue 150 buzzes the hangar in a steep climbing turn (Taras, later: "That wasn't *me*"), and the crew flashes Morse code at it with a spotlight. Dinner is a methodical surfeit at Hodel's; then everyone goes back to Shafter and sits around the trailer listening to Taras play the harmonica. Eventually most people turn in on the wing assembly mat, a 6′ x 30′ (1.8 x 9.1m) piece of flexible foam spread on the apron. Steve sleeps in a blanket in the van — he forgot his sleeping bag — and Bryan and Dave Saks share Bryan's pop tent. At 11:30 Sam Durán drives over to Baskin-Robbins and brings back sundaes for everyone.

Five hours later, Sam is out on the runway measuring the wind speed, and Ted, Taras, and Steve are getting up. The sky is gray-white and the air feels heavy and cold. In the center of runway 34 the wind is veering from north to northwest at about 6 miles (9.6 kilometres) per hour. There is no sound from the pop tent. The assembly mat is moved on to the runway, and the *Albatross* wing sections are eased out of the trailer one by one. After fifteen minutes of coaxing, Janet finally persuades Bryan to give up his sleeping bag. It takes a little over an hour to rig the plane, and by the time it is checked most of the crew has warmed up on the chase bikes. Bill Richardson arrives with his friend Jim Thorpe, who has volunteered the chase car, a red Cadillac convertible with the top down. Bryan is taped into the cockpit and makes a 25-second flight to check the controls. He begins the second flight low; there is a touch at 49 seconds, and a second one at 1′55″. Then the *Albatross* spreads its wings at last: Bryan pedals for 7 minutes and 5 seconds more, for a total flight time of 9 minutes.

The crew is elated. How did it go? everyone wants to know. Not too bad, Allen reports. The cockpit is fogged inside, and both of Bryan's wrists are tired because they have been flexed backward during the flight. We have him hold his hands where they are comfortable and note that the control axis should be rotated forward 30°. He has a red welt on his left palm; the gusset on the pitch control handle will have to be padded. "What about the power?" Sam asks. "About a third [horsepower] on the average, but maybe six-tenths in strong sink." Allen isn't breathing hard, but the *Albatross*'s power band is far too high for a really long flight.

That worrisome finding was confirmed two days later when the

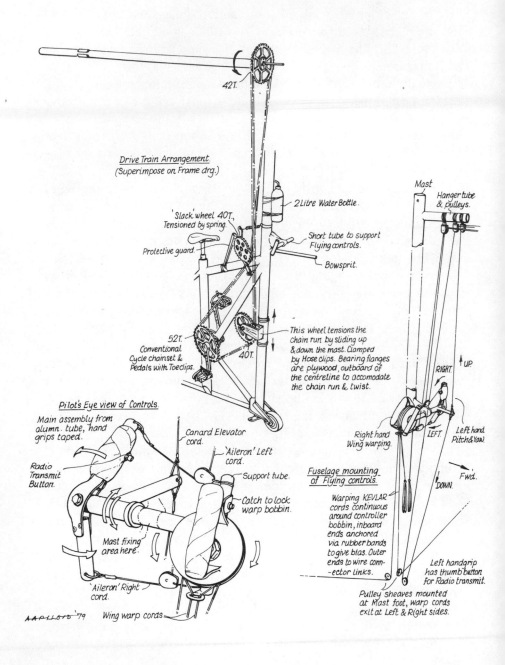

42T.

Drive Train Arrangement.
(Superimpose on Frame drg.)

2 Litre Water Bottle.

'Slack' wheel 40T,
Tensioned by spring.

Short tube to support
Flying controls.

Protective guard.

Bowsprit.

52T.
Conventional
Cycle chainset &
Pedals with Toeclips.

40T.

This wheel tensions the
chain run by sliding up
& down the mast. Clamped
by Hose clips. Bearing flanges
are plywood, outboard of
the centreline to accomodate
the chain run & twist.

Mast

Hanger tube
& pulleys.

RIGHT.   UP.

Pilot's Eye view of Controls.

Main assembly from
alumn. tube, hand
grips taped.

Canard Elevator
cord.

'Aileron' Left
cord.

Radio
Transmit
Button.

Support tube.

Catch to lock
warp bobbin.

Right hand
Wing warping.

LEFT.

Left hand
Pitch & Yaw.

Fuselage mounting
of Flying controls.

Warping KEVLAR
cords continuous
around controller
bobbin, inboard
ends anchored
via rubber bands
to give bias. Outer
ends to wire conn-
-ector links.

Fwd.

DOWN.

Mast fixing
area here.

'Aileron' Right
cord.

Left handgrip
has thumb button
for Radio transmit.

AA LLOYD '79

Wing warp cords

Pulley sheaves mounted
at Mast foot, warp cords
exit at Left & Right sides.

back-up pilots flew at Shafter. Dave Saks and Joe Mastropaolo made short flights in turbulent air, and neither one found the plane particularly easy to pedal or control. Kirk Giboney, the young Bakersfield bicycle racer that Bryan had recommended, piloted the plane for the first time that day. His two straight flights were only 30 and 40 seconds long, but his control was smooth, and he made a good crosswind landing. Ten days later Paul sent him a contract, and he became the last man to join the *Albatross* team before it went to England.

Giboney was 18 years old when he was hired, and he dropped out of his freshman year at Bakersfield College to go on the Channel expedition. He is tall and slender, with pale skin and a thin sensitive face, and the neatly trimmed mustache he wears makes him look even younger. Kirk was racing bicycles when he was 13, and he knew Bryan Allen for seven years. Two months before he soloed the *Albatross,* he began to take flying lessons from Bill Richardson and Sam Durán. He was a good student, and the flight instruction was invaluable; within a few weeks after joining the team Kirk became the principal back-up pilot.

When Ed Shenk first tested his Sonar altimeter in the *Gossamer Albatross,* he examined the airspeed indicator and decided that he could improve on it as well. On Saturday, April 14, the crew installed Shenk's new optical airspeed sensor, and a lightweight dual cockpit instrument that displayed both speed and altitude. That evening Bryan flew the *Albatross* for 15 minutes and 45 seconds, covering a distance of 3.2 miles (5.1 kilometres). It was a new world record, and would have been cause for celebration, except that the flight revealed many more problems than it solved. One of the simpler ones was underlined in the flight test log: *"We need motorcycles!"* The plane's flaws couldn't be fixed by a bike rental, however.

First of all, Bryan was worn out when he landed. The flying power was far higher than the 0.25 horsepower predicted by tow tests and flights the previous summer. It was certainly too high for a Channel flight. The controls had also deteriorated. Turns were mushy, and Bryan reported the "Climb response very poor, not

[*opposite*] 10. The drive train and flying controls of the *Gossamer Albatross.*

like it used to be." The drive chain kept slipping off the sprockets, and although the crew was by now expert at identifying "good chain," they had trouble finding lengths without internal voids.

The cockpit ventilation was so inadequate that Bryan could barely see through the fogged window when he landed. Since Allen transpires about 1 litre of moisture per hour during hard pedaling, Sam Durán had been worrying about moisture buildup in the cockpit. Before this flight he fastened tufts of red yarn to the inside of the fuselage covering to indicate the airflow. Most of the tufts hung limply the whole time; there was no through airflow except in a small area above the pilot's head. Despite these difficulties there were a few long stretches where Bryan reported that the "cruise power seems O.K."

The crew could handle the more obvious problems. Larger air vents with adjustable flaps were cut in the front and rear of the cockpit, and a long tube was installed to carry the pilot's exhalations out the rear of the fuselage. The new speedometer/altimeter was calibrated, and the turn and warp controls were rebalanced. The critical problem was power, and it seemed almost as elusive as turning the *Condor* had been. There were clues, those mysterious stretches where the plane flew so smoothly and easily, but the design team would not recognize the magnitude of the obstacle — turbulence drag — until months later, after the problem had been surmounted by persistence and good luck.

During these flight tests the construction crew at Hangar 522 was working on a new Kevlar-skinned propeller built to the M.I.T. specifications. They also built two more trailers to carry the parts of the *Gossamer Albatross 2,* now about 80 percent completed, and the *Gossamer Penguin.* The idea was that each plane would be driven up to Shafter for testing as it was finished, and then transported to England in its own trailer. The flight crew, however, was beginning to feel that even Shafter Airport was cramped for the distances that the *Albatross* had to master. Once again the Terminal Island Irregulars tapped their intelligence network to find a large unobstructed flying site with calm air. The one they came up with was Harper Dry Lake, 12 square miles (31 square kilometres) of flat, desolate, sun-baked clay northwest of Barstow in San Bernardino County. The nearest wide spot in the road was Lockhart; the only landmarks were two wells and Lynx Cat Mountain four miles to the southeast.

April 20 was the first day of testing at Harper. At 6:30 A.M. the temperature on the lake bed was already 64.4°F (18°C), and the wind speed less than 1 mile (1.6 kilometres) per hour. At 6:39 Kirk Giboney took off and flew for 17 minutes, another world HPA record. Sam Durán tracked the plane at 12 miles (19.3 kilometres) per hour. Kirk was followed by Dave Saks, who flew several 3-minute flights with a camera mounted in the cockpit. (These flights, which would have merited champagne at the early stages of the *Condor* program, are merely marked "short.")

The next morning at 5:30, Bryan Allen took off in still air, determined to log a flight that the team would consider "long." Sam, following the plane on a moped, noted that the left wingtip was fluttering, and that the wing gap covers and the propeller blades were wrinkling in flight. Bryan's time was 18 minutes, 38 seconds; it was a record again, but he was exhausted. The team had now learned that the R.A.F. transport would be at Nellis Air Force Base on April 27 — less than one week away. It was obvious that the offer of free shipment was wasted if the longest flight that the *Albatross* could make was 18 minutes.

The team's response to the problem was almost instinctive by now: Tighten up everything. They went over the plane piece by piece, lightening, streamlining, sealing gaps, and tightening the Mylar. The new propeller was finish-sanded and polished, ready to be fitted to the plane. With its slim, tapered gray blades, it looked more potent and less toylike than the transparent yellow-and-orange paddles that had moved the *Condor* and the *Albatross* up to now.

On April 25, at 4 A.M., the *Albatross* was assembled at what had become a small camp on Harper Dry Lake. Erection took an hour and a half, and every part and connection was checked twice. At 5:48 Bryan took off in calm air and immediately reported that the cruise power felt very low; he estimated it as 0.28 to 0.3 horsepower. The propeller turned smoothly at a steady 97 revolutions per minute, and the plane settled into a groove at an altitude of 9 feet (2.7 metres). Sam's moped gave out after a few minutes, and the crew followed the *Albatross* in the van at 10 miles (16 kilometres) per hour.

By 6:13 the team was aware that the *Gossamer Albatross* was on the step as no human-powered aircraft had ever been before. The fuselage was slightly bulged, pressurized by the warm air inside it. Over the radio Sam asked Bryan how he was doing. "Bring on Daedalus. I'll whop him," was the cocky and history-conscious answer. Allen was flying in a large triangle, and as the plane floated along the crew members had time to make subtle and detailed observations of the airplane's parts. More small changes were logged in this one flight than in the twenty that preceded it. Bryan pedaled on tirelessly; at 30 minutes he reported that sweat had begun to run into his eyes.

Jack Lambie has a magical memory of that flight. On the morning of April 25 he was flying his Fournier motor glider up to Harper Dry Lake from his home airport at Chino. As he approached the lake he saw, far below him, the slow, deliberate procession of the transparent *Gossamer Albatross* followed by its attendants. The shadow of the airplane was projected on the featureless clay beneath it, and Jack had the sensation that he was deep underwater, watching some strange marine creature floating over a vast, silent abyssal plain.

The flight went on and on. At one point Allen heard a popping noise, and noted that the wing warp guide had broken, which caused a slight mushiness in the controls. Sweat burning his eyes was still the major discomfort, although his left hand was beginning to ache from the pressure of the pitch control, and the seat had started to overheat. At 40 minutes a slight headwind came up, and Allen made a 180° turn to run downwind. Ten minutes later both his glasses and the bottom of the fuselage were beginning to fog despite the improved ventilation. At 58 minutes the temperature inside the cockpit had risen from 60° to 71°F (15.6° to 21.7°C). Bryan made a right turn and then another sweeping 180° turn that took 47 seconds to complete. At 6:56 he announced that he was hungry and thirsty, and was starting to land. When the *Gossamer Albatross* touched down, it had flown 1 hour, 9 minutes, and 3 seconds — by a tremendous margin the longest time that a man had ever supported himself in the air solely with his own power. Bryan was far from exhausted, and he was sure that with food and water he could have flown another one to two hours.

After a 9-minute flight by Kirk Giboney, the *Albatross* was dis-assembled and stowed in its trailer. As soon as the crew reached a telephone the news of the long flight was spread to the rest of the Gossamer team members, together with the word we had been waiting for: the Channel expedition was Go. That same day Bryan and Sam towed the *Albatross* trailer 170 miles (275 kilometres) from Harper Dry Lake to Nellis Air Force Base in North Las Vegas, Nevada. The next day the *Albatross 2* and the *Gossamer Penguin* arrived at Nellis in their trailers after a 300-mile (480-kilometre) drive from Terminal Island.

On the morning of April 27 — the day that the R.A.F. *Hercules* was due to arrive — the nine members of the Gossamer loading crew met the Thunderbirds, the pilots of the U.S. Air Force's crack exhibition flying team. The team's information officer offered the use of the Thunderbirds' hangar to store the HPAs until their transport arrived. The offer was accepted with thanks. The tired and mostly unshaven Gossamer crew were awed to find that the hangar was kept like a hospital, and that even the floor was painted with glistening white epoxy.

It was late afternoon when R.A.F. C-130 ASCOT 5681 landed at Nellis. Jack Lambie spotted the big brown-and-green camou-flaged plane between two hangars, but he was taken aback to find that not one of its weary crew members knew the first thing about the *Gossamer Albatross*. The only thing they did know was that they had to pick up several tons of ammunition, which would be lashed down in the center of the C-130's hold so it could be jetti-soned in case of emergency, and ferry it back to the United King-dom. That meant that none of the Gossamer team's trailers would fit into the transport. After a series of agitated telephone calls the matter was straightened out by Fred Hoerner and the British Mili-tary Attaché in Washington, D.C. The team was given permission to load their airplanes, their tools, and Sam Durán, but not the trailers, for the flight to England.

For the next five hours Bryan, Sam, Jim Burke, Norm Kozma, Jack Lambie, Jeff Stephenson, Sterling Stoll, Scott Strom, and John Volk struggled to fit the fragile parts of the three human-powered planes into the hold of the Herky Bird. The wing panels were hung 6 deep from the ceiling of the transport, but the fuselage frame of the *Penguin* was broken accidentally, and the foam leading edges and Mylar covering of the wings were damaged. Twenty-two cartons of tools and building materials had to be deferred to a commercial air freight flight because of the ammunition shipment. The highest priority boxes were numbered, labeled, and fitted into the corners of the hold like a three-dimensional jigsaw puzzle. (When the C-130 arrived in England Paul noted that the "packing in plane was phenomenal!") Early the following afternoon the crowded transport took off, only to return an hour later with an electrical fire in the cabin. Repairs were completed that day, and on April 29, at 10:47 Pacific Daylight Time, ASCOT 5681 left for Atlanta, Georgia, on the first leg of its four-day flight home. In addition to its crew and 6000 pounds (2727 kilograms) of live mortar shells, it carried the flight test chief of the *Gossamer Albatross* team, and the three human-powered planes that represented more than a year's work by him and his teammates.

14

Migrants

The Winds of Kent

SHORTLY AFTER ASCOT 5681 left Dover, Delaware, for England on May 1, 1979, the Royal Air Force copilot took a picture of Sam Durán flying the big transport from the left (Captain's) seat. Sam is wearing a smile of utter delight — he looks like a cherub in earphones. Judging by his expression, the stick time was adequate compensation for the C-130's noisy 340-mph (547-km/h) leapfrog across the United States. From Las Vegas the plane flew to Atlanta, Georgia; from Atlanta to Tampa, Florida; from Tampa to Pope Air Force Base in North Carolina; from Pope to Dover, Delaware, and from Dover, finally, across the Atlantic to England. Its estimated time of arrival at R.A.F. Lyneham, near Swindon, was 1:30 A.M. on May 2.

One of the last people that Sam saw before the C-130 took off from Nellis Air Force Base on April 29 was Jim Burke, leaving for North Las Vegas Airport. For Jim, it was like a space age blink: Piper Cherokee Six to Los Angeles; Laker Airways DC-10 to Gatwick Airport; British Rail express to Swindon; car to R.A.F. Lyneham. Paul MacCready, Jim Burke, Tom Horton, Bryan Allen, Kirk Giboney, and cameraman Louis Prézelin flew to London on the same Laker flight, arriving on April 30. With the help of Don Billett and Margret Clarke of Du Pont U.K., they arranged to rent two trailer trucks, and set out to find a base for the *Albatross* expedition somewhere in Kent before May 2.

The next morning it snowed in London, and Paul and Jim drove through a cold drizzle to Lympne ("Lim") Airport, from which Jim had flown years before, and where they had been led to expect the *Albatross* could be hangared. They found that in the intervening time it had been renamed Ashford, expanded mightily, and then abandoned — shades of Mojave. The *Albatross* project could have fitted into a corner of one of the huge empty hangars, but the owners refused to consider it. A sympathetic guard mentioned that there was a parachuting school on the east side of the field; perhaps they could help? Burke and MacCready, who were thinking about leaky tents at this point, drove over there, and met the first of many wonderful new friends.

The school director was Alex Black, a retired Captain of Sappers. His erstwhile occupation was parachuting at night with explosives and scuba gear, ditching the chutes, and swimming under things to blow them up. Black had given up this typically British sport to run a parachuting club in Kent, and he knew every airfield in the south of England. Within a few minutes he was telephoning generals, and a half hour later he, Paul, and Jim were flying over Kent in an old Percival EP.9 *Prospector,* prospecting. The flight was followed by a splendid lunch at Upper Otter Pool, the Blacks' sixteenth-century farmhouse near Sellindge.

By the time the trio returned to Lympne, the Old Boy network had worked its well-oiled magic: Alex turned from the telephone with a smile to say that the *Gossamer Albatross* team would be welcome at R.A.F. Manston. It was near Ramsgate, barely a mile from the coast of Kent, and there was a small but modern hangar available. Paul and Jim were on their way there while Black was still talking to the base CO, Wing Commander Colin Campbell.

At 4:30 that afternoon Burke and MacCready were welcomed to Manston by Wing Commander Campbell, who detailed Flight Lieutenant Vernon Gough, an electrical engineer, to be their guide. Gough showed them the hangar, which was quickly emptied of the snow blowers and grounds maintenance equipment stored in it. It was large enough for the partially assembled *Albatross 1,* as well as the components of the other two planes. "All great," Paul wrote in his notebook.

Colin Campbell was to be the *Albatross*'s landlord for the next six weeks, and the team could not have found a more thoughtful and good-humored host. With a fair complexion and sandy hair, he looked type-cast for the part of a Royal Air Force Officer, but we later learned that he had been born in Portsmouth, and was a renegade from a Royal Navy family. Despite his youthful looks,

Campbell's flying record included everything from Gloucester Meteor and F-86 jets to high-altitude reconnaissance over sensitive territory in the English Electric Canberra. (He received a discreet Queen's Commendation for that tour.)

Campbell is both flexible and used to Americans, but he remembers being amused after he offered the hangar at Manston, and Paul and Jim asked him, "Okay for this evening?" Given the assurance that it was, they continued their rapid carom across England, leaving for Swindon by train at 5:20, and arriving there at 11 P.M. that night.

Two and a half hours later, ASCOT 5681 rolled to a halt in front of a hangar at R.A.F. Lyneham, and its four 4000 horsepower Allison turboprops whined down to silence. Sam leaned out the window and waved; there on the ramp, freezing cold, were Paul, Jim, Bryan, and Kirk. The C-130 was towed into the hangar, and for the next five hours the crew unloaded the plane and transferred everything to the two waiting trailer rigs. At 6:30 A.M. they went to a Swindon hotel for a brief sleep (Jim was so tired by this time that he was sure the beautiful reddish glow on the horizon was sunset), and then Bryan, Sam, Jim, and Kirk left for R.A.F. Manston by train. The trailer trucks arrived at Manston on time at 3 P.M., and the crew was there 40 minutes later to unload them into the hangar. Paul drove down to Manston at eight that evening, and everyone collapsed in a Ramsgate bed & breakfast. The next morning Burke and MacCready drove up to Gatwick Airport, turned in their rented car at 11:15, and boarded a 12:15 Laker flight back to Los Angeles. The people they met in England were astonished by their pace, but even Jim's long tour of military service didn't alert him to the beginning of a pattern that he should have recognized: *Hurry Up and Wait*. Burke doesn't remember what time it was when he woke up at home in Sierra Madre; he does remember that the first thought he had was, "This is going to be really, really good."

Paul felt the same sense of excitement, but some dispiriting news was waiting for him in Los Angeles: Jack Franklin, a member of the *Gossamer Condor* team, had been killed in a hang gliding accident at Sylmar, California, on May 2, the day that the *Albatross* reached England. Ironically, the accident occurred at low altitude; Franklin was an outstanding high-altitude soarer, and had ther-

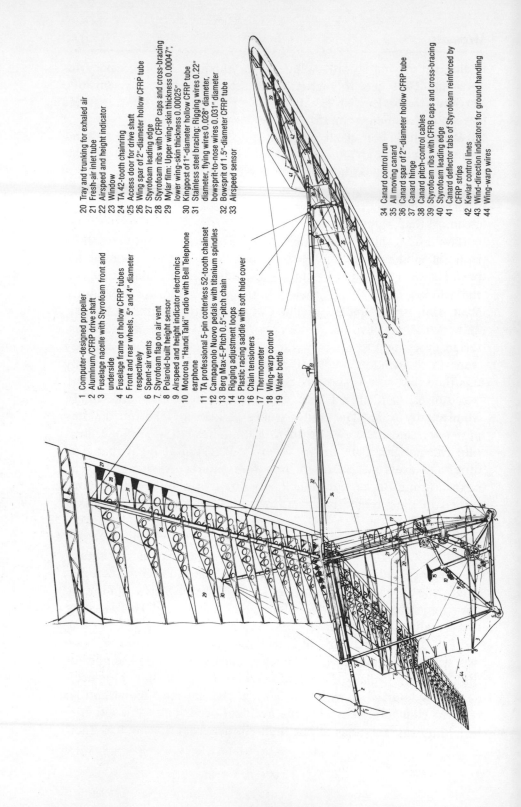

1 Computer-designed propeller
2 Aluminum/CFRP drive shaft
3 Fuselage nacelle with Styrofoam front and underside
4 Fuselage frame of hollow CFRP tubes
5 Front and rear wheels, 5" and 4" diameter respectively
6 Spent-air vents
7 Styrofoam flap on air vent
8 Polaroid-built height sensor
9 Airspeed and height indicator electronics
10 Motorola 'Handi Talki' radio with Bell Telephone earphone
11 TA professional 5-pin cotterless 52-tooth chainset
12 Campagnolo Nuovo pedals with titanium spindles
13 Berg Max-E-Pitch 0.5"-pitch chain
14 Rigging adjustment loops
15 Plastic racing saddle with soft hide cover
16 Chain tensioners
17 Thermometer
18 Wing-warp control
19 Water bottle

20 Tray and trunking for exhaled air
21 Fresh-air inlet tube
22 Airspeed and height indicator
23 Window
24 TA 42-tooth chainring
25 Access door for drive shaft
26 Wing spar of 2"-diameter hollow CFRP tube
27 Styrofoam leading edge
28 Styrofoam ribs with CFRP caps and cross-bracing
29 Mylar film: Upper wing-skin thickness 0.00047", lower wing-skin thickness 0.00025"
30 Kingpost of 1"-diameter hollow CFRP tube
31 Stainless steel bracing: Rigging wires 0.22" diameter, flying wires 0.028" diameter, bowsprit-to-nose wires 0.031" diameter
32 Bowsprit of 1.5"-diameter CFRP tube
33 Airspeed sensor

34 Canard control run
35 All moving canard
36 Canard spar of 2"-diameter hollow CFRP tube
37 Canard hinge
38 Canard pitch-control cables
39 Styrofoam ribs with CFRB caps and cross-bracing
40 Styrofoam leading edge
41 Canard deflector tabs of Styrofoam reinforced by CFRP strips
42 Kevlar control lines
43 Wind-direction indicators for ground handling
44 Wing-warp wires

malled up to 19,000 feet (5791 metres) at Telluride, Colorado, not long before. In one eulogy his friend Lynn Miller wrote that she was sure that Jack was "that tiny speck you saw thousands of feet above takeoff, heading into the distance on some incredible cross country flight . . . and now you don't even have to bother setting up your glider." For the Gossamer Squadron, it was a sad reminder that aviation, in any form, is a stern master.

As master or servant, it is usually swift, and perhaps it was appropriate that there was little time for the crew to dwell on the lesson. Within a few days the remaining boxes of HPA parts and materials were on their way to London via air freight. Soon afterward Jim and Lin Burke and Paul and Judy MacCready returned to England, together with all the other members of the *Albatross* team except Larry McNay and Parker MacCready (who had to finish school before coming over). By the second week of May the team was berthed in a cluster of small hotels in Ramsgate, Du Pont had installed a message center and public relations office in Deal, and Tom Horton and the film crew (Joe Thompson, Joe Thompson Jr., Louis Prézelin, and Tony Zapata) were ensconced in a spacious flat over a handsome old pub in St. Margaret's at Cliffe, a few miles down the coast of Kent. The weather was unseasonably warm, and the *Albatross* was soon set up, with 3 of its 4 wing panels assembled, in the R.A.F. Manston hangar to prepare for the qualifying flights required for the Kremer Cross-Channel Competition. During this tune-up all of the plane's instruments were reweighed. Here is the avionics package of the *Gossamer Albatross 1:*

2-way radio and instrument electronics:	320.3 grams	
Airspeed and altitude meters:	210.8	
Airspeed transducer:	39.7	
Acoustic altitude transducer:	48.2	
Cables and connectors:	56.7	
Total Weight:	(23.8 ounces)	675.7 grams

Neither the airspeed meter nor the altimeter was connected on May 9 when the *Gossamer Albatross* took off from English soil

[*opposite*] 11. A perspective of the *Gossamer Albatross* as it was erected at R.A.F. Manston.

for the first time. Bryan made two tuning flights into a variable 5–9-mile (8–14.5-kilometre)-per-hour wind. The first flight was about 5 minutes, the second 2 minutes and 51 seconds. The right wing showed marked polyhedral during these tests, and was re-rigged in preparation for the official qualification flight, which Sam Durán was confident could be made the following day.

The balmy weather held overnight, and at 4:15 A.M. on May 10 the wind at Manston was less than 5 mph (8 km/h) from the east. A number of R.A.F. officers were up with the Americans to watch the *Albatross* fly. Flight Lieutenant Vernon Gough had been designated an official AOPA observer; he was to witness that the plane could attain a height of 2 metres, and could make a flight of either 2 minutes' or 400 metres' duration. Bryan made an un-successful attempt to take off from an uphill apron and then flew a 2-minute test hop from a more level section of taxiway.

His third flight was declared an official attempt. The sun was a small yellow ball filtered through a layer of cirrus cloud on the horizon when Allen took off toward the east. He flew to the wind-sock at the end of the northern main taxiway, made a 180° turn, pedaled back to the hangar, flew over the 2-metre-height bar, and coasted to a landing. His flight lasted 4 minutes and 25 seconds, and surpassed all of the Kremer Competition requirements handily.

Kirk Giboney had also warmed up to qualify the plane. A few minutes after Bryan landed, Kirk took off again, and flew the entire length of the Manston main runway. En route he flushed a panic-stricken hare who, although used to jet engines, apparently thought that the silent *Albatross* was a new species of predatory bird. At the end of the runway Giboney made a U-turn, flew back to the taxiway junction, pedaled the length of the taxiway, crossed the T-bar, and turned 90° to touch down directly in front of the hangar. His airborne time was 9 minutes and 24 seconds, which became the new United Kingdom record for human-powered flight. After Kirk landed Lieutenant Gough confirmed in writing that the *Gossamer Albatross* had satisfied the Kremer qualifying re-quirements twice, and ". . . on both occasions landed without dam-age." As MacCready the optimist predicted, the first hurdle had been a piece of cake.

On May 14, a very warm day, Jim Burke went up to London

in a proper suit and tie and perspired his way from office to office to disentangle the team's 22 boxes of air-freighted parts and materials from U.K. customs. Human-powered aircraft parts were not, it seemed, listed in any British duty schedules. Eventually Jim pried them loose by writing a large check which the customs officer assured him would be refunded if we exported the stuff again. (As with the Kremer Prize entry fee, this actually happened.)

After the arrival of its missing tools and materials, the team split into several components. The pilots continued their training, bicycling on the roads of Thanet and working out on the ergometer in the Manston hangar under Joe Mastropaolo's direction. The building crew, which included everyone not occupied elsewhere, tightened up the *Albatross,* and worked on the *Albatross 2* and the *Gossamer Penguin.* The boat group, headed by Jim Burke, tried to solve the problems of marine escort, which were beginning to seem the most intractable of the lot.

The plan was to charter a large power boat equipped with radar and radio communications to set the course and lead the flotilla across the Channel. The *Albatross* was to follow the command boat at a distance of approximately 1000 feet (300 metres), and it was to be accompanied by three Zodiac inflatables, one immediately behind the fuselage and one abaft of each wing tip. Each Zodiac would carry two-way radios and wet-suited crew members who could rescue the pilot if the need arose. In addition, the crew of the center boat was to be equipped with hard hats and other gear that would allow the *Albatross* to land right on the boat, and one wing crew would have a rod and line that they could hook on to a fuselage shackle to tow the plane to shore.

Tom Horton had been working on the escort equipment for many weeks in California. Before the team left for Europe each rescue swimmer was fitted with a complete wet suit loaned by U.S. Divers Corporation in Santa Ana. Zodiac of France and America offered to supply the escort boats free, and Mercury Marine supplied eight new manual-starting 50-horsepower (37-kilowatt) outboard motors to the team's base at Dover, to use as long as we needed them. (These were recommended by Mercury as their most reliable motor for the job.)

Because of the Cinque Ports marine tradition, Paul MacCready had assumed, reasonably but incorrectly, that it would be easy to charter any number of large, fast power boats on the coast of Kent. Soon after his arrival in England, Tom Horton scoured the Kent ports and chartered the *Tartan Gem,* a 50-foot (15.2-metre) Colin Mudie–designed cruiser as a lead boat for the *Albatross* fleet. The *Tartan Gem* was owned by Norman Johnson, a Canterbury automobile dealer, and captained by Bernard Iverson, the proprietor of the Dover Yacht Yard. Her helmsman/navigator was Arthur Liddon, a lifeboatman from Dover. With roomy cabins fore and aft, a big bridge with radar, radios, and instruments, and twin GMC diesels that reputedly drove her at 18 knots, she looked ideal for the purpose. When the case proved otherwise, it was very difficult to find a replacement.

MacCready had also assumed that, given a calm day, it would be straightforward to put to sea on the day of the Channel attempt. Neither he nor anyone else on the team had anticipated the 20- to 30-foot (6- to 9-metre) tides along the Kent coast. On the crew's first trip to Folkestone, they were astonished to see a whole harbor full of boats sitting on the mud, their bulwarks propped up with poles. A few hours later the same boats were floating serenely in what looked like a normal anchorage. The Wellington Dock at Dover, where the *Albatross* boats were based, has a lock-gated harbor. The only times that boats can enter and leave are near high tide, and the gates are *shut* at published high tide with a great ringing of bells. This meant that the tide tables became the team's bible for the next month. The heavy boat traffic in and out of the lock gates also meant that in addition to our own transceivers, waterproof (and expensive) VHF radios were necessary equipment for all of the Zodiacs.

The first boat drill was planned for May 17. On the 16th, one Mark III, one Mark IV, and two Mark V Zodiacs, and the eight Mercury outboards were delivered to the Wellington Dock in Dover. That same day the American Embassy in London held a reception and press conference for the *Albatross* team. The plane was erected (with 3 of its 4 wing panels) above a reflecting pool in the lobby of the embassy. Between the elegant setting, and the suits and ties of the crew — some of them rented from Moss Brothers — the scene had a kind of unreal quality. Jim Ascher, the embassy information officer, shepherded the team around smoothly, and His Excellency Kingman Brewster, the American Ambassador to the Court of St. James, made a short speech in which he mentioned that he had been an airplane modeler as a boy. Maurice Brennan, the Chairman of the Man-Powered Aircraft Group Committee, represented the Royal Aeronautical Society, Don Kremer stood in for his father, and Paul and Bryan fielded the mostly good-natured questions of several hundred newsmen.

Du Pont was present in force: Dick and Joanne Woodward and Jack and Terese Conmy came over from Wilmington, and Jim Foght, the managing director of Du Pont U.K. Ltd., headed the British contingent. For many of the Albatrossers, this was a first introduction to two people who were to become invaluable helpers, treasured friends, and virtually members of the team: Don Billett, the public affairs manager of Du Pont U.K., and his multilingual and multi-talented secretary, Margret Clarke.

The crew returned to Ramsgate full of enthusiasm, to find that Jim and Lin Burke, who had stayed in Dover to run in the new outboard motors for the planned boat drill, had spent a miserable day wrenching their shoulder muscles. Only one engine had started, and the U.K. Mercury distributor was sending a technician from Poole — a five-hour drive — the next morning. The Zodiac part of the boat drill, at least, would have to be postponed.

The morning of May 17 was the *Albatross* team's first official meeting with the Dover port and Royal National Lifeboat Institution officers, Her Majesty's Coast Guard, the crew of the *Tartan Gem,* and others concerned with the marine aspects of the Channel attempt. It was held at the Royal Cinque Ports Yacht Club in Dover, and despite all the uniforms and formalities, went very well. Partway through the meeting Steve Elliott slipped in and whispered to Jim Burke that he and the Mercury mechanic had unstuck some poppet valves and started four engines in five minutes. Jim's normally cheerful face lit up for the first time in twenty-four hours, and the Zodiac drill was rescheduled for the following day.

After the meeting, part of the team boarded the *Tartan Gem* for speed tests in the Dover outer harbor. When the gates opened and the boat was given permission to pass out, the Channel was choppy in bright sunshine. With 16 people aboard — the number that Paul planned to have during the flight — the *Tartan Gem* rolled and yawed back and forth four times between the ½-nautical-mile markers on the Dover breakwater. All four runs were disappointing. The hull was not particularly seakindly, and the best speed was 11.7 knots (21.7 km/hr). That was not enough to keep up with the *Albatross* if there was a tailwind, and left scant reserve for maneuvering if there was not. The owner also disagreed with Paul and Jim's plan to use radar and a sequential plot to avoid ship traffic. The meeting ended on a discordant note, and Burke started worrying again.

If the *Tartan Gem* was a disappointment, the Zodiacs were a robust surprise. Although Louis Prézelin and Tom Horton had assured MacCready that during their years with Jacques Cousteau the inflatables proved equal to anything asked of them, some of the team members (and some of the Port authorities) regarded them as "rubber boats" fit only for paddling around the beach. On May 18 the Dover Harbour Patrol Boat led the four Zodiacs out through the crowded ship channel to an area east of the harbor. In bright wind and chop, the *Albatross* boat crews threw the inflatables around in circles, across the wake of the patrol boat, and raced back and forth with their 50-horsepower motors wide open. By the end of the test they were mightily impressed; the "rubber boats" were actually tough, maneuverable, seaworthy craft, and increased the team's confidence greatly.

Each time the Wellington Dock gates clanged shut behind the *Albatross* flotilla, an unconscious frown would cross Paul Mac-Cready's face. By this time the search for a takeoff point had eliminated Dover, and Paul was worried that the boats would be trapped in the harbor when the decision was made to fly. The most promising site for the plane to take off from was an area called the Warren, 5.6 miles (9 kilometres) west-southwest of Dover, and just north of Folkestone. The British Rail line parallels the coast not far above the beach here, and the shore curves sharply in below it. To prevent the chalk from eroding any further, a large groined concrete pad was built at the cliff base some years ago. The whole area is administered by British Rail, under the supervision of an engineer named Sid Turner and his assistant Bill Adams.

First, there was the question of permission: Could we take off from the Warren? Second, while the pad was not a convenient place to get to, there was a brick storage shed on it, used as a depot by an oil-spill laboratory. Could we store the disassembled *Albatross* there until we were ready to fly? Sid Turner speaks slowly and quietly, but it took only a few minutes in his cozy hut on the cliffside above the Warren to learn that both he and Bill Adams were ex-R.A.F. aviators. More remarkably, both of Turner's parents appeared as children in the famous 1909 photograph of Louis Blériot's landing on the grounds of Dover Castle after the first airplane flight across the Channel. A human-powered cross-Channel flight attempt? Sid made it seem as though nothing would be more welcome or easy to arrange.

May 18 was Paul and Judy MacCready's twenty-second wedding anniversary. Ann and Raymond Humphreys, the owners of the St. Hilary Private Hotel in Ramsgate where most of the team was staying, put on a gala dinner to celebrate the event. Parker MacCready and Larry McNay arrived to complete the team, and Paul confirmed that the Warren would definitely be the takeoff point. He also announced that the team would move down to Folkestone to be closer to it.

This decision was greeted with mixed feelings, since by now Ramsgate almost seemed like home. At Manston various team members had been treated to lager and lunch in the Officers' Mess by Wing Commander Campbell and Squadron Leader Robin Spooner, and Squadron Leader Paddy Brown had made us welcome in the comfortable fug of his cadet headquarters. Many of the R.A.F. officers were on a first-name basis with the team, and their wives were wont to come out to the *Albatross* hangar and see how things were going. (The project had also had a spit-and-polish visit from Vice Air-Marshal Sir Philip Lagesen.) Despite these thoroughly English adaptations and the reluctance of the Humphreys to give up Dave Saks, the move was made, and by May 19 the team was resettled in a string of bed & breakfasts along Wear Bay Road in Folkestone.

Three photographers came with us: Don Monroe, who had documented the career of the *Gossamer Condor,* and Otis Imboden and Jim Sugar, who were on assignment from *National Geographic.* Otis, an old acquaintance of Jim Burke, had directed much of the

U.S. moon rocket photography from Cape Kennedy and was a sailor and aviation buff; he soon became a helpful adjunct to the team. Perhaps it was Jim Sugar who said that it felt like bad karma to move; certainly the weather felt that way. Day after day the team woke to the wind howling along Wear Bay Road, interspersed with pelting rain. Off the Folkestone cliffs the Channel surged and smoked, and ferocious gray waves broke over the seaward face of the Warren. There was not a chance of flying.

On the morning of May 21, Paul, jogging with Joe Mastropaolo, hit a tilted paving slab wrong, twisting his foot sharply. "Run on it," Joe suggested, but the more Paul ran, the worse it hurt. Jack Conmy had now found the team a resident physician, Dr. Ingrid Dodd of Deal. She had served on a number of ocean liners, and was a specialist in immersion survival. Ingrid inspected Paul's ankle, popped him into a car, and drive him off to an orthopedic specialist in Canterbury. He came back on crutches, with a cast on his foot and a broken bone in his ankle. If there was ever a time when Mac-Cready's unquenchable optimism stood up, it was now. He refused help, insisted on hauling around his huge leather shoulder bag full of papers, and made a number of exceedingly bad jokes about his cast. Only when he was caught unawares, pulling himself up the stairs to his room, did the New England stoic underneath show through.

The *Tartan Gem* situation had not improved, and a meeting with Captain Peter White, the Dover Harbourmaster, impressed on everyone the need for a fast and reliable lead boat. By this time more than a hundred media people from various countries were following the team around, and their camera and television crews had staked out every reasonably fast power yacht on the Kent coast. On one foray, Paul and Jim approached the officers of the Royal Temple Yacht Club in Ramsgate. Though kept politely at arms' length, they were introduced to a yacht broker named Roderick Oates, who told them not to worry, that he would solve their problem in a few days.

On several of those days the team sent envoys to France to inspect landing sites and to make contact with the French maritime authorities. It was soon obvious that the only practical beaches for a landing lay between the small seaside village of Wissant, about

10 miles (16 kilometres) southwest of Calais, and Cap Gris-Nez, 3.7 miles (6 kilometres) farther in the same direction. Cap Gris-Nez ("Cape Gray-Nose") is the site of a major French Coast Guard station for controlling the Channel ship traffic. We were going to need an introduction to its commandant, and once again, a few phone calls were all it took for the aeronautical Mafia to unearth a new set of advocates and friends.

Monsieur Jean Louf is a pilot, a bon vivant, and a builder of ultralight aircraft. He is also Chef d'Exploitation, Chambre de Commerce de Calais, a title with even more influence than its length implies. Daniel Seité, the Press Attaché of the Calais Chambre de Commerce, is Louf's friend and colleague; both are frustrated race drivers. The rides they gave us from Calais to Cap Gris-Nez and back made a human-powered Channel flight seem like a cozy chat by the fireside. A few words from Jean Louf established the same atmosphere with the French authorities. In France, the Channel is *La Manche* — the sleeve. After we were introduced by Louf, M. Poupeville, the manager of the CROSSMA (*C*entre *R*égional *Op*érationnel de *S*auvetage et *S*urveillance *MA*nche) station at Cap Gris-Nez, and his assistant, M. Leborgne, offered us advice, charts, radar plots, and the hospitality of their post whenever we needed it.

The French connection was firmly established, but thus far the team's envoys had traveled to and from France only on large ferries and hovercraft. On May 24, a boat drill was planned in which the little *Albatross* fleet would cross to Cap Gris-Nez, led by the *Tartan Gem*. The day dawned bright and clear, with a moderate breeze. The flotilla was cleared to leave Dover on the noon tide, but because of heavy incoming ship traffic, Dover Port Control kept the boats circling in the harbor for an hour. During that hour the wind slowly rose to 25 knots, and when the Zodiacs finally cleared the breakwater it was into the kind of conditions that the Channel is famous for: a steep, breaking sea, whipped by shrieking spray-laden winds. The *Tartan Gem* bucked and wallowed, and the Zodiacs leaped from wave to wave, their propellers out of water half the time. In a few minutes Jim Burke, Otis Imboden, and Louis Prézelin reached the same conclusion independently and slowed their engines, but it took a half hour before the *Tartan Gem* came around and the boats straggled back into the harbor.

Although the crew was even more impressed with the inflatables, the rehearsal could hardly be called a success. A few hours after it was aborted, Roderick Oates raised everyone's spirits by keeping his promise and producing a splendid new lead boat. It was the *Lady Ellen Elizabeth,* a 36-foot (11-metre) twin diesel Moonraker with a top speed of 20 knots, radar, and all of the necessary radios. Her owner, John Ward of Sandwich, refused to accept any compensation other than the fun of being in on the flight. (In fact when Ward was around it was hard for an *Albatross* team member to get a hand on a lunch or dinner check.) Ward's crew consisted of John Groat, the Sandwich Quaymaster, and Frank Booton, an experienced sailboat navigator.

The addition of the *Lady Ellen Elizabeth* enlarged our squadron to six boats, but it was far outstripped by the press fleet, which was now up to about fifteen. Dick Woodward was very apprehensive about the conflicting goals of the media (coverage at any cost) and our flight (safety and a successful crossing). A conference of all the boat captains involved was organized at the Royal Cinque Ports Yacht Club, in the hope that we could convey the necessity of keeping unauthorized boats away from the *Albatross.* By this time the local authorities had realized that the team was both serious and responsible, and they were firmly on our side. At the end of the meeting most of the charter captains gave their assurance that they would resist the pressure of cameramen to get too close to the flight path.

Almost imperceptibly, the team was tightening up, building a routine sense of preparedness. At the Deal office Roger Morris spelled Jack Conmy and Maggie Masterton at fielding the insistent media questions. Jim Burke discovered a kindred spirit ("Another splendid Englishman") in Peter Allen, a Mercury engine dealer in New Romney who collected antique motors, and who not only provided lubricants that made our outboards run like watches, but who loaned us his own boat speedometer and compass as well.

The coordination of lifesaving efforts, in the unhappy event that we should need them, was in the hands of Chief Officer Peter Morris of Her Majesty's Coast Guard, Folkestone. Once again we went to an official agency for advice and came away full of strong tea and warm feelings, having made a friend not only of Pete Morris, but of his family as well. It was an extraordinary experience, especially for the younger members of the team who were visiting British families for the first time, and found themselves dandling children on their laps and telling stories about California. We were, after all, foreign competitors for a U.K. prize, and yet if we could have made it across the Channel on the help and good wishes of our British friends, the flight would have been a lark.

Everything cooperated except the weather. Day after day the monotonous forecasts came off the teletype at Deal from the London Mets, from Oceanroutes at Gravesend, from the R.A.F., and from the Varne lightship: *Winds 15 to 20 knots. Extensive fog. Thundery showers.* The cumulative meteorological data of the past ten years for the coast of Kent gave us a 1-in-5 chance of calm days at this season of the year. For Californians that seemed like a realistic enough estimate to launch the expedition. The team had now been in England for four weeks, and not once since the airplane and the boats were ready had there been a chance to fly.

The weekend of May 26 was even worse than usual; high winds and rain were predicted for the next 72 hours. Paul declared a holiday for all hands, and on Sunday the 27th, most of the team drove up to the Old Warden Aerodrome in Bedfordshire for a flying display by the Shuttleworth Trust Antique Airplane Collection. Weekend petrol shortages were endemic at this point, and our assortment of vans and minis made sporadic stops to persuade the owners of country stations to sell us more than £2 worth of fuel at a time. Eventually we arrived at Old Warden in time for the breathtaking opening show by the Red Arrows, the Royal Air Force aerobatic team. Most of us had seen the U.S. Air Force Thunderbirds and the Navy's Blue Angels, but the R.A.F. team seemed even more spectacular, staying close to the spectators and maintaining nerveless minimum clearances between their nine bright red Folland Gnats. The jet engines were almost drowned out by the camera shutters.

The flypast ranged backward through World War II and the 1930s to the age of the pioneers. Bryan Allen and Bill Watson watched thoughtfully while a 1912 Blackburn monoplane — the oldest operating British aircraft in the world — stuttered across Old Warden's grass runway and into the air. It was built only three years after Blériot's cross-Channel flight, and it was still flying.

Another reminder came along between the vintage aircraft

flights. A small ultralight airplane was assembled on the field. The closer it came to completion, the more familiar it looked to the Californians; it was unmistakably a Vollmer Jensen design. The commentator announced the Revell VJ-23, the first powered hang glider in the world to have crossed the English Channel. Meaningful glances passed between the *Albatross* team members. On April 14, before leaving for England, Ted Ancona had flown his motorized *Icarus V* hang glider 37 miles (59.5 kilometres) from Porterfield to Shafter, California.

The pilot of the VJ-23 started his 7.6 cubic inch (125cc) go-cart engine — the same size as Ted's — ran a few steps, and the plane buzzed into the air. Ted or Taras could have recited its specifications in their sleep: Wingspan, 32.6 feet (9.9 metres); empty weight, 100 pounds (45.5 kilograms); horsepower, about 10 (7.45 kilowatts). *Thirty Bryan Allens!* The blue-and-yellow Revell floated around the field, the wail of its little engine contrasting with a flight speed almost as slow as that of the *Gossamer Albatross*. The difference was that the VJ-23 could climb at a mere twist of the throttle, and when the pilot landed at the end of the demonstration he looked as though he was returning from a pleasant stroll.

The real lesson of the day was yet to come. After the flying display the Albatrossers toured the collection of historic aircraft in the buildings bordering the field. One display stopped the whole team short: Suspended from the ceiling of a hangar were *SUMPAC* and *Toucan,* two of the unsuccessful British contenders for the first Kremer Prize. We walked around stiff-necked for many minutes, staring up at them. "Fantastic," Blaine murmured. Bryan scanned the giant Meccano structure in the cockpit of *Toucan:* "Look at all that *metal.*" "Look at the woodwork," Janet countered. "They belong in the Victoria and Albert with Grinling Gibbons." One question could be read from the team's faces as we walked the length of *Toucan*'s 143-foot wing, appreciating as few others could the endless row of meticulously framed ribs. What happened when they crashed? "Six months' work," Bill Watson said. Everyone nodded; we knew what he meant.

For Paul it was a vindication of his theory of why the British had never been able to win the Kremer Prize despite their long head start. He had mentioned many times that the technology of the

Gossamer Condor was straightforward enough for it to have been built years earlier. He maintained that the crucial gap was one of philosophy, not materials. He hopped backward to get a longer view of *SUMPAC* and gestured with his crutch. "No one could mistake that for anything but an airplane."

"Aircraft," Blaine corrected.

"Right, aircraft. Like the name of the committee. If you call something the Man-Powered Aircraft Committee . . . you're probably going to build man-powered aircraft, not try to solve the problem of human-powered flight, which is something different."

Steve Elliott, a craftsman already seduced by the workmanship of British antiques, paid no attention to the logic of this pronouncement — he had heard it before — but gazed raptly up at *SUMPAC*'s sleek propeller fairing. "They are really beautiful."

"But they couldn't win the prize."

"Still . . ." There was unvoiced general agreement with Steve's point: Art over Science, at least for the moment.

From Old Warden we drove to R.A.F. Cardington, where the team had been invited to attend an indoor model meet in the huge hangar that had housed the ill-fated airship R-101, and where Daniel Perkins had built and flown his inflatable HPAs. It is hard to convey the feelings of historical resonance that affected all of us at one time or another in England; airship hangars are awesome structures to begin with, and this one had a weighty presence for any air-minded visitor.

The Tutankhamen factor was cheerfully ignored by the flyers testing their FAI microfilm models. These elegant featherweight airplanes are like miniature analogs of the *Gossamer Condor* and *Gossamer Albatross*. They have the same tubular booms, the same spiderweb of fine wire bracing, and the same air of flimsiness. Their covering is also transparent, but microfilm is thinner and more beautiful than Mylar; the wings of the models shimmered with iridescent Tiffany-glass colors.

The FAI planes span 25.6 inches (65 centimetres) and weigh as little as 0.03 ounce (1 gram). Their flight is languorous and dreamlike, and they impose similar constraints on their handlers. A man carrying a microfilm model moves in slow motion, as if he were in an underwater ballet. (At four in the morning, the men carrying the *Gossamer Condor* moved the same way, as silent as sleepwalkers.)

Paul was fascinated by the indoor models. Some of them were flying as long as 34 minutes that day, and he studied the delicate planes on their stands as if they held the secret to our Channel flight. We watched the magnificently bearded Ron Green launch his model on another half-hour flight. Paul stared up into the gloomy recesses of the hangar while the plane climbed in slow circles. A time trip: From the contest records of the Academy of Model Aeronautics, Washington D.C.:

> *Year:* 1941
> *Class:* Indoor Stick, Class D, Junior
> *Record Holder:* Paul MacCready, Jr.
> *Age:* 16
> *Longest Flight:* 6 minutes, 14.0 seconds.

The estimate for this expedition's longest flight was two hours, and many of the team members were thinking about the time difference on the long drive back to Folkestone. Jim Burke had given up his trip to Old Warden to replace a defective motor on one of the Zodiacs and to swing the boat compass. It was the last retrofit needed for the escort. What was needed now was calm weather, first to check the alterations that had been made to the *Albatross*, and second to attempt the Channel flight. There was still no sign of it, and on May 30 Paul decided to move the team back to Ramsgate.

15

Liftoff

The Edge of England

JUNE 1979: The month that Rear Admiral Goodhart must have been thinking of when he proposed his human-powered cross-Channel race after the *Gossamer Condor*'s successful Kremer Prize flight in August of 1977.

On June 25, 1909, at 4:41 A.M., Louis Blériot took off from Les Baraques near Calais in his frail *No. XI* monoplane powered by a 3-cylinder, 25-horsepower Anzani engine. "Pendant une dizaine de minutes, je suis resté seul, isolé, perdu au milieu de la mer écumeuse, ne voyant aucun point à l'horizon, ne percevant aucun bateau." ["For ten minutes I remained alone, isolated, lost in the midst of a foaming sea, unable to distinguish a single point on the horizon, or see a single boat."] At 5:17.30, after a meandering and chancy flight of 23.5 miles (37.8 kilometres), Blériot's plane glided down to a landing and gently nosed over in the Northfall Meadow near Dover Castle.

For the greatest naval power in history, these were 36 minutes that changed the world. The pioneer British pilot Sir Alan Cobham wrote, "It is vital to the safety of the nation that Britain should become a nation of aviators ... The day that Blériot flew the Channel marked the end of our insular safety, and the beginning of the time when Britain must seek another form of defence besides its ships."

During May and June 1979, many members of the *Gossamer Albatross* team made a pilgrimage to the spot where Blériot landed. It is a quiet clearing east of Dover Castle, reached by a narrow footpath and surrounded by tall shrubbery. There is a stone silhouette of the *No. XI* monoplane set into the grass of the sloping hillside, and a white flagstaff from which the French *Tricolore* flies. We never found another person there on our visits, and one taxi driver walked in with us, because, although he had lived all his life in Dover, he had never seen the Blériot Monument.

Like the *Albatross* team, Blériot was trying to win a prize, one of £1000 offered by the London *Daily Mail*. He had formidable competition, including the Comte de Lambert (Wilbur Wright's first pupil), Wilbur Wright himself, and the plucky but unfortunate Englishman Hubert Latham, who made two attempts that were both defeated by engine failure. One of these was made six days before Blériot's successful flight, so there was a genuine race.

Rear Admiral Goodhart was not the only one who anticipated a human-powered race for the Kremer Channel Prize in 1979. The *Canadian Aeronautics and Space Journal* for November 1978 carried a witty cartoon by Dubord picturing the Cliffs of Dover as the starting point for a flock of contestants, who between attempts took their refreshment at "Ye Olde Kremer Inn." Newsmen also like races; one of the most insistent questions that reporters asked the *Albatross* crew was about competition. "We're not worried about any competition that we know of," was Paul's answer. "It's the ones we don't know of." In fact, when we came to England we knew of no other HPAs that could even fly the original Kremer Course, and that was still the case when Kenneth Clark and Ron Moulton brought a list of the eight Channel Prize registrants to the Manston hangar. Early in June, we began to hear rumors about Paul and Stephan Maschelein, two brothers from Ypres, Belgium, who had built several human-powered planes and flown them at Calais. Jean Louf agreed to find out more about the Mascheleins for us.

There was little time to worry about competitors. MacCready's overall strategy was to use the much-repaired *Albatross 1* for tests and trial flights, and to keep the new and improved *Albatross 2* in reserve for a serious attempt on the Channel. Because of the need for escort and rescue drills, many hands were taken off construction, and the progress of No. 2 had not kept pace with the plan. Of course the rescue procedures were essential, and they had to be approved by the AOPA before any flight attempt. At the Man-

12. John Dubord's witty depiction of a cross-Channel race for human-powered aircraft.

ston hangar Dr. Ingrid Dodd and Dr. P. H. Garrard lectured the boat crews on various unpleasant scenarios, and it was agreed that the Zodiacs and cruisers would carry blankets, plastic warm-up bags, Brooke airways for mouth-to-mouth resuscitation, mucus extractors, and an all-body splint borrowed from the R.A.F.

The meteorologists predicted calm air on the morning of May 31, and at 3:45 A.M. the team assembled at Manston and waited for a lull that never came. The *Albatross 1* tuning flights were scrubbed again, to the disappointment of both the flight crew and the press. That afternoon the *Tartan Gem* led the Zodiacs out on a full boat test. The sky and the Channel were gray; there was light wind and a moderate swell. The small flotilla left from Folkestone, and at mid-Channel the *Tartan Gem* raised a buoy dead ahead, but it was Mid-Varne instead of Northeast Varne. This was a course-made-good error of 10° in only eight miles, a level of inaccuracy that the more experienced navigators on the project regarded as disastrous.

Navigation was not the only flaw. After the test Paul had a 2-page list of changes and improvements for the escorts. One discovery was quite unexpected. The Motorola radios brought from the U.S. for communicating between the escort boats and the *Albatross* were crystal-controlled on a frequency of 154.15 mHz. This turned out to be a Kent Police frequency, which made the radios illegal in the U.K. The only options were to replace the crystals, which were not available in England, or to get special permission from the Home Office to use the sets as they were. Paul immediately agreed to change the radios to an approved channel, and to order the necessary crystals from the United States. It was one more detail added to his interminable list of chores.

For MacCready this was the nadir of the expedition. He was hampered by his broken ankle, disappointed with the boat performance and the slow construction of the back-up planes, and burdened with the responsibility for the whole project. He also had less personal support: On May 29 his youngest son, Marshall, had called from Pasadena to say that he had finished school and had also had a bicycle accident. The garbled message didn't specify how bad the accident was, and Judy MacCready flew home the same day to bring Marshall back to England with her, assuming that he was all right.

To Jack Conmy, Paul looked worn and tired, and that is how he felt. "Organization seems to be in chaos . . . Is chaos," he wrote in his diary. He found the progress on the *Albatross 2* "agonizingly slow." Paul is not a flamboyant leader, but he never stopped pulling more than his weight, and when he pulled through this slough, there was no question of his leadership. The project could never have succeeded without him.

At midnight on May 31 the forecasters predicted another calm interval for the following morning. "Wolf! Wolf!" many of the crew members thought, as they stumbled out of bed after only two hours of sleep. At 3:30 the team was back at the hangar, and this time the wind was down to 4 mph (6.4 km/h) under a sky of high stratus clouds. Jack Conmy had notified the press and the television networks; when their representatives turned up in force, he and Roger Morris gave them a short talk about what not to do. The *Albatross* was brought out and assembled in front of the hangar, and just at dawn Bryan took off on a short flight to test a new 52-tooth pedal sprocket (the previous one had 62 teeth) and some changes in the cockpit ventilation.

The first flight went well; Bryan liked the 52:42 gear ratio, the flying effort was low, the wind stayed calm, and the tufting inside the fuselage indicated some airflow near the pilot's head and knees. Most of the newsmen were cooperative, although some of the foreign photographers didn't understand about the plane's bracing wires and kept running into them. The NBC crew immediately ignored all the rules and requests, a foretaste of their behavior on the Channel. The team had become increasingly wary of discourteous media folk, and Parker MacCready applied his foolproof technique: He kept a freeway salute showing in the camera's field of view until we were ready for them to shoot.

On his second flight Bryan took off to the northwest and pedaled a large, leisurely half-mile (0.8-km) S-turn to the west end of the taxiway in 2 minutes and 31 seconds. "Look at that," a British voice in the crowd marveled. "They are so very far ahead of all the others." The press was about to have an impromptu demonstration of another kind of advance. When the plane landed at the end of this flight, the front wheel abraded and cracked, unbeknownst to anyone. Bryan next attempted a downwind takeoff on an uphill section of the taxiway. He bore down hard on the pedals, the front wheel stuck, and the propeller shaft broke in the middle. "Well, of course," was the general media response. "Just like they all do." Some of the newsmen were veterans of the *SUMPAC* and *Toucan* days, and they began to pack up their cameras. Taras looked over the broken shaft, said, "Hmmm," and in five minutes had spliced it together with a short section of aluminum tubing, some carbon-fiber–reinforcing strips, and fiberglass strapping tape.

When Allen took off again and made a fourth flight, the reporters were incredulous. Paul, who had realized that with the lower gear ratio the hollow propeller shaft needed more foam stiffening plugs in it, fielded their questions with his usual equanimity. For the team, the test was useful in several ways. It indicated the final changes necessary to improve the cooling system, and it reminded everyone that there would probably be a few extra pounds of morning dew condensed on the wings at the time of the Channel takeoff. It wasn't the half-hour flight that the cameramen wanted, but it was just as impressive in other ways, and it strengthened the team's morale.

Anything that could accomplish that was welcome, because the weather was a relentless depressant to the Californians. The strain was especially hard on the younger members of the team, and it showed in occasional bursts of temper, in the need for extra sleep, and in a generally higher level of irritability. Jack Conmy, who had to deal with the media, showed it by chain-smoking. Du Pont had installed a telephone answering machine at the Deal office, and several times a day Jack recorded a patient reply for the insistent queries of the press: "This is Du Pont, and this is Jack Conmy. The weather forecast for tonight . . ." predicted 10- to 15-knot winds, day after frustrating day.

By now virtually everything was set except the weather. John Ward and his crew took Paul and Jim Burke on a practice crossing to Cap Gris-Nez and demonstrated the ample speed and competent navigation of the *Lady Ellen Elizabeth*. The *Albatross*'s broken propeller shaft was replaced with a spare aluminum one, and the cockpit cooling vents were improved once again. Finally the pre-flight checklist was rehearsed, and the plane was taken apart, trucked to the Warren, and stored in the oil-spill laboratory shed, where a night watchman was hired to guard it. The Zodiacs and the *Tartan Gem* were fueled and waiting at the Wellington Dock at Dover. Still, there was no letup in the wind and rain. On the night of June 5 Paul made an announcement: Because of the drain of time and money, an absolute deadline for the Channel attempt had been set at July 6.

Everyone on the team was depressed by this news. Many of the older members were on unpaid leaves of absence from jobs or simply playing hooky, but even Burke, who claimed, "If I don't get back to JPL soon they won't just fire me once, they'll fire me three times," was reluctant to acknowledge that we might fail by default. The response of most crew members was to push harder and try to buck up the next person. Kirk Giboney exhausted himself bike training that night, and slept 13 hours straight.

Several days earlier Sam Durán had had a surprise visit. Sally and Joe Sáenz, his sister and brother-in-law, were taking their first trip to England and turned up in Kent, having a wonderful time despite the weather. When Sam told them about the mood of the team they decided to cheer us up with a home-style barbecue. The three of them combed the grocery shops of Folkestone to find the ingredients they needed, and even discovered a box of *Fresno chiles,* far from home. With Du Pont's cooperation, they arranged to take over the Olde Cliffe Tavern (the pub in St. Margaret's at Cliffe where Tom Horton and the film crew were staying) for the afternoon of June 7.

The weather forecast that morning was poor as usual: unstable squalls, SSW winds of 12 knots, rain predicted for the evening. There was a fair amount of grumbling in the hangar, and Paul and Dave Saks had a run-in about the size of the prop shaft bearing support on No. 2. Joe Mastropaolo exercised his feelings on the ergometer, and then coached Bryan through a tremendous workout climaxed by a series of 5 grueling 30-second sprints. On the last of these Bryan was pedaling at an awesome rate against heavy resistance; as Joe counted him down, everyone stopped working to watch. The floor around the ergometer was soaked with perspiration, and Bryan was pulling in air like a bellows: "Five . . . Four . . . Three . . . Two . . . One . . . Stop! Well done!" The whole team burst into applause. Partly on the basis of that 0.8-horsepower performance Joe calculated Allen's still-air endurance limit in the *Gossamer Albatross* as 170 minutes, well over the 1 hour and 50 minute flight time that Paul estimated for the crossing. His water transpiration rate was 0.26 gallon (1 litre) per hour, an amount that had to be replenished at the same rate to keep his muscles functioning properly.

Bryan's unstinting effort cleared the air, and a little later Steve announced that everyone was invited to the Olde Cliffe Tavern for a California barbecue. The first reaction was puzzlement; in St. Margaret's at Cliffe? When we arrived, we found that Sally and Joe, Sam, Louis Prézelin, and Tony Zapata had been cooking all day, and that Sally had commandeered the only charcoal grill in St. Margaret's by inviting its owner to the party. It is unlikely that the tiny Kent village had ever seen this particular genre of feast. There were platters of homemade tortillas, homemade *salsa,* potato salad, tossed salads with avocado, guacamole, grill-your-own hamburgers and cheeseburgers, unlimited beer, and the *pièce de résistance,* an authentic *chile con carne.*

The Du Pont group left the media to the answering machine, the film crew abandoned their cameras, and everyone pitched into the food as if there were no tomorrow. The Californians were soon giving lessons in the proper assembly of *tostadas* to Penny, Melanie, and Yvonne of the pub owner's family. "My God," one of the Englishmen gasped, his eyes full of tears after tasting Sally's *carne,* "you people are unbelievable. You must have steel stomachs." The rain came, a soft classic drizzle (Burke: "The England we know and love"), and this time everyone sat out in it drinking and enjoying each other's company. It was a wonderful relief, and a momentary return to normality.

"Good vibes," Jim Sugar said, and two days later there was a sign that he was right. The weather forecast was dismal as usual — but the day was not. No one was prepared for the bubble of calm that drifted up from Portugal, and kept the wind light all day. "Missed it!" Paul wrote in his log, but we felt alerted. If there could be one bubble, there could be more. Although the prediction was still bad for Sunday, June 10, on Monday the 11th there seemed to be a break.

That morning Jim and Lin Burke were up in London prying a last carton of materials loose from Heathrow customs. Judy MacCready had returned from Pasadena, bringing the indestructible Marshall with her. They joined the rest of the team at Manston, where we worked on *Albatross 2,* and watched Joe Mastropaolo test himself with a routine as arduous as the one he had put Bryan through the day before. The results were impressive: Joe (who was admittedly heavier and therefore more powerful than Bryan) put out 0.32 horsepower for 2 hours continuously, which broke Bryan's own absolute ergometer record. "Not bad for an old man," Bill Watson quipped (Joe was 52 at the time).

Paul MacCready was famous in soaring circles for his intuition about the weather, and on the morning of the 11th he was watching it like a hawk. When we drove to the hangar he kept peering out the window at the sky, and he was soon on the telephone to the various forecasting centers. By this time the team was so closely knit that everyone sensed the air of expectancy, and quietly began

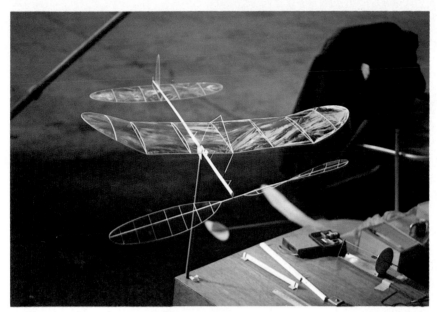

1. Forerunners, I. This microfilm-covered indoor model spans 25.6 inches (65 centimetres), weighs an unbelievable 0.03 ounce (1 gram), and is braced with wire thinner than a human hair. It is nearly a perfect miniature analog of the Gossamer airplanes. Indoor models have fascinated Paul MacCready for years; in 1941, at age 16, he was the U.S. junior record holder in Class D Indoor Stick.

2. Forerunners, II. Paul MacCready hang gliding in 1975. The wire-braced X-Y-Z frame of a Rogallo wing hang glider was MacCready's main inspiration for the structure of the *Gossamer Condor*.

3. From left to right: Jim Burke, Kirke Leonard, and Paul MacCready working on the first version of the *Gossamer Condor*. Mojave Airport, California, December 1976.

4. December 26, 1976: Parker Mac-Cready making the first 40-second flight in the *Gossamer Condor*. It covered 469 feet (143 metres) at an average altitude of 3 feet.

5. In January 1977 the *Condor* team tried to improve the plane's poor lateral stability by filling the space between the kingpost and the keel brace with Mylar. The experiment was not successful.

6. Greg Miller brought the powerful muscles of a bicycle racer to the *Gossamer Condor* project. Here he pedals a much-modified version at Mojave in January 1977.

7. The move to Shafter Airport near Bakersfield was accompanied by a complete redesign of MacCready's HPA. Here, clockwise, Paul MacCready, Vern Oldershaw, Peter Lissaman, and Jack Lambie work on the fuselage of the *Gossamer Condor 2*.

8. The new version of the *Condor* was not an immediate success. This typical crash took place in March 1977. Although it looks catastrophic, the plane was ready to fly again in a few days.

9. In April 1977, Greg Miller left the *Condor* project and was replaced as principal pilot by Bryan Allen. Here Bryan, on the left, shakes hands with Greg after a streamlined bicycle race in 1979. Behind them is Bill Watson, a member of the *Gossamer Albatross* team.

10. Under the direction of Dr. Joseph Mastropaolo, Allen began a strenuous training program to improve his ability to fly the *Gossamer Condor*. Here he works out on an ergometer.

11. Bryan Allen flying the closed-cockpit *Condor 2* at Shafter Airport, while Sam Durán rides the chase bike.

12. Allen's power and flying skills improved simultaneously. Here he practices flying the *Condor* over a height marker.

13. Tuesday, August 23, 1977, 7:30 A.M. Bryan Allen piloting the *Gossamer Condor* on the Kremer Figure-of-Eight Prize flight. Total flying time 7 minutes, 27.5 seconds; length of flight 1.35 miles (2.172 kilometres).

14. Part of the reward. At upper left the *Gossamer Condor* hangs above the North American X-15 in the National Air and Space Museum. At lower left are the wings of the Wright *Flyer,* and at upper right, the *Spirit of St. Louis.*

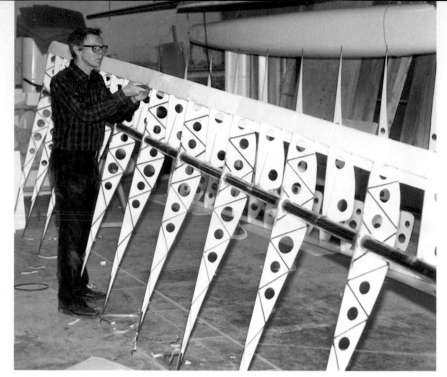

15. Beginning the *Gossamer Albatross*. In March 1978 Paul MacCready attaches the leading edge of a wing panel. Note the tubular carbon-fiber spar and polystyrene foam ribs.

16. By July 1978 the first *Gossamer Albatross* was ready for testing at Shafter Airport. Here it waits on the runway, with Parker MacCready in the pilot's seat.

17. Lighter and stronger than the *Condor,* the *Albatross* flew beautifully right from the beginning.

18. In December 1978 the *Albatross* project found a new home at Terminal Island, Long Beach, California. Here the plane is carried out for a test flight. Left to right, Steve Elliott, Bill Watson, Jim Burke, Sterling Stoll, Paul Mac-Cready, Marshall MacCready.

19. The *Albatross* was no more immune to crashes than the *Condor*. A failed wing wire connector caused this one in February 1979. Note the pilot stepping through the cockpit covering to remove his weight from the plane (the door is on the other side).

20. Hangar 522, Terminal Island. Taras Kiceniuk Jr. and Janet Grosser rig the canard of the *Gossamer Albatross* while John Volk and Scott Strom work on the fuselage. In the foreground, Mike Reagan, Ken Hamlyn, Mike Bame, and Steve Elliott cover the stabilizer of the *Gossamer Penguin*.

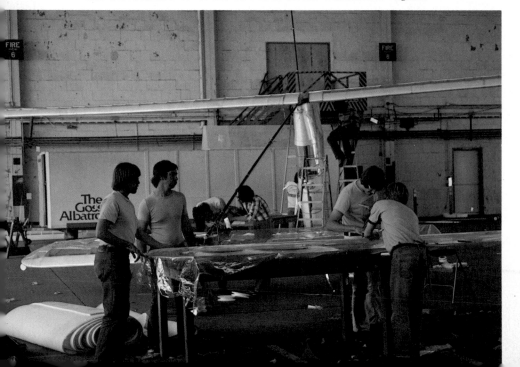

21. On April 25, 1979, Bryan Allen flew the *Gossamer Albatross* for 1 hour, 9 minutes, and 3 seconds at Harper Dry Lake, California, by far the longest human-powered flight ever made. On the basis of this performance, the decision was made to try the flight across the English Channel.

22. Building the *Gossamer Albatross 2* at R.A.F. Manston, Kent, England. Standing, from left: Dave Saks, Morton Grosser, Sterling Stoll. On floor, from left: Paul MacCready Jr., Tyler MacCready, Steve Elliott.

23. May 10, 1979, 4:15 A.M. at R.A.F. Manston. Bryan Allen flies the *Gossamer Albatross* on a 4-minute, 25-second qualification flight for the Kremer Cross-Channel Competition.

24. In the small hours of June 12, 1979, the *Albatross* is assembled on the Warren pad at Folkestone in preparation for the Channel attempt.

25. After an aborted takeoff, Steve Elliott, Taras Kiceniuk Jr., Dave Saks, and Bill Watson replace the *Albatross*'s broken front wheel. Du Pont's Dick Woodward does not look sanguine about the chances of success.

26. June 12, 1979: At 04:51 Greenwich Mean Time, the *Gossamer Albatross* lifted off the edge of England and set a course for France.

27. By mid-Channel the flight was far behind schedule. Bryan was low on water, the instrument batteries were failing, and the plane began to sink lower and lower.

28. At 06:26 Allen signaled that he had to give up and wanted a tow. When he climbed higher to clear the rescue boat he found smoother air and decided to go on.

29. More than 2 hours into the flight, with cramped legs and a fogged cockpit, Bryan struggles on toward the coast of France.

30. Over the beach at Cap Gris-Nez, paced by a crowd of well-wishers and crew members, Bryan is within 1 minute of his theoretical exhaustion limit.

31. The moment of landing. 07:40 Greenwich Mean Time, Cap Gris-Nez, France. Janet Grosser (in black raincoat) has just caught the *Albatross*'s starboard landing line. The total flight time was 2 hours and 49 minutes, over a distance of 22.25 statute miles (35.82 kilometres).

reviewing their roles for the flight. The London Mets reported that a small high pressure area was gradually moving southeast from the center of England, and at 3 P.M. the R.A.F. weather office at Manston predicted 5-knot winds, south to southeast, and 3-kilometre visibility for the dawn hours of June 12. The longer-range forecast included higher winds and sea fog. We had waited 35 days for this less-than-perfect chance. Paul made the hard decision: The flight was Go. His private written estimate of our chances at that moment was 1 in 6.

After five weeks of waiting, it was a relief to go into action. Standby calls were made to the crews of the *Lady Ellen Elizabeth* and the *Tartan Gem,* to the Dover Harbourmaster, the Coast Guard, the Royal National Lifeboat Institution, and R.A.F. Rescue. Since the boat crews had been advised not to carry passports in the Zodiacs, team lists were telexed to the French and British customs and immigration services. The French traffic control and beach group alerted the CROSSMA station at Cap Gris-Nez, Jean Louf, Daniel Seité, and Hoverlloyd, where Paul Dicken, the Research and Planning Officer, guaranteed us passage to Calais even though the hovercraft flights were all fully booked. The Du Pont office at Deal informed the media, which now included not only the British and American newspapers and television networks, but Polish, Japanese, and French TV, plus many magazine and aeronautical journalists. Paul made an apologetic call to the headquarters of the Kent Police to say that our replacement radio crystals hadn't arrived, and that we could ill afford to miss this opportunity to fly. The unruffled reply was that the world would not come to an end if we used one of their frequencies for a few hours, and by the way, "Very best luck."

At Ramsgate the team members checked their equipment lists for the nth time and dispersed to various restaurants for refueling. Their preferences were international and diverse: Some ate French food, some English; Paul and Judy had pizza, Sam, Otis, and Jim went to an Italian bistro, and Bryan, Sterling, and Joe had a Chinese dinner. Everyone tried to get a few hours of sleep before the flight, with varying success. Bryan turned in at seven, and when Sam woke the assembly crew at midnight, he let Bryan sleep an extra half hour before leaving for Folkestone.

Jim and Lin Burke returned from London to the welcome ex-

citement of preparation. By 7 P.M. Lin was at the Pegwell Bay
Hoverport with the beach crew, all of us loaded down with charts,
red smoke flares, and high-powered spotlights. (The landing light
code for the flight was Golf Alfa: --. .-, for *Gossamer Albatross*.)
The last hovercraft to leave Ramsgate that night was the 200-ton
Sir Christopher [Cockerell], and its 8 P.M. flight was indeed sold
out, but Hoverlloyd's Mr. Wright somehow found front-row seats
for Lin and Janet, and quietly mentioned to me that Captain
Ruckert would be delighted to have a guest from the *Albatross*
team in the cockpit during the flight.

While *Sir Christopher* was skimming across the Goodwin Sands
at 60 knots (and Jean Louf and Daniel Seité were racing to meet
it, doubtless at an equal speed), the boat crews were trying to
nap a few more minutes before what promised to be a long night.
The Dover lock gates were scheduled to open at 12 midnight. John
Ward had to make the same high tide to bring the *Lady Ellen
Elizabeth* out to sea from its mooring some 7.5 miles (12 kilometres) up the Stour River at Sandwich. The plan was for the
boats to rendezvous off the Warren by 3 A.M.; this meant that
the *Tartan Gem* and the Zodiacs would moor outside the Dover
Quay for several hours, while the *Lady Ellen* was making the
22.3-mile (36-kilometre) run down from Sandwich to Folkestone.

At 10 P.M., with the sky still light, the boat crew left Ramsgate
in its motley assortment of vehicles. (Jim, Dave, and Steve reached
Dover with only vapor in their gas tank and coasted down the hill
to the Wellington Dock.) It was even quieter than the forecast
promised; a few high clouds drifted across the moon, and there
was no surface wind at all. The four inflatables fired up their engines and idled across the dock pool, their wakes rippling the
reflections of the yellow dock lights in the water. At 12 midnight,
with the now-familiar clanging of bells, the lock gates opened,
and the *Tartan Gem* and its brood motored out to the Channel
side of the quay.

The Zodiacs tied up to the *Tartan Gem,* and their crews went
aboard the cruiser to catnap. They were rudely awakened when
a huge black bow bore down on them and was deflected at the
last moment by a tugboat. The bow belonged to the bulk carrier
Arco Severn, which moored next to the *Tartan Gem,* switched on

a blaze of floodlights, and began unloading coal through her steel conveyor chutes with a deafening clatter. Any further attempts at sleep were abandoned. At 1:30 Jack Conmy and Dr. Ingrid Dodd came aboard the *Tartan Gem* and distributed the medical supplies among the Zodiacs. A few minutes later all engines were started, and Dover Port Control gave permission for the flotilla to start for the Warren.

By this time clouds had covered the moon and left the Kent coast in darkness. For the next 40 minutes the five boats droned west along a smooth and empty stretch of black water like a war-time patrol. At the Du Pont office in Deal, where Margret Clarke was monitoring communications, the answering machine had been informing all callers since midnight that "Dr. MacCready has moved his troops from Ramsgate to the Warren at Folkestone." The troops included the five MacCreadys, crammed into one tiny car until Parker and Tyler were dropped off in Sandwich at the *Lady Ellen Elizabeth*.

Three of the callers to Deal were the Grossers and Lin Burke at Calais, who were put through for a final check at 11:30 and told that the flight was definitely on. A breathless half hour later the French detachment was delivered to the Cap Gris-Nez CROSSMA station by Jean Louf and Daniel Seité and welcomed by Officer-in-Charge René Richard. His watch-mates Olivier Malfoy and Jean-Charles Dupire made spaces to spread the team's British Admiralty charts of the Channel, and instructed the *Albatross* group in the operation of the French VHF radios and radar sets. Just as in England, the hospitality didn't stop there. Bunks were offered for any-one who wanted to nap (and gratefully accepted by Lin Burke, who had been on the move all day), coffee was made, and plotting and navigation rules were loaned for laying out the course of the flight.

Another caller to Deal was Ron Moulton, who with David Bryant and Nick Coles, the operator of a flying service at Lydd Airport, was one of the three official observers for the flight. At 12:30 Ron, Martyn Cowley, and Pat Lloyd were groping their way down the narrow rutted paths to the Warren by flashlight. When they opened the door of the storage shed they found the young watch-man listening to pop music on the radio and reading the *Kent*

Evening Post by the light of a kerosene lamp. Above him, the parts of the *Gossamer Albatross* hung on cords from the ceiling. Moulton says that he will never forget the atmosphere of that moment — for him, it was like walking into the Wright brothers' hangar at Kitty Hawk.

By 2:10 the *Lady Ellen Elizabeth* and the *Tartan Gem* were lying off the Warren in a safe depth of water, and the Zodiacs had moved in to about 50 metres from the seaward edge of the pad. A few moments later a rented mobile generating plant was started up, and the scene was starkly illuminated by its overhead lights. In blessedly calm air, Bryan Allen, Ted Ancona, Sam Durán, Taras Kiceniuk, Larry McNay, and Bill Watson carried the parts of the plane out of the shed and began to assemble it on the pad. They were helped by Larry's father, Dave, who had just arrived on his way to the Paris air show, and by Marshall MacCready. At 2:30 the inboard wing panels were lifted into place and bolted and pinned together, with Taras checking every connection twice. Bryan attached the canard, and checked the control rigging as he usually did at home — but this was definitely not home.

After the beautiful early morning solitude of Shafter, Mojave, and Harper Dry Lake it seemed bizarre to assemble the *Albatross* in the glare of movie lights and strobe flashes. By now the pad was crowded with newsmen and camera crews, and no conversation was safe from their probing shotgun microphones. Four policemen and a small squad of Royal Marines kept the spectators out of the wires, but Paul could not move anywhere without being followed by a cluster of reporters. His first answer as to whether the plane would fly was that "The wind here and at Cap Gris-Nez is still, but at mid-Channel it is five or six knots, and on that basis we would have too long a flight." The team weather queries were coming to Cap Gris-Nez at about 20-minute intervals, and the answer came back the same each time: "We have zero wind at Cap Gris-Nez."

Like Paul, Bill Watson was dubious about the attempt. He confided to Ron Moulton that this was going to be no more than a good full-scale practice. Ron played Bryan a tape-recording of Lord Brabazon's first aborted flight, which provided some light relief, while Bryan methodically fueled up on carbohydrates: two apples, two bananas, and a large fruit-laden sweet roll. By 4:20 the moon had reappeared, and a pale gray dawn was beginning to light up the Channel. A wisp of breeze slid down the cliffs behind the Warren and ruffled the water out to a few hundred metres from shore. The crew put down the takeoff runway — a strip of hardboard sheets laid end-to-end over the rough concrete surface of the pad, and the Zodiacs began to ferry everyone except the wing runners out to the boats.

When the escorts first arrived, the sea had been nearly level with the top of the pad; now it was halfway to low tide, and a strong swell pounded the inflatables against the slimy green steps at the edge of the Warren. Jim Burke was nervous about the ferrying operation, because he knew that the shelving bottom was covered with sharp groins and upended railway rails. He ordered the single-engined boats to stand off for fear they would damage their propellers, and paddled one Zodiac in to pick up some of the crew ·directly from the beach. The passengers, including Du Pont's Don Billett, photographer Don Monroe, and Paul and his crutch, were boarded soaking wet, and distributed to their various stations. By this time some 15 more press boats had arrived and were idling around the *Albatross* flotilla; it looked like a restaging of Dunkerque.

The expected dew load had indeed condensed on the wing and stabilizer, but although they were cleaned, we knew that wiping the surface often only redistributed the moisture and precipitated more condensation. Bryan stripped off his blue-and-white warm-up suit and knitted wool cap. His minimal flying outfit consisted of white shorts with three red stripes down their sides, black leather bicycle-racing shoes, a lightweight orange life vest, and a white bicycling helmet. (He had even considered changing from metal to plastic glasses frames for the flight, but decided to stay with ones that he knew were comfortable.) Sam checked that the two-litre water bottle mounted on the down tube was full, helped Bryan into the cockpit, and Bill Watson taped the door shut.

With his feet in the pedal straps, Bryan adjusted the ultralight earphone and microphone unit, and tested the radio press-to-talk button in the pitch control handle. The radio and instrument battery packs had been lightened to the limit; they were nominally good for two hours of continuous operation. One by one the boats verified their radio connection to the *Albatross*. The main reason for bringing radios from home was to have an internal communication system that was secure against eavesdropping and interference. The transmissions were recorded on our own equipment during the flight, but in a way it was a shame that they were not monitored by the press. Certainly they must be among the most clean-cut, considerate conversations in the history of experimental flight.

Marshall MacCready supported the stabilizer, Ted Ancona steadied the port wing, and Larry McNay balanced the starboard one while Bryan checked the radios and warmed up his legs. At 5:10 he reported that he was ready to take off; Sam radioed back that the boats were almost in position. By that time the wisps of land breeze had become a 3-knot zephyr angling across the Warren from the east. Taras called up the *Albatross*: "Perhaps the biggest problem is the crosswind takeoff. Remember to wait for your wind conditions." Bryan said he'd watch it, and Paul came on from Project Control aboard the *Lady Ellen Elizabeth* to instruct him about the red spotlight they would use as a follow beacon.

Bryan acknowledged the message, asked Paul to blink the light, and then, with the press cameras grinding, started his takeoff roll. A few seconds later the boat crews were stunned to see the plane suddenly slam to an abrupt stop and tip over forward. Sam came on the radio, his voice carefully controlled, "Bryan, this is Sam. Anything serious?" Bryan replied that the plane had crabbed off the left side of the hardboard runway, and the front wheel had apparently hit a crack in the concrete and disintegrated. Sam told Taras to go ashore and have a look at it. In a few minutes the drivers of the inflatables put Taras, Steve, Dave, and Bill Watson back on the pad again.

They found that the *Albatross* had run into an isolated deep hole in the concrete, and that the white plastic front wheel had shattered. The stop was so sudden that Bryan's glasses had shot off into the bottom of the fuselage; Dave Saks fished them out, fortunately unbroken. There was no other visible damage to the plane.

Bryan announced that they were going to replace the wheel with one of the old black ones and try again. At that point the press boats began nattering over the radio about "the great attempt that ended twenty feet from where it started." Jim Burke, who was familiar with the media's love for disasters from the moon rocket program, felt tense and angry. Dick Woodward, who had put hundreds of hours of work into the project, and the Du Pont Company's reputation on the line, felt even angrier. There is a now-famous picture of him walking away from the crippled *Albatross* with tightly folded arms and a truly black expression on his face.

Perhaps the team realized that even the repair of the broken propeller shaft at Manston had been valuable practice, because there is not a trace of tension or impatience in the radio exchanges between them during this time. In ten minutes Taras and Steve replaced the fractured wheel, improvising a missing spacer from duct tape. Chief Officer Peter Morris supplied a set of H.M. Coast Guard's tools, and when Taras needed an extra pair of pliers, one call brought dozens from car trunks and tool kits. Sid Turner found some sheets of British Rail plywood, and they were used to extend the runway toward the eastern edge of the pad. Bryan got back into the cockpit, and the door was taped shut again. The repair crew was picked up — the tide was so low now that each of the twin-engined Zodiacs damaged one propeller — and Paul anxiously scanned the rapidly lightening sky. At Cap Gris-Nez a faint easterly breeze had begun to come up — a headwind.

Nick Coles, the takeoff observer, waited patiently for the team to start their second attempt. Over the radio Paul reminded Bryan to keep the stabilizer lifting from the beginning of the takeoff run. "Roger on that. Clear." At 5:50 Sam radioed that the Zodiacs were in position again, and told Bryan to go ahead whenever he was ready. "Okay, there's a bit of a lull now, so I'm gonna go right now." This time the *Albatross* began to accelerate steadily, faster and faster as Bryan poured power into the propeller that was designed for efficient cruise rather than easy takeoff. Martyn Cowley and Pat Lloyd, running beside the plane, heard the wheel clicks between sheets of plywood as if they were rail joints and the airplane were racing with the train on the British Rail line a hundred feet above it. June 12, 1979: At 5:51 A.M. local time, 04:51 Greenwich Mean Time, the *Gossamer Albatross* lifted off the edge of the Warren near Folkestone, England, and set a course for France.

16

The Channel

Blériot, Nous Sommes Ici!

WHEN THE *Gossamer Albatross* lifted off the pad, the spectators behind it were cheering wildly. Bryan could not hear the applause. He had been concentrating so hard on the airplane and on keeping his mind clear and unfragmented that he had even forgotten about the water. The last time he remembered seeing it, it had been just below the level of the concrete. Now, as he cleared the edge of the pad, it was 20 feet (6 metres) below him — it was like flying off a cliff. "What a rush!" he called into the microphone.

The plane was heading east by north as it took off, and once airborne Bryan began a sweeping right turn that would line him up with the waiting escorts. A few moments later the *Albatross* was soaring silently over the four idling Zodiacs like the great white bird it was named for. Jim Burke remembers his heart beating fast as the plane crossed above him, and he gunned the throttle of his outboard to fall in behind the right wingtip. "Altitude fifteen," Bryan reported.

"Roger, let's see if you can bring it down to ten," Sam answered. "Looks beautiful . . . Let's go for it."

The two big project boats waited out in deep water with the press fleet and an R.N.L.I. *Waveney*-class lifeboat from Folkestone, their engines rumbling in neutral. Paul had set up his project control on the *Lady Ellen Elizabeth,* crewed by John Ward, John Groat, and Frank Booton. With him were his sons Parker and Tyler and two official observers, David Faulkner Bryant and Ron Moulton. For Moulton, the dream was still persisting. As the *Gossamer Albatross* curved gracefully toward them, growing steadily larger, he could not convince himself that the scene was real. Tyler stood at the stern, sighting across his thumbs on a ruler marked to correspond with the *Albatross*'s wingspan seen at a distance of 1500 feet (457 metres). "Let's go!" he called, and the Moon-raker's diesels opened up with a roar, accelerating the boat to 10 knots in a trough of white foam.

To starboard, the *Tartan Gem* followed the *Lady Ellen*'s course of 135°. Beside its 3-man crew, the *Gem* carried Don Billett, Jack Conmy, Dr. Ingrid Dodd, Don Monroe, Joe Thompson Sr., and Joe Thompson Jr. The other members of the film crew, Louis Prézelin and Tony Zapata, were in the fourth Zodiac with Tom Horton, Larry McNay, and Ted Ancona driving. The cameramen were ecstatic, and the temptation for the press boats to get a little closer, a little ahead of the plane, was already beginning to set in. In the right Zodiac with Jim Burke, Sam Durán, and Bill Watson, Otis Imboden exclaimed to himself after one shot, "That's a cover!"

"How're you feeling, Bryan?" Sam transmitted.

"Stabilized out very nicely, no problem." His legs pumping methodically at 80 rpm, Bryan was beginning to realize all the implications of the flight. ". . . So many things that we were doing for the first time. Flying over water, flying with all the boats out there . . . it struck me, what an audacious thing we were doing." Although most of us had pushed that thought to the back of our minds, it had occurred to everyone on the team at various times, and as a result the *Albatross* carried a number of private good luck totems. All of them were featherweight, since even a rabbit's foot seems heavy on a human-powered aircraft.

Under the starboard canard tip was the badge of the Kent Gliding Club, where several of the team members had qualified. On the fuselage, in addition to the three big oval Du Pont logos and the airplane's name on the upper fuselage fairings, there was a small "USA" badge on the right front, the badge of R.A.F. Manston symmetrically opposite it, a 10-pence airmail stamp on the left rear, and on the right side, Bryan's octagonal green "Nothing to Declare" sticker, brought back from a day trip to France.

"Control to *Albatross*. Stay . . . somewhat low, so you don't wear yourself out. Clear." Bryan followed this well-meant advice, dropping down to 10 feet, and almost immediately reported difficulty:

"Getting some odd turbulence there for a sec." Steve Elliott, driving the smallest Mark III Zodiac with Kirk Giboney and Taras Kiceniuk, speeded up a bit to cover the left side more closely. "Bryan, this is Taras. What's your flying speed?"

"Flying speed presently is six and three-quarters [on the arbitrary scale of the airspeed instrument], altitude is ten feet."

"Roger. Experiment for minimum power speed, and fly just a hair faster. Over."

"Check."

Fifteen minutes into the flight, most of the problems that were to dog the rest of it had begun to show up. The first one was depth perception. Even though he had an altimeter, Bryan was uneasy when he found that he could look right through the surface of the water, without being able to determine where it was. The second one was turbulence. At 05:06 Sam asked Bryan if it felt any different flying over water. "Yeah, there's a pretty definite interlinking between the water and the air. A smooth sort of bumpiness, but it's bumpy all the time." The third one was cockpit ventilation. Despite a 50-percent-reflectivity Mylar panel on the port side of the fuselage, the cabin interior had already started to warm up, and condensed moisture was beginning to fog the windows. Bryan reported that the airflow improved somewhat when he opened the rear adjustable vent. The fourth problem was interference by the press boats. They had been given diagrams and a patient explanation showing them why it was vital to the safety of the airplane that they stay behind and away from it. For some of them, it was clearly a waste of breath.

05:07: For the Zodiacs it was like formation flying. Dave Saks was driving the center Mark V, carrying Blaine Rawdon and Joe Mastropaolo (first and second rescue divers), and Sterling Stoll. As the press boats converged from both sides, Sterling asked Sam to move his Zodiac further out to the right to keep traffic away. Sam complied, and a moment later the first irritation could be heard in his voice: "Taras, check that boat out in front, get him outa there."

The *Lady Ellen Elizabeth* was maintaining contact with both the project boats and the shore radios. From the St. Margaret's Bay Radar Station, where Dick Woodward and Dave McNay had driven after the takeoff, a crisp and attractive female voice informed MacCready that H.M. Coast Guard was tracking the *Albatross* flotilla on radar. Judy and Marshall MacCready had meanwhile raced pell-mell to the ferry terminal in Folkestone, and just made it aboard the Sealink *Horsa,* bound for Boulogne. When the ship's purser asked Judy for their tickets, she explained why she hadn't had time to buy any and offered to do so then. The officer excused himself, and a few moments later returned with an invitation from the captain for Judy and Marshall to come up to the bridge. "The tickets . . .?" she asked.

"Just you go along and don't worry about them, ma'am, we'll sell you some in a bit."

Twenty minutes later the 5000-ton, 19-knot *Horsa* was following a course parallel with the *Gossamer Albatross,* and Judy and Marshall were watching the plane through the captain's binoculars. Not many of the *Horsa*'s other passengers could have realized how hard Bryan Allen was working. At 25 minutes into the flight his answers to radio calls were beginning to be punctuated by puffs for breath. "Bryan, what would you estimate it is, powerwise?" Sam asked.

"Hard to say, about point two eight [0.28 hosepower]."

"Roger. Oh, we're about three miles out now."

They were actually somewhat farther than that, but Bryan sensed that the flight was going slower than planned, and that he was beginning to fall behind. He looked over his left shoulder and was disheartened to find that he could still see the cliffs of Dover. The *Albatross* veered 30° off course, and he vowed not to look back again.

From the Zodiacs the *Horsa* seemed gigantic, even at the safe distance it maintained. There was enough mist to keep the project boats' visibility down to a few miles, but on the radar screens at Cap Gris-Nez, the Channel already looked like a busy thoroughfare. On an ordinary day about a thousand ships pass through the 22.3-mile (36-kilometre)-wide slot of ocean between the Warren and Cap Gris-Nez. Although the average ferry passenger sees the Channel as only an empty expanse of water, to the coast guards and the mariners navigating it, it is as cluttered as a city street with traffic lanes, buoys, lights, and obstacles. It is also cluttered with the wrecks of ships whose pilots have ignored or fallen afoul of those hazards.

On the big radar screens at Cap Gris-Nez the *Albatross* flotilla appeared as a cluster of luminous orange dots, a small amber Pleiades moving slowly — painfully slowly — across the main traffic lanes of *La Manche*. Every few times the scan cursor swept around the tube face, larger, brighter, and faster pips would appear at the top and bottom of the screen headed up- or down-Channel, at right angles to the *Albatross*'s course. As each ship came within range, it was called on the Coast Guard VHF frequency and warned in English, French, or German that a human-powered aircraft and its attendant boats were crossing the Channel at a speed of about 8 knots. Each ship also received the latest position we had plotted for the airplane and was asked to avoid interfering with its course if possible. Most of them were courteous and cooperative.

Up to this point the flight had progressed smoothly, almost monotonously, with Bryan turning the propeller at about 100 rpm and maintaining an altitude of 8 to 10 feet. His control motions were smooth and minimal, and he only varied from his normal position to sip some water or adjust his helmet or microphone. At 05:30 Sam asked for an altitude check, and received no answer. "Bryan, this is Sam. How're you feeling?" Still no answer. "Bryan, I'm not really getting you at all. Can you nod your head if you can hear me . . . Roger, okay." Allen could still receive the project radio transmissions, but he couldn't answer. At the time he thought that the perspiration running down his hands had short-circuited the press-to-talk button, but since there was no static or variation, he later concluded that one of the two fine wires to the button must have broken during a control motion.

By 05:52 Bryan had pedaled 9.6 miles (15.5 kilometres), and was abeam of the Varne lightship. Half of his water was gone, and the flight was about 22 percent behind Paul's original schedule. The flotilla had veered slightly north of the theoretically shortest flight path of 138° magnetic corrected to avoid a southbound ship track, and the 3- to 4-knot easterly wind that we had recorded at Cap Gris-Nez was also blowing in mid-Channel. The water, which had been relatively smooth for the beginning of the flight, now began to show ripples of turbulence and a short swell.

At that point Bryan dipped lower, partly because of perception problems, and partly to try to find smoother air. The flying effort went up immediately: "Altitude three feet," Taras cautioned. Allen realized that he was in a trap, because it takes much more power to pump the plane up to a higher altitude than to maintain it at a constant height. "Altitude! Two feet," from Taras and Sam simultaneously. "Bryan, this is Sam. Watch your altitude." Bryan nodded, but couldn't seem to get much above three feet; it was as if the air-water boundary layer was holding the plane down. At that point Paul MacCready's estimate of the flight's chance for success sank from 16 percent to zero.

One hour and seventeen minutes: "Altitude two feet!" Taras cried. "Bryan, this is Sam, on your right. Did you say you were tired?" Even though the media crews couldn't hear the radio transmissions they sensed that something was wrong. All courtesy went by the board as what Jim Burke now began calling the "press jackals" came roaring in, tossing the Zodiacs in their wakes. "Watch your altitude," Sam warned again, and then, "Taras, get that boat out of there. Get that boat *out of there!*" Steve and Jim gunned their engines to head off the press boats, but the wakes of the larger craft spread into the flight path. Taras sounded angry and alarmed, "Altitude three feet . . . Altitude two feet! ALTITUDE ONE FOOT! . . . Altitude two feet."

"That's better," Sam called.

The airplane stabilized a little higher, but the swells seemed to lick upward at the *Albatross*'s fuselage, and Bryan's control motions were more extreme. Sam pulled up close to the plane and Bryan was able to get across to him that his hand was tired. "Okay, Bryan, this is Sam. If it gets to the point that you really want to ditch it, or something like that, raise your right hand up over your head and we can move into position." Bryan acknowledged that. "Another thing, what we could do, if you want, we could give you a tow . . ."

"Altitude one foot. Altitude four feet," Taras reported. The lower Bryan flew, the higher Taras's voice went. Paul radioed to Sam that if Bryan needed a tow, they should be sure that he got it in time, and that they should turn the plane into the wind (to the left), and then slowly curve around toward England. While Paul was talking, the flotilla was being orbited in what Ron Moulton described as "curious fashion" by a small warship. This was the *Lyre,* a French ex-minesweeper converted to a patrol boat, and one of the two problem ships of the flight. We had called her repeatedly, asking her to report her position, and to please avoid the *Albatross* flotilla, but without any response. A commandant of the French Coast Guard eventually convinced her to reply and bear off.

Bryan meanwhile kept plugging ahead, but it was obvious that he was having trouble. His altitude dropped to one foot repeatedly over the wave crests. Still, he refused to quit. Paul advised Sam and Bryan that "There's another one and a half hours of flight time required to ... reach France." Bryan's receiver was noisy, and all he heard was "One and a half ... to reach France." His heart sank: "One and a half *what?* Hours? How can I do *that?* Never mind the headwinds, just pedal," he told himself, hoping that the message would reach down into his muscles. Pedal and fly. By 06:25 Paul could encourage Bryan with a milestone: "Control to airplane. We're just about two-thirds of the distance from England ... to ... France ... meaning that it's only about an hour to go. Clear." Sam asked Bryan to nod if he got a good copy. Bryan did, and Sam had hardly gotten, "Excellent, great, thank you," out before the *Albatross* dropped to one foot again. Kirk Giboney, the first back-up pilot, came in over Taras's radio, "Get it up, Bryan, get it up!" Bryan tried, but realized that he was close to exhaustion. "It's no use ... I'll have to ditch or take a tow from one of the Zodiacs," he thought. At 06:26 he raised his right hand, the signal to scrub the flight.

"OKAY, OKAY, WE'RE COMING IN!" Sam called. Bill Watson readied the modified fishing rod that carried the tow line. The catch ring was under the airplane's fuselage, near the front wheel. Bryan put out a tremendous burst of power and climbed to 15 feet (4.5 metres) so Sam's boat could get underneath the plane. Jim gunned the engine, and began what developed into an inadvertent and frustrating marine ballet between the *Albatross* and the Zodiac. Although the boat could match the airplane's speed perfectly, matching its lateral motion in the wave chop was almost impossible; the two craft veered sideways past each other again and again, while Bill stood up and tried to snag the fuselage, and Jim lay down in the bottom of the boat to avoid being hit by the plane's propeller. After the third unsuccessful try Bill suddenly realized that Bryan was intentionally trying to avoid him; each time he reached up with the rod, Bryan would pull the aiplane out of reach. After four minutes of this, the other boats were baffled. "Sam, can you give us a status report?" Sterling asked. By that time Sam's crew had heard over the drone of the outboard Bryan saying ". . . try it up here for a while."

"I had accepted the inevitable — I had to give up. Then, when I did climb up to ten or fifteen feet I found the air much smoother, and thought, All right! We can keep going!"

"Bryan's tryin' it up a little higher, to see if it's less turbulent. He didn't want us to hook him in . . . at this time," Sam reported to the other boats.

At 06:38 Allen's water supply ran out, and a few moments later Sam noticed Bryan tapping the altimeter. He realized that something must be wrong with it; in fact the battcrics were dead. For Bryan, this was one more burden; near the limits of his physical capability, he was learning a lesson that all seaplane pilots know by hcart. "I couldn't really judge my altitude from the wave or ripple size. I could look out to the side and estimate my altitude from the angle to the various boats, but that angle would change as they would get closer or farther away. There just wasn't a reliable reference point I could depend on. There's also something slightly hypnotic about flying over water, especially when you're flying close to it. It's a very smooth rolling surface. I would become hypnotized by whatever that was, ripple size or something. Then I would hear 'One foot!' in my earphones."

Despite their self-discipline, the crew's fatigue and edginess was beginning to show through. At 06:40 several of them saw a large dark shadow in the distance and thought, *France!* Unfortunately, it was not France, but the bulk carrier *Jacob Russ,* and it had been preoccupying the radar crew and the French Coast Guard for the past half hour.

All supertankers and large bulk carriers transiting the Channel are subject to special traffic controls. They are required to use assigned lanes, to report their position frequently, and to carry pilots for longer times than smaller ships. The *Jacob Russ* was one of these monsters, 922 feet (281 metres) long by 140 feet (42.6 metres) beam (the Wright brothers' first successful engine-powered flight could have been made *across* the deck of this ship). She was registered in Hamburg, and had a deadweight tonnage of 137,644 — more than one and a quarter million times the weight of the *Gossamer Albatross*. She was northbound in the Channel, and when her Dutch captain was first informed about the *Albatross,* he wanted no part of it. He made it clear in truculent terms that he refused to change speed or course, and that the flotilla would have to look out for itself. A few moments later he was notified by the Calais Pilot Board that he was expected to take aboard a pilot for the next section of the Channel passage. This precipitated a verbal battle that made our problem seem trivial, and tied up both Channel 6 and Channel 10 (the main intership and Coast Guard radio frequencies) for the next half hour.

Meanwhile the *Lady Ellen Elizabeth* was still leading the *Albatross* fleet on a bearing that was both north of the ideal line, and a collision course with the *Jacob Russ* as well. The British and French coast guards gave us special permission to use Channel 16, the emergency frequency, to call Paul and warn him to veer south in order to avoid the ship. Sam relayed the decision to the plane: "Bryan, what we're gonna do, is probably go behind this thing . . . It's probably gonna be a good mile ahead of us or so, we'll be behind him before we reach him." Bryan could only nod and pedal. At 06:49 the lead boat had reached the *Jacob Russ*'s track and found that the turbulence in its wake was no worse than what they were already experiencing. Paul called that to Bryan and told him that there was less than one-quarter of the flight remaining. Two minutes later the batteries for the *Albatross*'s speedometer ran out. Like the altimeter batteries, they had lasted almost exactly the two hours predicted; it was just that two hours wasn't long enough.

Allen was now flying without his crucial water supply, without a radio transmitter, and without instruments, in a cockpit that was getting increasingly fogged with moisture despite the vents. "One foot!" Sterling called. "ALTITUDE ONE FOOT, GET IT UP!" Taras trebled. Bryan put out another burst of energy and dragged it up to five feet. At that moment he grimly recalled that one of the Kremer Channel Prize rules was that the altitude of the plane must not exceed 50 metres. No problem there, he thought.

06:57: Sam, quietly, without an exclamation point: "Bryan, I think I can see land." For Bryan it is like a vision of Atlantis. There are still more than three miles to go, and he knows that he is fading rapidly. At two hours and ten minutes, he gets a stab of pain in his right calf, the first cramp. He shifts most of the pedaling load to the left leg, and the cramped calf eases, to be replaced by another one in the left thigh. He knows from experience that without water and rest they are not going to go away.

Slowly, the coast of France begins to materialize out of the haze. The camera Zodiac has already pulled ahead to land, and Sam reports that he can see the lighthouse at Cap Gris-Nez. At the CROSSMA station the French Coast Guards have changed shifts. The new detail, Christian Chaudru, Arnaud Souplet, and Olivier Tresca, are still helping the bleary-eyed *Albatross* crew to warn ships away until the flotilla crosses the inshore traffic zone boundary, when the newsmen begin to appear. Willem Van Loon of Du Pont Netherlands arrives to lend a hand, as does Jean Louf with the Maschelein brothers, who have driven all night from Belgium to be here for the landing.

Will there be a landing? Carrying red smoke flares and spotlights we race down to the beach at the foot of the cliff. The tide is near neap, and there is a large expanse of wet brown sand exposed. As we reach the water's edge the camera Zodiac beaches in the surf, and Louis and Tony jump ashore, cradling their movie cameras. With binoculars, one can just make out the plane, floating like a spectral creature in the white haze. It seems to be standing still, both to us and to Bryan: "I can make out the French coast, but it seems to come no closer . . ." "C'MON BRYAN, C'MON UP, C'MON!! . . . YOU'RE MUSHING!" "All right! Altitude two . . . Time of flight two hours and twenty-four minutes."

For the fourth time during the flight Bryan thinks, "Well, this is it. I've done the best I could . . . and I haven't made it." And for the fourth time, some voice inside him answered, "No, doggone it, I've still got a little bit left and I'm gonna keep going." The plane's airspeed was now about 12 miles (19.3 kilometres) per hour, against a headwind of half that. To everyone — pilot, boats, beach crew — it was like slow motion, as if the plane were suspended in some lucent gel instead of air. "Only one and a quarter miles to go!" Paul transmitted. Privately, he raised his estimate of success from zero to 20 percent. "Like a Kremer length," Sam answered. Bryan, listening, thought, "Less distance than for the original Kremer Prize . . . no headwinds or turbulence then, no thirst, no cramps . . ."

Still, he pedaled inexorably closer. When he was within 1 mile (1.6 kilometres) of shore the water became too shallow for the bigger boats to maneuver; at 07:30 the *Lady Ellen Elizabeth* turned sharp left, and the flight director's Zodiac took over the lead. "Heading straight into the sun, Bryan. Watch your altitude," Sam warned. As soon as he said it he flashed on Icarus, and Bryan, in the mute body of the *Albatross,* did the same thing. He was too tired not to smile. Now the plane was clearly visible and beautiful from the shore. We were *willing* him to reach land; it was a physical sensation that you could feel in your chest. "I talk to myself and sense that my friends are talking too: Don't give up hope now, you *can* do it."

On the beach we are dazedly aiming our spotlights at the plane in what is almost full daylight. At 07:31 I set off the first smoke grenade. It is disheartening; the brilliant red plume streams out nearly horizontal from my raised arm, straight toward the *Albatross:* pure headwind. "Okay, Bryan," Sam calls, "you should be able to see some red smoke over there." Bryan looks, and once again the altitude drops to two feet. A moment later the French television networks send up a small red helium blimp to lift their transmission antenna. It makes an ideal aiming point for the boats, but Bryan is almost too exhausted to care. Both his left and right thighs and his right calf are cramping now. "One foot! Don't head for those rocks." Sam's tone is more plaintive than commanding.

The rocks were like the final test in a classical ordeal. The massive wedge of gray-black stone pointed seaward, blocking the south end of the beach below Cap Gris-Nez. At that surreal moment it seemed that it must have been placed there only a few minutes before, when we weren't looking, to foil the flight at the last moment. The southbound tide was running at more than three knots, and the point deflected the stream out toward the slowly approaching boats. Jim Burke had to angle his Zodiac at 30° to the tide to maintain course, and behind him Bryan kept drifting to the right, south, below the rocks. A press boat, sensing his distress, moved close in to starboard, too close, and its outriggers nearly took off the *Albatross*'s right wingtip. "Stick with us, Bryan; don't go to the right. Watch your altitude," came Sam's reassuring voice. "C'mon Bryan, *hang on*," Sterling called.

For a moment Bryan considers crashing on the rocks; it would still be land. Then he changes his mind, and decides to fly around them, against the wind, and try to save the plane. "One hundred yards. I am flying on reserves I never knew I had." We light the second smoke flare to show the wind direction. The *Albatross* suddenly yaws seaward, away from the beach, and Bryan bears down on the controls. The canard tilts all the way over, straining at the anti-yaw cords; at a hundred feet from the beach Allen has the hideous thought that he has blown it, is going to crash in the waves at the last minute instead of making it to land.

It is Janet's job to catch the ground handling line when the *Albatross* lands and stabilize the plane. She is running down the beach toward it, waving her scarf, screaming at the top of her lungs, "COME ON, BRYAN!!" For an agonizing moment the canard remains tilted over, and then the plane responds. Everything holds. Suddenly it is past the rocks, floating toward us, growing bigger and more familiar every second. A crowd of newsmen and spectators is running alongside it; it is strangely quiet; we can hear the sound of their footsteps on the sand. Janet is running the other way, toward the plane, fixated on the starboard wing line. Bryan stops pedaling, and the *Gossamer Albatross* hovers in the air for a few seconds, as if it is loath to land. Then it slowly settles to the ground, and Janet catches the wing cord and balances it against the wind. It is 07:40, Greenwich Mean Time. The flight is over.

On the *Lady Ellen Elizabeth,* Paul can still not allow himself to believe that the flight is successful. Parker MacCready, over the boat radio, wistfully: "Sam, did he make it to the land?" There is no answer from shore, and then they can see that the *Albatross*'s propeller is stopped, and that the plane is stationary and upright.

"Bryan, from Control, *Congratulations! Wonderful!*" Paul calls. "Project boats and airplane, from Control. We just sighted a large shark in the water, right here, so, glad Bryan made it all the way."

Bryan, too, is glad. The flight has taken 2 hours and 49 minutes, exactly one minute less than the absolute endurance limit of 170 minutes that Joe Mastropaolo had predicted five days earlier. The great circle distance was 22.2583 statute miles (35.8212 kilometres), but Paul has calculated that the *Albatross* flew more than 35 miles (56.3 kilometres) through the air to cover that distance.

A few seconds after the plane lands the right side of the cockpit is mobbed by newsmen, all converging on the point where the flying wires are attached at the bottom of the fuselage. Cameras held overhead, strobes flashing, microphones thrust forward like prehensile auditory organs, the media have arrived. Between the crowd's treading on the wires and a shift in wind, the plane begins to tilt over to starboard, and dozens of willing but unschooled hands grab for the port wing line, trying to pull it down against the *Albatross*'s nearly infinite roll moment. "Turn it *into the wind,*" we shout, to no avail. More and more hands pull on the line, until the spar, able to survive the English Channel, but not the hands of would-be helpers, gives up and breaks inboard of the left wing joint. Bryan has punched a hole through the Mylar on the right side of the fuselage; as Sterling cuts the door open with a sheath knife Bryan looks up at the broken wing and murmurs, "That's a bit of a drag."

"Where's Ingrid? Where's Ingrid?" Jack Conmy, so excited he can hardly bear it, fights his way through the crowd to find Dr. Dodd holding Bryan's arm, right where she's supposed to be. (Conmy refused to empty his water-filled boots for hours, and finally used them to baptize the floor of the bar at the Hotel Normandy in Wissant. His telegram announcing the successful flight to his cohorts at Du Pont headquarters in Wilmington began, "Oh, Ye of little faith . . .") Ingrid finds Bryan in remarkably good condition: He can walk, he can smile, and he can drink, first champagne, and then, more importantly, water.

As soon as he is out of the cockpit, team members are hugging him, Sam, Blaine, Bill, Taras, Janet, Lin Burke. He is given a shy kiss by an American lady who lives nearby, and a nosegay of flowers by the Lady Mayor of Wissant. A crocodile of little French schoolchildren right out of *Madeline* stands watching solemnly. It is an altogether appropriate greeting.

Meanwhile, on the *Lady Ellen* John Ward has opened a bottle of champagne, and Sterling has radioed to say that Jim Burke is on his way out to pick up Paul. A few minutes later they are on the beach, once again soaking wet, and Paul hobbles over to Bryan on his damp cast and gives him a giant, grinning bear hug. His immortal words? "Well done, take the rest of the day off!"

Epilogue

Some Reflections on the Gossamer Projects

THE DAY OF THE *Gossamer Albatross* flight passed for most of us like a film seen from the outside. When the airplane landed the whole team was high on adrenalin, and stayed that way for several hours afterward. Paul had made arrangements to store the components of the plane temporarily in the yard of a house above the beach at Cap Gris-Nez, the Villa "Les Algues," owned by M. et Mme. Pierre Flahaut. We carried the parts up there and stacked them on a terrace surrounded by a low stone wall. While they were being secured, they were examined closely by a short, stout Frenchman and his equally short and stout dog. The man kept poking at the airplane, and we asked him several times to please be gentle; it was obvious to everyone that he really wanted a piece of it. Crew members kept coming and going, and after a while he realized that it was hopeless; there were simply too many people. When he turned to go, the dog, who had been receiving his master's frustration through his leash the whole time, suddenly growled, jumped on the polystyrene foam bottom of the *Albatross*'s fuselage, and took a bite out of it. *Faute de mieux,* we thought, as they trotted off without a word.

Down on the beach, Jim and Lin Burke were trying to set up a return procedure for the boats. The *Tartan Gem,* which was to escort the Zodiacs back to Dover, already had her anchor up when Jim hailed her. Her crew gave him ten minutes, and in that time he and Lin and the three MacCready boys rigged two of the inflatables for tow, and brought all four Zodiacs out through the surf. Accompanied by one of the smaller press launches, they made it back to the Wellington Dock just before the gates closed, and before the water pump on Jim's engine seized up. Parker, Tyler, and Marshall took the Burkes in tow, and that is how the boats came home.

The rest of the crew, some of whom had not slept in 30 hours, went to the Hotel Normandy in Wissant, where no one seemed to have enough energy to make a decision about lunch. Eventually, at about 3 P.M., it arrived. The wine was excellent, the food was delicious, but for most of the Albatrossers, it was too late; there are several photographs of team members literally asleep on their plates.

By the time everyone straggled back to England via assorted ferries and hovercraft, arrangements had been made to take the triumphant *Albatross* to the Paris Air Show at Le Bourget. The crew member who called a first-class hotel on the Northeast Périphérique for room reservations was told, "Sorry, we're completely full." He hung up, thought a moment, called back, and told the clerk that the rooms were for the man who had just flown the Channel. "How many rooms do you want?" was the almost immediate question.

It was a prophetic response. That trip was the beginning of a year of nearly nonstop prizes, awards, and lectures for Paul and Bryan. It suddenly seemed that everyone wanted to know about the *Albatross,* about the project, and about the people involved in it. Even the *Condor,* which was now world-famous among aviation buffs but relatively unknown to laymen, began to share in the limelight. In April 1979, shortly before the team left for England, Ben Shedd's film, "The Flight of the *Gossamer Condor,*" won an Academy Award for documentaries, and soon we began seeing it as a short before airline feature films.

Although many of the team members had already dispersed, ten of them described their parts in the project at a party at the Granville Hotel in Ramsgate on June 30, to which Paul invited everyone in France and England who had helped us, and who could be contacted. A few weeks later the Gossamer airplanes were on their way back to the United States via Seatrain container, and many of the crew members were back at their respective jobs.

The most important of the various awards that the team was to receive was the one we had set out to win: The Kremer Cross-Channel Prize. Some time after the official observers' letters had been forwarded to the British Aircraft Owners' and Pilots' Association, thence to the Royal Aeronautical Society, and ultimately to the Fédération Aéronautique Internationale, Paul received word that we had indeed won the Cross-Channel Competition. As before, the prize ceremony was to be combined with the annual awards of the Royal Aero Club, and the date was set for Tuesday, December 18, 1979.

That week it seemed as though England was trying to make amends for the weather of the previous spring. The team assembled in London on December 15, a crisp day that ended with the city silhouetted against a clear Canaletto sky. The next morning some of us went to choral matins at St. Paul's Cathedral and were rewarded with a beautiful sunlit service and the pleasant feeling that not everything was being rendered unto Caesar. The other important visits were obvious; team members kept running into each other at the Royal Aeronautical Society, in the aircraft gallery of the Science Museum, at Foyle's Bookshop, and at Fortnum & Mason. There was time for reunions with our British friends, with the Du Pont group — Dick Woodward came over from Wilmington and was joined at the prize ceremony by Don Billett and the irreplaceable Margret Clarke — and with erstwhile team members. We were especially pleased to see Bill Beuby, Bill Richardson, and Jim Burke's father, Richard, all looking pink-cheeked and debonair.

There was a sprinkle of rain as we taxied to the Royal Automobile Club on Pall Mall at 5 P.M. on the 18th. After months of boots and blue jeans, it was again surprising to see how handsome the team looked in street clothes. This time, we also had something that many of the crew had missed, and commented on: a generous sprinkling of ladies, dressed for the occasion. (For Lin Burke, Janet Grosser, and Judy MacCready, who had spent weeks on the expedition in the same sort of utilitarian garb as the rest of the team, the transition to designer dresses was even more startling than the males' suits and ties.) Now they were accompanied by Beverly Allen, Margret Clarke, Kathy Cleary (Bill Beuby's daughter), Polly Copeland (Lin Burke's mother), and John Lake's daughter, Monica, who was a student in Paris.

At 6:15 His Royal Highness Prince Charles arrived, was introduced by the President of the Royal Aero Club, and proceeded to award prizes for aeronautical achievements ranging from hot-air balloon flights to the British Gliding Championship. He presented Paul MacCready with a larger and heavier bronze sculpture than the one commemorating the *Condor* flight, and a box of medals for the team; these were to be individually awarded later by Henry Kremer. Prince Charles had just checked out in the new British Aerospace *Hawk T*. Mk I jet trainer, and gave an irreverent and amusing description of the flight and its preparations. He then praised our Channel flight at some length. No one could have smiled more broadly than Jim Burke when the prince classified us with "the wonderful eccentrics and mad Englishmen who are willing to try things other people won't do."

After his talk, the accompanying security guards asked the crowd to "Please clear a path for the prince." Behind them, their charge was paying no attention whatever. He began to circulate among the guests, talking enthusiastically about airplanes, and each member of the *Albatross* team was presented to him in turn. Beverly Allen renewed her acquaintance from the *Condor* award ceremony, and gave the prince a T-shirt autographed by the Channel crew to add to his collection. About an hour later Prince Charles left, from all reports well behind his tightly planned schedule. We had the impression that this group of aviators was one he enjoyed and with whom he felt perfectly at ease; certainly that is how we felt with him.

The Royal Aero Club reception was followed by a dinner at the Royal Aeronautical Society. Our group bused and taxied there, and were welcomed by the members of the Man-Powered Aircraft Group Committee, who were ultimately responsible for our being in England. There was one sad absence. Beverley Shenstone, who started it all, had died on November 9, at the age of 73. The other members of the committee were consoled to some extent by the thought that at least Shenstone had lived to see the two major Kremer prizes won, a satisfaction that had been denied Bob Graham.

The speechmaking at the RAeS was of the most informal kind, since everyone was busy socializing and talking shop. Paul gave another talk about the contributions of the team, Mr. Kremer awarded medals, and there was a show of slides and clips from the BBC movie of the flight. There was also an enthusiastically consumed dinner, and continuous signing of programs and photographs. When we came out on Hamilton Place at midnight the rain had disappeared, and we could see stars overhead. Many of us walked back to our hotels, still talking and trading anecdotes.

One of the Man-Powered Aircraft Group Committee members at the Kremer Prize dinner was Rear Admiral Goodhart, the proposer of the human-powered cross-Channel race. We were all curious about the progress of his *Newbury Manflier*. He told us that it was essentially completed and waiting, as we had, for decent flying weather. That finally came on January 1, 1980, only a few days after we returned to the United States. Given our experience, we could only be awed by the problems of a human-powered plane with two pilots and one and a half times the wingspan of the *Gossamer Albatross*. To Admiral Goodhart's great credit, the *Manflier* flew 400 yards (365.7 metres) on its first attempt. It suffered some spar damage on a second flight, but that was subsequently repaired, and by April 1980 the plane was ready to fly again.

In that month we lost another of our good friends at the Royal Aeronautical Society. On April 25, Kenneth Clark, who had been for years the secretary of MAPAC, died suddenly at age 75. Since the days of the first Kremer Competition, he had been our chief liaison with the RAeS and had supplied us with information, help, and generous encouragement. Perhaps even more than the British competitors, we appreciated the temperament that allowed him to answer the sometimes naïve and picayune questions of what must have seemed a bunch of lunatic sun-worshipers, without ever losing his patience and sense of humor.

And what about the sun-worshipers? It was clear soon after the *Albatross* team returned from England that the bonds forged between us were more than temporary. Since that time the group has been in more or less continuous communication. Paul has initiated several new projects, including a NASA-funded study of low-speed stability and control using the *Albatross 2,* and a Du Pont–sponsored conversion of the *Gossamer Penguin* to the first direct solar-powered airplane in the world. (In May 1980, without assistance from batteries or pedals, 13-year-old Marshall MacCready piloted the *Penguin* on the first human-carrying airplane flight powered solely by sunlight.) Members of the Gossamer Squadron worked on both of these projects, but even without formal contracts it is clear that some chemistry of creativity and mutual respect stronger than economic reward connects the whole group.

Why did the *Condor* and *Albatross* projects work? What were the factors that led to success where so many others had failed? Hundreds of people have asked us that, separately and together. Paul MacCready thinks that we succeeded because of four principles: First, *Single-mindedness:* keeping the goal in mind, and doing only what had to be done. Second, *Persistence:* having enough resolve to surmount the inevitable and recurrent stumbling blocks. Third, *Flexibility:* being willing (and able) to change the design and solve problems by evolution. Fourth, *Confidence:* being certain that the vehicles could be made to work. MacCready was particularly grateful that no limiting structural requirements were written into the Kremer rules. He regards the simple and lightweight structure of the *Condor* and the *Albatross* as one of two major contributing factors to their success. The other one was the safety and convenience for testing of a low flying speed.

In retrospect Paul thinks that much work and aggravation could have been saved by hurrying less and by more thorough theoretical work. He also believes that no one on the projects, himself included, realized the crucial effects of turbulence on aircraft that operate at such very low flying speeds and with such low power. Whether from air currents or erratic control motions, turbulence penalizes the Gossamer aircraft heavily, both through parasite drag and induced drag. The diversity and subtlety of these effects still intrigue MacCready, and he hopes to quantify them with the data from the *Albatross 2*'s tests for NASA.

When Bryan Allen is asked about his superb performance as the pilot/engine of the Gossamer aircraft, he often credits the direction and encouragement of his trainer, Dr. Joseph Mastropaolo. That citation would be echoed by everyone on the team, but allowance also has to be made for Allen's own modesty and sense of proportion. For most of us, his success would have to include the word "grit." (A year after the Channel flight, Paul MacCready was still awed and mystified by the physical and psychological resources that Bryan was able to draw on during the crossing.) The athletic aspect of the projects has also tended to obscure Bryan's natural talent and smoothness as a pilot. During the NASA tests with the heavily instrumented *Albatross 2,* the best flight data was recorded when Bryan was pedaling it. His flight was significantly smoother than when the plane was powered by an electric motor, or when it was flown by any of several highly skilled NASA test pilots.

John Lake and Peter Lissaman would say that the Gossamer projects worked because of the resources and sociology of California. Both of them cite the confluence of a great many talented people connected by a flexible social structure and a good communication network. Lake would also add technical and material resources, the convenient availability of incredible numbers of things that Californians take for granted. There is no question that it helped to be able to buy aircraft aluminum tubing, stainless steel wire, VHF radios, ten kinds of plastic foam, and a hundred different adhesives off the shelf in a few minutes. It also helped to be able to find precision machinists, aerodynamicists, tube etchers, and polymer chemists within a few miles of wherever one happened to be. Both are possible in California.

There is a corollary to Lake and Lissaman's theorem. The projects succeeded not only because of who people were, and what they could do, but also because of how they acted, and that, too, is different in California. Given the difference in their ages, positions, and putative wisdom, Paul's reaction to Bryan's criticism was not likely to be the same in a tightly structured organization or a traditional society. It was far from the only example of what would be an atypical response in a corporate setting.

On one occasion a somewhat stiff executive happened to be visiting the hangar when a disagreement arose over the construction of a part. "Do it this way," Paul said to the group working on it. A much younger member of the team replied with conviction, "That's really a dumb idea." The visitor flushed angrily — it was the unmistakable look of a guest who can barely resist spanking his host's child. Paul hesitated a moment. "Well . . . why?" The junior member explained why. Paul thought about it a moment, and said, "Okay, try it your way." (He didn't always say that, but when the decision went the other way, it was accepted.) The visitor's reaction was a mixture of surprise and indignation.

Visitors to the hangars were also often surprised by the way work was assigned. The construction chief, or whoever was acting fore-man for the day, would go over the airplane, and write down all the jobs that needed to be done. His list, usually written on several sheets of lined yellow paper taped end-to-end, was then posted on the hangar wall. Whenever someone finished what he was working on, he would stroll over to the list and scan it from top to bottom. "Hmmm," was a common audible accompaniment to this survey, followed by, "Okay, I guess I can do that." Occasionally this laissez-faire process resulted in entries like "Organization is in chaos." Most often, and ultimately, it resulted in people's doing what they were best at and producing a successful and well-crafted plane in a remarkably short time.

Summed up, the Gossamer Squadron's list of requirements for success doesn't look very novel: single-mindedness; persistence; flexibility; confidence; skilled direction; encouragement; grit; na-tural coordination and athletic ability; craftsmanship; quality ma-terials. To these I would add patience, mutual respect, and humor — there are many examples of good manners and few examples of short temper during the *Condor* and *Albatross* projects. "Well, of course," one thinks, "what couldn't be accomplished with all that?" And yet, there were teams in other countries who must have had many of these advantages as well; from meeting even a few of our colleague/competitors, we can be sure of it.

Though they are of different nationalities and grew up 6000 miles (10,000 kilometres) apart, Bill Beuby and Ron Moulton have, at least in part, an additional explanation, one to which Paul Mac-Cready has also referred at times. Since they are both aeronautic experts as well as wise and generous men, and since both were invaluable to the Gossamer projects, it would be crass to omit their viewpoint. During the team's stay in England, Moulton could not help noticing the unstatistical nature of our activities, and referred on several occasions to MacCready's "biblical connections." Beuby had long before made similar observations about the extraordinary coincidences that led to the team's coalescence. After the Channel flight, Paul felt that there was more to explain than our work could account for. He did not want to get any more specific than that, but he too felt that there were a remarkable number of coincidences involved in the activities of the Gossamer Squadron.

He was not dissuaded from that view when, three months after the Channel flight, he and Janet Grosser discovered that the lady who caught the *Gossamer Albatross*'s landing line on the beach at Cap Gris-Nez had been the teenage girl learning to fly the Piper L-4 at Brainard Field in Connecticut when Paul was learning to fly his Pratt-Read glider there in 1947.

On May 16, 1980, Paul MacCready was awarded the most prestigious prize in American aviation, the Collier Trophy. The trophy is named for Robert J. Collier, a president of the Aero Club of America, and is awarded annually for "The greatest achievement in aeronautics or astronautics in America, with respect to improving the performance, efficiency, and safety of air or space vehicles, the value of which has been throughly demonstrated by actual use during the preceding year." Some of its prior recipients include Glenn Curtis, Orville Wright, and the crew of Apollo 11. MacCready's citation was for "The concept, design, and construction of the *Gossamer Albatross,* which made the first man-powered flight across the English Channel — with special recognition to Bryan Allen, the pilot." It is a fitting summation to the history of the *Gossamer Condor* and *Gossamer Albatross.*

*　　*　　*

Paris, Spring, 1884: After twenty-one years of reconstruction, hundreds of Parian marble fragments found on the island of Samothrace by Charles-François-Noël Champoiseau in 1863, together with 26 blocks of Thasos marble weighing 3080 pounds (1400 kilograms) each, have been assembled into an incomplete but magnificent statue and its base. The figure dates from circa 190 B.C., and it is installed on the landing of a grand staircase, the Escalier Daru, of the Musée du Louvre. It is unveiled to tremendous critical and public acclaim, and soon becomes the most-photographed object in the museum. The statue, of a winged woman, lifts irresistibly upward from the stone that imprisoned it, symbolizing one of man's oldest dreams. It is named *La Victoire de Samothrace* . . .

ο'δεν νεον ὑπο τον ἑλιον

THERE IS NO NEW THING
UNDER THE SUN

APPENDICES
BIBLIOGRAPHY
ILLUSTRATION CREDITS
INDEX

Appendices

THE GOSSAMER SQUADRON

Although many people contributed to the Gossamer aircraft projects, the following roll includes those who worked on the projects for extended periods of time, or who made contributions of significant value. A superscript 1 identifies the *Condor* team, a 2 the *Albatross* team.

Bryan Allen[1,2]
Ted Ancona[2]
Mike Bame[2]
Bill Beuby[1]
Jim Burke[1,2]
Lin Burke[1,2]
Gary Cox[2]
Sam Durán[1,2]
Steve Elliott[2]
Phil Esdaile[1]
Jack Franklin[1] *
Kirk Giboney[2]
Janet Grosser[2]
Morton Grosser[2]
Ken Hamlyn[2]
Tom Horton[2]
Henry Jex[1]

Taras Kiceniuk Jr.[2]
Norm Kozma[2]
Chet Kyle[1]
John Lake[1]
Jack Lambie[1,2]
Karen Lambie[1,2]
Kirke Leonard[1,2]
Kirke Leonard Jr.[1,2]
Stan Levy[2]
Peter Lissaman[1,2]
Judy MacCready[1,2]
Marshall MacCready[1,2]
Parker MacCready[1,2]
Paul MacCready[1,2]
Tyler MacCready[1,2]
Joe Mastropaolo[1,2]

Paul McKibben[1,2]
Larry McNay[2]
Greg Miller[1]
Maude Oldershaw[1]
Vern Oldershaw[1]
Pete Plumb[1]
Bill Richardson[1,2]
Dave Saks[2]
Mark Schwinge[2]
Ed Shenk[2]
Jeff Stephenson[2]
Sterling Stoll[2]
Scott Strom[2]
John Volk[2]
Bill Watson[2]
Mike Reagan[2]
Bill Richardson[1,2]

The Du Pont team for the *Albatross* included Don Billett, Margret Clarke, Jack Conmy, Roger Morris, Willem Van Loon, Dick Woodward.

* Deceased

THE RULES FOR THE KREMER COMPETITIONS
AS ISSUED BY
THE ROYAL AERONAUTICAL SOCIETY
*
MAN POWERED FLIGHT

A prize of £50,000 is offered by Mr. Henry Kremer for a successful controlled flight of a Man Powered Aircraft under conditions laid down by the Man Powered Aircraft Group of the Royal Aeronautical Society. The official observers will be selected from a body approved by the Royal Aeronautical Society and the Aircraft Owners' and Pilot's Association.

The Regulations and Conditions governing the award, which is to be known as the £50,000 Kremer Competition, are as follows.

This competition shall be conducted by the Aircraft Owners' and Pilots' Association under the Regulations and Conditions laid down by the Royal Aeronautical Society.

REGULATIONS

1. GENERAL
   The prize will be awarded to the entrant who first fulfils the conditions.

2. PRIZE
   The prize is £50,000 sterling.

3. ELIGIBILITY
   The competition is international and is open to individuals or teams from any part of the world. Rights of appeal will be governed by the Competition Rules of the AOPA and the Sporting Code of the Fédération Aéronautique Internationale.

4. CONDITIONS OF ENTRY
4.1 *Aircraft*
   4.1.1 The machine shall be a heavier-than-air machine.

4.1.2 The use of lighter-than-air gases shall be prohibited.

4.1.3 The machine shall be powered and controlled by the crew of the machine over the entire flight.

4.1.4 No devices for storing energy either for take-off or for use in flight shall be permitted.

4.1.5 No part of the machine shall be jettisoned during any part of the flight including take-off.

4.2 *Crew*

4.2.1 The crew shall be those persons in the machine during take-off and flight, and there shall be no limit set to their number.

4.2.2 No member of the crew shall be permitted to leave the aircraft at any time during take-off or flight.

4.2.3 One handler or ground crew shall be permitted to assist in stabilising the machine during take-off, but in such a manner that he is unable to assist in accelerating the machine.

4.3 *Ground Conditions*

4.3.1 All attempts, which shall include the take-off run, shall be made over approximately level ground (i.e. with a slope not exceeding 1 in 200 in any direction), and on a course to be approved by the AOPA or in conjunction with its authorised representatives.

4.3.2 All attempts shall be made in still air, which shall be defined as a wind not exceeding a mean speed of approximately 10 knots, over the period of the flight.

4.4 *Course*

4.4.1 The course shall be figure of eight, embracing two turning points, which shall be not less than half a mile apart.

4.4.2 The machine shall be flown clear of and outside each turning point.

4.4.3 The starting line, which shall also be the finishing line, shall be between the turning points and shall be approximately at right angles to the line joining the turning points.

4.4.4 The height, defined as ground clearance, both at the start and the finish, shall be not less than ten feet above the ground; otherwise there shall be no restriction in height.

4.4.5 The machine shall be in continuous flight over the entire course.

4.5 *Observation*

Every attempt shall be observed by the AOPA or by any body or persons authorised by them to act as observers. It may take place in the Competitor's own country if it is affiliated to the FAI. In a country not so it could be advantageous to fly the course in a neighbouring country which is so affiliated.

5. APPLICATION FOR ENTRY

5.1 Entry Forms shall be obtained from, and returned to, The Secretary, Man Powered Aircraft Group, The Royal Aeronautical Society, 4 Hamilton Place, London WIV oBQ.

5.2 The entry fee shall be £1 (made payable to the Royal Aeronautical Society), which shall be refunded upon the attempt taking place.

5.3 Each entry form shall contain an application for Official Observation of the Competitor's attempt.

5.4 The entrant shall undertake to abide by the conditions for Official Observation as set out on the entry form and shall undertake to defray all expenses incurred in connection with the Official Observation of the attempt.

5.5 Final notice of the proposed time and place of the attempt requiring Official Observation may, if so wished, be sent to the RAeS later than the Entry Form. It must in all cases be received at least thirty days before the proposed date for the attempt. This time is required by the AOPA to arrange for Official Observation. Applications will be considered in order of receipt.

5.6 The Entry Form or the final notice of the attempt must be accompanied by the sum of £15, made payable to the Aircraft Owners' and Pilots' Association.

5.7 *Competitor's Annual Licence*
This licence is required for all pilots taking part in the Kremer Competitions. It is not required for other flights. Application forms may be obtained as in paragraph 5.1.

6. GENERAL CONDITIONS

6.1 *Insurance*
The entrant must take out on behalf of himself, his pilot(s), crew, representatives or employees, an adequate insurance to indemnify the Society against any claims. Evidence that such insurance has been effected must be produced to the Official Observers before the attempt.

6.2 *Eligibility*

In any question regarding the acceptance of entries, eligibility of entrant, pilot, crew or aircraft under these Regulations, the decision of the RAeS shall be final.

6.3 *Supplementary Regulations*

The RAeS reserves the right to add to, amend or omit any of these regulations and to issue Supplementary Regulations.

6.4 *Interpretation of Regulations*

The interpretation of these Regulations or any of the Regulations hereafter issued shall rest entirely with the RAeS. The entrant shall be solely responsible to the Official Observers for due observance of these Regulations and shall be the person with whom the Official Observers will deal in respect thereof, or any other question arising out of this Competition.

6.5 *Revision of Regulations*

These Regulations shall remain in force until such time as the Royal Aeronautical Society considers it necessary to amend them, or the prize has been won.

REGULATIONS AND CONDITIONS FOR
THE £100,000 KREMER COMPETITION
FOR A FLIGHT FROM ENGLAND TO FRANCE
OCTOBER 1978
THE ROYAL AERONAUTICAL SOCIETY

*

MAN POWERED FLIGHT

A prize of £100,000 is offered by Mr. Henry Kremer for the first successful controlled flight of a Man Powered Aircraft from the mainland of the UK to the mainland of France under the following Regulations and Conditions laid down by the Man Powered Aircraft Group of the Royal Aeronautical Society (RAeS). The Official Observer or Observers will be selected from a body approved by the Royal Aeronautical Society and the Royal Aero Club of the UK.

The Competition shall be conducted by the Aircraft Owners' and Pilots' Association (UK) on behalf of the Royal Aero Club under the Regulations and Conditions which follow.

The award is to be known as the £100,000 Kremer Cross-Channel Competition.

REGULATIONS AND CONDITIONS

1. GENERAL

The prize will be awarded to the entrant who first fulfils the conditions.

2. PRIZE

The prize is £100,000.

3. ELIGIBILITY

The competition is international and is open to individuals or teams from any part of the world. Rights of appeal will be governed by the Competition Rules of the AOPA (UK) and the principles of the Sporting Code of the Fédération Aéronautique Internationale (FAI).

4. CONDITIONS OF ENTRY
4.1 *Aircraft*
    4.1.1 The machine shall be a heavier-than-air machine.
    4.1.2 The use of hot air or lighter-than-air gases shall be prohibited.
    4.1.3 The machine shall be powered and controlled solely by its crew over the entire flight.
    4.1.4 No device for storing energy during any part of the flight shall be permitted except as described in 4.4.4.
    4.1.5 No part of the machine or its equipment shall be jettisoned during any part of the flight.
    4.1.6 The machine shall not receive aerodynamic assistance from any vessel or aircraft.

4.2 *Safety*
    4.2.1 Prior to any competition attempt, the machine must have made an officially observed flight of at least two minutes' duration or 400 m (437 yds) distance and landed without damage. Any such demonstration flights, including the take-off run, shall be made over approximately level ground (i.e. with a slope not exceeding 1 in 200 in any direction) within the United Kingdom, and on a site to be approved by the AOPA (UK) or in conjunction with its authorised representatives. If the machine is modified after the demonstration flight it may be required to make a further flight. There is no restriction on the course covered by the flight except that at some point between take-off and landing, the aircraft shall exceed a height of two metres above the ground.
    4.2.2 For the Cross-Channel attempt the entrant(s) shall be responsible for making adequate arrangements, which are to be approved by the AOPA (UK) prior to the attempt, to ensure the safety of the crew following a forced landing on water.
    4.2.3 Any attempt shall be escorted by at least one suitable vessel, vehicle or aircraft, capable of rescuing the crew. The escort arrangements shall include provision for operating in shallow water. These shall be provided by the entrant.

4.3 *Crew*
    4.3.1 The crew shall be those persons on the machine during take-off and flight, and there shall be no limit set to their number.

4.3.2 No member of the crew shall be permitted to leave the aircraft at any time during take-off or flight.

4.3.3 No drugs or stimulants shall be used by any member of the crew. The definition of drugs or stimulants shall be that of the International Amateur Athletic Federation current at the time of the flight.

4.3.4 A maximum number of three ground crew shall be permitted to assist in stabilising the machine during take-off, but in such a manner that they do not assist in accelerating the machine.

4.4 *Take-off Conditions*

4.4.1 For the Cross-Channel attempt the location of the take-off shall be subject to the approval of the AOPA (UK) or their Official Observer.

4.4.2 The starting point of the take-off is defined as the most forward point of contact between the machine and the surface from which it takes off.

4.4.3 The starting point of the take-off run shall not exceed 30 m above Ordnance Datum.

4.4.4 The take-off may be from a fixed artificial ramp, the total fall of which does not exceed 6 m (19.7 ft).

4.4.5 Take-off is permissible also from water or from a stationary vessel. In this case the starting point of take-off shall not exceed 30 m above water. The entire machine must then fly over land directly connected to the UK shore line, and uncovered by the sea at the time of the event. An Official Observer must verify that this has been done.

4.4.6 No external connection between the machine and the ground, or sea or any other object, shall be permitted during the take-off or any part of the flight except as may be required to fulfil paragraph 4.3.4.

4.5 *The Course*

4.5.1 The course shall be from the mainland of the UK to the mainland of France.

4.5.2 The machine shall be in continuous flight over the entire course.

4.5.3 During the flight, the height of the lowest part of the machine shall not substantially exceed 50 m above the sea for any period of three minutes.

4.5.4 The machine will have deemed to have completed the course when it lands on the French Mainland which is uncovered by the sea at that time.

4.6 *Observation*

    4.6.1 Every attempt shall be observed by the AOPA (UK) or by any organisation or person(s) authorised by them to act as Observers.

    4.6.2. Every attempt shall be continuously observed from take-off to completion of the course.

5. APPLICATION FOR ENTRY

5.1 Entry forms shall be obtained from, and returned to The Secretary, Man Powered Aircraft Group, The Royal Aeronautical Society, (RAeS), 4 Hamilton Place, London W1V oBQ.

5.2 The entry fee shall be £10 (made payable to the Royal Aeronautical Society) which shall be refunded upon the attempt taking place.

5.3 Each entry form shall contain an application for Official Observation of the competitor's attempt.

5.4 The entrant shall undertake to abide by the conditions for Official Observation as set out on the entry form, and shall undertake to defray all expenses incurred in connection with the Official Observation of the attempt.

5.5 Final notice of the proposed time and place of the attempt requiring Official Observation may, if so wished, be sent to the RAeS later than the Entry Form. It must in all cases be received at least thirty days before the proposed first day for the attempt. This time is required by the AOPA to arrange for Official Observation. Applications will be considered in order of receipt.

5.6 The Entry Form or the final notice of the attempt must be accompanied by the sum of £15, made payable to the Aircraft Owners' and Pilots' Association (UK).

5.7 *FAI Sporting Licence*
This licence is required for all pilots taking part in the Kremer Competition, or making record attempts. Application forms for those who do not already possess an FAI Sporting Licence issued by their NAeC may be obtained from The Royal Aeronautical Society, 4 Hamilton Place, London W1V oBQ.

6. GENERAL CONDITIONS

6.1 *Insurance*
The entrant must take out on behalf of himself, his pilot(s), crew, representatives or employees, an insurance to indemnify the Society against all claims arising out of the attempts in the terms of the

Standard Policy obtainable from the RAeS at their address mentioned above. Evidence that such insurance has been effected must be produced to the Official Observers before the attempt.

6.2 *Acceptance of Entries*

In any question regarding the acceptance of entries, eligibility of entrant, pilot, crew or aircraft under the Regulations and Conditions, the decision of the RAeS shall be final.

6.3 *Supplementary Regulations*

The RAeS reserves the right to add to, amend or omit any of these Regulations and Conditions and to issue Supplementary Regulations and Conditions.

6.4 *Interpretation of Regulations and Conditions*

The interpretation of these Regulations and Conditions or any of the Regulations or Conditions hereafter issued shall rest entirely with the RAeS. The entrant shall be solely responsible to the Official Observers for due observance of these Regulations and Conditions and shall be the person with whom the Official Observers will deal in respect thereof, or any other question arising out of this Competition.

6.5 *Revision of Regulations and Conditions*

These Regulations and Conditions shall remain in force until such time as the Royal Aeronautical Society considers it necessary to cancel or amend them, or the prize has been won.

MEMBERS OF THE ROYAL AERONAUTICAL SOCIETY
MAN-POWERED AIRCRAFT GROUP COMMITTEE
AS OF JUNE 12, 1979

Mr. M. J. Brennan — Chairman
Mr. K. W. Clark
Rear Admiral H. C. N. Goodhart
Mr. C. F. Joy
Professor G. M. Lilley
Mr. R. G. Moulton — Vice Chairman
Squadron Leader J. Potter
Mr. M. S. Pressnell
Mr. B. S. Shenstone
Dr. K. Sherwin
Mr. F. W. Vann
Professor D. R. Wilkie
Mr. J. C. Wimpenny

Bibliography

PRIMARY SOURCES

Much of the research for this book was in the form of personal interviews and shared experiences. These were seldom recorded; where recordings were used, as in the case of narrated personal histories or radio transmission tapes, they are listed below.

Manuscripts

Allen, Bryan. Letters to author and to Paul MacCready; notes on the Gossamer aircraft projects; pilot's logs of the *Gossamer Condor* and *Gossamer Albatross,* March 1977 through June 1979.
Beuby, William. Autobiographical notes; letters to author.
Burke, James D. Letters to author; notes on the *Gossamer Albatross* Channel expedition.
Champagne, Isabelle MacCready. Letters to author.
Giboney, Kirk. Letter to author; pilot's log of the *Gossamer Albatross,* April to June 1979.
Goodhart, Rear Admiral H. C. N. Letters to author; specifications of the *Newbury Manflier.*
Gronen, Wolfgang. Letters to author.
Jex, Henry. Autobiographical notes; flight dynamics calculations for the *Gossamer Condor.*
Kiceniuk, Taras, Jr. Autobiographical notes.
MacCready, Edith Hollingsworth. Diary notes.
MacCready, Paul B., Sr., "A Father Looks at Flying"; diary notes.
MacCready, Paul B., Jr. Autobiographical notes; calculations, drawings, and original design studies for the *Gossamer Condor* and *Gossamer Albatross*; diary notebooks for June 1976 through July 1979; letters to author.
Mastropaolo, Joseph. Autobiographical notes; letters to author; physiology calculations for Bryan Allen, Paul, Parker, and Tyler MacCready.

Plant, Anne MacCready. Autobiographical notes; letters to author.

Richardson, Bill. Letters to author.

Shenk, Edwin K. Autobiographical notes; design criteria and circuitry for *Gossamer Albatross* altimeter.

Recordings

Beuby, William. Autobiographical tape recording.

Gossamer Albatross Team. English Channel flight radio tapes recorded on 154.15 mHz, 12 June 1979; debriefing tapes recorded 13 June 1979.

Jex, Henry. Autobiographical tape recording.

Lake, John. Autobiographical tape recording.

SECONDARY SOURCES

Books

Angelucci, Enzo, and Paolo Matricardi, *World Aircraft* (Chicago: Rand McNally, 1979).

————, *World War II Airplanes* (Chicago: Rand McNally, 1978).

Barringer, Lewin B., *Flight Without Power* (New York: Pitman Publishing, 1940).

Bianconi, Piero, *The Complete Paintings of Bruegel* (New York: Abrams, 1967).

Burke, James D., *The Gossamer Condor and Albatross: A Case Study in Aircraft Design* (Pasadena, California: Aerovironment, 1980).

Dalton, Stephen, *The Miracle of Flight* (New York: McGraw-Hill, 1977).

DeDera, Don, *Hang Gliding: The Flyingest Flying* (Flagstaff, Arizona: Northland Press, 1975).

Dwiggins, Don, *Man-Powered Aircraft* (Blue Ridge Summit, Pennsylvania: Tab Books, 1979).

Foote, Timothy, ed., *The World of Bruegel* (New York: Time-Life, 1968).

Fouquet, Richard J., ed., *Pilot's Guide to California Airports* (Los Altos, California: Optima Publications, 1974).

Getty Oil Company, *Getty in California* (Los Angeles, 1978).

Gibbs-Smith, Charles H., *Aviation: An Historical Survey from Its Origins to the End of World War II* (London: Her Majesty's Stationery Office, 1970).

Gilbert, James, *The Flier's World* (New York: Grosset & Dunlap, 1976).

Green, William, ed., *The Aircraft of the World* (London: Macdonald, 1965).

Gunston, Bill, *The Complete Story of Man's Conquest of the Air* (London: Octopus Books, 1978).

Guttery, T. E., *The Shuttleworth Collection* (Biggleswade, U.K., 1976).

Jameson, William, *The Wandering Albatross* (New York: William Morrow, 1959).

Kimura, Hidemasa, *Man Powered Aircraft Since 1963* (Tokyo: Nihon University Research Institute of Science and Technology, 1977).

Poynter, Dan, *Hang Gliding* (Santa Barbara, California: Parachuting Publications, 1977).

Reay, David A., *The History of Man-Powered Flight* (Oxford: Pergamon Press, 1977).

Riedel, Peter, *Start in den Wind* (Stuttgart: Motorbuch Verlag, 1928).

Robins, James G., *The Wooden Wonder* (Edinburgh: John Bartholomew, 1974).

Rüppell, Georg, *Bird Flight* (New York: Van Nostrand Reinhold, 1977).

Schmidt-Nielsen, Knut, *How Animals Work* (London: Cambridge University Press, 1972).

Schulze, Hans-Georg, and Willi Stiasny, *Flug Durch Muskelkraft* (Frankfurt am Main: Verlag Fritz Knapp, 1936).

Sherwin, Keith, *Man Powered Flight* (Watford, U.K.: Model & Allied Publications, 1975).

———, *To Fly Like a Bird* (Folkestone, U.K.: Bailey Brothers & Swinfen, 1976).

Simons, Martin, *Model Aircraft Aerodynamics* (Watford, U.K.: Model & Allied Publications, 1978).

Taylor, J. H., and David Mondey, eds., *The Guinness Book of Air Facts and Feats* (Enfield, U.K.: Guinness Superlatives Limited, 1973).

Udvardy, Miklos D. F., *The Audubon Society Field Guide to North American Birds: Western Region* (New York: Alfred Knopf, 1977).

Various authors, *Man Powered Flight: The Channel Crossing and the Future* (London: The Royal Aeronautical Society Third Man Powered Aircraft Group Symposium, 1979).

Welch, Ann, *The Book of Airsports* (New York: Arco, 1978).

———, and F. G. Irving, *The Soaring Pilot* (London: John Murray, 1957).

Articles

Allen, Bryan, "Winged Victory of Gossamer Albatross," *National Geographic,* 640–651 (Washington, D.C., November 1979).

Brechner, Berl, "Mojave — An Airport in the California Desert with a Spirit of Rebellion," *Flying,* 134–141 (New York, June 1979).

Hacklinger, Max, "Theoretical and Experimental Investigation of Indoor Flying Models," *Journal of the Royal Aeronautical Society 68,* 728–733 (London, 1964).

Hewish, Mark, "How Gossamer Condor Was Pedalled Through the Sky to Win £50,000," *New Scientist,* 28–29 (London, 6 October 1977).

Jones, Michael, "Interview: Bryan Allen," *Glider Rider,* 33–36 (Chattanooga, Tennessee, August 1979).

Lambie, Jack, "In the Beginning — The First Hang Gliding Meet," *Hang Gliding,* 14–20 (Los Angeles, California, December 1978).

————, "The Gossamer Condor," *Air Progress 40,* 41–45, 71–73 (Canoga Park, California, January 1978).

————, "The Story of the Gossamer Condor," *Aeromodeller,* 138–143 (Hemel Hempstead, U.K., March 1978).

Le Cheminant, A. N., "So the Kremer Prize Has Been Won," *Canadian Aeronautics and Space Journal 24,* 399–402 (Ottawa, November/December 1978).

Lissaman, P. B. S.; H. R. Jex; and P. B. MacCready Jr., "Aerodynamics of Flight at Speeds under 5m/sec."

Larrabee, E. Eugene, "The Screw Propeller," *Scientific American,* 134–148 (New York, July 1980).

Long, Michael E., "The Flight of the *Gossamer Condor*," *National Geographic,* 130–140 (Washington, D.C., January 1978).

MacCready, Paul B., Jr., "Developments in Ultralight Gliding," *Soaring,* 23–29 (Los Angeles, California, June 1976).

————, "Flight of the Gossamer Condor," *Science Year 1979,* 85–99 (Chicago, Illinois, 1979).

————, "Flight on 0.33 Horsepower: The Gossamer Condor," *AIAA Paper No. 78-308* (Washington, D.C., February 1978).

————, "Soaring Bird Aerodynamics — Clues for Hang Gliding," *Ground Skimmer,* 17–19 (Los Angeles, California, October 1976).

McMasters, John H., "An Analytical Survey of Low-Speed Flying Devices — Natural and Man-Made," *AIAA Paper No. 74-1019* (New York, 1974).

————, Curtis J. Cole, and David Skinner, "Man-Powered Flight," *AIAA Student Journal 9,* 5–17 (New York, April 1971).

————, and George M. Palmer, "At the Threshold of Man-Powered Flight," *Astronautics & Aeronautics,* 60–70 (New York, September 1977).

Moulton, Ron, "Progress with Human Power," *Aeromodeller,* 102–104 (Hemel Hempstead, U.K., February 1977).

————, "The Gossamer Albatross — If the Wind Don't Blow and the Chain Don't Break," *Aeromodeller,* 533–542 (Hemel Hempstead, U.K., September 1979).

Potter, John, "Jupiter: Man Powered Flight Project 1972," *Society of Experimental Test Pilots Fifth Annual Symposium* (London, 1973).

Reinach, Salomon, "La Victoire de Samothrace," *Gazette des Beaux-Arts,* 89–103 (Paris, February 1891).

Seehase, Hans, "Menschenkraftflug: Ein konstruktiver Beitrag," *Flugsport 18,* 491–497 (Frankfurt am Main, 1937).

Shenstone, B. S., "Engineering Aspects in Man Powered Flight," *Journal of the Royal Aeronautical Society 64,* 471–477 (London, August 1960).

Vann, F. W., "Structural Materials for Man Powered Aircraft," *Royal Aeronautical Society Third Man Powered Aircraft Group Symposium,* 125–132 (London, February 1979).

Wilkie, D. R., "Man as an Aero Engine," *Journal of the Royal Aeronautical Society 64,* 477–481 (London, August 1960).

Wright, Charles, "Flight of the Albatross," *Aviation Quarterly 5,* 72–87 (Plano, Texas, 1979).

Illustration Credits

Index

Aachen Aerodynamische Institut, 59
Academy of Model Aeronautics, 54, 226
Adams, Bill, 218, 219
Adidas U.S.A., 178
Aerochem, Inc., 88
Aero Club of America, 264
Aeronca Champion (private aircraft), 120
Aerovironment, Inc., 65–65, 70, 85, 146, 181, 183
Ag-viation, Inc., 124, 145
Airco (de Havilland) D.H. 2 (World War I fighter), 83
Airco (de Havilland) D.H. 4 (World War I bomber), 102
Aircraft Owners' and Pilots' Association (U.K.), 104, 119, 188, 258
"Albatross Heights" (apartment house), 195
Alfano, Ray, 183
Allen, Brook, 119, 147
Allen, Beverly, 125–126, 143, 145, 158, 194, 258, 259
Allen, Bryan, 114, 124, 158, 160, 161, 171, 176, 187, 195, 207
   Albatross piloting, 165–166, 177–178, 180, 185, 189, 191, 201, 203, 204, 205–206, 214, 231, 239–255, 264
   Albatross project management, 187, 192–193, 262
   Awards and prizes, 194, 258, 264
   Background, 107, 122, 125–128
   Bicycling experience, 122, 126
   Condor piloting, 123, 127–129, 131, 132–133, 135–136, 137–145, 147
   Cross-Channel flight, 239–255
   Education, 126–127
   Endurance, 233, 254, 261
   English Channel expedition, 209, 211, 214, 223, 224, 231, 235
   Flights in England, 214, 231
   Flying experience, 126, 127
   Hang gliding experience, 107, 127, 181
   HPA construction, 164, 184, 198
   Icarus piloting, 135
   Physical training and condition, 126, 127–128, 130, 138, 140, 145, 168, 175, 189, 203, 233, 251, 252, 261
   Power output, 168, 175, 233
   Record flights, 137–138, 143–145, 203, 205–206, 239–255
Allen, Marvin, 125, 126, 143, 158, 194
Allen, Peter, 222
American Aeronautical Corporation, 15
American Institute of Aeronautics and Astronautics, 90
American Meteorological Society, 181
AMF-Voit, Inc., 178
Ancona, Ted, 135, 161, 200
   Albatross construction, 198
   Background, 171–172
   Cross-Channel flight, 238, 240, 243
   Flying experience, 224
Antelope Valley, 83
Apollo 11 (spacecraft), 264
Arco Severn (bulk carrier), 236
Armstrong, Tom, 127
Arnold, Alan, 64
Ascher, James, 216
ASCOT 5681 (R.A.F. C-130), 207–208, 209, 211
Ashford Airport (England), 210
Ashton-Warner, Sylvia, 160
Aspect ratio, 47, 74
Atlantic Richfield Company (Arco), 178
Avery, Robin, 123, 194
Aviette (aerocycle), 1–5, 6, 47
Avro 504 (trainer), 18

BAC Concorde (supersonic transport), 41–42, 191

Ballet Russe, 5–6
Bame, Mike, 195
Barnes, J. L., 35
Barstow (California), 204
Batso (hang glider), 71, 78, 134, 186
Batten, Barton, Durstine, and Osborn, 183
Beatles, 69
Bennison, H. G., 25
Berlin Air Transport Museum, 13
Beuby, Bill, 108, 113, 158, 258, 263
   Albatross construction, 167
   Background, 102–103, 119
   Condor construction, 114, 131–132
Bicycles, high-speed, 90–91
Billett, Don, 209, 217, 239, 243, 258
Black, Alex, 210
Blackburn monoplane (pioneer aircraft), 223
Blaue Maus (glider), 8, 59
Blériot, Louis, 157, 223
   First cross-Channel flight, 219, 227–228
Blériot monument (England), 222–228
Blériot *No. XI* monoplane (pioneer aircraft), 227–228
Boeing aircraft:
   707-320 (transport), 45, 174
   720 (transport), 174
   747 (transport, freighter), 157, 199
   747SP (transport), 37
Boeing Airplane Company, 199
Bond, Kathy, 194
Bonomi, Vittorio, 16
Booton, Frank, 222, 242
Bossi, Enea, 15–17, 20, 103
Bowlus, Glenn, 59
Bowlus, Hawley, 102
Bowman, Bryan, 46
Brabazon of Tara, Lord (J. T. C. Moore-Brabazon), 238
Brainard Field (Connecticut), 57, 264
Breguet 901 (sailplane), 61
Brennan, Maurice, 217
Brewster, Kingman, 217
Bristol Aeroplane Company, 76
British Aerospace Corporation, 197
British Aerospace Hawk T. (jet trainer), 259
British Aircraft Corporation, 25, 41–42
British Petroleum, 25
British Rail, 218, 241
Brown, J. R., 22
Brown, Paddy, 219

Brustmann, Martin, 9, 18, 21
Brustmann-Lippisch human-powered ornithopter, 9–10, 18
Bryant, David Faulkner, 237, 242
Budd *Pioneer* (stainless steel amphibian), 15
Buhl LA-1 Bull Pup (private aircraft), 58
Burd (human-powered aircraft), 48
Burd II (human-powered aircraft), 48
Burke, Caroline Copeland (Lin), 106, 149, 150, 158, 194, 213, 217, 234, 235, 258
   Cross-Channel flight beach crew, 236, 237, 254, 256–257
Burke, Jim, 96, 98, 101, 117, 120, 158, 161, 183, 194, 207, 219, 259
   Albatross English Channel expedition 209–211, 214–215, 232, 234, 235
   Albatross design contributions, 162
   Albatross hangar, 182
   Background, 93–94, 106
   Condor design contributions, 106, 109
   Cross-Channel flight, 239, 242, 243, 247–249, 253, 255
   Cross-Channel flight escort boats, 215, 217–218, 221, 222, 226, 232, 236, 256–257
Burke, Richard, 258

Calais (France), 221
Calais Pilot Board, 250
California Condor (*Gymnogyps californianus*), 1, 2, 80, 83, 111
California Highway Patrol, 91
California Portland Cement Company, 64
California State Historical Landmarks Commission, 193
Cameron, Donald, 179
Campbell, Colin, 210–211, 219
Canadian Aeronautical Institute, 22
Canard configuration, 54, 77, 85 [*fig.*]
Cap Gris-Nez (France), 221, 232, 235, 245, 246, 251, 252, 256, 264
   Weather, 238, 241, 246
Carbon fiber, 162–168, 166 [*fig.*], 174, 175, 197
Casco, Emilio, 17, 20
Catapult launching, 8, 10, 17
Centre Régional Opérationnel de Sauvetage et Surveillance Manche (*CROSSMA*), 221, 235, 237, 246, 251

Cessna 150 (private aircraft), 83, 172, 200
Chambre de Commerce de Calais, 221
Champoiseau, Charles-François-Noël, 264
Charles, Prince of Wales, 159, 160, 258–259
Chaudru, Christian, 251
Church, Chris, 35–36
Churei, Kazuhiko, 47, 48, 100
Ciba-Geigy Corporation, 178
Clark, Kenneth, 147, 150, 151, 157, 179, 228, 260
Clarke, Margret, 209, 217, 237, 258
Cleary, Kathy, 258
Cobham, Sir Alan, 227
Coefficient of lift (C_L), 67
Cohu Electronics, 62, 63
Coles, Nick, 237, 241
Collier, Robert J., 264
Collier Trophy, 264
Comte de Lambert, 228
Conmy, Jack, 197, 217, 220, 222, 230, 232
    English Channel expedition, 237, 243, 254
Conmy, Terese, 217
Consolidated PBY Catalina (patrol bomber), 94, 196
Consolidated PB2Y Coronado (patrol bomber), 182
Copeland, Nancy, 61, 106
Copeland, Polly, 258
Cousteau, Jacques, 181, 218
Covert, Eugene E., 48
Cowley, Martyn, 237, 241
Cox, Gary, 195
Cranfield College of Aeronautics. *See* R.A.F. Cranfield
Cranfield Institute of Technology, 22
Crawford, Fred, 182
Curtis, Glenn, 264

Daily Mail Prize (London), 228
Davey, Christopher, 179
"Decimetre" Prize, 7, 26
de Havilland Aircraft Company, 24, 28, 29, 30, 31, 35
de Havilland aircraft:
    D.H.82 Tiger Moth (private aircraft), 112
    D.H.91 Albatross (transport), 29
    D.H.88 Comet (racing plane), 29
    D.H.98 Mosquito (bomber), 24, 29

D.H.104 Dove (light transport), 84
    T.11 Vampire (jet trainer), 112, 194
De Witt, Alden, 104
Diaghilev, Sergei, 5
Dicken, Paul, 235
Didier, Paul, 7, 20
Dodd, Ingrid, 220, 229, 237, 243, 254
Doolittle, James H., 102
Douglas Aircraft Company, 59, 92
Douglas aircraft:
    A-20 (attack bomber), 102
    B-26 (attack bomber), 112
    C-133 (military transport), 83
    DC-8 (transport), 102
    DC-9 (transport), 77
    DC-10 (transport), 209
Dover Harbour Patrol, 218
Dover Harbourmaster, 220, 235
Drag, 74, 87, 89, 101, 103, 131, 136, 204, 261
Dubois, George, 7, 20
Dubord, John, 228, 229 [*fig.*]
Dumbo (human-powered aircraft), 41–42, 44, 46
Dunlop Company, 30
Dünnebeil, Karl, 10, 20, 21
Dupire, Jean-Charles, 237
Du Pont Company, 163, 166, 179, 199, 258, 260
    Albatross sponsorship, 176, 179, 182–184, 197, 199
    English Channel expedition, 213, 217, 232, 234, 251, 254
    Solar aircraft sponsorship, 260
    Sponsorship aims, 183–184
Durán, Sam, 114, 121, 126, 127, 129, 130, 132, 142, 143, 144, 158, 159, 161, 171, 176, 194, 203
    Albatross flight director, 198, 201, 205–207
    Background, 107–108
    Cross-Channel flight, 238, 239, 240, 242–255
    English Channel expedition, 232–233, 235
    Flight to England, 207–209, 211
    House father, 195, 201
    HPA piloting, 180

East, Fred, 25
Eastman Kodak Company, 178
Eaton, Alfred, 119, 139, 141
Eaton Corporation, 178
Eco-Flight Systems, 195
Edward G. Budd Company, 15

Egret (human-powered aircraft), 41, 99
Egret II (human-powered aircraft), 47
Egret III (human-powered aircraft), 47
Eipper 17 (hang glider), 108
Elliott, Steve, 201
  Albatross construction, 186, 198
  Background, 186
  Channel crossing boat crew, 217, 236
  Cross-Channel flight, 241, 244, 247, 249
  English Channel expedition, 225, 233
Emery Air Freight Corporation, 182
Engleman, Mia, 59
English Channel crossing by human-powered aircraft, 157, 235–255
  Distance, 254
  Landing, 253
  Landing point, 220–221
  Plan, 215
  Rescue arrangements, 215, 229
  Ship traffic, 245–246
  Takeoff point, 218
  Time, 254
  Weather, 238, 239, 240, 241, 245, 246, 252
English Electric Canberra (bomber), 21, 211
Eppler 193 (model airfoil), 199
Ergometer, 92–93, 96, 128, 175, 189, 198, 215, 233, 234
  Albatross project ergometer power output record, 198, 234
Esdaile, Phil, 124, 129, 132, 143, 144, 158, 172, 194
  Background, 124
Exxon Company U.S.A., 178

FAI microfilm models, 225–226
Fairey Aviation Company, Ltd., 19
Fairey Long Range Monoplane, 19
Fédération Aéronautique International (FAI), 99, 258
Flahaut, Pierre, M. et Mme., 256
Flanders, Mike, 107
Flight of the Gossamer Condor (film), 192, 257
Flour Mining & Metals, Inc., 178
Flying Tiger Line, 178
Foght, James, 217
Folland-Hawker Siddeley Gnat (jet trainer), 223
Ford Trimotor (transport), 119
Fortnum & Mason, 258
Fournier RF-4 (motor glider), 206
Foyle's Bookshop, 258

Frankfurter Polytechnische Gesellschaft, 10, 11
Frankfurter Polytechnische Gesellschaft Prize, 10, 11, 12, 15, 20, 26
Franklin, Jack, 102–103, 113, 211–212
Franzgrote, Ernie, 196
French Coast Guard, 221, 235, 237, 246, 249, 250, 251

Garrard, P. H., 229
Gen-Mar Company, 63–65, 69, 70, 77, 106, 151, 163, 167, 181
Getty Oil Company, 107, 130, 178, 198
Gibbons, Grinling, 224
Giboney, Kirk, 198
  Albatross backup pilot, 203, 205, 206
  Background, 203
  Cross-Channel flight, 244, 248
  English Channel expedition, 209, 211, 214, 232
  Record flights, 205, 214
Gloucester Meteor (jet fighter), 210–211
Goering, Clyde, 127
Goldberg, Rube, 164
Goodhart, Molly, 159
Goodhart, Nicholas, 155–157, 158, 159, 227, 228, 260
Goodyear-Zeppelin Company, 59
Göring, Herman, 11
Gossamer Albatross (human-powered aircraft), 16, 44, 79, 80, 86, 89, 90, 125, 135, 170 [*fig.*], 176 [*fig.*], 212 [*fig.*], 257
  Airfoils, 85 [*fig.*], 162, 175, 199
  Assembly and disassembly, 198, 200, 201, 205, 238, 256
  Awards and prizes, 258–259, 264
  Base in England, 210–211
  Channel boat escort, 215–216, 218–219, 221–222, 229–230, 236–237
  Control problems, 179, 180, 191, 196, 201, 203–204
  Crashes, 180, 189, 191, 192, 198, 240
  Cross-Channel flight, 235–255
  Design elements, 162, 174–175
  Dimensions, 176 [*fig.*], 200
  Drive system, 174, 202 [*fig.*], 231
  English Channel Expedition, 186, 209–235
  Expedition deadline, 232
  Expenses, 175–176, 179, 181–182, 199
  First flights, 172–173, 177–178
  Flight durations, 180, 185, 189, 191, 197, 201, 203, 205, 206, 207

Gossamer Albatross (*cont.*)
Flights in England, 213–214, 231
Instrumentation, 169, 187, 191, 200, 203, 213, 230, 239–240, 246, 249, 250
Materials, 162–168, 174–175, 177, 196, 197, 204, 262
Naming, 162, 169–170
Origins, 160, 162
Pilot position, 175
Pilots, 197–198, 203
Power to fly, 175, 191, 201, 203, 205, 245, 247
Press and public relations, 181, 197, 216–217, 222, 230–232, 235, 240–241, 244, 247, 253, 254
Project management, 184, 186–187, 192–193, 230
Propellers, 162, 198–199, 204, 205
Qualification flights, 213–214
Radio communications, 200, 230, 239–240, 246
Safety procedures, 189, 193, 215, 222, 228–229
Sonar altimeter, 169, 187, 191, 213, 249
Spar construction, 164–165
Speed, 173, 178, 179, 246, 251–252
Sponsorship, 175–176, 178–179, 182–184, 197
Structure, 164–168, 166 [*fig.*], 170 [*fig.*], 174–175, 212 [*fig.*]
Trailer, 184, 198, 207
Transportation, 199–200, 205, 207–211, 257
Ventilation, 201, 204, 206, 231, 244, 250
Weight, 173, 199, 200
World record flights, 203, 205–206, 235–255
Gossamer Albatross 2 (human-powered aircraft):
Construction, 196, 197, 215, 234
Origin, 185
Stability and control studies, 260, 261, 262
Transportation, 199–200, 205, 207–211, 250
Weight, 199
Gossamer Condor (human-powered aircraft), 14, 16, 19, 72 [*fig.*], 75, 84, 92, 93, 118 [*fig.*], 125, 155, 159, 174, 175, 219, 225, 226, 257
Airfoils, 85 [*fig.*], 85–86, 116, 131
Awards and prizes, 151, 155, 158–160, 257
Control problems, 96, 105, 106, 108–109, 115, 116–117, 121–122, 130
Crashes, 95, 101, 105, 116, 128, 135, 136, 139, 148
Design elements, 85–87, 106, 109–110, 131, 175
Drive system, 89–90, 128
Evolution, 109–110, 114, 131
Expenses, 97, 108, 150–151, 168, 176
First flights, 94–97, 115
Flight durations, 95–96, 101–102, 115–116, 128, 135, 138, 139, 140, 142, 144
Historical marker, 112, 193–194
Instrumentation, 117
Landing fee, 194
Last flights, 161
Materials, 86–90, 119, 121, 133, 138, 163, 174
Models, 70, 75, 77, 106
Museum exhibit, 151, 161–162, 166
Naming, 80
Number of flights, 130, 161
Origins, 66–82
Pilot position, 89, 175
Power to fly, 101, 103, 115, 121, 131
Press and public relations, 99, 138, 139, 141, 142, 145, 146, 147, 148
Prize-winning flight, 142–145, 171, 227
Project duration, 80
Propeller, 85, 86, 89, 103, 205
Prototype, 79–82
Record flights, 115–116, 142–145
Speed, 96, 102, 145
Structure, 73–74, 86–89, 95, 98, 119, 121, 130, 133, 136, 140, 197
Weight, 81, 117, 138, 140, 145, 161
Gossamer Penguin (human-powered aircraft):
Construction, 197, 215
Conversion to solar aircraft, 260
Dimensions, 185
Origin, 185
Speed, 185
Transportation, 200, 203, 207–209, 257
Weight, 199
Gossamer Penguin (interim name for *Gossamer Albatross*), 162, 169, 171
Gough, Vernon, 210
Official AOPA observer, 214

Graham, Robert, 22, 259
Background, 19
And Kremer Prize, 24–25, 97
Granville Hotel (Ramsgate), 257
Green, Phillip, 42
Green, Ron, 226
Green flash, 130, 200
Griswold, Lee, 87
Groat, John, 222, 242
Grosser, Janet, 57, 169, 201, 258, 264
Albatross construction, 184, 198
Cross-Channel flight beach crew, 236, 237, 246, 251, 253, 254
Grosser, Morton, 169
Albatross construction, 184
Cross-Channel flight radar and beach crew, 236, 237, 246, 251–252, 253
Ground effect, 43, 87, 134
Grumman Ag-Cat (agricultural aircraft), 111, 112
Grumman Mallard (amphibian), 94, 196
Grumman TBD Avenger (torpedo bomber), 124
Gulf Oil Corporation, 178
Gutermuth, Hans, 8

Haessler, Helmut, 10–13, 20, 21, 74
Hamlyn, Ken, 195
Handley Page Aircraft Company, 45, 46, 76
Handley Page, Frederick, 46
Hang glider structure, 71, 73
Hangar 522 (Terminal Island), 182, 184–185, 196, 197, 198, 204
Hangar meeting rules, 171
Hannover Technical Institute, 9
Harper Dry Lake, 204–207, 238
Weather, 205, 206
Hatfield, Bryan, 25
Hatfield Man-Powered Aircraft Club, 28–31, 35–36, 39, 40, 41, 44
Hawker Siddeley Aviation, Ltd., 25
Her Majesty's Coast Guard, 217, 222, 235, 241, 245
Hertfordshire Pedal Aeronauts, 45–47
Hewlett-Packard Company, 85–86, 142
Hodel's Restaurant, 130, 141, 171, 201
Hoerner, Fred, 200, 207
Hoffmann, A., 11–12, 20
Hollingsworth, Edith Margaret, 50. *See also* MacCready, Edith Hollingsworth
Hollingsworth, Norman, 57

Horner, Jackie, 61
Horsa (Sealink Channel ferry), 245
Horton, Tom:
Albatross public relations director, 181–182, 193
Background, 181
Du Pont sponsorship, 182–184
English Channel expedition, 209, 213, 215, 216, 218, 233, 242
Hotel Normandy (Wissant), 254, 257
Hoverlloyd Ltd., 235, 236
Human power output, 11, 27, 33, 34 [fig.], 233, 234
Humphreys, Ann and Raymond, 219
Hurel, Maurice, 47, 74
Hurel Aviette (human-powered aircraft), 47, 74
Hutch's Coffee Shop, 129, 170

Icarus (human-powered aircraft) 134, 135, 149, 161, 164, 181, 186, 197
Icarus I (biplane hang glider), 134, 186
Icarus II (biplane hang glider), 134
Icarus V (hang glider and ultralight aircraft), 134, 172, 224
Imboden, Otis, 219, 221, 235, 243
Induced drag, 74, 87, 261
Inland Crop Dusters, Inc., 145
Institut für Aerodynamik und Gasdynamik (Stuttgart), 36
International Business Machines Corporation (IBM), 176, 178
International Human-Powered Vehicle Association (IHPVA), 90, 91
Irving, H. B., 22
Italian Government Human-Powered Flight Prize, 15, 16, 17, 20
Itford Hill (England), 9
Iverson, Bernard, 216

Jacob Russ (very large bulk carrier), 249–250
James, Thurstan, 23, 27
Jankowski, Paul, 163
Jensen, Vollmer, 224
Jet Propulsion Laboratory, 93, 196, 232
Jex, Henry, 96, 108–109
Condor design analysis, 108–109, 114, 117
Johnson, Norman, 216
Julkowski, Everett, 119
Junkers Flugzeuge und Motorenwerke, 10, 18, 19, 20
Junkers Ju52 (transport), 18

Junkers Ju87 (dive bomber), 19
Jupiter (human-powered aircraft), 42–43, 74, 158
　World record flight, 43, 100
Justice, La (newspaper), 7

Karsavina, Tamara, 6
Kato, Takashi, 47, 99
Kent Coast:
　Tides, 216, 236, 239, 241, 242
　Weather, 220, 221, 223, 226, 229, 230, 232, 233, 234, 235, 238, 239, 240, 241
Kent Police, 229, 235
Kern County (California) Department of Airports, 84, 119, 194
Kiceniuk, Taras Jr., 141, 149, 181, 201, 224
　Aircraft designs, 71, 78, 134–135, 197
　Albatross construction, 164, 184, 198, 200
　Albatross construction head, 171, 187
　Background, 134–135, 186
　Cross-Channel flight, 238, 240, 241, 244, 247, 248, 250, 254
　English Channel expedition, 231
Kilroy, Jim, 182
Kimura, Hidemasa, 39, 41, 44, 47, 93, 99, 100, 158, 159
　Background, 19–20, 37–38
Klassen, Larry, Enterprises, 145
Klemperer, Eleanor, 60
Klemperer, Mia, 59
Klemperer, Otto, 59
Klemperer, Wolfgang, 8, 59
Koken Long Range Monoplane, 19
Kozma, Norm, 195, 207
Kremer, Don, 217
Kremer, Henry, 24–25, 29, 40, 46, 63, 97, 147, 157, 158, 160, 259
　Background, 24
　Physical fitness interest, 24, 189
Kremer Cross-Channel Competition. *See* Kremer £100,000 Competition
Kremer £50,000 Competition, 7, 19, 44, 45, 48, 63, 69, 70, 74, 76, 77, 82, 92, 97, 115
　Attempts, 104, 137–139, 141–145
　Competitors, 32, 93, 99–100, 156, 225
　Course, 26, 112–113, 116, 135, 141, 142–145
　Duration, 32, 144–145
　Entries, 27, 93

Evolution, 40, 46–47
Licenses, 93, 100, 120, 123
Official observers, 103–104, 119–120, 138
Origin, 24–25
Prize award, 151, 158–160, 176
Registration fee, 149–150
Rules, 25–27, 149–150, 261, Appendix
Winning flight, 143–145
Kremer Figure-of-Eight Competition. *See* Kremer £50,000 Competition
Kremer £5000 Competition, 40
　Attempts, 40–41
Kremer £100,000 Competition, 156–157, 257
　Entries, 189, 228
　Optimum weather window, 191
　Origin, 157
　Qualification flight, 189, 213–214
　Registration fee, 189
　Rules, 157–158, 159, 160, 179, 188–189, 250–251, Appendix
Kremer £10,000 Competition, 157
Kyle, Chester, 90–91, 92, 94, 100, 148
　Background, 91

Lady Ellen Elizabeth (cabin cruiser), 222, 232, 235
　Cross-Channel flight, 236, 237, 238, 240, 242, 243, 244, 250, 252, 253, 255
Lagesen, Sir Philip, 219
Laidlaw, Robert, 77, 84
Lake, John, 108, 113, 114, 117, 120, 122, 123, 124, 127, 131–132, 161, 196, 258, 262
　Background, 104–105
　Condor structural contributions, 119
Lake, Monica, 258
Laker Airways, 209, 211
Lambie, Jack, 80, 81, 87, 94, 106, 108, 146, 148, 158, 161, 193, 194, 206, 207
　Background, 78
　Bicycle design work, 90–91
　Condor construction, 79, 86, 88, 91, 113, 122, 132
　Heat shrinking contributions, 117–119
Lambie, Karen, 78, 161, 194
Lambie, Tom, 80
Lamont, Douglas, 66
Larrabee, Eugene, 199
Laser Engineering Ltd., 24

Laser Engineering (Development) Ltd., 24
Lasham Gliding Centre, 29
Lassière, Alan, 27, 34
Latham, Hubert, 228
Leborgne, M., 221
Le Bourget Airport, 257
Lennon, John, 75
Leonard, Judy, 56, 61, 62, 106. *See also* MacCready, Judy Leonard
Leonard, Kirke, 56, 61, 77, 79, 81, 94, 96, 105, 106, 108, 113, 121, 122, 171
  Albatross construction, 184, 185
  Albatross design contributions, 162–166, 178
  Background, 63, 106
  Condor construction, 77, 79, 86, 87, 88, 91, 96
  Condor design contributions, 86
  Gen-Mar Company, 63–65
Leonard, Kirke Jr., 122, 171, 184
Leonard, Parker, 56, 57, 59, 64, 113
Leonard, Tippy, 56, 61
Licher, Lloyd, 77, 104, 116
Liddon, Arthur, 216
Lilienthal Hang Glider Meet, 71, 78, 134
Lilienthal, Otto, 8
Lilley, Geoffrey M., 27, 158, 161
Lindbergh, Charles A., 102, 162
Linnet (human-powered aircraft), 38–39, 41, 74, 99
Linnet II (human-powered aircraft), 41
Linnet III and *IV* (human-powered aircraft), 41
Lippisch, Alexander, 9, 10, 18, 20, 21, 27
Lissaman, Peter, 62, 64, 78, 79, 94, 98, 117, 125, 134, 135, 141, 146, 148, 158, 159, 171, 183, 194, 196, 262
  Airfoils, 85–86, 95, 116, 131, 134, 135, 138, 162, 175
  Albatross design contributions, 162
  Background, 76–77, 106
  Condor design contributions, 106–107, 108–109
Liverpuffin (human-powered aircraft), 44–45, 158
Lloyd, Pat, 237, 241
Lockhart (California), 205
Lockheed C-130 Hercules (military transport), 200, 207–208, 209, 211
Lockheed P2V-1 Neptune (patrol bomber), 21

Loken, Halvar, 167
Lopez, Donald, 151
Los Angeles Times, 178
Louf, Jean, 221, 228, 235, 236, 237, 251
Low Speed Aerodynamics Research Association (London), 22
Ludington-Griswold Company, 55, 56
Luftschiffbau Zeppelin GmbH, 59
Lympne Airport (England), 209–210
Lyre (French patrol boat), 248
LZ 126 (dirigible), 59

MacCready, Anne, 50, 51, 52, 74–75
MacCready, Edith Hollingsworth, 50, 56, 57
MacCready, Isabelle, 50, 51
MacCready, Judy Leonard, 62, 63, 77, 142, 158, 159, 162, 187, 194, 213, 219, 230, 234, 235, 245, 258. *See also* Leonard, Judy
MacCready, Marshall, 62, 79, 94, 96, 142, 194, 230, 234, 238, 240, 245, 256–257
  HPA piloting, 185
MacCready, Parker, 62, 63, 67, 71, 80, 93, 94, 101, 142, 171, 213
  Cross-Channel flight, 242, 253, 256–257
  English Channel expedition, 219, 231
  HPA piloting, 96, 98, 101, 102, 161, 172–173, 179, 180
  Physical conditioning, 93, 96
MacCready, Paul Beattie, 50, 51, 52, 53, 54, 56, 57, 58, 59
MacCready, Paul Jr., 14, 49, 66–75, 78–82, 84–87, 91, 96, 105, 106, 112, 113, 115, 116, 124, 137, 140, 143, 157, 158, 159, 160, 161, 173, 187, 219, 264
  Awards and prizes, 54, 55, 60, 61, 62, 65, 151, 159–160, 176, 192–193, 257, 259, 264
  Biography, 50–65
  Cross-Channel flight, 235–255
  Education, 53, 55, 56, 58, 59, 60, 61, 75, 106
  English Channel expedition, 187–188, 209–226, 230, 233, 234
  Hang gliding experience, 63, 67, 71, 78
  HPA piloting, 95, 116, 161, 179–180
  Model building background, 52–55, 56, 70, 75, 79, 86, 98, 225–226
  Physical conditioning, 93, 96, 100, 220

MacCready, Paul Jr. (*cont.*)
  Project direction, 184, 187, 192–193,
    199, 230, 235, 261, 262
  Soaring experience, 57–59, 60, 61, 62,
    113
  Solar aircraft project, 260–261
MacCready, Tyler, 62, 63, 69, 70, 71,
    80, 93, 94, 101, 102, 116, 142, 143,
    144
  Background, 77
  Cross-Channel flight, 237, 242–243,
    256–257
  HPA piloting, 94–95, 101, 103, 104,
    114–115, 122–123, 139, 161
  Physical conditioning, 77, 93, 96
MacCready Factor, 79–80, 95, 168
Malfoy, Olivier, 237
Man-Powered Aircraft Committee
    (Cranfield), 22–23, 24, 25, 26, 149,
    158, 225, 260
Man-Powered Aircraft Group Commit-
    tee (Royal Aeronautical Society),
    23–24, 25, 26, 44, 147, 150, 157,
    158, 159, 259, 260
Man-Powered Aircraft Group Sympo-
    sium, 196
MAPAC. *See* Man-Powered Aircraft
    Committee (Cranfield)
Marsden, Anne, 27, 31
Martens, Arthur, 8
Maschelein, Paul and Stephan, 228, 251
Massachusetts Institute of Technology:
  Albatross propeller design, 199
  Human-powered flight program, 48
  Student Information Processing
    Board, 199
Masterton, Maggie, 222
Mastropaolo, Joseph, 91, 94, 148
  Albatross backup pilot, 197–198, 203
  Background, 91–92
  Cross-Channel flight, 244
  English Channel expedition, 220, 233,
    234
  Physical training programs, 93, 96,
    100, 127–128, 140, 168, 197–198,
    215, 233, 234, 254, 261
May, Derek, 46
McCartney, Paul, 76
McCown, William, 196
McKibben, Paul, 133, 167
McMasters, John, 48, 156
McNay, Dave, 195, 238, 244
McNay, Larry, 195–196, 213, 219
  Cross-Channel flight, 238, 240, 243

Mercury (human-powered aircraft, ex-
    Dumbo), 42
Mercury Marine (Kiekhaefer Mercury
    Division of Brunswick Corpora-
    tion), 215
Mercury outboard motors, 215, 217,
    218
Meteorology Research, Inc., 61, 62, 63,
    113
Michelin Prize (powered flight), 7
Microcell Limited, 24, 25
Midnight Flyer (railroad handcar), 186
Miller, Dave, 196
Miller, Greg, 120, 128, 158
  Background, 100
  Condor piloting, 101–102, 103, 104,
    115–116, 121, 138
  Pilot instruction, 120
Miller, Lynn, 213
Miller, Richard, 71
Ministry of Supply (U.K.), 22, 24
Mobil Oil Corporation, 178
Model airplane building, 52–55, 70, 75,
    79, 87, 94, 98, 100, 102, 106, 113,
    117, 126, 130, 167, 172, 186, 225–
    226
Mojave (California), 83–84
Mojave Airport, 77, 82, 83–84, 94, 98,
    111, 112, 186, 238
  Weather, 95–96, 99, 101, 103, 105
Monroe, Don, 219, 239, 243
Morris, Peter, 222, 241
Morris, Roger, 222, 230
Mouillard, Louis-Pierre, 155, 160
Moulton, Ron, 158, 159, 160, 171, 228,
    263
  Chairman of Kremer £100,000 Com-
    petition Rules Committee, 159,
    160, 179, 188
  Cross-Channel flight official observer,
    237, 238, 242, 248
Mufli (human-powered aircraft), 10–
    12, 14, 17, 21, 28, 29, 74, 156
Musée du Louvre, 264

NAMC YS-11 (transport), 38
NASA (National Aeronautics and
    Space Administration), 260, 261,
    262
National Aeronautic Association, 104,
    119, 147
National Air and Space Museum, 151,
    161–162, 166
National Geographic magazine, 219
National Geographic Society, 182

Neiswanger, Gordon, 58, 62
Nellis Air Force Base (Nevada), 200, 205, 207–208, 209
Nettleton, Lee, 53, 57
Neubert, Hans, 87
Newbury Manflier (human-powered aircraft), 156–157, 159, 260
Newell, A., 23
Nieuport, Édouard, 6, 21
Nieuport, Société Anonyme, 3, 6, 21
Nihon University human-powered flight program, 38–39, 41, 47–48
  World record flight, 99–100
Nijinsky, Vaslav, 6
Nonweiler, T. R. F., 23, 27
North American F-86 Sabre (fighter), 83, 211
North American YF-100A Super Sabre (fighter), 21
Northrop Corporation, 76

Oates, Roderick, 220, 222
Oceanroutes, Inc., 188, 223
Okamiya, Munetaka, 39
Okamura N-52 (private aircraft), 38
Old Warden Aerodrome (Bedfordshire), 223–225
Olde Cliffe Tavern (St. Margaret's at Cliffe), 213, 233–234
Oldershaw, Eugene, 145
Oldershaw, Maude, 113, 114, 129, 132, 133, 137, 139, 140, 143, 145, 149, 150, 158, 160, 161, 194
  First woman-powered flight, 149
Oldershaw, Paul, 114
Oldershaw, Vern, 119, 129, 132, 138, 141, 142, 144, 145, 146, 147, 148, 149, 158, 159, 176, 193, 194
  Background, 113–114
  Condor construction and design, 121, 130, 133, 137, 138, 140, 161–162
Olympian ZB-1 (human-powered aircraft), 48–49
Orlik (sailplane), 60, 61

Parasite drag, 74, 89, 261
Paris Air Show, 238, 257
Parks, Bob, 199
Pasadena Museum of Modern Art, 79
Pedaliante (human-powered aircraft), 16–17, 21, 22, 29
Percival EP.9 Prospector (private aircraft), 210
Perkins, Daniel, 36, 37, 73, 225
Peugeot, Robert, 4, 6, 7, 155

Peugeot Prizes. *See Prix Peugeot*
Phillips, Hewitt, 199
Phillips, Jimmy, 31, 32, 35, 38
Phillips, Manny, 104
Piggott, Derek, 29, 31, 32, 33, 35, 40, 158
Piper Cherokee (private aircraft), 120, 209
Piper Cub (private aircraft), 55, 56, 58
Piper L-4 (trainer), 57, 264
Plumb, Pete, 123–124, 130, 134
Polaroid Corporation, 169, 176, 187
Port of Los Angeles, 182
Potter, John, 42, 158
  World record flight, 43, 99–100
Poulain, Gabriel, 3–6, 8, 20
Poupeville, M., 221
Power needed to fly, 15, 68–69
Pratt-Read glider, 55, 57, 58, 264
Pressnell, Martyn, 45, 158
Prézelin, Louis, 209, 213, 218, 221, 233, 243, 251
Price, Humphrey, 196
Prix Dubois, 7
Prix Michelin, 7, 20
Prix Peugeot, 3–7, 20, 26, 40
Puffin (human-powered aircraft), 28–31, 35–36, 38, 39, 42, 45, 112, 158
  World record flight, 35, 43
Puffin II (human-powered aircraft), 36, 38, 39, 40, 41, 42, 45
Python, Monty, 69

Queen Mary (passenger liner), 196

R-101 (dirigible), 36, 225
R.A.F. Benson, 43
R.A.F. Cardington, 36, 37, 225–226
R.A.F. Cranfield College of Aeronautics, 22, 23, 76, 149
R.A.F. Halton Apprentice School, 43
R.A.F. Lyneham, 209
R.A.F. Manston, 210, 211, 213, 234, 235
  Weather, 214, 235
R.A.F. *Red Arrows* exhibition flying team, 223
R.A.F. Rescue Service, 235
Ranger (space probe), 93
Raspet, August, 21
Rawdon, Blaine:
  Albatross construction, 186, 198
  Background, 186
  Cross-Channel flight, 244, 254
  English Channel expedition, 224, 225

Reagan, Mike, 195
Reeves, Christopher, 194
Reimer, Dwight, 112, 148, 194
Reluctant Phoenix (human-powered aircraft), 37, 44
Rettig, Sigmar, 7, 20
Revell VJ-23 (ultralight aircraft), 224
Rhön-Rossiten Gesellschaft, 9, 18
Rhön-Rossiten Gesellschaft Human-Powered Flight Prize, 9, 20
Richard, René, 237
Richardson, Bill, 119, 129, 139, 141, 142, 158, 194, 201, 203, 258
  Background, 119–120
  Official observer of *Condor* prize flight, 145, 147
Roberts, Sean, 76, 84
Robertson England-to-Australia Air Race, 29
Robinson, Heath, 164
Robinson, Johnny, 57, 60
Rockwell International Corporation, 178
Rogallo, Francis M., 70
Rogallo, Gertrude, 70
Rogallo wing glider, 70–71, 72, 104, 134, 172
Roper, Chris, 42–43
Rose Bowl, 78, 79, 80, 81, 83
Rosemont Pavilion, 78, 80, 82, 106, 108
Rossiten (East Prussia), 9
Royal Aero Club, 159, 258, 259
Royal Aeronautical Society, 23, 24, 25, 26, 29, 34, 35, 45, 47, 93, 147, 150, 151, 157, 158, 159, 160, 179, 187, 196, 217, 258, 259, 260
Royal Air Force, 200. *See also* R.A.F.
Royal Air Force Museum (Hendon), 159
Royal Automobile Club, 159, 258
Royal Cinque Ports Yacht Club, 217, 222
Royal College of Art, 160
Royal National Lifeboat Institution (R.N.L.I.), 217, 235, 242
Royal Temple Yacht Club, 220

Sabovich, Dan, 84
Sáenz, Joe and Sally, 232–234
St. Hilary Private Hotel, 219
St. Margaret's Bay Radar Station, 244–245
St. Paul's Cathedral, 258
Saks, Dave, 134, 135, 171, 195, 201
  Albatross backup pilot, 197, 203, 205

Albatross construction, 198
  Background, 172
  Cross-Channel flight, 236, 240, 244
  English Channel expedition, 219
San Diego Air and Space Museum, 181
Schmitt, Stephen P., 119, 194
Schwarzer Teufel (glider), 8, 59
Schweizer, Ernie, 57, 70
Schweizer, Paul, 57, 70
Schweppes U.S.A. Ltd., 178
Schwinge, Mark, 195
Science Museum (London), 159, 258
Screamin' Wiener (sailplane), 58–59, 60
Seagull Hang Glider Company, 184, 195
Seehase, Hans, 13–14
Seehase human-powered aircraft, 13–14
Seité, Daniel, 221, 235, 236, 237
Shafter (California), 111–112, 146–147
Shafter Airport, 108, 111–112, 145, 146, 161, 176, 238
  Albatross flight test base, 171, 172–173, 176–177, 179–181, 197, 200–204
  Condor base, 108, 111–112, 161
  Historical marker, 112, 193–194
  Weather, 108, 112, 120, 128, 131, 135, 136, 139, 140, 141–142, 143, 161
Shaklee Corporation, 182
Shedd, Ben, 99, 103, 115, 192, 257
Shell Oil Company, 25
Shenk, Edwin, 169, 187, 191, 203
Shenstone, Beverley, 20, 21–23, 27, 48, 158, 259
  Background, 18–19
Sherwin, Keith, 44–45, 158
Shimofusa Naval Air Base, 47, 99
Shuttleworth Trust Collection, Old Warden Aerodrome, 35, 47, 223–225
Sir Christopher (SR.N4 hovercraft), 236
Skarin, Ron, 100, 120, 121, 128
Sloman, Chris, 80
Sloman, Easy, 80
Sloman, Nancy, 80
Sloman, Scotty, 80
Smith, Lowell H., 102
Smithsonian Institution, 151, 155, 161
Soaring Society of America, 77, 104
Society of Experimental Test Pilots, 200
Sony Corporation, 178
Souplet, Arnaud, 251
Source Perrier S.A., 178

Southampton University Department of Aeronautics, 27, 158
Southern California Soaring Association, 113
Spirit of St. Louis (transatlantic record aircraft), 162
Spooner, Robin, 219
SS-1 (Japanese high-altitude research plane), 37
Stearman PT-13 (biplane trainer), 60
Stearman PT-17 (biplane trainer), 56
Stephenson, Jeff, 195, 207
Stinson Reliant (private aircraft), 120
Stoll, Sterling, 187, 195, 207
  Albatross project business manager, 184, 185, 187
  Background, 184
  Cross-Channel flight, 244, 249, 250, 253, 254, 255
  English Channel expedition, 235
Stork (human-powered aircraft), 38, 47–48, 99, 100
Stork B (human-powered aircraft), 48, 99–100, 101, 116, 159
  World record flight, 99–100
Street, Mike, 37
Strom, Scott, 195, 207
Struck, Henry, 55–56, 57
Sugar, Jim, 219, 234, 235
SUMPAC (*Southampton University Man Powered AirCraft*), 27–35, 39, 41, 47, 158, ·161, 224–225
Supermarine Spitfire (fighter), 18, 124
Systems Technology Inc., 96, 109

Tachikawa A-26 (long-distance transport), 37
Tartan Gem (cabin cruiser), 216, 217–218, 220, 232, 235
  Cross-Channel flight, 236–237, 238, 243, 256
  Navigation, 229
  Seakeeping, 218, 221
  Speed, 218
Taylor, Albert E., 104
Taylor, Stanford, 70
Terminal Island (California), 182, 184, 185, 191, 198, 204, 207
Texas Instruments Incorporated, 178
Thierrard, J. Pierre, 47
Thomas-Morse S.4 (World War I trainer), 102
Thompson, Joe, 213, 243
Thompson, Joe Jr., 213, 243
Thorpe, Jim, 201

Tokyo University Aeronautical Research Institute, 19
Tombach, Ivar, 64, 107, 108
Toucan (human-powered aircraft), 45–47, 158, 224
Tresca, Olivier, 251
Turbulence, 103, 136, 143, 204, 244, 246, 261
Turner, Sid, 218–219, 241
Turning problems (human-powered aircraft), 34, 35, 47–48, 99, 100, 105, 109, 117, 121, 122–123, 130, 131

Union Oil Company, 178, 182
United Kingdom Meteorological Service ("London Mets"), 188, 223, 235
United States Hang Gliding Association, 104
Ursinus, Oskar, 8, 9, 10, 11, 12, 21
U.S. Air Force *Thunderbirds* exhibition flying team, 207, 223
U.S. Air Racing Association, 104
U.S. Divers Corporation, 215
U.S. Naval Flight Test Center, 200
U.S. Navy *Blue Angels* exhibition flying team, 223
U.S.S. Los Angeles (dirigible), 59
U.S. Steel Corporation, 178

Vampyr (glider), 8–9
Van Loon, Willem, 251
Vann, F. W., 196–197
Varne lightship, 246
Verdon-Roe, Sir Alliott, 22
Versailles, Treaty of, 7
Vickers Viscount (transport), 21
Victoire de Samothrace ("Winged Victory"), 264, 265
Victoria and Albert Museum, 224
Villa "Les Algues," 256
Villinger, Franz, 10, 13, 20, 21, 27, 74, 156
Volk, John, 195, 207

Waltz, Samuel Jr., 176, 182–183
Wandering Albatross (*Diomedea exulans*), 153, 154, 171
Ward, John, 222, 236, 242, 255
Warren (Folkestone), 218–219, 232, 237, 238, 239, 241, 245
Wasserkupe, 7–8, 9, 18, 55, 57, 59
Watson, Bill, 134, 135, 141, 164, 171, 172, 186, 195
  Albatross construction, 164, 166
  Background, 166

Watson, Bill (*cont.*)
  Cross-Channel flight, 238, 239, 240,
    243, 248–249, 254
  English Channel expedition, 223, 224,
    234
Weir, J. G., Air Commodore, 25
Weissenberg, Chuck, 144
Wellington Dock (Dover), 186, 216,
  218, 232, 236, 256
Welsh, Dick, 183
Westland Aircraft Ltd., 25
Weybridge Man-Powered Aircraft
  Group, 41, 42
White, Peter, 220
Wilkie, D. R., 27
Williams, David, 27, 33
Wills Alpha 185 (hang glider), 181
Wilson Sporting Goods Company, 178
Wimpenny, John C., 28, 31, 35, 40, 41,
  43, 158
  World record flight, 35, 43
Wimwell, John, 41
Winfred M. Berg Inc., 89
Wing loading, 8, 67, 69, 73–74, 95
Wing warping, 109, 117, 121, 122–123
Wissant (France), 220–221, 255, 257
Woodcock, Alfred, 67
Woodford, Tony, 200
Woodford human-powered aircraft
  group, 42

Woodward, Joanne, 217
Woodward, Richard J., 183, 184, 197,
  217, 222, 241, 244, 258
Worley, Brian, 21
Wortmann, F. X., 36
  Airfoils, 36, 42
Wright, Orville, 8, 155, 264
Wright, Peter, 44, 73, 164
Wright, Wilbur, 7, 155, 228
Wright brothers, 6, 15, 45, 68, 174, 238,
  250
Wright *Flyer* (pioneer aircraft), 162

Xerox Corporation, 178
Xonics, Inc., 181

Youngren, Harold, 199

Zaschka, Englebert, 14
Zaschka human-powered aircraft, 14–15
Zanussi Grandi Impianti S.P.A., 179,
  182, 183
Zapata, Tony, 213, 233, 243, 251
Zinno, Joseph A., 48–49, 96
Zodiac inflatable boats, 215, 216, 217,
  218, 232, 235
  Cross-Channel flight, 236–257
Zodiac of North America, Inc., 215
Zodiac S.A., 215